THE AUTHOR AND HIS

David Northcroft spent the earlier part of his boyhood in Worcestershire and Sussex. When his father became exciseman at Cragganmore Distillery, Ballindalloch, Banffshire, however, he moved up to the North-east. He has seen no reason to live anywhere else ever since.

He attended Aberlour High School, followed by degrees at the Universities of Aberdeen, Cambridge and a doctorate at Stirling. His career has been in education, firstly as a teacher of English at Aberdeen Grammar School, then as a member of staff at Aberdeen College of Education (later Northern College). By the time of his early retirement he was Vice Principal.

He has divided the happy years since then between helping to look after granddaughters and researching in, first, Scottish school education, and latterly in oral history, where he has concentrated on building up an archive of personal reminiscences from North-east folk. He is responsible for two earlier books: *Scots at School* (Edinburgh University Press, 2003) and *North-east Identities and Scottish Schooling* (Aberdeen University Press, 2005).

He has lived in Muchalls for some 45 years. He is married to Kathleen and they have two sons: Jonathan, who as Football Correspondent to the *Sunday Times* is forced to watch Man U and Chelsea rather than the Dons, and Mat, who is both a head teacher in the Mearns and a Grade 1 referee. Jonathan and Jan are located in Liverpool with their very young daughter, Ishbel. Mat, Elaine and his other three granddaughters also live round the corner in Muchalls and, like the wee Liverpudlian, are a constant source of wonderment and delight.

Grampian Lives purports to offer a collective portrait of the shape and texture of daily life in the north-east of Scotland, as experienced by the folk who have spent their formative years there. The personal recollections which appear in this book are extracted from the recorded words of the 350 people David Northcroft has interviewed and recorded during the last 12 years. Invariably the interviews have been made in the subjects' own homes and been conducted in an informal, conversational style. The selection of witnesses – usually based on word-of-mouth recommendation or newspaper letters and stories – has been guided by the wish to cover a representative range of places, occupational backgrounds and ages.

The present volume focuses on the more recent generations, those who have been able to recall life in the second half of the last century and the opening decade of this one. In that respect it acts as a successor volume to *Grampian Lives 1900-1950,* which appeared in November 2011. It is hoped that this volume will be followed by one more: *City Lives 1900-2010,* which will draw upon the reminiscences of those who were brought up in Aberdeen itself, as opposed to the country, coastal and small town people of the first two books.

Readers are invited to get in touch with observations and also recommendations of further interviewees. (35 Nethermains Road, Muchalls, AB39 3RN or 01569730621 or David@davidnorthcroft.wanadoo.co.uk)

Published in October, 2013

A catalogue record for this book is available from the British Library

ISBN 978-0-9570999–2–0

Design and typesetting by Leopard Press
LePress@btconnect.com

Printed and bound in Scotland by
Robertsons, Forfar

Published by Leopard Press
Auld Logie, Pitcaple, Inverurie, Aberdeenshire AB51 5EE

GRAMPIAN LIVES

Eyewitness accounts of growing up in the towns of North-east Scotland

Volume 2: Twentieth Century Lives and Memories 1950–2000

David Northcroft

LEOPARD
PRESS

DEDICATION

To Ishbel: where this book ends, she begins

ACKNOWLEDGEMENTS

No book can ever be produced without the help of others: in the case of *Grampian Lives* that has been especially so.

While the great majority of the photographs which illustrate the reminiscences in the pages that follow have been provided by the speakers themselves – people who have trustingly allowed me access to precious family collections – I must also thank a number of other helpers. Brian Watt has once more generously opened up his extraordinary collection of old postcards for me to plunder. Similarly, the two marvellous on-line libraries of images run by the Alford Image Library and the Glenbuchat Heritage Archive have been most helpful and forthcoming. In this latter connection I must mention Peter Duffus. The Buckie Fishing Heritage Museum has been similarly generous. Some dozen images have been purchased from Aberdeen Journals and here I must thank Tom Cooper for effecting this business in such a friendly and speedy manner.

On a more specific basis, Brenda Ogilvie of Muchalls has tracked down and handed over the photographs of Mary Geddes and Bridge of Muchalls School which appear in the chapter, 'Going to School'. For the same chapter, Anne Burgess supplied the photo of Craigdam, and David Dixon generously handed over images of his father, Dr Dixon. Iain Macaulay is responsible for 'Fisher Jessie' in 'Off-shore On-Shore'. Emma McGuire kindly gave me the lovely shot which acts as the frontpiece to 'The North-east'. Mike Pickering sent me the photos of the Muchalls jubilee celebrations which appear in 'Life in the Community'. Gavin Shaw readily produced the photos of Tom McGregor ('Life on the Land'). Muriel Sinclair has faithfully sent me news and birthday photos (up to age 106!) of her aunt, Alexina Fleming.

A number of people have been helpful in other ways, either by facilitating contacts with likely speakers or by readily answering specific queries. They are: Susan Bennett; John Black jnr; Margaret Black; Bob Cooper; Allan Fraser; David Hartley; Ian Lakin; Wilma and George Lawrence; Alison McCall; Joe McDowall; Viveca McNeil; Alison Mitchell; Joan Ritchie; Susan Shaw; Edith Stephen; Carol and Hamish Strang; Ian Russell and Alison Sharman, both of the Elphinstone Institute, University of Aberdeen.

Once again, I must also offer up heartfelt thanks to Lindy Cheyne and Ian Hamilton of Leopard Press, whose enthusiastic and inspiring co-operation has exceeded the normal bounds of professional assistance. Not only have they performed a highly skilled and creative task in editing and laying out the presentation of *Grampian Lives*, they have been very fine folk to have worked with.

I would dearly like to thank my family for being just that – my family, a constant source of life-giving support. The names of this incomparable set of North-east people are Kathleen, Jonathan, Jan, Mat, Elaine and young Erin, Abby, Rachael and Ishbel.

But above all else, my gratitude belongs to all the people who have opened up their memories to me. Once I had exhausted the circle of my own relatives and friends I became dependent upon the willingness of complete strangers to welcome me into both their homes and their lives, there to ply me with fly cups, home bakes and their own very human stories. The names which appear in this book confirm the truth that the North-east of Scotland contains some of the finest folk you could hope to meet anywhere. I hope they will accept this second volume of *Grampian Lives* as my further tribute to them.

Cover Photograph

At a time when, we are informed, the average wedding now costs some £25,000, this shot of a family wedding breakfast from the beginning of our period in 1950 offers a salutary reminder of how things used to be. Picture supplied by Wilma Machray whose cousin, Margaret, is celebrating her marriage in an aunt's back garden in Banchory.

Notes

The words which appear in this book are taken from transcriptions of recordings of the recollections offered by the contributors to this book. In each case, scripts were sent back to the speakers for their amendments before an agreed version was arrived at. The accounts set out in *Grampian Lives* are selected extracts; the typical interview lasted 90 minutes and generated over 4,000 words. Editing has been kept to the minimum necessary to smooth out repetitions and hesitations.

Witnesses spoke in their own accents and dialect. As these ranged along a continuum of usage rather than falling into any distinct 'Standard English/ Doric' category – often within the one interview – the decision has been made to render their words in the one Standard form, excepting reported instances of direct speech. Here a more immediate, localised form has seemed to be more appropriate.

'Grampian' refers to the former Grampian Region as it was composed before the local government re-organisation of the 1990s. That is the historical counties of Aberdeenshire, Banffshire, Moray and Kincardineshire.

The place names which appear after each speaker's name refer to the locations focussed on in their specific recollections, not their birth places. The names of the interviewees appear as given to me and, in the case of women, are usually in the married and not the maiden form.

Many more interviewees have given of themselves than I have been able to squeeze into this present volume. I hope that they will not take their omission as being enforced by anything other than exigencies of space. My great discovery in researching this book is that everyone – especially in the North-east – has a worthwhile story to tell, whether I have managed to find room for it or not.

Sadly, but inevitably given their age range, some of my witnesses have subsequently died. As, however, it has been difficult to ascertain exact dates and occurrences, the decision has been made to give the year of birth only. I can, however, report that Alexina Fleming – the first person to appear in *Grampian Lives* (Volume 1) – did live on to 2012, when she reached the age of 107.

Alexina tackling the cake on her 106th birthday.

CONTENTS

LIFE IN THE FAMILY 10

The North-east owes something to them .... Bill Sleigh   **Tolquhon, Tarves**   12
Hobbling up the aisle .... Anne Stephen   **Bridge of Muchalls**   14
Who am I? .... Ian Robertson   **Forres**   14
A rural education .... Allan Presley   **Craigdam**   18
He was Victorian in his attitudes .... Iris Wilson   **Dailuaine**   21
Respect .... Gavin Joiner   **Buckie**   22
The community scribe .... Jane Yeadon   **Dunphail**   24
A child at school, an adult at home .... Nancy Davidson   **Laurencekirk**   26
It must be 250 years old .... Janette Anderson   **Luthermuir**   28
Granny Nicol .... Eleanor Fordyce   **Gartly**   30
Paying your way .... Colin McLennan   **Muchalls**   32
Alone but not lonely .... Shona Barclay   **Cammachmore**   34
Up the close .... George Paul   **Elgin**   36
Work hard, play hard .... Lorna Johnson   **Stonehaven**   38
We didn't do friends .... Moira Cameron   **Muchalls**   40
There was always something going on .... John Duncan   **Inverbervie**   43
A reality check .... David Shiach   **Dailuaine**   45

LIFE ON THE LAND 48

Carry on cooking .... Nina Smith   **Netherley**   50
Running faster just to stay still .... Tom McGregor   **Auchnagatt**   52
Don't make me laugh! .... Bob Souter   **Netherley**   55
A farmer's life is all ups and downs .... John Robb   **Echt**   57
Give me the shallow end! .... John Copland   **Strathdon**   59
Rise and fall of an agricultural industry .... Duncan Forbes   **Fetterangus**   60
From town to country .... Brian Robertson   **Rothienorman**   63
Great fun, all of it .... Douglas Aberdein   **Tarland**   64
Get on! Get on! .... Charlie Allan   **Methlick**   66
It must have been the smell .... Davie and Evie Alexander   **Ellon**   68
How hard everyone had to work .... Janet Byth   **Fintry**   70
Eggs and horses: how it used to be .... Gavin Sim   **Cuminestown**   72
Hard! Windy! Cold! .... Maggie Fraser   **Bridge of Muchalls**   73
That's just the way I like it .... A Life-long Farmer   **Mearns**   74
A mug's game .... Kevin Gilbert   **Kintore**   76

ALL MANNER OF FOLK: Part 1 80

The health educator: so little has changed .... Horace Thomson   **Lossiemouth**   82
The gala queen: just a fun week, really .... Aileen and Bill Allan   **Macduff**   85
The building magnate: hard work and honest effort .... Stewart Milne   **Tough**   87

The photographer: a special light . . . . Andy Hall **Stonehaven** 89
The radical activist: still committed . . . . Corrie Cheyne **Durno** 92
The student: the future comes from the past . . . . Kirsty Strang **Torphins** 94

GOING TO THE SCHOOL 96

Thirty-four years in PE: I think I'll hold on to that! . . . . John Black **Fraserburgh** 98
The retired teacher: that's what's made it all worthwhile . . . . Moira Jolly **Stonehaven** 99
An outstanding Head . . . . John Cummine **Inverurie** 102
The school bus: lessons in life . . . . Clark Simpson **Johnshaven** 104
The curriculum adviser: school must work for everyone . . . . Andrew Dick **Buchanhaven** 104
The new methods: my position was impossible . . . . Douglas Aberdein **Lumphanan** 105
Into digs at 12: I'd had enough . . . . Elspeth Dey **Glenbuchat** 107
The born teacher: I'd always wanted to teach . . . . Wilma Machray **Inverurie** 108
The retired Head: it's not so easy now . . . . Pat Walker **Tough** 111
The Qualifying exam: parting of the ways . . . . Mary Harvie **New Byth** 113
A Fifties education: I just took to it . . . . Richard Bennett **Alvah** 114
A small rural school: oh yes, I had the Geddeses... . . . . Alan Blacklaws **Muchalls** 117
Dominie at 24: always on duty . . . . Roddy Duncan **Fetterangus** 119
Secondary education: I wish I could say something positive . . . . Daphne Frances **Aberlour** 121
The incomer: from Sussex to Tin Academy . . . . Janet Pickering **Ballindalloch** 123
The dyslexic: complete frustration . . . . Martin Sim **Stonehaven** 125
The walk to school: I've been fearful ever since . . . . Betty McCorkindale **Banff** 126
The tawse: I detested that dominie . . . . Gavin Sim **Cumminestown** 127
The Journalist: I can trace it all back to my Primary school . . . . . Norman Harper **Alford** 128
The teacher: I really enjoy it . . . . Craig Sim **Elgin** 130
The school leaver: developing my own voice . . . . Jenni Keenan **Stonehaven** 131

GOING TO THE KIRK 132

A music heard no more . . . . Charles Birnie **Strichen** 134
What can you put in its place? . . . . Pierre Fouin **Bieldside** 135
You just jumped . . . . William McRae **Peterhead** 135
A protesting Catholic . . . . Dorothy Shaw **Blairs** 136
A bit of ritual . . . . Charlie Allan **Methlick** 138
Son of the manse . . . . Ian Campbell **Inverbervie** 138
Daughter of the manse . . . . Gwen Haggart **Cuminestown** 139
A forgotten hero . . . . George Philip **Fyvie** 141
The Reverend Jean . . . . Jean Montgomerie **Culter** 142
Let us gather by the river . . . . Andy Hall **Maryculter** 144
It was doing my head in . . . . Roseanne Fitzpatrick **Peterhead** 145
Amidst God's nature . . . . Henry Irvine-Fortescue **Kingcausie** 147
The new ministers . . . . Fiona Squires **Newtonhill** 148
Not a pulpit but the people . . . . Tony Stephen **Banchory** 148
Sometimes I don't strike people as a minister at all . . . . Ian Murray **Dufftown** 151

Uganda, not South Africa . . . . Rachael Adams   **Kinneff** 153

It doesn't stop me believing . . . . Jenni Keenan   **Stonehaven** 155

ALL MANNER OF FOLK: Part 2   158

The local historian: a lot to be proud of . . . . Patrick Scott   **Huntly** 160

The farmer's daughter(1): we all had to pitch in . . . . Sybil Copland   **Foveran** 162

The story-teller: writing from memory . . . . Mary Munro   **Ballater** 165

The councillor: only in it for themselves? . . . . Raymond Bisset   **Keith Hall** 167

The fiddler . . . . Paul Anderson   **Tarland** 170

The prisoner: I've learned so much . . . . Prisoner #70351   **Aberdeenshire** 173

THE WORLD OF WORK   176

The travelling shop . . . . James Gordon   **Alford** 178

The signalman . . . . George Lawrie   **Lumphanan** 180

The distillery worker . . . . John Goodbrand   **Longmore** 181

The machine operator . . . . Alex Rennie   **Fraserburgh** 183

The bus conductress . . . . Anne Stephen   **Stonehaven** 184

The waitress . . . . Margaret Hay   **Tillyfourie** 185

The garage mechanic (male) . . . . Bill Allan   **Banff** 188

The joiner undertaker . . . . Norman Duguid   **Oldmeldrum** 189

The storeman . . . . Alan Riddell   **Turriff** 190

The printer . . . . John Smith   **Montrose** 192

The hairdresser . . . . Martin Sim   **Stonehaven** 194

The builder's apprentice . . . . Colin McLennan   **Newtonhill** 196

The demolition man . . . . Gavin Sim   **Cuminestown** 196

The butcher . . . . Jim Collie   **Kemnay** 197

The painter decorator . . . . Duncan Naysmith   **Inverurie** 198

The bakery director . . . . Bill Deans   **Huntly** 199

The garden centre director . . . . Marion Bell   **Kellockbank** 202

The apprentice cooper . . . . Ian Murray   **Dufftown** 203

The garage mechanic (female) . . . . Laura Ironside   **Cammachmore** 205

LIFE AT THE BIG HOUSE   206

The chauffeur's daughter . . . . Dorothy Shaw   **Milltimber** 208

A lovely gentleman . . . . Isobel McRobbie   **Ballogie** 210

Outsiders don't understand . . . . Elspeth Dey   **Glenbuchat** 212

A certain social grace . . . . Charlie Allan   **Methlick** 213

What, still here, Burnett? . . . . Bill Burnett   **Boyndlie** 214

The jewel in Banffshire's crown . . . . Clare Russell   **Ballindalloch** 215

A figure of authority . . . . Lena Burr   **Rickarton** 220

The keeper of the castle . . . . Andrew Bradford   **Kincardine o'Neil** 221

Maintain, protect, improve . . . . Henry Irvine-Fortescue   **Kingcausie** 226

ALL MANNER OF FOLK: Part 3 · 230

The motorcyclist: the first lady biker . . . . Anne Stephen — **Muchalls** 232
The mineralologist: learning how to keek . . . . Ian Cameron — **Ballater** 234
The newcomer: it takes a village to bring up a child . . . . Joel Sandé — **Alford** 237
The folk singer: song and the Doric were all about me . . . . . . Barbara-Ann Burnett — **Tyrie** 241
The female referee . . . . Morag Pirie — **Parkhill** 243

ONSHORE AND OFFSHORE: Life along the coast · · · · · · · · · · 246

Skill and hard graft . . . . A Life-Long Fisherman — **Moray Firth** 248
Sold down the River Lossie . . . . John Thomson — **Lossiemouth** 250
The oil, the sea and overfishing . . . . William Cowie — **Portessie** 255
The fisherfolk are my tribe . . . . Jack Findlay — **Portknockie** 257
The salt of the earth and sea . . . . Celia Craig — **Gourdon** 260
Nae guid'll cam o' a quine aboard! . . . . Roseanne Fitzpatrick — **Peterhead** 262
No messing about with my mother . . . . Iain Bruce — **Peterhead** 263
Oil, the new frontier . . . . Eric McNeil — **The North Sea** 265
From Buckie to Baku . . . . George Smith — **Portsoy** 270

LIFE IN THE COMMUNITY · 274

Fun and games in the village

Now there's only the football . . . . Ally Irvine — **Cuminestown** 276
The highlight of the month . . . . Isobel McRobbie — **Ballogie** 278
The mighty *Dauntless* . . . . Clark Simpson — **Johnshaven** 279
Loo with a view . . . . Heather Bisset — **Peterhead** 280
The travelling players . . . . Ian Law — **Keig** 282
From St Ninian's Park to Auchenblae Golf Club . . . . Kenny Morgan — **Auchenblae** 282
A magic experience . . . . Martin Sim — **Stonehaven** 285
The whole community joined in . . . . Janet Byth — **Fintry** 286
Childhood games: life-long lessons . . . . Irene Watt — **Gardenstown** 287

Moving with the times

The big night out – Fifties style . . . . John Goodbrand — **Glenlivet** 289
Jolson and a smart white suit . . . . Alan Robertson — **Kintore** 290
How else to meet the opposite sex? . . . . Duncan Naysmith — **Inverurie** 292
The real bee's knees . . . . Alistair Black — **Keig** 293
A real fashionista . . . . Roseanne Fitzpatrick — **Peterhead** 294
Raves were all the rage . . . . Marianne Bell — **Inverurie** 295

Pillars of the community

The bobby: commonsense, that's the thing . . . . Stanley Rothney — **Culter** 296
The country store: nobody had heard of pizzas . . . . Gertrude Mowat — **Newtonhill** 299
The country doctor: who would you rather be? . . . . Pierre Fouin — **Culter** 301

The rep: too much for the poor lassie . . . . Robbie Gordon   **Alford**   304

The escapee – keeping up the record   . . . . Heather Bisset   **Peterhead**   304

The savings bank: correct to the last penny . . . . Aileen Allan   **Macduff**   305

The postmistress: more than just a business . . . . Doreen Aldridge   **Archiestown**   306

The postie: daily visitor, trusted friend   . . . . Alan Riddell   **Turriff**   308

Scotland's last handloom weaver   . . . . Janette Anderson   **Luthermuir**   309

The railway signalman: our water came by train . . . . Eleanor Fordyce   **Udny Station**   311

The landlord: local worthies at the bar . . . . Ian Murray   **Dufftown**   313

ALL MANNER OF FOLK: Part 4 314

The local businessman: skylarks and ironmongery   . . . . Stuart Watson   **Inverurie**   316

The government administrator: I owe a lot to Tyrie . . . . Mary-Helen Bayne   **Tyrie**   319

The farmer's daughter: it gets in the blood . . . . Moira Ross   **Craigievar**   321

The international footballer   . . . . Neil Simpson   **Newmachar**   325

The concert pianist: talent and hours of hard work . . . . Joseph Long   **Muchalls**   329

HOME AND AWAY, HERE AND NOW 332

Here and there; changes in the community

We pass but never speak . . . . Ally Irvine   **Cuminestown**   334

Sounding like a grumpy old man . . . . James Coull   **Peterhead**   335

An empty countryside   . . . . Eric Brown   **Stonehaven**   336

Mutual respect, that's the key . . . . Clark Simpson   **Johnshaven**   337

End of an era . . . . Evelyn Hood   **Turriff**   338

Only a place to sleep? . . . . Ian Law   **Alford**   339

It's changing so fast . . . . Douglas Aberdein   **Coull**   341

My generation had the best of it . . . . Charlie Allan   **Methlick**   343

In harmony with the environment? . . . . Richard Bennett   **Torphins**   343

You can't stop the clock . . . . Ian Campbell   **Inverbervie**   345

The village shops are going . . . . David Hutchison   **Auchenblae**   345

They'll grow out of it . . . . Rachael Adams   **Kinneff**   346

Councillor at 18 . . . . Jenni Keenan   **Stonehaven**   346

The soldier's tale: National Service

The experience made me grow up . . . . William McRae   **Maud**   348

I got discipline all right . . . . Ian Stevenson   **Keith**   349

I'd never been out of Scotland before . . . . Duncan Forbes   **Kininmonth**   351

Among the best years of my life . . . . William Sinclair   **Quilquox**   351

The stuff of the North-east

I've come across plenty of laughs . . . . Jack Benzie   **Huntly**   353

Civic action . . . . Donald Munro   **Montrose**   354

The North-east in action . . . . John Kemp   **Rhynie**   354

A country village . . . . Margaret McArthur   **Fettercairn**   356

A real earthiness . . . . Cathy Macaslan   **Old Deer** 357

The book of the North-east . . . . William Malcolm   **Aberlour** 357

A land worth fighting for . . . . Maggie Fraser   **Bridge of Muchalls** 358

The morality of the North-east . . . . Norman Harper   **Alford** 359

Going away showed the value of home . . . . Irene Watt   **Gardenstown** 360

A sense of belonging . . . . Fiona Squires   **Stonehaven** 361

My wee Kincardineshire village . . . . Eric McNeil   **Muchalls** 362

A close knit spirit . . . . Ian Murray   **Dufftown** 364

The very air seems different . . . . Sarah Malone   **Peterhead** 365

GRAMPIAN LIVES: CHANGE AND CONTINUITY

Volume 2 of *Grampian Lives* means what it says on the cover: a continuation of the story begun in Volume 1, 1900-1950. Its purpose is to draw upon a storehouse of individual reminiscences and photographs by which to track the everyday experience and familiar human concerns of a broad cross section of North-east folk, as their lives have carried them through the final decades of the 20th century and into the opening years of the present one: 1950-2010.

The guiding ambition has been to gather together significant episodes, culled from some 350 remembered lives, and then to make of them a collective diary of a region and of its people as, day by day and year on year, they have moved from the static black-and-white of the immediate post war era into the instantly mobile, multi-faceted, brightly coloured Facebook world of today.

At the point reached at the conclusion of Volume 1, the majority of rural and coastal North-east people were still leading lives that would have been intimately recognisable to those at its beginning. In 1950, 'Grampian' endured as a self-contained and largely self-sufficient region of a single large city, one which was surrounded by a stretching hinterland of agricultural terrain, dotted by industrious rural villages and fringed by a chain of fishing settlements.

Out there, beyond the urban boundaries, farming and the fish remained the dominant occupations. For the most part, its workers and their families subsisted in small cottages, lit by Tilley lamp and heated by an open grate fire. Frequently, their water had to be fetched in buckets from spring or well, and sanitation meant a shed out at the back, while transportation was by push bike and Alexander's Bluebird. The weekly groceries were purchased by hard won cash at a family run local shop or delivered in its van. Domestically, entertainment came from the 'wireless' or a pack of cards, communally by a dance, a whist drive, WRI meeting in the village hall, or the yearly Christmas party for the bairns and the summer charabanc outing to the links at Banff or the Pleasure Park at Turriff.

Education was divided into 'Senior' and 'Junior' courses and while all received a thorough grounding in the Three Rs and General Knowledge, nine out of ten pupils quit school at 15. If male, they then moved out into the adult world of a job in a practical trade, a position on a nearby farm or a berth on the family trawler; for the female counterparts, a shop, office, hotel or – still – domestic service, to be followed by a life-long marriage leading to child rearing (always in that order) and housekeeping, were the predetermined destinations.

Above all, life appeared to be predictable, familiar and thoroughly local: offspring walked to the same local school that their parents had attended, fell into the same occupations, courted and married within the same circle, spoke the same Doric, attended the old parish church, participated in the fixed annual round of communal events, and regarded the local bobby, the local dominie, the local minister and the local doctor as the fixed pillars of the one society. To walk down the village street was to encounter a host of familiar faces and engage in easy conversation about the shared features of a known and unproblematic world. Youth culture, pop music, foreign holidays, the car at the door, daily commuting, suburban owner occupation, multi-channel plasma screen television, North Sea oil, supermarket shopping, open heart surgery, multi-culturalism, legalised equality in racial, gender and sexual rights, bar codes, a chorus of instant tweetings, the personal computer and the universal mobile phone, would – all of them – have been conjectured, if at all, as the visitations of a distantly futuristic universe.

We have, from that simple starting point, come a long way, have we not? That would, however, depend on what you are looking at. In material terms there is no doubt that everyday life has been transformed and assuredly for the better. That much would be readily agreed by each one of the witnesses in our pair of books – but then, having nodded their assent to the proposition that daily existence 60 years on has become more affluent, more comfortable, less restricted and more various, they would go on to invite you to peer beneath these externals and into the character of the lives within. And here, the verdict becomes less certain. The elders' generation, those who grew up against the solid background of the older values, is often troubled by the less securely knowable swirl of late century challenges they have been asked to mature into. Drug taking, family break ups, binge drinking, obesity, promiscuity, credit card debt, youth unemployment and youth indiscipline, a culture of benefits taking, the spectacle of empty churches and abandoned village schools, and, running through it all, the erosion to the good old virtues of thrift, piety, work ethic, respect, neighbourly support and hospitality – all these may be cited as evidence of the way in which true contentment has been supplanted by a sickly and bloated individualistic materialism.

But it would be misleading to use the accumulation of years represented by the span of our two volumes to draw up a facile balance sheet of quantitative gains and qualitative loss – to seek to match the teenager's centrally heated, Wi-Fi'd bedroom against the cosy family hearth, the convenient ready meals against the plain oatmeal fare, the Guidance staff counsellor rather than the leather tawse, the greater tolerance now given to race, creed and sexual orientation against the firmer social disciplines of a past age.

What counts are the people themselves and the extent to which the North-east has enabled them to make something worthwhile out of their lives. And here the story shifts from one of brute change to that of simple human continuity. Look into this book and compare its accounts with those of the earlier volume. Set the Torphins of Kirsty Strang (born 1990) against that of Jimmy Morrison (1917), or the Jenni Keenan's (1992) Stonehaven against that of Bel Wilson (1903), or the Buckie of George Smith (1976) against Isabel Harrison's (1926), or the teaching commitment of a Craig Sim (1972) compared to that of Mary Geddes (1904) and the self deprecating devotion to maintaining the family farm of Kevin Gilbert (1967) to the good humoured tales of orraman toil of a Dod Forbes (1914) – and you will discover that the same essential concerns endure: to fashion a decent, well made life out of what the North-east has thrown at you, one in which useful endeavour, parental nurture and neighbourly service are the true measure.

Indeed, what has been most striking among the younger testimonies has been the willingness of their speakers to embrace the past, to view their parents and their grandparents not as tiresome relics, but as mentors and as valued companions. Far from being rejected, the example given by past lives has been grasped as a bequest to build upon. And beyond the immediate domestic circle, those who have followed on would see the village and the family, their family and their village, as a ticket of membership into the wider community of inherited experience. To them, 'society' does indeed exist and their own North-east is seen as a preciously coherent and life-giving version of it.

The circumstances change but the people endure. This, after some 350 separate interviews in which the birth dates have ranged from the first to the final decade of the 20th century, is the conclusion to be drawn from *Grampian Lives*, Volume 2, as well as Volume 1. That it is one which emerges from the stories individuals tell about their own circumstances shows something else as well: the binding power of personal recollection. Here, memory acts as something more than a kist filled with the inert data of an historical past; rather it is the golden thread by which members of today's generation join their biographies to those who have gone before.

Without exception, my witnesses have been concerned to lay claim to the shape of their parents' and their grandparents' careers as the essential context in which to set their own. They have been anxious, too, to establish their native heath as the place which has informed their own adult strengths and imparted to them a sense of what being part of a community should be.

This is as true of an international football star like Neil Simpson, looking back to the infant days of kicking a ball among the dubs and mire of his grandfather's farm near Cluny, as it is of a seven year-old Paul Anderson discovering that battered old fiddle beneath the bed in his granny's glory hole and becoming inspired to take up the bow of a great North-east tradition. And it is also true of the future English teacher Richard Bennett recalling the days when his widowed mother would hasten to Jupps Sale at Aberlour Orphanage to pick up the discarded bundles of books that would feed his growing appetite for reading – and also of Andrew Bradford being prepared for the responsibility of sustaining a costly inherited castle by a Spartan boyhood regime of log chopping, freezing bedrooms and no television. And so it goes on: there is the teenage Rachel Adams embracing the Baptist faith of her parents as the call to donate a year's missionary work to the streets of Entebbe; and Mary-Helen Bayne lauding the early schooling she received at Tyrie because it laid down the standards of rigorous application which enabled her to rise to the very top of the British Civil Service down in Whitehall; and Bill Deans determined to build upon the family business which began in the small kitchen of an ordinary Huntly council house, where his mother baked shortbread to raise funds for the local Pipe Band. All of them – and the many rest – are representative of the long line of witnesses who give proud and grateful testimony to the extent to which their early North-east experiences have enriched their own sense of identity and implanted it in a firmly rooted growth.

These are the formative experiences, ones of place and of history, which the folk who fill the pages of the two books find themselves reaching for when they are invited to return to their own upbringing. And this act of telling and of retelling is the process by which they are bringing the past not only into the present, but, by projecting its values and its lessons forwards, into the future too.

All changed, certainly – but changed utterly? Not at all. Reading through this collective biography, and looking at the North-east faces which stare out at us across the years, we become aware that what really concerns people remains much the same. Birth, growing up, going to school, then out to work, seeking to pass on a better life to one's children and, on the way, meeting the common challenges of sicknesses, land and weather, the daily struggle to earn a living, and to hold together a settled family life, the responsibility of playing a part in the life of one's community – these are, and always have been, the real stuff of human concern.

It would be fascinating to speculate what dramatic developments a 'Volume 3, 2010-2050' would record. But whatever wonders and disturbances that coming era will bring, the record of continuity through change, to be encountered in the two antecedent books, is sufficiently strong to encourage us to think they will remain truly 'Grampian'.

LIFE IN THE FAMILY

Anderson family line up, Thistle Cottage, Luthermuir, 2012, on the occasion of Janette and Francie's 46th wedding anniversary. From left: Francie, George McDonald, Michelle, Hamish, Murdoch, Hazel, John Souttar, Martin, Janette, Harry Souttar, Mhiran Souttar, Heather, Jack Souttar, Heather Souttar. In front are Rory, Charlotte and Archie.

11

'That large and rambling house': the Dower House at Newstead of Tolquhon in the 1940s.

Although my father never, to my knowledge, rolled his sleeves up and set to work in the fields, he took an intense interest in his cattle and was always thinking of ways to improve his stock.

The North-east owes something to them

I was born in 1937 at Newseat of Tolquhon, Tarves: the old dower house to Tolquhon Castle. My father's family could go back to four generations of farmers. I grew up in a social milieu that has almost faded from our memory now. At that time very few of the farmers we knew actually worked, at least not in the physical sense. That isn't to say they took no interest in their land. Although my own father never, to my knowledge, rolled his sleeves up and set to work in the fields, he took an intense interest in his cattle and was always thinking of ways to improve his stock. He was a noted breeder of Shorthorns and he'd go round each day to confer with his stockman as to the herd's progress and welfare. He would go to all the shows and kept up with the literature on the subject. Latterly he exported to the Americas and to Canada, too.

Just about the only time he'd go out into the fields for some physical labour would be at hairst time. But he wasn't necessarily welcomed. Once he decided to take over a tractor which was pulling the trailer on to which men were forking up the stooks; he kept driving in a jerky fashion with the result that the man at the back was in constant danger of being jolted off. After observing this performance for a while, the grieve came up to me and muttered, 'Ach, wull ye tell yer faither that hi's nidded back in the hoose fer his tea!'

In those days there were a number of old well-established farming families in the area, families such as the Mackies, the Durnos, the Fowlies and the Campbells. They had evolved their own gentleman farmer culture. Everyone knew everyone else and there would be a lot of cross visiting. This could entail a deal of formality. If a new family moved into the area, the ladies of our houses would call by and drop a visiting card. Then, after a decent interval – a fortnight or so – they would phone up to invite the newly arrived to come round for afternoon tea on such and such a date. This would serve as initiation into local society.

The farm runs to 500 acres now, quite sizeable by the standards then. We employed a team of up to 14 and always had a pair of live-in housemaids. We were brought up to avoid getting over-friendly with them but always to be polite and, above all, kind. We took their presence for granted. I would come down at about eight in the morning and there would be Janet with the fire lit and the breakfast properly laid out. I'd say something like, 'What a nice morning, Janet!' and never think that to her it must already be well into her working day

For the most part, life ran very smoothly. We all sat at table to take a meal together, as the one family unit. To do that would have been regarded as a vital social function, a bonding process and the opportunity to exchange views and display proper manners. Nowadays we all live better, have more varied diets and, of course, are far less formal in our behaviour – but it's difficult not to think that something has been lost that has been valuable in binding the family together. One of the factors in this has been the changing role of women. In my young day the wife was looked upon to ensure that everything in the household ran smoothly, that when the men came in for the evening meal at six o'clock everything would be set out for them, on time, all in its due place. But now most

wives look to have their own lives and don't regard the running of the home as a full or exclusive concern. People have different expectations now and I can't say I blame them – but a little something has gone in the process, I think.

Looking back, this way of life can seem highly privileged, even pampered. But to us then it wasn't like that at all. My father had his due place in the community and was aware that he had social responsibilities. People worked for him and although their pay might not be great they would be taken care of. There was an implicit bargain: care in return for service. If a farm servant fell ill, my mother would call round with the offer of help. At Christmas, mother held a party for all the children, with presents all round. To my parents working on the farm meant more than a contract of employment: it meant 'care'.

I come from a class which even in the Fifties was dying out. The work that used to keep ten or so in employment is now done by two or three. The idea of a gentleman farmer who contented himself with a hands-off oversight is now almost unthinkable; all my relatives who are still in farming have to work from morning to dusk. But in their time, my parents' class played its part in maintaining not only agricultural efficiency but in making their communities well ordered and content. The North-east owes something to them.

No longer part of a bygone social milieu: Bill Sleigh in 1986 when he was working in business in the south of England.

Bill Sleigh, born 1937, interviewed 2011: Tolquhon, Tarves

Thank goodness for a long dress and a supportive groom: the newlywed Mr and Mrs Stephen, Fetteresso Church, 1961.

In those days it was the custom to blacken the feet of the bride beforehand.

Hobbling up the aisle

My wedding was due on the Saturday in Fetteresso Church and in those days it was the custom to blacken the feet of the bride beforehand. So by the Thursday night I was looking out for something to happen. Sure enough I heard this car drawing up at the farm. 'Ah, ah!', I thought, 'something's up'. Then a second car came along and pulled up. I could hear voices so I came to the conclusion it was time to be making myself scarce. My plan was to escape down the road. But it was dark and the lights of the car blinded me; I landed up in a ditch surrounded by bramble bushes. I tried to get to my feet but found I just couldn't. Something was very wrong with my leg.

By this time my visitors were shouting that they were going to come and get me. I called out that I was in the ditch and couldn't move. They thought I was just joking and reached down and pulled me out quite roughly, laughing all the time. But one of them was a nurse and she realised that something was wrong all right. She got me into the house and plonked my foot into a pail of cold water so as to bring down the swelling.

I went to my bed thinking that all I had suffered was a sprained ankle. But the next day things were no better and my father decided I'd have to go to Foresterhill to get the thing checked over. When they told me my leg was broken I just couldn't believe it. The doctor put my leg in plaster and wrote on it, 'She's getting married in the morning!'

Well, there was no putting off the wedding: the church and the reception were all booked and the invitations out. I got through it; the dress was nice and long and completely hid the plaster; my father and I proceeded up the aisle, he with his stick, me with mine. The minister had placed a chair for me to sit on but I did manage to stand for my vows.

As you can imagine, the honeymoon was somewhat marred! I had to cut it short because I needed to get back for more x-rays at the hospital. Still, we had one night at the Station Hotel, Carnoustie and then a couple of nights over at Oban. I've still got the receipts – for the two of us, bed and breakfast at Carnoustie, it was 12/6; Oban was a wee bit more expensive – 13 shillings! The cake had cost all of 12/6.

We would have had our Golden Wedding this very year, but sadly John passed away 16 months ago. He was a gentle and quiet man, devoted to his family. My John, we miss him so much.

Anne Stephen, born 1937, interviewed 2011: Bridge of Muchalls

Who am I?

Who am I? Well, that's a question I've been trying to answer for some time! Now, the BBC programme, 'Who do you think you are', has a whole team of researchers who are able to present their famous subjects with the answers about their past on a plate; I've had to do it all myself. I've been deeply involved in genealogical researches, on the internet, visiting registry offices, writing letters, getting on the phone. Gradually I've been able to piece together an answer to that question, 'Who am I?'

I've always known I was born in 1939, immediately boarded out, fostered and then, when I was 17, adopted by my foster parents. Fifty years later, I went onto the Scottish People website; all I had was this document, 'Ian Robertson, born July 1939 in Scotland'. That was it – no specific place, no exact date. I tried to dig deeper but when I clicked onto the General Registrar of Scotland site all I got back was 'No matches'. I discovered that in the whole of the country for July 1939 there had been registered 18 'Ian Robertsons', but apparently I wasn't one of them!

But, if you search for 'Ian Simpson' you'll find him – it's me. Now, I'd realised from the start that I was born illegitimate; I did have contact with my mother whose name was 'Simpson'. If you use that name rather than Robertson you'll unearth what is referred to as 'a corrective entry' and then you'll discover the exact place of my birth. You'll have read your Dickens – imagine something like Dotheboys Hall in *Nicolas Nickleby*. Like that, my birthplace was a big square building, a real institution that dates back to Victorian times. It was called 'Balblair House'. It looks quite imposing in the photograph I've got, but really it was what was commonly termed the 'Poor House' for Nairn.

'**Like something out of Dickens**': Balblair house, Nairn, birth place of Ian Robertson.

Balblair House was demolished in 2000. But in its time it was what was called a 'combination hospital' and most districts had one. The authorities had come up with the notion of organising all the odd private and charitable 'hospitals' they'd inherited from the 19th century into a series of centralised institutions. If you read an official report of 1946, you'll come across terms like 'Mental Defectives', 'Homeless Lunatics', 'Indigent Poor'. And that's the place where I entered the world!

'**Just this old man leaning on a stick**': the grandparents Ian never really met.

At the time of my birth it had 52 beds; you could say that they were used to shut off from the outside world all those difficult cases which society couldn't deal with in any other way. It's obvious that illegitimate births were one of them and that my mother went – or was sent – to Balblair House to have her child delivered in a private location, after which she could go back and resume her life.

The matron in charge of the register at the House had made this entry under respective columns: 'Name of inmate – Elsie Simpson'; 'Address – Moy Carse'; 'Date of arrival' – June, 1939; 'Date of departure' – a week after my birth. Then there's this: 'Disease on admission – pregnancy'.

As I've said, I always knew my blood mother. She would visit my adopted home at birthday and Christmas times. She was a hard working domestic servant and cook. She'd made a career, looking after widower or retired farmers as a housekeeper. Then she went to Lord Melville's as resident cook in Glenferness House, a large estate on the banks of the Findhorn.

My adoption when I was 17 came about, I suppose, because I was now on the brink of adulthood and was nearing conscription age. It was time to turn what had begun as fostering into a more formal set up. I'd lived with the Robertsons all my life and had been treated as a member of the family, so I was quite happy at this turn of events.

Why had the Robertsons decided to take me in? Perhaps they'd wanted a companion to their son, Bill, but what you've got to remember is that back then fostering was quite

'**The ta'en in bairn**': Ian, aged eight.

The brother he hadn't seen for 56 years: the reunion with Michael (left) at Elgin, 2011.

I knew I hadn't been the only child he'd fathered with my mother and that I had a full brother. One day the phone rang; I picked it up and heard the question, 'Do you know who I am?'

common out in the country. The phrase used was to be 'ta'en in' – and that was me, 'a ta'en in bairn'. I was never told about my father, but as I was growing up I did manage to put two and two together to some extent.

The Robertsons were farm workers. They had a brother, a Jimmy Robertson, who spent his working life on farms in the Buckie area. He was deaf and dumb but could use sign language. I'd see him at family gatherings such as funerals, making signs to other people; I learned to pick up on some of what he was saying. From this I gathered that my natural father was a man called James Watt, and that he was a career soldier. He eventually married Janet Robertson, a sister of the Robertsons who had fostered me.

I knew I hadn't been the only child he'd fathered with my mother and that I had a full brother called Michael. One day, much later, the phone rang; I picked it up and heard the question, 'Do you know who I am?' His voice had traces of Morayshire in it and I answered, 'Yes – it's Michael isn't it?' This was my brother whom I hadn't clapped eyes on for 56 years. He was living in Luton but was coming up on a visit and would like to see me.

I knew that he'd gone into the services when he was 17/18. He'd had a career in British Aerospace and was now retired. Unlike me, he hadn't been fostered out and had stayed with our mother all through his childhood. She'd been able to keep him in her small flat at Glenferness House where her employers had accepted her situation. He was three years younger than me but a fair bit taller. I now introduce myself as 'his little-big brother'.

He was able to fill me in on more family detail. He said, 'You do know we've a sister, don't you?' I'd always suspected there was someone else; when my natural mother came to see me she'd be asked, 'An fa are y' aff tae, noo?' as she was leaving and she'd reply, 'Oh, to see Jeannie!' So this was now confirmation.

I only ever saw my grandfather the once. I was 18 and had newly got my driving licence. My mother had come over on a visit on the bus and Innes Robertson – the man I called my father – suggested that I might like to drive her back to Glenferness House in his car. Well, it was something special to be entrusted with the family car so off we went. On the way, she said, 'Oh, I'd like to caa in at ma faither's hoose; I'll show you far it is'. Just as you leave Forres you come to a row of pensioners' cottages called 'Ferry Road'. We pulled up in front of one of them. A man came out and leaned on the gate. He asked, 'Fa's that ye've gat wi ye?' 'Oh, it's Ian,' my mother said. 'Ian fa?' 'My Ian!' It was semi-dark, we couldn't see each other clearly, and he was just this old man leaning on a gate. And that was that – we never met again.

As for my father, I likewise only saw him the once – I think. He and I were at a funeral and he was in the crowd that gathered at the house afterwards. But nobody introduced us and I never spoke to him or him to me. But, as I said, he did get married to Janet Robertson, the sister of my adoptive father, and they had five or six children – my half siblings. So James Watt became both my father and an uncle!

The Robertsons didn't have a good name for him. He'd been known as a 'bit of a lad'

Together at last:
Ian's natural parents,
Elsie and James Watt
finally man and wife,
late 1980s.

Sixty years earlier:
with Michael (left),
a neighbour (right) and
Drift the dog, 1950.

**'Love makes
memories':**
the shared headstone.
Ian's mother is the
'Second Wife.'

and a womaniser. I got hold of a copy of the medical papers he had when he joined the Gordon Highlanders in 1932. His height is given as 5 feet 3 inches – my height. James Watt must have had a silver tongue to have gone from one woman to another and have children by some of them. But when he met my mother he was in his prime, had been all over the world as a soldier and no doubt there was something glamorous about him.

But here comes the climax of the story. In July 1961, when I was 22, he and my mother finally got married. I've got a photo of the couple taken from the *Forres Gazette*. His wife, Janet Robertson, had died the year before and here he was, 22 years after my birth, marrying the woman who was my mother. Naturally, I'd known nothing of this turn of events, nothing at all. There's a headstone which the family erected. On it, Janet Robertson is described as 'the beloved wife of James Watt' and my mother, Elsie Simpson, as 'the second wife'. He lived till 1995, dying at the age of 86; my mother had passed away in 1997, aged 76. On the headstone are the words, 'Love makes memories'…

Ian Robertson, born 1939, interviewed 2011: Forres

I was
probably the
only one in
the class who
had a parent
who spoke
English in
the house
at all
frequently.

A rural education

L ife in Craigdam revolved round the school, the church, the family and the farming. There wasn't much else. For a start, there was no electricity. My father was a fairly well-to-do farmer and we did run a car, but we were the only ones. Hardly anyone had a phone.

My father was a big farmer in that he actually owned his land. I was the only one among my school mates who had a father in that position. The rest were tenant farm children or the kids of crofters, of tradesmen, the shepherd, jobs like that – and all connected in some way or other to agriculture. It was a widely scattered parish.

The school wasn't just a matter of going to the classroom for us: it was the centre of our natural lives. At dinner-time we'd all disappear into the woods just beyond the glebe land that bordered the school. At the end of the harvest the farmers would put these portable hen houses out among the stubble for the hens to scratch around for any grains of corn that would be left and we'd hop into the fields and steal the eggs. Or at other times we'd go and forage for neeps. We'd spend our lunch times doing that kind of thing.

You could say we were living our lives according to the rhythm of the seasons and the ways of the land. Everything revolved around the subject of farming. That's what we would be talking about, not football or pop music. I remember there were these two famous shorthorn breeders – Billy Strachan and Jim Durno – and we'd spend hours arguing about who was the better of the two. Or we'd argue over the merits of different tractor makes – to the extent of fisticuffs too. These were the days of the binders still and a road had to be cut out along the edges of the harvest fields to let them in. When we got back after the summer holidays there'd be great rows as to which of the farms had achieved the honour of being the first. And at the other end of the harvest, there'd be furious discussions over who had taken in the last sheaf the earliest. These were the things that shaped our outlook in life.

There would have been a social hierarchy at work and a rather obvious one at that, essentially based on land and the ownership of land. At its most basic it was the 'big farmers' and the rest. I was aware of our position – after all, we had a car. There was also the question of accents. My mother was a graduate teacher and mostly spoke English, although she could lapse into the Doric for her local friends. My father was a Doric speaker almost always. But I was probably the only one in the class who had a parent who spoke English in the house at all frequently. Although she never actually insisted on our doing so, we would tend to modify our speech when we were talking with her. And in the classroom the Doric was forbidden, of course. This didn't appear to create much difficulty – it was accepted that the school was the school and its language was English. In the playground we all reverted automatically to the Doric – and I was always careful to join in and to conceal any tendency to use English as my personal language. I wanted to be thought of as one of them.

But this experience did make me aware of the signs by which social differences could show themselves. I was aware that English was the language of aspirations; I wouldn't say

'There wasn't much else': the farming community of Craigdam.
IMAGE BY KIND
PERMISSION OF
ANNE BURGESS
WWW.GEOGRAPH.CO.UK

my mother was exactly a snob over this, but her attitude implicitly reinforced my sense of the possession of English as important in order to get on. I don't think many of my other classmates were in that position.

At Primary stage the whole community attended Craigdam as the local school. This would be the children of the big farmer, the minister and so on. It was run by one teacher and this was Miss Buchan. She was one of the old school with worsted thick stockings, brogues, hair up in a severe bun. She was regarded by the locals as something of an incomer – she'd come from Maud – but was also accorded a certain status in the village as 'the teacher'. You could sense this by the way she was treated at events like the school sports and the Christmas party. She was a respected body who held herself slightly aloof from the rest of the community. She lived in the school house and was thought of as one of the pillars of the community – like the minister, the doctor, the bobby, the big farmers.

Craigdam gave me an excellent early education. The small school offered a cohesion you wouldn't get in a bigger place. All the kids of the village were mixed in together. We did all kinds of things together, not just the Three Rs, but skills like music, art,

There were fancy dress parades – I went as a ghost – and you'd get prizes for bringing the best collection of flowers or of grasses

knitting – I learned to knit at that school – and PT, even if that was hardly Miss Buchan's forte! The teacher did everything, including playing the piano. The versatility of those old village school-mistresses was amazing.

The year was punctuated by events. We had an annual sports day, with the three-legged race and all the rest of it. There were fancy dress parades – I went as a ghost – and you'd get prizes for bringing the best collection of flowers or of grasses. We were in touch with the countryside around us. My own kids didn't know one tree from another but we certainly did. One year we needed a Christmas tree for the school party. We told Miss Buchan, 'We'll get one, Miss, if we can only get hold of an axe'. We did and a few of us toddled off to the woods – they belonged to a farmer called Captain Manson who'd lost an arm in the First World War but was still a crackshot. He was feared by the kids, so some of us kept watch while the rest jumped over the fence and chopped down this big tree – too big, but we simply chopped the top off and took it back to the school in triumph for our Christmas party. No kids in the city could have experienced anything like this. In some ways our lives were unregulated; we had the freedom of our environment, to roam and do what we liked. Miss Buchan simply took the view that she should leave us to it; she stayed in her school house and waited for us to appear with our prize.

But like the school, the church eventually closed. This had been part and parcel of our lives. Most of us came from families that had an attachment to the church and most of us did attend the Sunday school. The minister was a part of the community, someone who you would automatically expect to see at any community event.

Craigdam now has street lights and has grown a significant number of up-market houses. It's become commuting country. But back then you could say I was brought up in a definite North-east environment. My attitudes have been coloured by the agricultural, small community environment I grew up in and went to school in. I do recognise descriptions of values and North-east character that talk about integrity and hard work and straightness in behaviour and talk. But I think that these are what you might call rural values, the product of living in an agricultural setting; when I read about Laurie Lee's Somerset upbringing in *Cider with Rosie* I can see the familiarity of it all. And the historical setting is so important too. You've got to remember how very different the times were just after the war to the age we're living in now. Think of the fantastic changes that have come about in that time. In the village when I was growing up there was this old cattleman who'd only really ever been out of the place when he served in Flanders in the First World War. And the only thing that he seemed to have brought back from all that was the memory of digging holes and trenches. During my boyhood we went from horses to tractors and fields full of beasts to large-scale arable farming. And since then we've moved on to the computer and the mass ownership of cars and television sets…

Allan Presly, born 1941, interviewed 2003: Craigdam

After the fire: rebuilding the Orphanage, Aberlour, 1932. Iris's father, Jack Simpson, is in the back row, fifth from left.

He was Victorian in his attitudes

My father was a distillery worker. He ended up as head maltman – heid mattie, at Dailuaine, then Convalmore, Dufftown. He was a very sensitive man, very kind. I'd go up onto his knee and he'd sing to me – till I was 12. Then it was arms' distance. He was very Victorian in his attitudes. His belief was that it was the girl's parents who were the ones responsible for good morality. The males could sow their wild oats, that was to be expected, but the girls must be kept under strict control. Mother wasn't allowed to go to the WRI – that was 'women running idle'. He was severe in that way. She wasn't allowed to go into other people's houses. She could visit her mother, which she did as often as she could, maybe too often. The Aviemore train came into Dailuaine at nine, for Aberlour. Under the guise of taking me to school she would accompany me on it and then pop in to see her mother.

He had left school at 14. He was a very honest man, my father, and held cheating to be like taking the money out of someone's pocket. He was sitting this French exam and the teacher accused him of cheating! That was the end of it as far as my father was concerned. He walked out of the exam there and then, having just written 'J'ai'.

He was very keen for me to get on; he valued education. I remember him sitting poring over the *Pears Cyclopaedia*. I'd go home and say, 'I can't do this' and he'd get down to it with me.

Still time for some fun: Iris, aged four, 'marrying' her cousin, Angus Taylor, at her sister's wedding, 1946.

The distillery man: Jack Simpson with the Dailuaine team, outside the Exciseman's office, 1928; second back row, second left.

My father encouraged me, but he did have the opinion women should give way to men in the job market. If a woman and a man were applying for the same job, then in his view the man should always get it. I would argue, 'What if the woman was the one better able to do it?' But as far as he was concerned that just didn't come into it.

Iris Wilson, born 1942, interviewed 2004: Dailuaine

Respect

Religion and its organisations had enormous power. On Sundays we had the BB, then the church, then homework. That was it: no going outside or playing. The woman next door was disabled and the Sally Army would come and play at her door, but we weren't allowed to go to the window to watch. If you tried to go out you'd get a thrashing. There was hard discipline at school and hard discipline at home.

Buckie had, and still has, one of the largest Boys Brigade companies in the UK. 1st Buckie is attached to the South Church; to be a member was considered quite an honour. As well as the usual badges, sports and the Bugle Band, it ran a Saturday night social club where you took your girlfriend and learned to dance – once you were 15. But the Sunday morning Bible Class was in the church and all the officers and boys attended. The catalyst to its success was the Captain, Mr Duncan, who was Head of Science at the school and who ruled the company with an iron rod. The other officers were mostly

Note the hairstyle!
A youthful Gavin Joiner
(left) with sister Vera.

made up of teaching staff too, so respect for adults was instilled into us all. I believe that the present Captain is also a teacher and that the tradition of respect is being maintained.

My mother seemed to be afraid of us going astray. If you did manage to get to university but then had to return with nothing to show for it, you'd be an embarrassment to your family and pointed out in the street as such. Buckie was the kind of place where everyone knew everyone else and failure would instantly become the subject of common gossip.

When we were children we expected far less. I remember my mother had a pair of trousers made for me out of two legs from my father's old pairs. Children would be affronted nowadays if they didn't have the latest gear. But we weren't aware of our deprivation. At school everyone seemed to be on the same level, to wear the same kind of clothes, eat the same diet, have the same holidays.

When you died, the local paper would publish details if your estate was worth more than £1,000. I remember my father wouldn't buy a new car in case his savings went down below the £1,000 mark and he would fail to make it into the paper after his death. You all had to save – that was respectability.

It was a very orderly routine. Hands up when you wanted to speak. From day one, respect for the teacher. Stand up when she came into the room and salute the Headmaster whenever you passed his way, both inside and out of school. We all wore the school uniform: short trousers with long socks, gold and black stripes at the top and

The fantastic Coronation Year trip. Feeding the pigeons, Trafalgar Square with sister Vera, 1953.

The first Banffshire Boys Brigade recipient: being presented with the Duke of Edinburgh Silver Award, aged 17, 1961.

garters to hold them up straight. When you got home, change into your plain clothes so as to preserve the school ones. And when you were called to your tea there was no question of, 'Just a minute'; you jumped to it. You spoke when you were spoken to. Any misbehaviour or cheek at home then out to the back passage and the belt – swish! All parents were like that then. I remember a fisherman's son, coming to school with a gash down his face. His mother had hit him and her wedding ring had caught the skin.

We always had a car. The first one was AJA 728. It had a wooden floor. We used to take our holidays in it. We'd pack the crockery into a large metal tin and sleep and eat in the car. We'd park it in some quarry and sleep there. The seats would be removed and stowed in the boot and all four of us would sleep on the floor. In 1953 we were all packed into the car and drove off to London for the Coronation. It took days to get there and days to get back. It was a fantastic trip. We parked the car at Wembley and slept in it overnight.

There were benefits in being brought up in that way. It was harsh but it did teach you respect. I now find it hard when young people try to call you by your first name – we wouldn't have dreamt of doing that. You respected adults and that stuck. Even as a professional man I couldn't call my bank manager by his first name.

Gavin Joiner, born 1944, interviewed 2003: Buckie

The community scribe

My father was a tenant farmer at Tombain near Dunphail in Morayshire. He was also Ian Macpherson, novelist, writer, broadcaster. My mother – Elizabeth Macpherson – was also a writer.

But my father died suddenly in a motorbike accident when I was no more than six

'A wonderful mother' – six days of the week. A young Jane with her mother, writer Elizabeth Macpherson, at the family farm, late 1940s.

The man I came to call 'Dad': Dod with car, Tombain.

The young nurse – taken after Jane left the farm to embark on her nursing career.

weeks old. This left my mother in sole charge of the farm, with the responsibility of bringing up two young daughters. She also kept up her writing.

Tombain ran to about 50 acres of arable land and several hundred acres of hill grazing for sheep. It was viable, but needed constant hard work to make it so. I loved that farm and I loved growing up in the midst of real country life. You had great physical freedom and could wander wherever the fancy took you. I suppose that although I never knew my father I inherited this great feel for rural life. He'd been a university lecturer but had found academic life enclosing; his spirit had demanded the freedom of the outside natural world and there was a lot of that in me too.

My mother was the daughter of a Highland Church of Scotland minister and she'd scandalised the world by running away to marry my father whilst she was a young probationer teacher. So you could say my mother was very much a free spirit too – and that amuses me when I think the extent to which she expected us to lead conventional lives in properly paid positions.

Anyway, I must salute her for the way in which she kept things going and brought us both up. She had to run a difficult farm and then each week to turn out her piece for the *Bulletin* magazine. How she would have loved today's word processors instead of the old typewriter she had to hammer away at! She was a very fine writer. My sister, Elizabeth, and I have put together a forward to the compilation *Leaning on the Gate* and there we talk about how we used to dread that one day in the week when she ceased to be our mother and became the dedicated author, shutting herself away so as to get the article done before

Author daughter of an author mother.
A recent photograph.

Elizabeth Macpherson:
photograph on the cover of the collection of her writings put together by Jane and her sister, Elizabeth Baillie.

the deadline. Every other day of the week, she was always there for us, a wonderful, humorous, intuitive mother, but on those Mondays she became tense and withdrawn and definitely not to be approached.

But she did have help in running the farm. There was the grieve, Dod, who took his duties most seriously and was a skilled and progressive farmer. He came to marry my mother and become the man I called 'Dad'. He did a superb job on the farm and complemented my mother well: she was more the observer and he was very much the man of action. He liked throwing himself into the hurly burly of the weekly round; she would reflect upon it and write about it.

She had an honoured position in the community. People didn't resent the fact that she might be watching and reporting them; she was a lady of letters, after all, and when folk came to an event like a death which demanded correspondence and form filling she was there to help. In some ways she was the community scribe.

Dod had an old car, and we could stand in the back of it while he drove us around. I say 'stand' because the back seats had been removed to make room for the farm's chickens and the calves. I can still remember the number – AGD 495 – and now I have difficulty recalling those of any other more recent vehicles we've owned.

Jane Yeadon, born 1944, interviewed 2011: Dunphail

Jane went on to enjoy a notable career in nursing; she has brought out two books on her experiences: IT WON'T HURT A BIT!'; IT SHOULDN'T HAPPEN TO A MIDWIFE [Black & White, 2010 and 2011].

A child at school, an adult at home

My mother died when I was 13. It meant there was just Dad and me left. We just soldiered on. He was brilliant, a lovely man. We had our ups and downs, but on the whole we got on great.

At school I could have gone on but I lost interest after the death of my mother. I did the schoolwork well enough but, really, I was more interested in getting everything in the home right for my dad. I was always anxious to get home, to get the floors scrubbed or the mince on. I was a child at the school but an adult at home. The teachers would have known about my situation, but I wasn't aware of any special treatment because of it. Their world was the school, mine was my home and that was that.

I was just focussed on the home all the time: 'Must get to the butcher to get the mince, must pop over to the baker's for the bread for his piece for tomorrow…' And then there was the washing. Oh, that wash house, how I hated it! We had our set days and mine was Tuesdays. So home from school, out to the wash house, fill the blooming boiler, get it lit. Then once I'd finished you had to clean up the floor after yourself. We had a late tea that night; when my father came home from his work, he'd help me. We had to turn the old fashioned mangle. Oh dear…

Just the two of them left: Nancy with her father, late 1950s.

The doctor eventually came at 8.30a.m. and by that time the cyst had burst and the poison was all through her.

The dearly missed: Nancy with her mother, early 1950s.

Her death was very sudden. She came home from work one night, a Friday. She'd been in and out of the hospital periodically before that, but her trouble had always been put down to inflammation of the gall bladder. But this time she was in terrible pain. I can remember Dad sending me round to old Dr Buchan; he wouldn't come, as he was just about to go into his evening surgery. I was sent back at eight o'clock and he gave me two pills with a 'Take them home, girl!' Then my dad went for him later that night but he was just about to go to bed: 'Oh, I've just gone to bed, boy! If she's no better in the morning let me know'. Well, my dad was up all night; she was in absolute agony. It was now Saturday morning and my dad went round for him again. 'Oh, I'm not up yet, boy!' He eventually came at 8.30 and by that time the cyst had burst and the poison was all through her. She was rushed to Stracathro and operated on. But they accidentally cut the right ureter and she developed peritonitis. I got to see her on the Tuesday; she rallied but then had a relapse; she died the following Wednesday.

It was Mrs Allen, the chemist's wife, who came across with phone message. Dad was at work. We had to phone Mrs Nicoll at the level crossing gates for my father to get on the line to Stracathro. When he came home that night he just sat down and wept; he couldn't tell me what had happened. But then his brother came to the door and he'd on a black tie. I knew then. All I could think of was that my dad would need his best black shoes, so I started to polish them. I remember the tears dripping down and mixing in with the polish. Then there was the white shirt and the tie for the visit to the undertaker and the Registry.

Years later I can still hear his, 'Now lassie, we'll hae aa these jobs to do…!' I always remember he wore these double fronted, van Heusen shirts with unattached collars. Oh, trying to iron those things! And he was a very pernickety man was my father. But I got the hang of it eventually – we used to laugh about it years later. We got on with it; he was good to me; I wanted for nothing. But it was so hard.

Nancy Davidson, born 1945, interviewed 2004: Laurencekirk.

Family line up, 1904. The year Janette Anderson's forebears took possession of Thistle Cottage, Luthermuir. Her grandmother, Jessie Kirkland, is far right with, going left, her great grandfather, William, and great-grandmother, Charlotte, in the doorway; the other family members are their two daughters and two sons.

It must be 250 years old

I was born in 1947, in Luthermuir, in this very house – just like my mother before me. My great-grandfather bought this house back in 1904, for £50. I haven't been able to date it exactly, but I do know it's one of the original clay cottages, so I imagine it must be 250 years old or so. If you go into the walls you'll see that it shows the same red as you find in the clay fields all around here. The stone walls are really thick and were

Anderson Family line up, Thistle Cottage, Luthermuir, 2012: Janette Anderson and Francie, her husband, third and fourth left, on the occasion of their 46th wedding anniversary, with their children and grandchildren.

bound together by straw and this red clay. I can't get my head round how with simply that sort of rough materials brought in off the local fields, the houses have stood for so long and are so solid.

I had a lovely childhood. Most of the time we would have been playing outside, in the woods and fields. My brother was a great bird watcher and he'd look for nests, trying to count up the number of different species he could find. My cousin and I played in the back garden. The toilet was a shed at the bottom; Father would put its contents in a midden in the garden. Once our inside toilet arrived Father cleaned out the midden and this made a sunken area we could play in. The apple tree became our bus and if we wanted to go to far off destinations, we'd clamber along the furthest out branches.

We worked too. Once you got older you'd be expected to go out and lift tatties and that was important because the cash would kit you out for the winter. It was always a big event when, on the final day of the tatties holidays, you'd be whisked into Aberdeen to Markies to purchase the gabardine coat. Even to get to the city was a huge expedition: you had to catch the bus into Montrose and then wait an hour for the connection to Aberdeen, so the whole day was needed. Going to the town was exciting enough, but I found that the noise of the traffic and all the bustle of people going about soon wearied me and that I was pleased to get back to the peace of Luthermuir. Once a year for the town was quite enough!

Back in the Seventies the village could support four shops. We ran a general merchants and newsagent, from this house. For us the big steady thing was the papers. People would call in for the *Courier* and usually buy one or two odds and ends while they were about it. Of course, we knew all our customers – well enough to trust them to look after themselves. Often my gran would be sitting in the back or be out in the garden when a customer popped in. They'd shout out, 'Jist in fae ma *Courier*, Jessie! The money's on the coonter.' But Luthermuir was like that then. If, as a child, you were out playing

The toilet was a shed at the bottom; Father would put its contents in a midden in the garden.

Before Thistle Cottage got its plumbing: Brother George in the garden, 1944. The small shed is the toilet, the larger one the hen house.

Eleven years on, Janette and brother, George McDonald, 1955.

Her mother's generation: Luthermuir WRI outing with Janette's mother, Lottie McDonald, front row, far right.

and came a cropper then you'd know you didn't have to run off home, because as sure as anything some adult would come out and doctor you up. Changed days: I was horrified when the other day I came across this small girl who'd fallen over and was crying. I went to her to offer my help but she rejected the whole idea: 'I don't know you! My mummy says I'm not to speak to a stranger!'

Janette Anderson, born 1947, interviewed 2011: Luthermuir

Granny Nicol

I was very much in awe of my paternal grandmother. Born in 1879, she left school at the age of 12 and in the same year, her parents decided the family should emigrate to America. She refused to go and they sailed off to Illinois, leaving her behind. They kept in touch by letter, but she never saw them again. My grandmother married William Nicol to whom she had 11 children; now in his 90th year, my father is the last of her children to survive.

I remember her as a formidable character. By the time I came along, she'd only one eye and a slit where the other should be. She told me the cat had scratched it out and I never doubted her. As a four-year-old, I would trot behind her down to the burn to drown another sack of kittens – a common practice in the country when the place became over-run by cats – but I remember thinking it was some sort of getting her own back. It was only as an adult I learned that the eye had been lost because of a brain haemorrhage.

When I was growing up in the Fifties, I spent a lot of time in her company, feeding hens, picking elderberries, listening to her stories and trying to please her by making

The grandparents: studio photograph from the 1930s.

Helping Granny with the hens. Eleanor at Hamewith, early 1950s.

myself useful. She was a matriarch, a Scottish female equivalent of the Godfather to a huge extended family with all their dramas and feuds.

Granny Nicol was a woman who embodied all the traditional North-east qualities: strong, unflinchingly realistic, thrawn, hard-working; full of practical wisdom and absolutely undaunted by whatever life threw at her.

Widowed not long after I was born, she was completely independent all her days. I can still picture her standing at the stone sink at the window, peeling the tatties, there in her black flowery overall – the uniform of women of her generation – or chopping up carrots and neeps for the soup. She was quite a small woman, her hair already white by the time I knew her. It was very long and every morning she would twist it into two plaits which were then folded over the top of her head and tightly secured with hair pins. At night the hair came down and was brushed out before she retired to the recessed bed in the kitchen.

We had the eerie experience of going back to the old house recently. The derelict building was filled with her presence even after 40 years. Her father-in-law had been a master joiner and had made the furniture when she married. Pieces of the dresser he'd crafted were strewn on the floor; the stone sink was still in place. I half expected her to appear from the pantry beside it. Up the rickety stairs, in the loft, were remnants of the green bed chair. I saw her then, sitting by the fire, twiddling her thumbs round and round, stories pouring out in her low Doric voice.

But she could be a devious old lady, hard and uncompromising. Up until her death at

Visiting granny:
Eleanor and father, William (the signalman at Gartly Station), outside Hamewith Cottage, 1952.

Return to Hamewith Cottage: Eleanor's father – the last surviving of Granny Nicol's 11 children – revisits the old family home, 2011.

Undaunted: Granny Nicol, now in her 80s, stares the camera out.

When he bought his new car, an Austin 100, he just went down to the showroom with the cash all there in a bag.

ninety, every Sunday she'd write a letter to each of her daughters and daughters-in-law. Despite little formal education, these letters were perfectly written. However, every now and then, my mother would receive the wrong one, the envelope addressed to herself, but the letter inside would be the one written to Jean, Mary or Meg, containing comments designed to stir things up. This happened too often to be an accident.

Right up until her death in 1969, Granny Nicol stubbornly clung to all the old ways and a hard-working lifestyle: up at six, bed at nine, to rest for the next day's labours – and no work on the Sabbath, of course. Once, my parents explained they were going away to Austria for a week. 'Austria,' she commented scornfully, 'and fa div ye ken there? Weel, I'll nae be here fin ye come back.' Ironically, she wasn't – she was in Foresterhill, having tripped over a stone and broken her hip.

For all her contrariness, she was always kind to me, sending a lollipop, apple or some treat from the grocer's van home with Dad; allowing me to read her 'love story' magazines despite my father's disapproval. I often wondered what she must have thought of me still at school at 17, when she had left at 12 to start work.

I can't recall Granny Nicol travelling any further than her native Aberdeenshire. My husband and I are very fond of Spain and friends often ask, 'Why don't you move there?' It's then I think of her and the momentous decision she made as a young girl. I enjoy writing poetry and the poem *Bidin* is a celebration of my grandmother and a reminder of my Scottish roots. The last lines sum up the effect she has had on me:

'I canna win awa; it's far I'm fae.
It's fa I am, an far I wint tae be.'

Eleanor Fordyce, born 1948, interviewed 2011: Gartly

Paying your way

My father was a salmon fisher from out of Newtonhill. Discipline in the home was really tough; often a leather job round the bare legs. He was very conservative. He lives in his own little but-and-ben still. Best to rough it out than get fancy things you might not be able to afford. When we were first married the only way we could afford a colour TV set was to get one with a 50p slot attached to it – pay as you view. The old man came round one night, 'What's this? A colour TV, how the hell can you afford one of those?' As far as he was concerned, the 50p business was living on tick. Later he relented and would come round to watch the football – but he brought his own 50p piece with him. And when he bought his new car, an Austin 1000, he just went down to the showroom with the cash all there in a bag and handed it over, got the keys and drove it away – completely paid for.

Colin McLennan, born 1948, interviewed 2004: Newtonhill

A salmon fisher from out of Newtonhill: Colin McLennan's father is second left, pictured with Jimmy Mason (from Catterline), John Morrison and John Craig.

Lodge Croft a century ago: Shona's grandparents and great-grandfather.

Alone but not lonely

My parents lived at Lodge Croft, Cammachmore, where my father ran a croft, as a sideline to his job as an insurance agent. We raised pigs, hens, cows, and ducks and chicks from eggs in an incubator. My mother fed the hens and ducks, but she was afraid of the cockerel – a big fierce bird that would chase after you. My father's advice was to get hold of a thick stick and hit him over the head to keep him off. Well, my mother did exactly that – with the result that the cockerel fell down at her feet, eyes closed, quite motionless. My mother was convinced she'd killed the creature, but when my father went to have a look he discovered the cockerel staggering around, dazed but alive. She also made butter and cheese, which she sold locally.

I loved this side of our life. I was an only child and the animals acted as company for me and were pets, not just working animals. I fed the calves and I could milk one of our three cows, though I usually left that to my father. We had one cow which would only consent to be milked by him; if anybody else attempted she would allow them to fill up the pail and then promptly kick it over.

I revelled in the environment of the croft; I'd spend hours just wandering around by myself, haunting the woods, musing to myself or taking my book to have a quiet read. My father was very much at home among nature and he introduced me to the wild fruits of the woods. He knew where to dig down for earth nuts and how to clean them with his knife. He could tell which mushrooms were edible and which were venomous. He told me all the names of the various trees and could identify each one by its leaf and twig shape. He didn't need to see a bird to name it accurately; its song was enough for him.

'I usually left that to my father': milking one of the family cows in the 1950s.

Primary 4 Mackie Academy, 1955/56. Shona is front row, far right.

At night he could take me out and point out the stars and constellations.

I was quite happy on my own; I was never afraid. Oddly enough, I once went back into my bluebell wood, to collect a certain kind of leaf I knew would be there – and suddenly felt a real shiver of fear. As a child I'd been there constantly without a thought and now the atmosphere struck me as eerie and disturbing; it was almost as if a murdered body was lying in the undergrowth and I was about to disturb it.

I'd also play with an old tennis ball by myself, knocking it backwards and forwards against a wall. I'd construct whole matches against an imaginary rival – somehow I'd always emerge as the winner! But I did have one real friend and that was Irene who stayed in a cottage about a mile away. We'd go into the woods and make a little den. We both went to Mackie Academy from the age of five and in the evening we'd come off the bus and pop into our hidey-hole. We stashed our own sets of pencils and paper beneath some stones for drawing and writing stories. This meant we didn't get home till five, but nobody worried about us.

And at the croft I made my very own housie in a shed. I got a lot of furniture from a friend of my mother's and was able to kit it out with curtains, chairs a table and a wee doll's house, complete with tea set. I could entertain my mother and friend in my very

own house – although the tea was entirely imaginary.

I was a great reader, with Enid Blyton my absolute favourite – *Chalet Girls* and *Malory Towers*. My mother didn't approve of actually buying books, but the school library kept me going. I loved *Children's Hour*, five o'clock on the Home Service each evening.

No, I was never bored, nor would I have been allowed to be. 'Boring' simply didn't feature in our vocabulary. Today's girl would find my very homely, quiet life, back in the Fifties, laughable, but it was a more simple age for everyone and I knew no different. In fact, I often wish things could return to that time, when we lived at a slower pace and were content with what we had.

On my mother's side we also had deep roots in the area, though this time over at Muchalls. My grandmother stayed in Strathbarrel Cottage – the very house I now live in. This had originally been built by my great-great grandfather in 1856 and handed down through the generations until it has arrived at me.

After my grandparents' deaths, my own parents came over to Strathbarrel Cottage and now, in my turn, this has become my home. Of course, it's been extensively refurbished and done over since those days – but as the fifth generation to live here, with me, my family can claim 156 years of continuous occupation. That's something, isn't it!

Shona Barclay, born 1947, interviewed 2012: Cammachmore

Up the close

Seceder Close was a 16th century block, with cobbles and flagstones outside, just off the High Street. Entrance was over a very old worn stone at the threshold. My father once had the bright idea of getting a crowbar and lifting it up so as to turn it over – only to discover that the underside was equally worn. Someone had obviously had the same idea – about 200 years previously!

Our home was basically one room that you entered from a close through a small hallway. Our flat was on the left, the Camerons were to the right and then up the stairs there was a pair of other apartments with families. Really, like a city tenement. So you could say that my first years were spent in an environment you might think of as more urban than rural, even though we were living in a modestly sized country town – almost a piece of Glasgow in Morayshire.

Our home was a room with a small alcove off it, separated by a curtain. This was the sleeping area, with a bed for me and my brother as well as a dressing table. My parents slept in a settee bed and there was a pair of easy chairs, a table with two more chairs, and a sideboard. By the window was the sink which had a cupboard beneath it.

It must have been very cramped, with us three sons, but my main memory is of how dark and gloomy it was. There was only one window and often in the winter the wall-

'Not raining': with brother Iain (on trike), mother at the door, 1951.

mounted gas lights had to be on all day long. Heating was by open fire; we burnt coal and coke and this had to be fetched in a pram or wheelbarrow from the gas works. Bathing was in the big tin bath put in front of the fire and filled by kettle. The toilet was an outside affair which had to be shared with the other three families of our close. But

'Just off the High Street': Elgin in the 1930s, as it was in George's father's time.

'Like a city tenement': Seceder Close is nowadays uninhabited and inaccessible. This 2012 shot is of the nearby Gordon's Close.

everyone took their turn and the place was kept spotlessly clean.

The domestic economy was very tight and things could only be kept going through unremitting labour and good organisation. Dad repaired our shoes and Mum knitted socks and pullovers. She also made coats for us out of her own mother's worn out coats. We wouldn't have had many clothes, just one set on and the other in the wash.

We played outside as often as we could. My father's attitude was, 'It's not raining – why aren't you outside?' There were plenty of other children around us and we all got on – doolies, skipping, ball games, that sort of amusement. With Cooper Park nearby we were often there, playing on the swings and roundabout. That's where the library was, too, and although there were few books in the house, we were regular readers.

Our social life was limited to visiting relatives and friends – there was a lot of that back then. People wrote letters to each other – no telephones in the house; calls could be made from public boxes but were reserved for serious news. Sunday visits to an aunt were a regular event – though her command was always, 'Mind, you can hae butter or jam on your bread for tea, but nae them baith!' We also took long walks to Spynie, or along the Lossie, or out to Oak Woods. Basically, we sought to get out of the house as much as we could.

If you ask me how I look back on what has come to seem a remotely primitive way of living, then I can only say how normal it seemed at that time. The sort of existence we were leading in our little close was the common lot 50, 60 years ago. The people around us were similar to ourselves: my father was an electrician and our neighbours were posties, plumbers, joiners – time served tradesmen. Everyone worked hard and hung together. The values I imbibed were exemplary ones – hard work, co-operation, ordered living, sobriety, thrift, neighbourliness. I can't recall any trouble with any of our neighbours, not a moment's insecurity and disturbance.

When I go back to Elgin I give the old place a glance, though no more than that. It's a strange experience to revisit the spot where I passed my early childhood, half a century ago. I find myself thinking, 'If I just turn that corner, I'll bump into so-and-so'. The close is still there – but the buildings, not the people.

George Paul, born 1948, interviewed 2012: Elgin

Work hard, play hard

Children are undoubtedly more indulged nowadays. But despite that I find they will still be prepared to listen to a friendly adult's point of view. For example, I remember my niece once telling me, 'I'm going to blag a new outfit off Dad for a party.' This after her parents had laid out a lot of money for a school trip to China. I found that attitude appalling, so I had it out with her. And she must have listened because she turned up at the party in one of her old frocks.

In fact, I find that among my nieces and my nephews there's still this strong family

spirit. It's a testimony to the caring and common-sense way in which my parents brought us up in Stonehaven in the Fifties and Sixties. It's a childhood I'm grateful for and look back on fondly.

As I moved through my teens I did become quite a high spirited young lady. I'd go off to the dances at Laurencekirk. I'd get a lift with some guys in their car. To us this was simply 'fun' but our parents must have worried about it and seen us as 'wild'. I remember staying at this girl's house while her parents were away, with only the grandfather there. I remember having breakfast before we went to bed, so that he would know I was there and could vouch for it. I was 17 at the time.

We'd listen to the Billy Steel Combo, to Chris McClure. Like most people of my age I was into the pop music of the day; I preferred the Stones to the Beatles, who were a bit too groomed for my taste; I was looking for something with more of an edge to it.

But I always worked hard at the school. I had a deal with myself, that during the week I would study diligently and then at the weekend I could go off and let my hair down a bit. From the age of about 13 we'd go to the cinema in the town – Elvis, Cliff Richard's *Summer Holiday*, *Easy Rider*. You'd all go off together and then you'd buy a bag of chips at Larnarch's, on the way home. But really, it was all quite tame. In a place like Stonehaven you knew that if you stepped out of line at all, then your parents would hear about it

'A strong family spirit': Lorna, parents and brothers out on a picnic, Ballogie, late 1950s.

And at home a few years later: Back, Dad John and Mum Mary; front L–R James, David, Lorna, John.

The Birse family together, late 1950s.

before you'd even got home. I'd push at the boundaries, but never really wanted to go beyond them.

Most of my contemporaries were the same. For example, the dances at Laurencekirk usually featured a fight or two – but they were always fair fights with equal numbers on each side. The girls would put their handbags on the floor and dance round them till you got the tap on the shoulder and an invitation to go up with some guy or other. There could be the odd rammy, but I never got involved. The most we did might be to buy a bottle of cider and take a drink out of it before we went off and then at the Commodore to nurse a half pint. We couldn't afford more!

Drugs? I certainly never got involved, but I do remember an incident at Mackie when, in 1972, two guys got suspended for taking pot. There was this lad I knew – a nice guy – but he became hooked on heroin and died. That drove it home to me that drugs were a poison to be avoided. But these were isolated incidents. In those days you had to go looking for drugs; now the dealers seem to come looking for you.

Lorna Johnson, *née* Birse, born 1953, interviewed 2011: Stonehaven

We didn't do friends

We didn't do friends. This was because of Dad's drinking. Ever since I can remember he would get drunk whenever he could, night after night. He never explained why; he always refused to discuss the problem.

We learned to live our own lives behind closed doors. By 1966 my father's effort to hold down his job with the railways was becoming too much: he got the sack because of the drink and then just drifted from job to job.

His drinking dominated our lives. Every night he'd be out at the pub and then, when he came back, there'd be rows. But back then such matters were regarded as strictly domestic affairs and there was little in the way of outside help available. Once the police did take action and we were able to get him sectioned into Cornhill under the Mental Health Act. The month he spent there was like a holiday, but once he was out again things returned to normal – or what we had to regard as normal.

As a child I couldn't go to anyone's house because we could certainly never have them back here. At home we were left to battle on with all our difficulties by ourselves. There were some evenings when our father would barricade us all in the house while he went on one of his drunken rampages. He would love to have us at his mercy so he could abuse us. Mostly it was verbal with the foulest curses against us that you could possibly imagine. I would have to climb out of the skylight, go along the roof and jump down at the back so as I could run to the phone box and call the police.

I don't know how Mum managed to keep going with household bills or how she managed to feed us all. Dad would spend his pay on drink as soon as he got it. I've still got one of the old pay packets from the railways, the one which had one old penny in it – he had taken an advance on his wages for his drinking, When I reached the age of seven or eight and could ride a bike, on pay day, I would cycle some three miles to the pubs in a nearby village. When I found him, I would plead with him to come home, or I'd ask for some money for Mum. This was usually refused and at times I would steal cash from his pocket when he was very drunk so as to have something to take home to help with the bills and food. People just wouldn't take the problem seriously or would decide to regard it as our business and turn a blind eye.

No one to my knowledge tried to restrain his behaviour, to tell him he'd had enough and ought to think about the wife and children at home. I'm not sure we understand the damage alcohol can do any better now, but at least there would be more in the way of help for the family. In those days there was nowhere for Mum to turn, no place of refuge for her to go to. The attitude was that this was our own domestic situation which we had to cope with as best we could.

My childhood completely revolved around home. There was my father and I also had a younger brother, Jeams, who was a Down's syndrome child. He was born in 1963, so by the time I was at Secondary school most of my spare time was taken up with helping to look after him while Mum went off to work in order to get some income.

'There was my father...' Moira's parents at the door of their home, 1989.

> There were some evenings when our father would barricade us all in the house while he went on one of his drunken rampages.

No end of problems: an invasion of cattle into the Cameron garden, 2011.

That was my life, as a teenager. No clothes shopping, no pop music, no going out to the pictures or to dances. The community wasn't all that understanding of Jeams's condition. Oh, some of the adults were nice, but there were others who seemed to take a pleasure in telling us what he'd been up to and demanding that we do something about it, even when he hadn't been there – for example, paying for breakages.

There was nothing for Jeams in those days, no school or nursery provision. I remember just after Jeams was born coming home from school one day to find my mother in tears. She told me that my little brother was a 'Mongol' – they didn't use the term Down's Syndrome in those days. The advice we got from our GP was to put Jeams into an institution because he would never be anything but a burden, would never be able to walk or to speak. But Mum took the view that, 'He's my son and we'll look after him here at home'.

Jeams was born with a congenital heart defect which led to his passing at the age of 31. With modern technology his condition could probably be corrected by surgery but this was, alas, not possible back in the 1960s.

While some found Jeams very endearing, others found it difficult to tolerate him and his mischievous ways. He led a full and active life and while we undoubtedly became unpopular with some on the village because of Jeams and his antics, he was loved by many neighbours and certainly by his family.

Moira Cameron, born 1954, interviewed 2006: Muchalls

There was always something going on

A s children we enjoyed a lot of freedom. As long as we turned up back at the house for the next meal nobody bothered. Inverbervie and Gourdon were one big playpark to us children and we were left free to enjoy it. We learned how to take risks, how to keep within sensible limits. We'd make up our own carties out of any old pram wheels and bits of wood. On any summer evening you'd see 30 kids running around on their bikes, all over the village. In the summer the fish merchants would sometimes send out a demand for buckies and that would be our signal to descend on the beach and collect them onto our carties. We'd lug our loads off to Gourdon and collect the shillings for each hundredweight. I always spent my share on the way home by buying home-made tablet from Andrew Freeman in the Gourdon Post Office.

In the summer there'd be strawberries and raspberries to pick; in the autumn tatties; daffodils in the spring. We all took part; the pay was an expected part of the family budget and was used to set you up with new footwear and clothes for the winter. I started when I was seven; I did it every year right up till University. You'd get picked up on a trailer each morning and taken out to whichever farm was organising the picking. Then I had my paper round; there were also jobs like delivering leaflets for the VG shop and Bob-a-job for the Cubs. We were expected to keep busy and show enterprise. If ever a parent caught you sitting around the house they'd urge you on to go out 'and do something useful'. The work ethic was engrained into us; we were shown that if you

Taking part right from the start: helping at the Gourdon fish market, aged two.

'Every organisation going': Fancy dress party run by Inverbervie WRI, 1965/66. John is back row, in top hat.

at the Bervie ATC summer camp, Doncaster, 1975. John is fifth right.

There was the Scouts, the Air Training Corps and, for the girls, the Guides. Almost all of the children in the village would be a member of one or other.

wanted something then you had to go out and do something about it.

The Cubs and the Scouts were another big thing. My eighth birthday actually fell on the very day of the Cubs meeting, so I could run down to the hall and join up. A great day! Then there was the Air Training Corps and, for the girls, the Guides. Almost all of the children in the village would be a member of one or other.

In the winter you couldn't go out so freely, but we all seemed to be guided by a calendar of events which pulled you through the dark months. Halloween meant guising from house to house; Christmas would bring parties – all the various organisations had one for the children. Then New Year was a huge event: first footing could go on for days and it would be a good week before you had done everyone. January had Burns Night. My mother seemed to be in every organisation going – the WRI, the Guild, the Red Cross, the RNLI. Each of them had sales and fund raising activities and social evenings, so there never seemed to be a shortage of things to look forward to. A lot of effort in the late Sixties was put into raising money for the refurbishment of the burgh hall.

Besides, we would play card games and draughts in the house as a family. There were Beetle Drives and Sales of Work and Whist Drives. There was always something on the go. When I became a teenager there was the Youth Club started up, initially by the Church, then in the school. The Church Youth Club put on shows in the church hall.

Nowadays people worry about child and teenage lethargy and obesity. They're just not out and about the way we were. We're trying to bring up our two so that they have something of the freedom and the responsibility we enjoyed at their age. But already when I compare Andrew's life with mine at that age I can see a difference. When I was seven I'd be out doing something all the time, at the park on the swings, into a paddling pool, messing around on the beach, sailing boats at the pond, all the things that Health and Safety regulations, as well as parental fears, have put paid to. Our children's activities are much more organised than ours ever were – and, of course, we drive them everywhere so they can do them.

John Duncan, born 1961, interviewed 2007: Inverbervie

A reality check

There was no fear of strangers; everyone knew everyone else.

My boyhood was spent within the one small area, in the Speyside community of Dailuaine, where my father worked in the distillery. It was a fantastic place to grow up in. I suppose by today's standards it would seem to have its dangers, with the river Spey just a couple of hundred yards away. Then there were large woods stretching up the higher banks and all around us to the east. But for us young boys it offered plenty of opportunities for exploration and hiding out. At that time there was no shortage of other kids to join up with; the Terrace was still occupied by distillery workers and was full of young families.

We did have boundaries, but our parents never seemed to need to spell them out too heavily. We just seemed to know that the Spey was off limits, that there were points in the woods that we shouldn't stray beyond. In any case there was a fair mix in the ages of the kids and the older ones could be trusted to see that the rest of us didn't do anything

too silly. There was no fear of strangers either; it was a community where everyone knew everyone else.

The community support was strong and based on this kind of intimate knowledge of each other. When I was young I suffered badly from asthma. The croft had no phone so

'No better view anywhere': looking down the Spey, Dailuaine Terrace.

A Speyside heritage. David Shiach's father, Joseph, (second from end) and two grandfathers, James Stewart McHattie (at the head) plus Alexander Shiach (third from right) leading out the famous Kinermony herd of Aberdeen Angus in the 1950s. Note the small size of what then constituted prize winning cattle.

what my mother did was use her washing line as a way of summoning help if I was into another attack. She would put a certain combination of towels out, the two men who worked down at the distillery chemical works just below the house could look up, see something was wrong and use their phone there to send a message across to the distillery for my dad. Or, if another particular combination was set out, they would know to phone for the doctor straight away.

We led an outdoor life, playing football, going off to explore various places in the woods. I noticed the difference when I went to the Secondary school in Aberlour and suddenly found myself coming up against guys from Dufftown and Rothes and they seemed to have a different approach to what they did in their spare time. They would hang around street corners – we didn't even have any streets, only the woods and the fields. We always seemed to have somewhere to go and something to do when we got there. I remember cycling over to someone's house in Dufftown and when we got there, all that happened was that we stayed indoors and watched TV. A round cycle of 16 miles just to watch the telly! Most of the lads I got friendly with at the High School were from small places like Glenlivet or Tomintoul and had a similar outlook. We called those who came from Rothes and Dufftown 'toonsers'.

We were brought up to respect adult authority – maybe we are the last generation to be like that. Teachers were generally held in high regard and so was the doctor. Dr Caldwell would come out on home visits, even in the middle of the night. He did that for me with my asthma. But any adult had power over us. I remember getting a crack round the ear from the father of a friend because we'd put a ladder up on his shed and as I was the oldest one present it was held that I should have known better. He then took me home where my dad gave me an even bigger whack. It's not like that now.

They set them to work young back then. A two-year old David busy at the logs, Dailuaine, 1970s.

I did Forestry at Aberdeen University, but I'd still go home every other weekend or so. I still found that my favourite night out would be a game of pool and a pint or two in the pub at Aberlour, followed by a 10 o'clock bag of chips. For me, that beat any city night-club in Aberdeen. You'd see the familiar old faces and be able to chat in the same old way. Going back was a reality check; university life can be a bit surreal and Aberlour and Dailuaine to me was still the real world.

I suppose that what I am describing is a rural upbringing rather than something peculiar to Speyside. I once had a job attempting to sell hoovers door to door. This was a hellish task, which I could only stand for a month, but that was long enough to realise that the country areas offered you the best in the way of friendliness and hospitality. One day you'd be slogging your way round Cults, encountering a series of unpleasant, rude people, the next you'd be up on a farm north of Inverurie with the wife opening the door and inviting you in for a bowl of soup and sandwich.

I still visit several times a year. To stand at the end of Dailuaine Terrace and look down onto the Spey – there's no better view anywhere.

David Shiach, born 1970, interviewed 2006: Dailuaine

We were maybe the last generation to respect adult authority. Teachers were held in high regard and so was the doctor, who would come on home visits, even in the middle of the night.

LIFE
ON
THE
LAND

The age of the machine: bringing in the hairst, 21st century style, near Torphins, September 2012.

Saturday mornings I'd do the baking for the week: scones, pancakes, loaves, sponge cakes. Never anything ready-made or out of a packet.

Carry on cooking

When I look back now all I can see is me at the kitchen. The routine was that Bill would have a cup of tea at six then he'd go off to see to the cattle. At nine he'd be back for his breakfast and that meant bacon and eggs. If they were going to be working over at the other side, he'd go off with a flask for his 10 o'clock, then at 12 he'd be back in the kitchen for his lunch – and this had to be a full cooked meal – soup or a pudding and meat and veg. For the afternoon he'd be off with another flask and a piece. When he returned in the evening at five or so it would be another cooked meal. He was working all day, long, hard physical work, and he needed all this intake, believe me.

That was my weekday routine; Saturday mornings I'd do the baking for the week: scones, pancakes, loaves, sponge cakes – a whole tray full of stuff. Never anything ready-made or out of a packet. As for pasta or a pizza – no, certainly not! It had to be good old fashioned meat, tatties and vegetables. I remember once when there was a bit of a potato shortage and we were being encouraged to turn to alternatives and I served up his mince with a helping of rice: 'Fit's aa this? Rice, that's for puddins!'

Then I did my share of mending and dress-making and making a spot of money from that. Looking back, I don't know where I got the time for it all – the days must have had more than 24 hours in them then. But I could never not be doing something. You know, it's only in the last year or two that I've been able to sit down in an evening without some cooking or a spot of dress-making to do and not feel guilty about such idleness. 'Look, what do you have to do that you can't take a wee bit of time to yourself?', I'll tell myself. But it doesn't come easy, I can tell you.

But, you know, it wasn't all grim toil, not by any means. We worked hard, both in the kitchen and the fields, but we also knew how to enjoy ourselves. The farming routine was broken up by Farmers' Balls in a range of venues – St Cyrus, Stonehaven, Auchenblae; then there was the monthly WRI, the Church Guild, visitors from Canada, Sunday School outings, events at the local school, regular outings in the car and holidays all over the UK – I think we must have visited just about every mart north of Oxfordshire!

Nina Smith, born 1930, interviewed 2008: Netherley

No longer run off his feet. Tom McGregor at his home in Newtonhill with some of his prize-winning blooms, 2011.

The bank was aye at your heels. Just a treadmill, it was. When you went to the mart to sell your cattle, you had to accept a knock-down price

Running faster just to stand still

When I started out the horse was still king and it was a big thing to work them. It made you a real farmer. You needed a lot of patience to get the best out of them, so it was a bit of a challenge to do it well. But then the tractor came in and we had to put the horses away. I can still see the day – 1955 it was – when the last one went. He was called Pride and he'd been with us for nigh on 10 years, a good and faithful beast. I could hardly bear to coax him onto the float and stand there and watch it disappear down the road. Pride was off to work on a farm over at Tarland, a good enough life ahead of him, no doubt, but real sad for me.

I stopped work when I was 68. During those last years I'd been running faster and faster just to stay still. We now had the machinery, but the financial side of things was just driving us on and on. The bank was aye at your heels, telling you that you were this much overdrawn and what arrangement would you be proposing to do something about it. Just a treadmill, it was. When you went to the mart to sell your cattle, you found yourself having to accept a knock-down price just to get some money in.

At the end I was working 100 times harder than at the start. When I set out as a cattle raiser there was little hard pressure; you might not have much money, but then nobody else did either. You had time to stop and have a news with your neighbour. Things went at a slower pace, the pace of the man on foot and his horse. But then the machines moved in and in one big sweep the labour force was decimated. There was no neighbour around you to chat to now. You'd get a glimpse of him up in his tractor cab, all shut off from the outside world. He'd go up and down, listening to his music through his earphones above the roar and rumble of his machine and he'd never drop into the tattie shed to tell you what was going on in his world.

I mind the first time I took the plough behind the horse and the grieve was watching me go and do my furrow. 'Weel, Tom, 'he said, 'that furrow's sae stricht an sae lang that ye cud open that gate an let it run richt oot o it!' Could you imagine that happening now? Then the ploughman, even with the early tractor, he could stop his work if he came across a peewit's nest and lift it gently to one side so as not to damage it. Now he'd be over it before he could get a glimpse of it, the tractors are that big and that powerful. The countryside's become a silent, empty place. When I was a lad and off to bed at eight of an evening the last thing I would hear before I went to sleep was the cry of the oyster catchers and the peewits. There used to be skylarks, but then the heavy roller just crushed their eggs out of existence.

A few years back I was up doing a job with Scott Annand at Bograxie, near where I started as a boy. I quite fancied making a return, but what a disappointment that was. Up the glen, there had been three, four farms on each side; now there was nothing. It used to be alive with birds and wild life. 'Bit, Scott,' I said, 'the auld place, it's jist deed'. We were there three whole days and in all that time all I heard was one crow, one single crow. Yet when I was little, those big backit craws were hated by us all because they would come and prey on the small chicks. And now you were almost pleased to hear it as one sign of life at least. It was a sad, sad return for me.

I understand the modern methods had to come in. Wild life won't feed the nation. But it does make our lives more pleasant, more human somehow. Now kids are quite cut off from the land. If you talk to them of tatties then they think of packets of crisps. The kids here see nothing of the fields; they take their bus to their school of a morning and come back on it at night and that's the nearest they get – a few fields from out of the window and a whole crop of new houses. We would walk to the school and we'd take twice as long coming back as in the morning – because we'd be stopping to watch the birds and to talk about all the life around us.

The modern farm employs only one or two men. The farmyard used to be a cheerful, human kind of place, where people worked at a slower pace and as a gang together. There was time for chat and song and music. How often nowadays do you hear anyone going about with a song on their lips or whistling a tune? When I started out there were plenty of tunes which everyone knew; one person would start up a whistle and soon everyone would be joining in. But by the Eighties all this pop music came in and the tunes died away. Even today I can pass a whole evening listening to someone like Gordon Patullo playing all the old favourites on one of his CDs – Strip the Willow, the Canadian Barn Dance, The St Bernard's Waltz – music with a tune and life to it! That's the sort of stuff I'd whistle when I went about my work; but when the Eighties came in the younger ones began going on about all this pop music and how much more modern it was than my old fashioned stuff. 'Ga'n,' I'd tell them, 'if it's sae wonerful, whistle or hum sam o it an gie me a treat.' But I just couldn't make head or tail of it – just a noise, a tuneless noise!

In my opinion the farm was a lot happier in the old days. I started tattie picking when I was eight. You'd work an eight-hour day and get eightpence an hour. You'd be bent

Where he was brought up. Tom's father was blacksmith at Burnhervie, near Inverurie. Pictured here with Auntie Mary and the family's blue coo.

When the horse was still king – and there was time for a chat and a piece. Tattie picking at Maitland Mackie's farm, near Tarves, 1930s.

over the rows, picking up the tatties, putting them into the buckets for taking away and then into the sacks. Hard, hard work, but you'd be in a squad with time to chat and sing and whistle. You'd get something taken out to you in the forenoon and again in the middle of the afternoon; at midday you'd all go into the farmhouse for a dinner – soup, a plate of porridge, mince and tatties, all of you would be sitting round the table, laughing and joking. I remember how the servant girl would come out of the house with a basket of tea and pieces in the afternoon and how the horseman would take the first bite and then say, 'Ach, Bella, ye've dane it agin. This tastes o paraffin!' She'd been working at the paraffin lamps inside the house and then had packed up the pieces without bothering to wash her hands. But we would wolf down what she brought us and have a laugh about it all. Paraffin or not, it still tasted good to us.

But by the Eighties it was all finished; the machines had taken over. For me, that's when the really big changes in farming took over: farms became bigger and bigger, the EEC subsidies and the entire form filling came in, the machinery and the chemicals for spraying got more and more sophisticated; winter cereals and rape oil were all the thing. The work became non-stop. The machines drove you on until you became a machine yourself, just going from one job to the other with scarce a moment to get a hold of your own thoughts. I'd find myself dressing tatties in the shed and the rollers would be going one way and the machine would be going the other and sometimes you wouldn't know whether you were coming or going, you'd be that dizzy with it all.

But no use moaning about it; you can't turn the clock back. It's as the grieve would say when I came to end of the day and got through all the tasks he'd set out for me and I

would tell him, 'Weel, I managed it aa,' and he would reply, 'Weel, I kent ye wad. Naethin else fer it is there? Ye jist hae to kip gaein – that's the hale bloody thing – isn't it - jist tae kip gaein,'.

Tom McGregor, born 1931, interviewed 2011: Auchnagatt area and Newtonhill

Don't make me laugh!

I left school at 14 and went straight onto the family farm. My first idea was to go for a job on the railways, but my father wouldn't hear of it: 'Na, na – ye'll jist wark wi me on the fairm.' So that's what it had to be – the farm.

The farm belonged to my father, a nice 65-acre holding, well drained, good clean land. I had to start off as the orra loon, just doing all the jobs about. That was the normal way, while you were still growing and coming into your strength. You'd be the youngest one and not yet ready for the heavy lifting jobs, so there I was at the top of the mill receiving the sheaves as they were forked up so as to pass them on to the feeder. That went on till I was big enough to fork the sheaves myself. That took about a couple of years.

Then came the carrying of the bags of corn and that was no easy job, I can tell you. The barley bags were two whole hundredweights; my God they were heavy all right! You had to get them up on your back and shoulder, then carry them up the stairs. And you couldn't fail at it, not if you wanted to show that you were now a man and fit enough for anything the others could do. The only time someone got hurt that I can mind was

Those early tractors could be a hell of a beast to get going, especially on a cold winter's morning.

'I never cared much for the horses' – but for Bob's father that was all there was. Pictured here with 'Pride' and foal at Cairnbeg, 1920s.

when Charlie was carrying this bag over his shoulder and he was walking with it below the belt; well, he'd been doing it that way, the bag high up on the shoulder for years, but this time the belt caught him bang! Right on his head, knocking him over. What a mess of blood he was! But he got up, got his head bandaged and just carried on.

That's the way we were brought up – just get on with it, show you could do it. They speak about the good old days, but I couldn't call them that. I started off at the back end of the horse age and that was hard going, believe me. I never cared much for the horses: they had to be fed and fed, morning, afternoon and night and then rested in the middle of the day too. When the tractors came in things did get better, though the first machines needed some handling too. You had to lift whatever you were needing to put on the back by hand and get it in position – the plough or the harrow or whatever. That was a hell of a job, getting out and trying to push the bloody thing into its right position. Then you had to use a handle and if you didn't hold it in the right way the kick-back could break your wrist. Those early tractors could be a hell of a beast to get going, especially on a cold winter's morning when your hands were numb.

Did farming pay well? That's a laugh! In the Fifties you'd get no more than £7.10 a week and that was as a married man and the only wage earner. I was working for my father and that wasn't easy, believe me. He was a hard taskmaster; he'd bawl you out and for nothing at all as soon as look at you. Even when I was still at the school I was expected to help about the farm, early in the morning beforehand and when I came home. I mind one early morning when the bruiser was on the go and I was rushing backwards and forwards with bags into the boiler house. I was pushed for time and was fleeing on; I tripped over myself and got my little finger stuck in the door. Well, I near ripped my crannie clean off, it was so badly torn and twisted around. Dr Watson had to come up from Stonehaven to stitch me up, right there on the kitchen table. Eight stitches I needed, right round the finger. Did I get any sympathy? Did I hell! My father simply shouted away at me for being so careless; I'd got what was coming to me.

But I learned a lot and kept healthy. I've aye been blessed with good health. I can put that down to a strong constitution and the way I was brought up. We had a good simple diet and plenty of physical work to keep us going.

Bob Souter, born 1932, interviewed 2008: Netherley

Ups and downs of the farming life

When I left the school my first idea was to become a mechanic. I got a job as a showroom assistant at Claude Hamilton's in their big showroom on Union Street. I was doing well and was all set for a career in the motor trade. But one day I noticed that my mother was standing at the window peering in for me. She'd come to tell me that my father had taken a heart attack and that I was to come home.

My father was never the same man again. So I had to come back to the croft full time. I realised that the way to make it pay was to expand. We had hens, but only 100 or so, so I built two deep litter houses and got the number up to 500. Then I started with pigs and had 12 sows and 100 pigs and that did very well. Later, in 1959, I took a larger farm at Dunecht, an 80-acre farm, and when a 40-acre one came on the market right next to mine I took that on as well.

Leaving the Rhynie home with mother, cousin, brother and foster brother. John Robb is in the white hat, 1938.

I was now married and things were going well. It was a November Saturday and I had a squad in to lift the tatties and we were hard at it all day. When we'd finished I couldn't stop for any supper because the cows needed milked. That's when the disaster struck. There I was in the byre, milking away when a strange cat came running in, attracted by the smell of milk no doubt. The cow behind me took a fright and gave me a hard kick. It smashed my leg; my heel and my toes were twisted completely round.

So there I was in agony just, holding on to my wellington boot and shouting out for help. Daisy was up at the house, but her brother was out helping me with the milking and he was able to get her. When Daisy came she took some convincing that I had actually broken my leg: 'Ach, it'll be a sprain, jist.' 'A sprain! Jist tak a look at far ma taes are pintin!' Well, the ambulance came quick enough and drove me off to Aberdeen. But they never put any splints in and I was left holding onto my wellington and the vehicle was speeding over bumps and round corners and it was absolute torture.

The first harvest at Bervie, with Moss the dog, 1959.

When I got to ARI I had to wait in the A&E before the surgeon came. It was a Saturday night and Aberdeen had been playing Celtic and the waiting room was full of football fans who'd been drinking and fighting. Some of them were staggering about and I was aye feared they'd be crashing into my broken leg. They were calling out to me, 'An fit are you here fer, Jock?' – as if it wasn't quite obvious. When the surgeon did come he took one look and said, 'A very bad break; you'll need an operation to have a plate put in'.

This was a big setback. It was 1962 and I was only three months married. I'd been in

Bringing in the harvest at Tillioch, 1982.

that farm only three years. I did get a man in to help and he had some experience as a dairy baillie, but really, he was pretty useless. One day my wife came in and told me a heifer was lying dead by the small byre. I was on crutches by this time and I hobbled out to see what was up. As soon as I got there I knew what the trouble was. He was an awful careless worker and he'd been giving the hay as feed by simply cutting through the twine that held the bales together and then, instead of removing it, just letting it dangle loose. The heifer would have swallowed the twine along with the hay and choked on it. And it was a cracking wee beast, too – killed by sheer carelessness. The vet came and confirmed that a big ball of twine had been found in her stomach right enough. Well, that same night I just went up to the man and told him he was to go. I would just manage without him.

It was a great struggle for the next few months, but we got through it. I think my biggest mistake was never to have owned my farms; if I had, I could have borrowed against the asset and built things up faster and bigger. And the landlord would keep putting up the rent, especially if you were doing well. But I did well enough. A good farmer needs to work hard and to have plenty common sense and be good with his hands.

One day – it was in 1979 – I was out at the plough when the laird's Landover drew up. They were offering me the farm over at Tillioch, Echt. It was a big 26-field farm, but it had been run down and was in a bit of a mess. They wanted me to take it, but I had to decide that very day. I'd just put a new kitchen and although the new

Still carrying the effect of that broken leg. Tillioch, 1990.

farm house would have 12 rooms, I doubted my wife would agree to the move. I told them this. 'Oh, but we'll compensate you for the kitchen. We'll get our surveyor in and fix a fair price.' So we went.

It was 220-acres, but fair run down. I realised the fastest way to build things up would be to go for beef cattle. There was nothing for it but work, work.

I retired 10 years ago when I was 67. I could have gone on longer as I was quite fit, but my son was keen to take it over and now he runs it. He actually went to University and had a good post with an oil company, but he got fed up sitting at a computer all day long and felt the call. He does a good job; it's good to see him carrying on the family tradition.

John Robb, born 1932, interviewed 2009: Echt

Revisiting Cairnmore, Rhynie, 1992. With wife Daisy, son and son-in-law.

Give me the shallow end!

My career was as a rep for an agricultural supplies firm, SAI. My work would take me up into the really remote farms in Donside and I was always struck by just how different the way of life could be in those parts. Communication was quite a challenge, especially in the early days when the winters were harder and there weren't so many cars around; you could be on the road and not pass another vehicle for a half-hour at a time.

But they managed. Folk were so hospitable. When I started going up there I could find myself drinking seven cups in a day. I remember the first time I was in Glenbuchat and it was my last call of the day. 'Ye'll hae a cup o tea afore ye gae.' I'd already drunk and drunk all day long; you could hear the stuff swishing about inside me as I walked. But I also wanted to be polite, especially as this was my first visit, so when I turned the

A good farmer needs to work hard and to have plenty common sense and be good with his hands.

> This hen came waddling in, sat down beside me and proceeded to lay an egg. Nobody batted an eyelid.

offer of tea down, and the woman of the house came back with, 'Weel, maybe ye'd like a glass o milk', I reckoned I just had to say yes – it would at least be a change from all that tea. But it turned out to be goat's milk, a whole glass of goat's milk. I had one hell of a job in getting through it but, out of politeness, I felt I had to force the horrible stuff down and then say how nice it had been. But all that meant was that on my next visit, four weeks later, I was immediately served up with another glass of this infernal goat's milk. I became known as the man who preferred goat's milk to tea.

Sometimes you'd get your lunch at a farmhouse up some remote glen. I remember once in Strathdon I was sitting on the couch after my meal and this hen came waddling in, sat down beside me and proceeded to lay an egg. Nobody batted an eyelid; apparently this was the hen's regular routine, one she did every day, right there on the couch.

I remember this large family over at Tornaveen. The father was a fee'd farm servant and there were 11 children and they all had to live together in a small house. This meant that the children had to sleep three to the bed. Years later, I was speaking to this chap who'd been one of the family and he was telling me that one of his younger brothers was in the habit of peeing the bed. Now these were the days when you couldn't expect to find an inside toilet in such a house: usually the men would go out to the midden while the females would make use of the hen house near the back door. But getting up in the middle of a cold dark winter's night was no fun and this younger brother often just peed where he was, in the bed. He told me how his mother would ask him, before the three of them got into the bed, 'George, fit side o the bed wad you like the night?' and he would reply, 'I dinna care, Mither, as lang as it's the shallow end!'

John Copland, born 1936 interviewed 2008: Lumphanan

The hands-on approach. Eddie Gray testing out his firm's front loader, 1958.

Rise and fall of an agricultural industry

I started at Gray's as a welder blacksmith in 1960; two years later I was made a charge hand and two more years later I was foreman and then works manager. At our height we had 80 staff, a huge employer for a small village like Fetterangus. We were making a vast range of products, all serving the agricultural sector. There were rollers, buck rakes, hammer mills, loaders, saw benches and so on. We might have begun as a local firm, but by now we were serving customers all over the UK and also exporting.

Yet when we started we were no different from many small firms scattered all over the North-east. Old man Gray – he was called that even though he died when he was only 54 – he was the one who'd grown it. He'd started out with small scale wooden products, back in 1929, making things like chicken coops, made out of wire meshing and wooden planks – the kind of thing you'd have found in any back garden in those days – and the odd wooden trailer. Then in 1949 he went over to steel, first of all with simple products such as hay sweeps and buck rakes. He had great drive.

Eddie Gray came from an ordinary farm background. He developed the firm in a

A parade of Gray
front end loaders,
Aden Park, 1980.

'Practical solutions to everyday farming problems.' The Gray overhead loader at
work, delivering bales onto a cart.

home grown manner: no University-trained engineers, just trial and error. He'd spot a
need or someone would come to him with an idea and he'd make up a piece of
equipment and then try it out. He invented a tipper for a trailer by fashioning a
mechanical arm that lifted the load up, long before the hydraulics came in, and then won
a huge contract with the Ministry of Agriculture. He made a front-end loader which
could hoist its load right over the head of the tractor and deposit it in the trailer behind.
We traded under the slogan, 'British built for British farmers'. He knew what the farmer

Royal approval.
Duncan showing Prince
Charles the works,
2000.

Main Street, Fetterangus, packed with trailers, ready to transport Gray products all over the UK, 1960.

Still the enthusiast.

Duncan at home with two of his extensive collection of vintage tractors, 2011.

wanted – simple practical solutions.

I can still visualise the main street of the village, packed with trailers waiting to be shifted to Mintlaw Station for transportation all over the UK. Nothing could stop him, not old man Gray. But it was never the same after his death. It passed on to the next generation, but they hadn't the same flair, didn't stick at it the same, somehow.

I finally left in 2000; one year later the firm came to its end. It had been my life. I stay just a few miles from Fetterangus yet I can't bring myself to take a look at what's happened to the old site. Just too sad.

Once we'd dealt with a network of 600 dealers all over the UK; we had three reps permanently on the road. I really miss the phone, now I'm retired. I'd be sitting in my office and messages would be pouring in from all over the place: reps, dealers, suppliers, farmers with a new job – I was in the thick of it. When I went home of an evening the phone would be switched through to me, so I was at it from early morning to night.

All this from a small village factory which was hidden behind the houses so that you'd scarcely know it was there – and now it's disappeared completely. Go into Fetterangus, up the main street, turn right at the pub, then first left and walk up to the gate in front of you and just look over and what will you see? Nothing, just a barren site. Ah well, I suppose it's the way of the world; you read about the fall of yet another local example of industry going to the wall all the time and its works site being converted into housing estates and retail malls. Sad to think that the firm that was once so thriving, so busy, has gone that way, too.

Duncan Forbes, born 1936, interviewed 2011: Fetterangus

From town to country

We had just moved into the farmhouse at Burnside of Folla, one mile on the Inverurie side of Rothienorman, from a bungalow at 32 Camperdown Road in Aberdeen. I was eight years old. My Dad said that living in the country would be safer for us than in the big city during the war. Burnside was a small farm, only 44 acres, and on the north-east side of a steep hill – not a very good farming position for oats or barley. On reflection, I think perhaps my dad used the safety issue as an excuse to buy the farm he had always wanted. He had previously had a poultry farm in South Africa before he got married and since returning to Scotland what he really wanted to do was to be a farmer again.

'Aa ye need is one pair,' my Father was immediately advised by a neighbour, who obviously doubted the abilities of this man from Aberdeen to manage Burnside. 'They've aye hid jist the ane pair o' horse at Burnside.' My Dad muttered his thanks, but even then I knew he was not having any horses. He was determined to try new ways.

We had a new home, new school, new life and a very different house. It was dark inside, with a bed recess in the kitchen, no electricity, an outside toilet and a hand-operated water pump in the wash house at the back door, connected to a well in the nearest field about 100 yards away.

I remember visiting about a month before we moved in and the bed in the recess of this large dark kitchen was on this occasion occupied by an old man. There was a door (as you might have into any room) lying in the middle of the kitchen floor, one side propped up precariously with a stick about 25 cm (10 inches) high. I was curious and was immediately informed by Nellie, the incumbent tenant farmer's kitchie deem, what it was all for. The string going from the stick to the hand of the old man in the bed was so that they could kill the rat by bringing the door down on top of it. It had been pestering them in the kitchen for weeks and if I took a careful look under the door I would be able to see the tempting lump of cheese waiting for the unsuspecting rat. I did, but quickly returned to my dad's side.

The next time we visited was just prior to moving in. It was to attend the roup. My mum and brother and sister were also there. All the implements and furniture from the house were laid out in the nearest field alongside the muck, carefully moved from the yard midden and built into a neat rectangular structure so that it could be sold per cubic yard at the roup along with everything else. We didn't know it at the time, but unfortunately this was built right on top of the concealed well that supplied the washhouse pump. When we eventually went to use the pump what came out looked just like beer – complete with a white frothy top. I can remember my mother crying. She was a city girl and had come from her new bungalow built in Aberdeen in 1940 – complete with all the modern conveniences of the day, to what she regarded as a complete backwater.

Brian Robertson, born 1936, interviewed 2011: Rothienorman

I knew my Dad was not having any horses. He was determined to try new ways.

Building a city bungalow in the country: the new Robertson house taking shape behind the old 'dark' farm house. Brian is on the pony, brother Alan and sister Helen alongside.

Someone would play the squeezebox, accompanied by a 'moothie an speens'. My contribution would be a comb, some brown paper and some pretty horrible noises.

Even as a toonser, I was always keen on farm life. This was due to the Andersons of Wester Beltie. The boys had to deliver milk every morning to all the villages around, before going off to school. You'd hear old Donald Anderson's tackety, clackety boots coming up the close after five am on a frosty winter's morning, when a warm bed seemed the only good place to be, and his voice shouting up at them to be good and ready. He'd find nobody there as they'd escaped out the front door; then he'd go back to the milk lorry and find Angus [Covie] and Donald waiting for him all the time. I loved all that –- but then I hadn't had to do that for several years and then rush off to the school for a rest.

I enjoyed going around with the deliveries, during the holidays, and finding the money for the week's milk always left out in the empty bottles on the doorsteps. Changed days! You'd go round all the places –- Lumphanan, Glassel, Torphins – and meet the folk and hear all the chat. And one of the year's highlights was the arrival of the packman on a summer's evening and seeing him lay out his multitude of wares on the kitchen floor and listening to the haggling and the banter, which were always jovial.

When I went to the University to do Agriculture I had a spell in the dairy farm at Dounside, Tarland – they took in students to give them experience. This was a wonderful time for me. I was 18 and part of a warm, happy group of people. We stayed out in the bothy, but got our meals in the Ranna farmhouse kitchen from Bert and Ruby Thomson, parents of Linda and Bertha. There was always something going on among us – salt in your tea when your back was turned; a newspaper you were behind suddenly catching fire; or, after 40 winks, finding your boot laces had been tied together – always something to keep you on your toes. Good fun days.

The milking was under the supervision of another famous Anderson family. Norman was father to Ian and grandfather to Paul, David and Heather, all well known as fiddle experts. I was forced into taking part in any devilment and often Norman turned the tables on us. The milking wasn't hard going and the byre was a cosy place on a cold winter's morning. Starting at six am the first job was to muck out with a graip and barrow and then set to the milking of the pedigree Freesians. The climate was more severe back then and we often had to wade through the drifts.

But the kitchen and the bothy always seemed to have a good fire going and we would sit around it of an evening. Someone would play the squeezebox, accompanied by a 'moothie an speens'. My contribution would be a comb, some brown paper and some pretty horrible noises. It was great fun, all of it.

The under-manager had a room in the house and he would warm his stout by the fire. Someone covered the chimney with a divot and the room filled with smoke. On investigating he was of the opinion the wind must have suddenly changed direction – until the divot was spotted and a ladder produced to remove it. While he was up there on the roof, the ladder was taken away and a hosepipe fetched to wash him down – just in case he were to catch fire.

He was also keen on a certain young Tarland lady. On his return one night he found

At the barnyard dance, 1957.
Douglas is second right; others from the left are Bill Reid and partner, Geordie Taylor and Charles Bannerman.

his bed missing. An early morning phone call informed him that it had been set up in the said young lady's front garden. And then there was the good-looking milk recorder girl who had a tattie stuck up her car exhaust; before the joke could be rectified, the under-manager had the vehicle towed away to the garage because it wouldn't run and she had to get a bus to convey her back to the town.

Bill Reid VC was an agricultural adviser at that time. He was just one of the lads; when trying to cape (castrate) cattle his language was fully equal to the worst of us. I still can't believe that this unassuming man was one of the bravest pilots ever to have flown with Bomber Command, a country boy who gained the VC at 23 for sheer gallantry, having been shot to bits in a raid over Germany.

I saw the last of the horses and the heavy manual work. Everything was done by muscle power and horsepower then. Farm work was 100% physical; now it's 100% mechanical. If you go to the mart nowadays and look at the men there what you will see are fat, red-faced types; 40 years ago they would all have been lean and hungry looking.

Farming was quite different then, much more of a human and communal affair. When the corn was being thrashed at the rucks, a good Collie dog was all important. They were home to a multitude of rats; Nicky tams were essential as they would be jiggling around, seeking what cover they could find. The dogs went into overdrive and it wasn't unusual to have 100 dead rats laid out. I recall my father-in-law, Willie Jamieson, when farming in Canada in the 1920s, having a rat run up his trouser leg and asking, 'Fit div I dee noo?' He survived – I'm not so sure the rat did!

Piece time was a longed for moment. You'd been hard at it, at what seemed like never-ending work, always on the lookout for the farmer's daughter or kitchie deem coming across the park with the basket containing the goodies and the tea. And you'd all sit down and eat the bread and drink the tea. Plain loaf and jam seemed like a great delicacy then. You'd take your 15 minutes fly, chat and then up and at it again till the next time.

I can still smell the various scents: the clover, the hay, the broom, the horse, the cattle and falling in the midden. Farms were bursting with life then. Evening competitions in the close with neighbouring worthies ended up with all the local gossip. There were the geans and rowans in blossom, the sounds the oyster catchers, curlews and the spectacular peasie. In the summer you'd go out shooting rabbits with the 'big loons' or fish for trout in the burn. There'd be dooking in the larger pools accompanied by certain manly capers in the hope of impressing any local talent that might appear. And I'm sure that all of the girls of that time would have wiped the floor in any modern beauty competition…

Douglas Aberdein, born 1938, interviewed 2008: Tarland

Get on! Get on!

Although the farmyard was our great boyhood playground we understood that its work was a serious matter. We knew that there was nothing more important in the year than getting in the harvest or, during the day, the cows in for their milking. We lived in an atmosphere of 'Get on! Get on!'

As we got older we'd be expected to lend a hand. One of the low points of my childhood is when I was entrusted with the tractor between the stooks. It was a simple matter of applying the pressure with the foot on and off as the situation required, but that was something I found tricky. So I blundered along to the cries of 'Ca canny wi that fut, man!' As soon as one of the older lads came along I was turfed off as obviously unworthy. I was very put out; to be seated up there in control of the tractor was a glamorous position and here I was being sacked from it.

These were good years for farming, the 1940s and Fifties. The rush was on to

The 1954 hairst squad. Charlie Allan and father John R. Allan on the left.

bring as much land as possible under cultivation in order to make the country more self-sufficient in food. Ours was a mixed farm: dairy, tatties, barley, oats, beef and all the usual by-products of dairy farming. I saw myself as growing up as a farmer's boy; I identified with the work and with the place – and I still do. I'm retired from active farming now,

but I can sit here in my conservatory and look over a whole sweep of typical Aberdeenshire landscape. It's a spread of fields, with the odd knot of woodland, that stretches over west towards Bennachie. I get great satisfaction from hearing the whack of my own windmill as it thrashes round and round in a stiff breeze and know it's producing enough electricity to keep us warm in my old age and enough over to sell to the National Grid, too. Personally, I like the sight of windmills marking the landscape. They work best on an upward slope and the North-east has plenty of those, as it does wind. Wind is going to be a good local crop over the coming years.

But farming has suffered a downturn over the last 30 years. A few farmers have become very rich in terms of the assets they are sitting on, but there has never been a decent return on that capital for most of them. The number of farmers has reduced dramatically since 1945. What has happened is that a few clever ones have managed to take over the land so that large concentrations of wealth are now in relatively few hands. The average price per acre is now £4,000 and that is the price my father paid for his whole farm, which came to near on 250 acres. It is now worth, on paper, some £1,000,000, a huge percentage gain. But then father ran it with seven men and now my son-in-law does it himself and holds down another job as well.

My father would take three weeks to get in the harvest with his seven men plus help from me. We'd be at it day after day; other people from round about would come in to lend a hand. There would the cutting, the stooking, the waiting for it all to dry out – an endless business. Now one visiting combine with the contracted-in driver and my son-in-law will do it in a couple of days. In the old days we'd be at the ploughing all through the winter, up and down the fields, dragging along a small eight-inch single furrow plough; now a large reversible model can do the lot in two days.

When I was a boy there were enough families living round the farm to make it a

We'd be ploughing all through the winter, dragging along a small eight-inch single furrow plough.

community in itself. The kids would all play together; we'd walk in droves down to the school. The adults would meet up for bothy nichts; there would be home made musical entertainment; at New Year there would be some furious communal activity. Now that's all gone: the farms are empty now; usually there's the farmer and his own family and that's that. We do have neighbours who live in the old farm houses and cottages, but they no longer work on the land; mostly they are commuters who drive into Aberdeen each day. With some of them I don't even know their names.

Charlie Allan, born 1939, interviewed 2006: Methlick

Charlie Allan has produced a series of articles and books on the theme of North-east agriculture, including the autobiographical THE TRUTH TELLS TWICE *and* THEM THAT LIVE THE LONGEST.

It must have been the smell...

Not yet met: Davie and Evie when each was 11, in 1953.

Davie: In 1957, as soon as I left school, I started as a tractorman, but Evie's granda could see I was itching for something a wee bit better, so he said to me, 'Weel, tak a dairy jab; ye'll git mair oot o that than ye div at the tractor'. He was right: a dairyman did get more pay – but at a price. Whereas the tractorman begins his work at seven and then stops at the fixed hour, a dairyman has to go on till his work's finished - you can't just turn the beasts off like the engine of a tractor. But I reckon his work is more satisfying: you're dealing with living things and getting in among all their little ways and characters.

Evie: That's how we met, in the dairy. I was a dairymaid and he was the dairyman. I did the washing and the bottling. Cleanliness is vital in the dairy; you're constantly having to watch out for mastitis. You have to shave and wash the udders; you have to clip the cows when they come into the byre for the winter, before they start lying down among the straw and the sharn and getting covered with muck. You kent hygiene was vitally important and if you didn't, then the Milk Inspector would soon let you ken about it. This was Miss Douglas from the Milk Marketing Board and she would visit us once a month, inspect all the utensils and see that everything was in order. And if you weren't washing the udders right she would soon show you!

You get to ken the beasts; some of them you get to like and some you don't – and some of them take to you and others don't. Some of them can be real gentle, but some can be real coorse. Just like people. There'll be those which kick out every day and there'll be those which take to the milking in a wink of the eye and are never any bother.

The dairyman's family: Evie Alexander, left, with brothers and sisters, 1940s.

Davie: By the time I stopped, in 1977, the dairy business was becoming quite scientific. You had a milk recorder who would come out from the College and he would check on

the amount of feed each single cow took against the quantity of milk she gave. He'd weigh it all, taste the milk, check its quality and then give the cow the right amount of feed.

When the cow was running dry the machine would come off automatically and you

At one of the several schools:
Davie, as son of a farm worker, attended. Garvock School, 1950, second left, back row.

Same year, different school:
Evie at Esslemont School first row, left.

The young dairyman: Davie, 1960s.

knew to move onto the next beast. It was all becoming quite mechanised and that meant you were beginning to lose the close contact with the animals. When I started you would get to ken each single cow as an individual and they would get to ken you and to respond to you. You'd come into the byre and they would carry on feeding quite content, but if a stranger came in then their tails would be cocked and they would look round to see what was going on. And if the vet appeared there would be complete pandemonium! They'd follow his each move, to see which one was going to be getting the injection next.

Evie: If you worked in the dairy then you aye carried a certain smell about you. At the end of the week you'd scrub and scrub yourself ready for your time off, but the smell remained; it got into the very pores of your skin and no matter how hard you scrubbed it just clung onto you.

Davie: I'd go and visit the folk at the Bridge of Don, all nice and clean, and I'd come in and at once there would be, 'Ach, we kent it wis you withoot even lookin – it's aye that same aul' stink o' coos ye bring wi you'. So maybe it's a good job we married who we did. Maybe it wasn't love; maybe it's because we kent each other's smell. It's like with fish workers – a cattleman can never get rid of the smell.

Davie and Evie Alexander, born 1942 and 1944, interviewed 2008: Ellon

How hard everyone had to work

My main recollection is how hard everyone had to work just to keep going. We were involved in the life of the farm from quite a young age. We learned to drive the tractor as teenagers. My allotted task was feeding the hens and collecting the eggs, a job which I hated. They'd come at you with their sharp little beaks, pecking away at your bare legs. We had a threshing mill and my job on a Saturday morning was to feed sheaves into it.

The farm was quite isolated and we'd no car, so getting into Turriff was something my parents had to do by bike or bus. We children seldom saw much of the outside world. When the annual Turriff Show came round we'd all go to see the sights, though we'd watch from the grass banks, not the ringside seats – too expensive!

My three brothers and I spent hours as young children just pottering about on the farm land. There was an old sand quarry and this was our sandpit. Down at the back there was the King Edward burn where we could paddle and the boys would fish for brown trout. Occasionally you'd catch sight of an otter.

As the only girl, I didn't have much company, but I was fairly self-sufficient, with books from the local library and books given to me as occasional presents. They were mostly the 19th century classics, such as *Little Women* and *Jane Eyre*. For me, one highlight of the year was the summer holidays and the chance to spend a fortnight over at my aunt's at Alford.

The farmer's daughter. Janet Byth aged seven with parents and brothers John, Max and Duncan.

The first car, 1957. Note the farmer's priorities – first the tractor then the car!

The hard work is rewarded: the first tractor, 1951.

The house was near the road, so you could see all the comings and goings. And you could walk into the village and do the shopping. I even watched football matches!

I only ever got one doll and that was a Christmas present from Santa. It came wrapped in brown paper. For the rest it would be books and jumpers – nothing frivolous. But our parents gave us a good upbringing. Although they were usually taken up with the daily effort of keeping the farm going, they were kind and caring and fun. But my childhood was socially limited: there were few other children around and I learned to live in my own world, or simply potter around by myself.

All this seemed good enough at the time. You see, the work ethic was important and that applied to us children too. Thrift was another great value: clothes would be handed down from your cousins and would be patched and mended. I was brought up to knit and sew. You behaved yourself; you were expected to be a 'good' child and to learn a sense of respect and responsibility. There were some community entertainments, like barn dances in the Fintry Barn, whist drives, the odd concert. We children were taken along – it was the only way the parents could attend – and you sat and watched the adults dancing and sipped your bottle of lemonade. Today's young people might not think much of my childhood, but it was of its time – before country folk, other than the big farmers, had a car, a TV or even a telephone. I certainly don't regret any of it.

Janet Byth, born 1944, interviewed 2011: Fintry

The hated task – but this time Dad has taken on the feeding of the hens.

Eggs and horses: how it used to be

I was brought up at Newstead farm, Cuminestown. I went into partnership with my father and after his death I continued to run it. I sold out about 20 years ago. To start with, it ran to 300 acres; by the time I was finished with it, it was up to 800 acres. My memory of the farm was work, work and yet more work! My father worked round the clock and expected the same from me. I remember I was approaching the time of the Qualifying exam. My mother was keen for me to do some swotting, but my father just said, 'Fit the hell div ye wunt him tae dae that fer – he's jist gaein anta the ferm ony bloody way!' My father wasn't somebody you could argue with. When I got to 14 I told him I was thinking of joining the Merchant Navy. His response: 'Ye're here tae werk wi me an the ferm an that's aa there is tae it'.

Right from the start I was expected to do my share. Even when I was at the school I'd be sent to mucking out the pigs and gathering in the eggs. Hens were a huge part of farming then. We had some 600 hens and sent off crates of about 1,000 eggs a week. Hens were the basis of farming economy in those days. Granda told me that back in the Twenties he kept 400 hens and that was enough to support a house, a maid, two men and still leave enough to bank a bit each week besides.

You don't see that sort of thing on the average North-east farm nowadays. All the farmers now seem to live on their subsidies. But back in the Fifties they all had maids. We always did: a live-in maid. After all, the house was large, the wife was fully occupied with the hens and there would be farm workers to feed at midday too. We had a team of four labourers.

Machinery has wiped all that away now. I remember when we took the step of moving from horses to tractors. On the day Judy, our last horse, left I shed a tear or two. I'd been fond of the horses and would like to pet and to talk to them. My father told me not to be sad, that Judy would be going off to a nice place somewhere on the Islands – but I later found out that he'd sold her off to a dealer who was going to move her on to a knacker's and then to be sold as horsemeat in Holland.

The very next day our first tractor arrived. This was a petrol-paraffin Fordy with steel seat and no cab and bumpy steel spad wheels. When you started her up the petrol-paraffin mixture took alight and you'd see flames shooting up in the air from the exhaust pipe. I missed the horses, but there's no denying that the tractors were much more efficient. It was great to see the man following the horse as he ploughed – but a horse would take a whole week to get through one acre while a tractor even then could do it in an hour. Nowadays they have highly sophisticated machines: eight-furrow reversibles with

> Our first tractor was a petrol-paraffin Fordy with steel seat and no cab and bumpy steel spad wheels.

'A large part of farming back then.' A typical North-east farmyard of the 1950s: Sunnyside, Quilquox. Picture supplied by William Sinclair, who grew up there.

250 horse-power beneath the bonnet. A neighbour of ours has one that's controlled by sat-nav. This means he'll always plough dead straight; he can stop spraying for an hour while he goes off to eat and when he returns the sat-nav will tell him where to go to the exact spot he left off at.

Gavin Sim, born 1949, interviewed 2011: Cuminestown

Hard! Windy! Cold!

Life, as an organic farmer, has been hard, hard work. Hard! Windy! Cold! That's how I would sum up the last 20 years. When we told people our plans they would give us a polite hearing and then nod at each other – 'They winna lest twa years at that organic caper, twa years and they'll be oot!' The year we managed to get as much oats per acre as they did they started to knock at the door and enquire after our methods. We told them how we undersowed the cereal with clover, so that the cattle would then feed on it later and their dung would go on the land, that what we were aiming to recreate was a natural cycle. We've made a living, not an opulent one, but a living.

We've 40 acres of arable land here. Our main crop is winter vegetables – swedes, leeks, cabbages, parsnips, carrots. After a couple of years we decided it wasn't worth dealing with supermarkets. They give you a lot of hassle; they are very demanding. The strawberries are completely my department and we had this rep from Safeways come to look at them. He refused to talk to me; it was John he assumed he should be addressing. We walked up to the field, he looked and tasted and then said, yes, they would be interested. At that point John went off to do something else and left me to negotiate, but the Safeways man still didn't seem to understand who he should be talking with. I asked him what his price would be. I told him I was getting £1.10 the pound at Stonehaven market, but he wouldn't give me his figure; he was obviously waiting for the man of the place to return. I told him I didn't like his attitude: I was the one who had selected these strawberries, I was the one who'd overseen their growing and I would be the one who dealt with their sale. I then told him that I thought his prices were rubbish, that he would be taking my entire crop and throwing some of it away as 'not perfect'. I told him not to come back.

I couldn't really tell you what the future is for organic farming. When we started we knew that it would be labour intensive. Since we naturally don't use herbicides, our biggest bill is for weeders. We sow in the spring; in the early summer we plant our vegetables and then it's weeding, weeding. When August comes round everyone imagines 'harvest home', that we reap all our crops and put our feet up over the winter. But we have to keep going: we have cucumbers and tomatoes in the polythene tunnels; we have the root vegetables to pull up. From September through to March we're outside, picking, picking. There's no rest for the organic farmer.

The food policies of the last 60 years have done a lot of damage to the nation's health.

I told him
I didn't like
his attitude:
I was the one
who had
selected the
strawberries,
I was the one
who'd
overseen
their growing
and I would
be the one
who dealt
with
their sale.

After the restrictions of the war and the rationing, people were pretty lean and fit. There was no fast food and little money for extras. Now children are brought up to eat when and what they like. No wonder we're now plagued with obesity, with allergies and childhood asthma. This is tragic: we are supposed to be more sophisticated and better informed than our grandparents ever were and yet we don't know how to eat properly or where our food comes from. When I was living in South America there were three things that everyone knew about Scotland: the bagpipe, the kilt and the excellence of Scottish education. And now look at us!

Maggie Fraser, born 1956, interviewed 2008: Bridge of Muchalls

That's just the way I like it

I enjoy almost all aspects of farming. I like being on the go. I hate just standing around. The worst time on the farm is a winter's afternoon. In the morning and late afternoon you have the cattle and the pigs to feed, so that's fine. You're out in the steading and it's three o'clock and it doesn't seem worth starting on a new job and it's getting dark and the weather might be closing in…

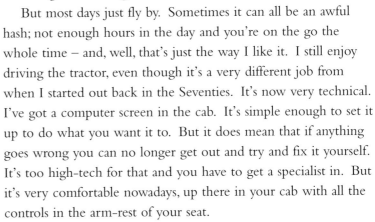

But most days just fly by. Sometimes it can all be an awful hash; not enough hours in the day and you're on the go the whole time – and, well, that's just the way I like it. I still enjoy driving the tractor, even though it's a very different job from when I started out back in the Seventies. It's now very technical. I've got a computer screen in the cab. It's simple enough to set it up to do what you want it to. But it does mean that if anything goes wrong you can no longer get out and try and fix it yourself. It's too high-tech for that and you have to get a specialist in. But it's very comfortable nowadays, up there in your cab with all the controls in the arm-rest of your seat.

The satisfactions of a well turned field.

The Mearns farmer keeping a firm uphill line.

But you still have to do the steering and there's an art in ploughing a good straight furrow. I really enjoy that, trying to make a well turned job of a field. That's not as easy as you might think and some days you seem to be better at it than others. That's the case here where we have a lot of fairly flat fields, but also some side ones where you have to have a good touch in steering so as to compensate for all the awkward slopes and make sure there are no overlaps and that you don't miss a patch. You have to have an eye for how the ground lies and steer accordingly.

How much you do depends on the size of the plough. I'm presently working a four-furrow reversible and that means I can get through six acres in a yokin. When I started that would have taken more than twice as long. And although you did have a cab at the sides and the front, it was open at the back and gey cold at times. Now you're completely closed in and have a heater too. You can have a CD player and the radio as well. The

A farmer's pride and joy: showing off the new tractor.

model's a 160-horse power and has an electronic fuel management for extra power when you need it. It's also automatic and changes the gears by itself.

I also enjoy the combine. When it's a fine day and you're sitting up there in that cab at the controls and everything's going well, then that's a great feeling. I love the sensation of going steadily up and down through the corn and seeing the field being cleared behind you.

You don't see as many people about a farm as you used to. If I want to communicate then it's the mobile phone that does the job. When I started there was a team of five or six of us and you'd be able to chat and have a laugh together. Now I have to rely upon my radio in the cab to get a bit of noise about the place.

Nor do you get so many company reps calling. In the past you might have a rep coming in with grass seed or fertilisers to show you; it's all done on-line and by phone nowadays. You do miss that; some of those salesmen would have been all over the region and be able to give you all the news of the day. And the farming community's changed too. The workers are no longer there to fill the cottages and a lot of them are sold off. So many of the old steadings are now converted into executive houses. That does keep people in the countryside, I suppose, but you never really get to know them. They aren't part of the farming community.

I still enjoy the farming. It's never been a well paid job; it's quite amazing to compare the low rate of pay to the value of the equipment and the livestock we have to handle each day, but that's the way of things. Then if you think of the sort of money people in the oil industry can get, well…

It's little wonder that so few young folk go into farming nowadays. It used to be just about the biggest employer in the North-east, but now it's very much a minority trade. But farming's in the blood, I suppose. It's not just a job with a wage, it's a whole way of life. It's something that never leaves you. Often enough, on a Saturday evening I'll jump in the car and have a tour just to see what's going on in the fields all about. I get great satisfaction at seeing the fields in good order, in being able to look out on a well ploughed field, with the earth all fresh and straight and nicely turned over. I hate to see the furrows all squint and trash not buried. There's no excuse for that kind of sloppiness, not with the modern tractor and plough and a tractorman who takes the trouble to see it's done in the right way. Straight! That's how a furrow should be, dead straight. It's very satisfying to see a long big field where the furrows stretch out into the distance nice and straight.

So although I doubt whether there are going to be many young folk leaving school this year and rushing into farming, I've no regrets. Farming – it's what I am.

View from the cab: keeping those furrows straight.

Farming used to be the biggest employer, but now it's very much a minority trade.

Ready to tackle the A90. Off to deliver the bales 15 miles down the road.

A life-long farmer, born 1960, interviewed 2011: the Mearns

A mug's game

Farming generally has suffered over the last 15 years. I stick it out, but if you ask my two elder sons whether they feel like following on in the family business their immediate answer is, 'Farming, no way! We're never going to go into that.' The returns are so uncertain now and the farm itself is so tying that it's difficult to see anyone coming into it from the outside.

The worst aspect of farming today is the incredible amount of bureaucracy and regulations we now have to work under. I have to do it all myself. Just look at my hands and tell me if they're what you would expect to see on a working farmer. Look, they're as soft and as clean as an office worker's – and that's what I've now become, a glorified office worker. Each cow has to have its own passport. When I took over from my father in 1989 you could just choose your own cattle, take them back to the farm, open the gate and let them run free. Now you have to make sure they're fitted out with two tags for their ears and that the numbers tally with each other and with the passport.

Then there's the non-stop stream of inspectors that come to the farm and have to be prepared for. There's people from the Pharmaceutical Society come to check on the drugs that we put into the feeds, visitors from Animal Health Office to check on the presence of any animal meal in the rations; then there will be inspectors from Aberdeenshire County Council to look at trading standards. This year we've had to become subject to something called IPPC – Integrated Prevention of Pollution Control. I have had to get a licence at the cost of £3,500 to be approved; as I keep pigs I have to fork out another £2,800 on top of that. All this means that a representative from Health & Safety comes round every four months to check on my pollution control. I have to prepare an odour management plan, a noise pollution plan, a slurry management plan. Each March people come out from Thainstone to check on our cattle tags and match them with the written records. These bodies address me as if I have a staff of various managers who can see to each of these tasks, but it's only me rushing around, putting on these various hats.

It's all very expensive and time consuming. It's also a bit demoralising because it's not what I came into farming for. One of the great attractions was to be my own boss, but how can I feel I'm that when I have so many other people to satisfy?

Farming nowadays is a mug's game. The people I feel really sorry for are my employees. I was speaking to someone in the oil industry the other day and he was telling me he gets £50,000 a year. But I've got someone here who is a fantastically talented engineer; but all he'll get for his year is £20,000 and that's only because he's prepared to do plenty of overtime. They get 29 days holiday a year, but their mentality is such that they rarely take all of it; they know there's always something more to do, that this is a job that never ends. I'm amazed they've stuck it so long – over 20 years. They work very hard, are skilled and devoted to the job, they handle equipment worth tens of thousands of pounds, yet they are never valued in the same terms as others in society.

I suppose I only continue because of the emotional attachment to the farm, because my father built all this up from next to nothing. It's what I've grown up to do; I find it

Just look at my hands. They're as soft and as clean as an office worker's — and that's what I've become, a glorified office worker.

difficult to imagine myself doing anything else. In any case I cling to the notion that things must turn one day, that land is a sensible investment – after all they're not making any more of the stuff. But in terms of the here and now it's all quite crazy. I've spent £1,250,000 on the pig unit and yet in only one of the last four years have I run at a profit. Any money I get in goes on the staff or is invested back into the farm.

The pig farmer at work. At the time of interview Kevin was noted for the scale and innovative efficiency of the operation he was carrying out at his Womblehill farm.

I don't think the general public have a clue about this. When I go into the village I can get remarks like, 'Here comes the Laird of Kintore'. I'm not sure that at a farm like this we can even regard ourselves as country farmers. The housing comes so close now that you have to be careful about spreading the slurry in case the smell drifts over to all those new houses which have been packed in by the bypass. Probably that's my main impact on the people who live there – I'm the guy who makes a stink!

Farming can be great if it's a fine day and you're out on your own land, going around and seeing your stock and how well the fields are looking – well, you can have a sense of pride in all that but, really, we've become a commodity industry, at the mercy of the big supermarkets. I tell you it's a cut-throat business. The supermarkets have so much control. They can switch suppliers just like that if they think they can get a better deal elsewhere. Tesco's motto is 'Every day lower prices' – and what they mean is '… for the farmer'.

So that's been my life over the last 17 years: running this farm. Sometimes you can't help but feel that it's a dying way of life. Do you know that there used to be 13 farms on Womblehill? And now there's only one – mine. It's all big scale production. If a farm comes on the market then only someone who's already big enough to be able to borrow the necessary cash will be able to buy it.

That's why the country is becoming emptier and emptier. The number of small farms of the old days each had several workers and their families too. Now there's hardly anyone left. Not only has the number of farms gone down, but the need for labour has too. Take the guy who farms along the road: he has two sons, but one of them works as an engineer and the other is out on contract work elsewhere. There just isn't the work to sustain all three of them. You need at least 250 acres to support one family nowadays.

I believe the average age of a farmer in this part of the world is now up to 57. And some of the old socialising that used to make the farming folk a real community has passed too. When I go to the mart it's for a particular purpose, to buy or to sell. I'll just pop along in my boiler suit. You can see what it used to be like by looking at some of the old guys that still turn up each Friday, dressed up in a sports jacket, best bonnet, collar and tie. For them it's a social occasion still, a chance to chat and to catch up on the latest

The changing agricultural scene.
A group of bison blinking in the November sunshine, Muchalls, 2012.

news. But a lot of these older guys are actually retired.

My wife speaks of this place as 'the family burden'. It's as if Womblehill has been handed over to us on the basis of, 'Here's the family farm; it's now your responsibility to keep it and to run it and then to pass it on to the next generation'. But, as I said, no one actually pressurised me into doing that. I just sort of fell into it. Maybe it's been a lack of imagination or the fear of the unknown, but I know I've always had this model of a way of life in front of me and I've just naturally gone into it. And I suppose I do like the freedom, that I wouldn't have taken to driving into an office each day and spending my time sat behind a desk.

So maybe farming is something I just can't help myself doing. Am I optimistic? But of course! They say that in 15 years' time there'll be a real need for more food production and that farming will be on the up again…

Kevin Gilbert, born 1970, interviewed 2006: Kintore

ALL MANNER OF FOLK: Part 1

'**Something for the whole community.**' Corrie Cheyne, her mother
Lindy and brothers Gavin (extreme left) and Angus, Brighton 1980s.

The family business: a 1923 advertisement for Horace Thomson's father's famous Cod Liver Cream.

I ran the family business till 1965 and had my eyes opened to the weaknesses of the politics and ethics of the North-east.

The health educator: so little has changed

My father and grandfather ran a chemist's shop in Elgin High Street. They developed a prescription for children's growth and development which they marketed as 'Thomson's Cod Liver Oil Cream'. His success necessitated the building of a separate factory in Abbey Street to meet the demand for the product. It was used by the Royal family, but the only reference we were allowed to make was that it was 'Under Royal Patronage'.

You could say I was brought up to the family trade in that I went in for Medicine, but I must admit I was something of a rebel at school. I got regular skelpings on my backside; I was naturally rebellious and independent minded. I grew to think of school as a machine for the confinement of the young; you were expected to sit there and take whatever the authorities deemed important, which had little to do with my own developing interests. These experiences gave me what turned out to be a life-long interest in educational reform.

I graduated as a doctor in 1944. But my father suddenly died. I had to return home and see to the family business. I ran it till 1965 and had my eyes opened to the weaknesses of the politics and ethics of the North-east.

I was Chairman of the Moray and Nairn Education Committee from 1962 to 1964 and was keen to push the cause of outdoor and sporting activity. But the drive to get swimming pools into schools proved to be controversial; the editor of the local paper said that 'education should come before sport'. That shocked me to the core. To me, sport is an integral part of a rounded personal development.

There's a lot of sport in my family background. My father was the Annual Moray Open Tournament Champion on many occasions. He had a handicap of plus two in his best years. I served as Captain of Elgin Golf Club in 1950-51.

When I went into Medicine I became interested in the links between social background and health. I have a restless mind. To me at the centre of our search for a good life is the human body and, within it, the human brain. How can we best use that body? That's why I went into the College of Education and got involved with the training of young teachers. I took up my appointment as Medical Officer and Lecturer in Health Education at Aberdeen in 1966.

This was the same year as the Abortion Act which gave women the legal right to seek termination of pregnancy. Before then, abortion was certainly practised, but as a back street business with all its attendant miseries and mutilation. The act was a great step forward but there were still difficulties. A stipulation was that the woman had to make a case out for it and I found that some people are unable to communicate such an intimate problem with any verbal confidence. There was a cultural block, a social reticence in discussing such matters. This applied to even the supposedly well educated students at the College: they had been taught to write but not to speak. I got them to write an essay outlining their situation and that made all the difference.

I found that the sex education of the typical female student had been neglected. The fact that many unwanted pregnancies fell nine months after Christmas and New Year told

90 year-old rivals, Horace Thomson (left) and Bill Campbell in a rerun of their 1951 Moray Open Trophy final, fought out at Lossiemouth Golf Club, 2011.

its own story. My approach was to give explicit advice and never to moralise. 'Look, if you want to go in for high jinks over the festive period, then make sure you're on the pill.' Whether that was right or wrong from a traditional viewpoint didn't concern me; my duty was to make sure these young women were in control of their own bodies.

In my younger day sex was considered a taboo subject; young people were to be kept on the straight and narrow by blanket moral prescription. When I arrived at the College, the traditional authoritarianism still prevailed. The female students were held to a strict code of behaviour and dress by the Dean of Women. If a girl became pregnant, her course was terminated forthwith.

I was determined to help my students cope with their ignorance and lack of support. I decided that any female who became pregnant would be allowed to continue her course, provided she submit evidence that she was regularly attending antenatal examinations by her GP. The college policy had been to eject any girl falling pregnant from the student hostel immediately. I arranged that they could have abortions done at a private clinic in town for £50 and that the operation would be performed over the weekend so that they could return to the hostel for the following week without the warden having to be informed.

I organised a series of lectures on 'Social Education' where students were given information concerning venereal disease, nutrition, drugs usage, contraception. Notices were posted in the student union encouraging students to come to me as soon as possible

The reunion: Horace (back row, third left) with a group of old College colleagues, on the occasion of the closure of its Hilton campus, 2005.

after unprotected intercourse.

These policies reduced the pregnancy rate. In 1975 I organised a research project into the state of sexual knowledge in schools; I knew it was important to get at the 14-year old age group. I realised that to send out questionnaires to them would be challenging the traditional attitudes of the North-east. I was careful to get the approval of both the college governors and the Director of Education, James Michie. Even so, I stirred up controversy. I was attacked by a Roman Catholic priest in Keith: 'a dangerous invasion on the privacy of the child…it could do untold harm for any child to be associated with this project'.

The cause of education and medicine has always been dear to me. I hope I've made some contribution to opening up attitudes. But when I look back over a long lifetime I'm astonished at how little education has really changed. I'm frustrated at how little curiosity young people are encouraged to develop into the physical world. There's so much to amaze us about the animal world. Here at Lossiemouth we have the din of fighter jets taking off and landing at the base. They require so much thrust to get up into the air and come down again and so much of their energy is simply expended on noise. Look at a bird and see how silently it goes about its flying. It can utilise wind and temperature to soar and glide and can land on a twig with an efficiency humans, despite all our technology, can't even begin to emulate.

Man is the great threat to the environment. We are the creatures that damage the world we share with the animal kingdom. Yet our educational system is content to leave our children – the rulers of tomorrow – in a state of ignorance about our own bodies. Biology departments spend hours on field trips to examine the dandelion, but never think to invite old folk into the classroom so that the ageing process can be examined.

I've enjoyed my career, but I'm frustrated that, despite all that has been tried and fought for, so little has changed since the days when I was a rebellious boy going to school for another round of boring desk-bound studies.

Horace Thomson, born 1921, interviewed 2008: Lossiemouth

The gala queen: just a fun week, really

Aileen: From the age of 16 you'd be allowed to go to the dances – but only so long as you respected the rules your parents laid down for you. The music was still quite traditional: three-piece bands with guitars, drums and accordion and the boys and the girls lined up on opposite sides of the hall. But we did take note of the arrival of rock 'n roll. I remember going along to the cinema in Banff with the girl who lived next door to see an Elvis film and she started to scream. She was normally straight-laced, very churchy and strictly brought up and here she was screaming her head off!

At home we'd watch *Top of the Pops* and *Ready, Steady, Go!* My mother would sit there shaking her head and muttering about all 'that racket' and we'd accuse her of being 'past it' – and then later I found myself doing exactly the same when our son went through his Heavy Metal phase.

I liked the fashions too – all those underskirts and sticking out dresses that you could swirl about at the dances. And I just loved the stilettos. Mum would warn me that I would suffer for it later on in life, but I just laughed it off and continued to stride out in my high, high heels – and then in later life I had to have an operation for bunions. I thought of Mum looking down on me and saying, 'Weel, I telt ye!'

But the dances were innocent affairs compared to today's carry on. There was no alcohol, just a small shop at the top of the stairs where you could get lemonade and crisps. The boys might have visited the pub beforehand, but not us: young women simply didn't

A royal line: the contestants for the title of Macduff Gala Queen, 1961. Aileen Allan is second left.

A Queen does her duty. Aileen escorted up the harbour steps at Whitehills by the Provost.

go to pubs in those days, not in Macduff. And we had to keep proper hours. On a Sunday night I would have to be back in by nine; if I wasn't then I knew I wouldn't be allowed out the following week. Can you imagine telling a 17-year old nowadays that they have to be back home by nine? That's the time when they're just going out! I can remember my father with a Tilley lamp, standing at the top of the hill, waiting to give my sister a telling off because she was 10 minutes after time.

I was the Macduff Gala Queen, when I was just 18. The town ran an annual gala week and on the Saturday we went to the dance in the Town Hall and that's where the queen and her attendants were chosen. The first I knew of it was when I was tapped on the shoulder by the player-manager of Deveronvale FC, Billy Smith. He and his wife had been given the task of watching us all and then selecting the one they judged to be the queen for that year. It all came as a complete surprise to me.

The actual Gala Week I was kept very busy performing all my duties. I had to go to Whitehills and sit in the lifeboat while it sailed across the bay and then go on to the shore, where I was greeted by the Provost. I was escorted up the pier and a big crowd turned out to watch. Then I had to go to a public park and deliver my Queen's speech, which had already been written out for me.

The crowning moment. Billy (manager, Deveronvale FC) and Mrs Smith choose Aileen as their Queen. Her attendants are Marlene Davidson, left, and Maureen McHardie.

Then there were other events like a children's fancy dress parade and a swimming gala at our open air pool, Tarlair. All very exciting, but nerve-wracking too; I was a young girl, really, and had never been used to the limelight. I found the whole week something of an ordeal, but I kept smiling and waving and got through it. People were very friendly and I took confidence from the fact that I was among folk that I knew. As a memento, I was invited to go to the jeweller's shop and choose a gift for myself. I got a travel clock and a crystal necklace, which I still have to this day,. A memorable week – but I was glad when it was all over.

Bill: I had to stay in the background and keep a low profile. I was very proud of Aileen, but I must admit that I kept worrying that some rich farmer or fishing boat owner might come along and sweep her away in his fancy car.

Aileen: No such luck! After the week was over we were able to resume our normal lives together and that suited me fine. It was really just a fun week and the fact that I got chosen just the luck of the draw. The odd thing is that I was the very last Macduff Gala Queen; 1961 was the last year they ran the event.

Bill: Well, they knew they couldn't improve on you...

Aileen and Bill Allan, born 1943 and 1940, interviewed 2011: Macduff

The building magnate

His other role.
Stewart in the Board
Room of Aberdeen FC,
where he is the long-
standing Chairman.

My parents stayed at Tough; the whole of their married life was passed in the same house and this was the old schoolhouse there. I had a fairly basic upbringing. My father didn't marry till he was 53 and then he had five sons in five years. No electricity, just Tilley lamps and rudimentary conveniences.

My background is farming. Father was self-employed. He'd go round the farms and built up a strong reputation as an expert in draining and ditching.

To be honest, I regarded school-work as drudgery. I got through it well enough, but I never found anything of real interest there except sport and, later, Technical. I actually spent quite a lot of my time in class daydreaming, usually of football.

My success has been a combination of a lot of things, including luck. But I believe that the fundamental things are what I acquired from my upbringing. My father was a great believer in hard work. He would tell us to treat life like a bank account: what you get out depends on what you put in. He himself was a really determined character and came up through many difficulties.

He had a very basic education and left school at 13. But he always took a great interest in the wider world and was a great reader. Just working with the farming community from all around gave him a great insight into how things work in life.

Discipline was forceful, both at school and at home. I never resented it. I still genuinely believe that, if administered in a controlled way, corporal punishment has a role to play. My father would certainly give me a clip round the ear to reinforce his message.

Origins: Tough School which Stewart Milne attended in the 1950s and 1960s.

I have learned that you must confront, not hide. You mustn't carry on kidding yourself that all is well.

My commitment is that if you take something on then you have to see it through to the finish. A lot of people assume that the Milne Group has ascended upwards to success in a straight, unbroken line. Far from it. We have had to come through difficult times – and done so because our basic philosophy is that if you work hard then the rewards at the end of the day will justify the effort. What I have learned is that you must confront, not hide. Whatever you do, you mustn't carry on kidding yourself that all is well; you must stop, assess and work out a different route.

I think that this does have something to do with the North-east. The people I interfaced with were of a kind to give me a solid attitude towards life. I'm really talking about the rural community. I found it a huge step to move into the city. I had grown up in an environment where folk went about things in a certain way. Often my father would go for weeks without being paid, but he knew the day would come when things would be settled properly. There would be a great evening when, every two months or so, these big farming characters would come along to the house to pay up. They would spend the whole evening over it, have a dram and discuss the world at large. It was fascinating to sit quietly by the fireside and just listen to them all.

There would be detailed discussion of what my father had done for them. He'd go into the job thoroughly and then a happy argument – over a dram – would ensue as to its real worth. He really did have this belief that if you did the job properly and explained yourself clearly then the reward would come. But the city wasn't necessarily like that, I found. There, I often detected a desire for the reward before the job was half done.

Maybe this is something that has developed over the generations. Back in the 19th century, life in the North-east was very hard. The land was something that had to be won, made fit for cultivation by hard effort. Inevitably it's changing. Over the last 30 years or so, people have moved in from all parts of the country; the villages have become bigger, the old culture is being diluted. The North-east is now a more cosmopolitan place. That's not altogether a bad thing. Even 30 years ago you would have noticed a great gulf between the country and the city, in terms of amenities and living standards. That gap has now closed. When I think back to Tough, in the Fifties and Sixties, it's obvious we had a lot less compared to families in the town.

I still go back to Tough from time to time. Mum and Dad are both buried out there and I've held on to the old house. But, you know, even after we'd grown up, Father didn't want much change. The house still had its outside toilet; he did get the electricity in, but whenever I tried to persuade him to let us build on a new kitchen and bathroom he resisted the idea.

I still think back to those sessions round the fire and over a dram, in the old house when the farmers came to pay their bills and discuss the world with my father. They were able to record so much – all that had happened to them and their community over 50 years past, and with such vividness too. There was a lot of wisdom in those people.

Stewart Milne, born 1950, interviewed 2003: Tough

The photographer and the teacher

Maryculter was an idyllic place for me to grow up in. I stayed at 2 Fernieslack Cottages, almost directly across the road from Maryculter East School, now closed, where I received a very happy rural primary education in a school of only 40 pupils in total. I feel strongly that the carefree childhood and the very personalised education that I received there have been major influences on the formation of the person that I am today.

All of my primary schooldays were at Maryculter, the majority of them under the tutelage of Ronnie Mackay. As a head teacher of a small rural primary school myself in later years, I became aware of how significant a role Mr Mackay had played in my formative days. As well as providing me with a very solid grounding in reading, writing and numeracy – solid enough for me later to acquire a Bachelor of Education degree – he had an ability to fire the imaginations of the children in his class. A love of poetry and literature also began in his classroom. In creative writing, the immediate school surroundings were the principal learning environment. He was very much ahead of his time for the early Sixties.

This early influence has shaped my career as an educationalist and as a landscape photographer. At Maryculter, our leisure time was almost entirely out-of-doors, absorbing and observing the changing seasons. In my childhood, I was immersed subliminally in the changing light on the land, the patterns in the fields, the texture of the bark on trees and the colours of the wildflowers in springtime.

Unfortunately, my father died at the young age of 53 when I was only 12. By then,

A happy Primary education. Andy Hall (fifth right, back row) at Maryculter East School, 1965. His inspirational Head is Ronnie Mackay (end, back row).

Camera at the ready: Andy Hall, photographer and educator

**Capturing the spirit
of the North-east.**
Arbuthnott, Lewis
Grassic Gibbon
country.

I've been
privileged to
have opened
the eyes of
generations
of children
to the
literature,
poetry,
music, art,
history and
culture of
a very special
corner of
Scotland.

we'd moved to the North Lodge of Ury Estate near Stonehaven. He'd had a house built in the grounds of the lodge but, sadly, we were only in it for three months when he passed away. Subsequently, my mother and I moved down into Stonehaven where, apart from a 10-year spell when my career took me away, I've lived ever since. During the intervening time, I've enjoyed life in the small seaside town. I married Sylvia, younger daughter of the late and much-respected GP Dr. Brian Hopper and we have brought up two children in Stonehaven, both now making their own way in the world.

I discovered a love of photography quite late on, into my mid-thirties. If Maryculter instilled a love of the land, the Kincardineshire coast has inspired a deep attachment to the rugged, rocky shoreline and the beaches, particularly atmospheric at the beginning and at the end of a winter's day.

Notwithstanding the allure of the coast, I've also grown to love the landscape of the Mearns, lyrically described by Lewis Grassic Gibbon in *A Scots Quair*, which I studied as part of my degree. I try to explore, through the medium of photography, similar themes to those that Grassic Gibbon described in his writing, themes of the enduring nature of the land, the sense of longing for and belonging to a place and the relationship between the landscape and the people who lived in it, who worked on it and left it behind.

In recent years, I've become a published photographer which has allowed me to explore these themes more fully in a Scotland-wide sense with *A Sense of Belonging to Scotland* and, more locally, in collaboration with an artist friend, Francis Boag, in a publication entitled *The Mearns Distilled*. Although I've travelled thousands of miles throughout Scotland for the *Sense of Belonging to Scotland* book project, Stonehaven is the place I return to, allowing me to hone my photographic skills and to 'keep the vision', as a friend of mine once described it.

I go through a process when I'm taking photographs which goes beyond making a mere record of the location. In every case, my aim is to capture 'the decisive moment', a phrase used by iconic French photographer Henri Cartier-Bresson. It is the moment when all the elements of light, movement, colour and composition come together in perfect harmony. It is in that moment, described by Cartier-Bresson in an interview with the *Washington Post* in 1957, that the photographer becomes a creative artist. A moment later and the image is gone, never to be repeated. The art is being able to anticipate, wait for and eventually capture the exact moment when all of the elements harmonise. Timing is everything for the creative photographer.

The process begins for me with absorbing a location in every sensory aspect, often without my camera. Gradually, I distil the experience which attracted me to capture an image there in the first place and, most often on a tripod, I put together a balanced composition in the viewfinder that pleases me. The next stages of the process are linked; anticipating, waiting for and capturing the 'decisive moment'.

My favourite times of the day for photography are the hours before and after a sunrise when the light is cool and the shadows are shortening, and the hours before and after sunset when the light is warm and golden, with shadows lengthening.

In the morning 'magic hours' I'll be found down at Cowie shore, next to Stonehaven, to capture the subtle soft light of pre-dawn, or I'll be above Dunnottar Castle to photograph a silhouette. In the evening, I'll be in the middle of a ploughed field in Arbuthnott capturing deep shadows in the furrows or, during the post-sunset afterglow, standing above the north end of St. Cyrus beach facing the estuary of the North Esk at Montrose.

My favourite season for landscape photography is winter when the sun never really rises very high in the sky, offering cool and golden light almost all day long. Dunnottar cloaked in snow in the late-afternoon sun is an unforgettable experience.

Even on a dull day, there is a multitude of opportunities, whether it is eroded sandstone rock formations on the coast or melting ice in the River Carron, or the joy of capturing the bluebells in Dunnottar Woods. There are shadows on the bridge over the River Cowie, reflections on the still water of a harbour morning or the delight of the unique Carron Restaurant, the finest example of Art Deco architecture that I've seen in Scotland. I run weekend photographic courses every spring and, without exception, the participants cannot believe the amount of diverse photographic opportunities that can be discovered in and around Stonehaven.

For me, the North-east of Scotland has had a huge influence on my life. In education, over my teaching career, I've been privileged to have opened the eyes of generations of schoolchildren to the literature, poetry, music, art, history and culture of a very special corner of Scotland, one with its own character and identity. I have also had the opportunity to interpret photographically the very distinctive, characteristic clear light of one of the most beautiful parts of the country.

Andy Hall, born 1954, interviewed 2006: Maryculter and Stonehaven

'The most beautiful collection of photographs of Scotland I have ever seen'
– Ewan McGregor. Cover illustration from Andy's SENSE OF BELONGING – The Complete Collection, Birlinn 2007.

Still active: Corrie as she is today.

> I can still relive the wonderful spirit of optimism, the feeling that we could actually change the world.

The radical activist: still committed

A t 18 I was off to London to university. I couldn't wait to get away. Looking back, I can see that I'd become a stroppy young woman who couldn't see much good in the older generation; it was obvious that Aberdeen was a pokey wee backwater and that the bright lights and the buzz lay elsewhere.

I studied 'Communication and Sociology'. The course fed my interest in contemporary society and the situation of the individual within it. I'd always had a strong radical left-wing bias, a feeling that that 'they were out to get us', that is, to turn us into drones, obedient consumers and voters. My dissertation was on the 'Rise and fall of the counter culture movement of the 1960s', which I saw as prime example of the manner in which the capitalist system would take up any individual or dissident movement, and commodify it.

The most obvious example for me had been the way in which the upsurge of the new, young energies that had marked the Sixties had been absorbed into the mainstream of the music and fashion industries. As a child of the Eighties I had personally joined a second wave, one that was characterised by a free party culture and active protest. In my mind, I can still relive the wonderful spirit of optimism which gripped young people like me, the feeling that by coming together in social protest we could actually change the world. By then I'd come to see how the state – oh, don't I sound like an old hippy! – had tolerated us for a while and then found ways of throttling us.

My involvement led me to join a squatters' group in Brighton. I'd now graduated and was anxious to join an alternative life-style movement rather than become swallowed up in the prevailing rat race.

I was part of an era when there were environmental protests against new roads and when there were free parties and festivals. You'd descend upon a nearby field, set up a sound system and party all night and feel you were striking a blow for freedom. You'd refuse to pay exorbitant landlord rents and, by setting up a squat in some vacant warehouse, would draw attention to the number of empty properties they were sitting on.

All this was done in a joyous, celebratory manner; partying, music, drugs were part of what we were about. We wanted to demonstrate that the freedom to enjoy yourself in noisy, colourful ways was also our way of showing that life shouldn't have to be a matter of grey, respectable conformity.

We were based in an old brewery complex in the middle of Brighton, which we called 'The People's Free State of Trumpton'. We were well organised. The squat we set up had phones, running hot water, a washing machine. We paid our bills.

The introduction of the Criminal Justice Bill, criminalising squatting and free parties, galvanised us. In protest we squatted an old courthouse, which hadn't been used for years. We made an arts centre out of it, by repairing the roof, painting the woodwork, connecting the phone lines and getting electricity running. We ran a crèche, set up meditation sessions and yoga. It became a thriving hub of local life. We did home baking, made soup. We invited the locals in to see what we were doing and to consult with them about our next moves. The community backed us.

Of course, there was a certain amount of naivety in all this. I genuinely thought that all you had to do was to explain yourself to people and they would see the light and rise up. I remember one day when I said to my mate, an older, hard bitten Scouser, 'I'm just knackered!' and he replied, 'Eeh lass, when you've spent the years I ave kickin against the pricks you'll cum to realise that all you get is a sore toe!'

But back in those heady days I was excited by being down south where the action was. I'd return to the North-east for Christmas and I'd feel that we were a decade behind in our thinking.

In the end, I did come back, first to Edinburgh, then to the North-east. I'd gone to the south because I thought that's where it was all at, where the centre of social activism and the excitement were. I hadn't been disappointed – I've not regretted living in any of the places I've stayed in and have met some wonderfully interesting people, people I still keep up with.

Social protest:
Putting the Criminal Justice Bill on trial with Corrie Cheyne as judge.

But I found the longer I spent away, the more I was missing my old home area. I'd go down to the shore at Brighton and see this brown sludgy stuff feebly lapping a shingle beach and compare it to the North Sea and the sands at Aberdeen. I'd see the South Downs and think of them as pimply hills when set against Bennachie and the Grampians. Everything seemed so crowded down there and I was missing the wide spaces of Aberdeenshire. The great stretching fields and farmlands of Buchan had an elemental character which made the douce countryside of Sussex appear tame stuff. Landscape has always meant a lot to me and the North-east has it all – hills, water, sea, forest, river valleys.

By going to Edinburgh I'd imagined I was satisfying my longings to go back home. But it gradually dawned on me that it was the North-east I needed. I came to realise just how distinctive our corner is. The sense of thrawn-ness among the people is the best way to sum it up – that acceptance that life is a struggle. The emphasis on hard work and community effort, which probably springs from our peasant background and is maybe a characteristic of all rural areas, seems to be more deeply ingrained in the North-east than most parts of the UK. There's a line you cross somewhere between Brechin and

Laurencekirk which tells you that you're entering a different region, that you are coming home.

But I'm still committed to my old causes. My great concern is that here in the North-east we've been sucking at the oil teat for so long we are ill prepared to confront the post-carbon era which is fast approaching. We will have to work out a new life style if we are to adapt to a world without on-tap gas and oil. The global energy gap is terrifying, as is the pressure on such basic resources as water and food. The present world of freewheeling capitalist economies, built on the assumption of perpetual growth, cannot last.

Perhaps the old North-east virtues will rescue us. Our inbred understanding that life is a grudging, hard affair, that you won't get anywhere truly worthwhile without hard work and community co-operation, might see us through – I hope!

Corrie Cheyne, born 1969, interviewed 2012: Durno

The student: future comes from the past

I appreciate the fact that I've been able to grow up in a small community with fields, woodland and river all around. Torphins still has the feel of a village, with its own identity. But it's being threatened. There's a plan to open up its green belt to the developers for housing and a business park.

I'm very much an environmentalist and believe that the green spaces are precious to retaining the integrity of a distinct community like Torphins and shouldn't be surrendered to the march of the Tescos and the Stewart Milnes.

For me, the opportunity to create is central to the good life. In the last few years I've been at St Andrews University. My present course is 'Scottish Society and Culture', part of a Scottish Literature and Creative Writing degree.

I'm deeply involved in live music. I work for the Students' Union as their music promoter, arranging gigs and festivals and bringing in artists. I play the flute and appreciate classical music, but folk music is my real passion. I love a real live performance: to watch and to listen while something is being created, well, that gives you a real sense of being not just a consumer, but a participant. The atmosphere, the noise, the excitement – nothing else can match that!

I think that in the UK generally one of the most hopeful things is the way in which there is so much creative work going on – artists, writers, people working with various materials, fashion, music. It's something we are good at and it should be celebrated. And Scotland plays a very big part in all that. I feel very Scottish; I love its landscapes and its musical heritage. We are a great little country, one that maintains a real identity and stands up for itself.

I'm optimistic about the future. Of course, there's plenty to be angry about. I'm concerned at the way we've been trashing the environment and squandering its natural riches. For me, ethics and conservation go hand in hand. When you look at wars, the

Growing up in a nourishing setting.
Kirsty Strang with brother Peter, Torphins Primary School, 2000.

I'll always appreciate the stable base my Torphins childhood has given me.

banking crises, the growing gap between the rich and the poor, well, it's no wonder that a young person like myself is becoming increasingly left-wing.

I'm looking forward to what is to come as I go out into the world. But I'll always appreciate the stable base my Torphins childhood has given me. For me, continuity is important; I've learned such a lot from older folk; I've picked up cooking at their side, I've listened to stories and to folk lore and memories and, above all, I've experienced how to live in a community together, with all ages and types of people.

I'm proud I have deep roots in the Deeside landscape. Peter Strang, my grandfather, was the head gamekeeper at Craigendinnie – part of the Glen Tanar Estate, by Aboyne. He would take me into his garden and point out the plants and showed me how to draw the various shapes of the animals we could see around us. Above all, he gave me wisdom and showed me how to treat others with kindness and understanding. He made me feel part of my community, one which finds its identity through its links with the past as well as its physical environment. As a young person to be taken into all those memories, why, that's been a priceless experience.

Kirsty Strang, born 1991, interviewed 2011: Torphins

Undergraduate no more. Kirsty brandishing her First Class Honours degree, St Andrews University, June 2013. She also won the prize as the best student in her class.

GOING TO SCHOOL

The day he became Provost of Gordon District, 1992.
Raymond Bisset, Head Teacher at Kintore Primary School,
celebrating with some of his pupils.

Equipment was fairly rudimentary: vaulting horse, buck and box – all wooden with heavy leather tops.

Thirty-four years of PE

On my release from the Army, I was accepted for teacher training at the emergency Physical Education College at Woolmanhill, Aberdeen. The organisation, the discipline, quality of teaching, discipline and high expectations set by the Principal and staff became my model throughout my career. I was fortunate as a student to observe and appreciate the efficiency of the PE department at Aberdeen Grammar School during teaching practice there.

Joining the staff at Fraserburgh Academy in 1949, I soon realised that I had many obstacles to overcome – but this is the case with every young teacher. And problems which arise early in any walk of life do seem trivial with experience.

So it was for me. In those days, equipment was fairly rudimentary: vaulting horse, buck and box – all wooden with heavy leather tops – climbing ropes, beams, benches, wall-bars and the usual small apparatus of bean bags, hoops and so on. There was no field, the nearest one being half a mile away, so single periods had to be limited to formal gymnastics. Indoor football (three-a-side) would have been an anticipated treat on the week preceding holidays.

But in the spring of 1953, I introduced the House system and the co-operation I enjoyed, from both within and without the PE department, ensured its well being. Then the opening of the new academy by HRH Princess Margaret, in September 1962, heralded an expansion of facilities. By the end of that decade, we could boast two new gymnasia, playing fields and a shared swimming pool – and all now

Checking the results. Sports Day, Fraserburgh Academy, 1959. John Black is furthest right; the others, from the left, are Sheila Black (PE and John's wife), Susan Macdonald (Business Studies) and James Crawford (Technical and later first Principal Banff & Buchan College).

available in a 40-minute period.

All this meant that the PE curriculum could now be extended to include a greater variety of games and individual activities, thereby catering for the special aptitudes of more pupils. Pupils responded in excellent fashion, as our many achievements at county level and beyond showed. I took particular satisfaction over the years in our success in the North of Scotland Football Cup competitions.

My aim was always to strike a balance between teaching /learning, practice/ improvement and achievement /competition. Something for everyone at any stage. The House system helped me to fulfil this aim. I retired in 1983, having served the school for some 34 years.

There's a postscript to this. In May 2003 I phoned the Academy to ask to speak to the rector, someone I'd never met. I told him that it was now the 50th year since the house system had been introduced. He knew nothing of it and, sadly, he gave me the impression that he didn't consider any such system could be of significance to his school.

I suppose I did feel disappointed at the snub. Perhaps I had spawned a monster that had outgrown its lair.

My final thought is when an earlier predecessor, W.D. Kennedy, had made the response to my plans for a House system back in 1953: 'Well, boy, go ahead – but we'll know who to blame if it doesn't work out!' As to whether it did, I quote from the 'Rector's message' in the 1954 *Fraserburgh Academy Magazine*: 'The House system has been in operation for a full year and has proved to be an unqualified success'.

I think I'll hold on to that!

John Black, born 1928, interviewed 2008: Fraserburgh

Fraserburgh Academy Under-13 football team, 1961-62. Rector W. Kennedy is on the left, John on the right.

The retired teacher

I certainly don't regret becoming an English teacher. I loved it from the very start, even though beginning in Archie Watt's department at Mackie was somewhat daunting. There was a strict hierarchy: he kept the top sets for himself; his Special Assistant had the B classes, while I, as a mere probationer, was allocated those repeating their Highers. I remember all the candidates being summonsed to Archie's room to hear the results of the prelims – and there was little doubt that the teachers were being judged, too! I can recall squirming with embarrassment when he made it quite clear that a grammatical error by one of my pupils could be traced back to an omission on the part of his teacher.

The memories from 37 years though are overwhelmingly happy ones – and that is thanks to the hundreds of young people whose lives I shared. Two of them speak out: one

from my early years, the other from my final year of teaching.

I'll always remember this girl from Drumlithie. She came from a difficult home and married early as a way of escape. She found herself trapped into a round of housekeeping and family rearing. I met her later and she told me, 'Do you know what's helped me when it's all a bit too much and I find myself chained to the kitchen sink? I can look out of the window and catch a glimpse of something from those poetry lessons you gave us. I can see the harvest fields and think of Keats's "stubble plains touched with rosy hue", and that gives me a lift, it really does'.

Or a bottom class I once had, a set of Christmas leavers who were just putting in time before they could leave. I gave them – at their request – some Shakespeare: *Macbeth* it was. We concentrated on the witches and the murder scenes, and the class, these academic failures, got stuck into it. It's the moment when one of them remarked quite spontaneously, 'I widna hae her fer a mither!', thus summing up the whole character of Lady Macbeth in a flash, well, that was just as rewarding as getting a class of high fliers through their O grades.

That's what makes teaching worthwhile: not the obvious things like the examination successes, but the sudden, unexpected human moments, and the thought that you've brought something to the ones who might so easily have been written off by the system.

Moira Jolly, born 1934, interviewed 2008: Stonehaven

All in a good cause: dressed as Paddington Bear and surrounded by members of her S2 Register class, early 1970s.

The Mackie Academy staff, mid 1970s. John Fraser, Rector, is seated dead centre and Moira, now PT English, is three along to his left.

An outstanding Head

There's no doubt Dr Dixon was a magnificent man, someone of whom I cannot speak too highly. He's just about the only person I've met in teaching who I reckon would have gone to the top, whatever profession he had followed. His great gift was boundless energy and a tireless attention to detail. He also had a great understanding of pupils' needs, of pupils from any background and ability. We were all in awe of him.

He was famed for knowing the name of every single pupil in his school – and of their parents too. He was a great person in the community. These were still the days when the October holiday was definitely the tattie holidays but, latterly, the numbers going picking were beginning to tail off as pupils were becoming unwilling to get up early and spend a day with their backs bent in some dirty field or other, not for ten shillings pay. So, Dr Dixon would take it on himself to go round the school and try to drum up support. He came into my class and decided to address one or two pupils directly: 'What about you, Colin? Surely you'd like to earn some extra cash, wouldn't you?' Now, Colin had spent a lot of his time down in England and spoke with a pronounced southern accent. 'Sorry, sir, but I've got the pipers!' 'Why that's wonderful! I didn't know you played in a band, Colin!' 'No sir, not the pipers – I've got to deliver the newspipers!' But Dr Dixon wasn't someone to concede the final word; he left the room, only to return a moment later. 'Colin's just reminded me – does anyone here know what a bison is?' Various answers came forth, but most agreed that a bison was a large hairy beast from North America. 'No, no,' came Dr Dixon's triumphant response. 'A bison is what you wash your fice in – isn't it Colin?'

He was only of medium height, but he was a real bundle of energy. He would prowl the corridors during the day, always in his gown, on the lookout for anything that might catch his eye and tell him what was going on in his Inverurie Academy.

Every exam taken by every pupil in the whole school, why, he'd take a look at each paper in each subject himself and then either pass it with a tick or write a comment on it. If you were in the top six this would be, 'Please see me' – to receive his congratulations – but if you were in the bottom six there'd be a curt 'See me!' If that happened more than three times you got the belt. I gave up using the belt myself very early on in my teaching – I found it degrading. But Dr Dixon did employ the strap, though never prolifically. His motto was, 'Seldom and memorably'. He was of his time.

Once you'd left the school he wasn't finished with you either. He was always watching out for your later progress. To each former pupil who went to university and graduated, he would send a personal letter of congratulation. To him, they would always be his pupils.

John Cummine, born 1935, interviewed 2011: Inverurie

Towards the end of a memorable career: as caught by his son, David Dixon.

He would have known each of their names. Dr Dixon with head prefects and senior pupils, Inverurie Academy, early 1970s

> Everyone pitched on to it and none could be avoided – the rough and the tough, the ragamuffins, the swots and the timid ones.

The school bus: lessons in life

I travelled daily into the Mackie on a rickety Alexander bus. It was termed a utility bus, a very basic vehicle that had wooden seats and draughty windows. You'd walk up to the top of the road and then clatter and rattle your way up the 15 miles into Stonehaven. This journey became a big part of our daily lives and the school bus was a significant sociological feature, an institution in its own right. Everyone pitched on to it and none could be avoided – the rogues, the rough and the tough, the ragamuffins, the swots and the timid ones. You were part of this motley crew for 40 minutes, twice a day, winter and summer, and had to learn how to make the best of it.

The main lesson you learned was how to survive among the name calling, among the intimate conversations, the whispered observations, the by-play between the sexes, the young and the senior. Last minute homework was done, allegiances were forged and courting was carried on. There was a definite hierarchy, dictated by age largely. When you got up to the fifth year you could occupy the back seat by virtue of your seniority. You would then be entitled to the services of a younger minion who would rush out and reserve your place for you while you strolled along.

Clark Simpson, born 1935, interviewed 2011: Johnshaven

The curriculum adviser

I started school at the small two-teacher establishment in the village. It was a terrifying experience. My first teacher ran a regime of blame and instant retribution. I was in constant trembling, frightened to go to school each morning. I could see the playground from our house and if I didn't see anyone in it I'd panic that I must be late, even though there was a whole hour to go. In the evenings, I'd return with my back black and blue from the constant pencil jabbings it had received at the hands of the teacher. Pupils were scared to ask permission to go to the toilet. I've seen boys wet themselves – and worse – rather than put their hands up and receive the inevitable, 'No, you must wait till the interval'. Yet I was one of the bright ones! For the slower pupils, the pressure was constant; she operated a regime which showed no patience with those who couldn't grasp the work immediately.

This was our Primary 1-2 teacher; the following two years a different person was in charge. Well, it was just like heaven to get away from that dragon and encounter a teacher who was at least half decent. By the time I got into Primary 6-7, the transformation was complete. Here we had a male teacher, someone who wasn't afraid to come into the school with a smiling face and give us some praise for our efforts. I think those early experiences have coloured my whole view of what education should – and shouldn't – be.

The education I received was efficient enough. But I can't accept the commonly held belief that in those days everyone left school fully literate and a master of spelling and of the semi-colon. National Service exposed the fact that a huge number of 18-year-olds were in need of basic education. That's why the Army had to run a large Education Corps.

The truth is, our Scottish education served the bright, hard working minority pretty well. But it also generated a large number of casualties because it adopted a 'one system fits all' approach that was intolerant of the less able. It was a thoroughly divisive and repressive system; if you didn't make the grade at age 12 – and three-quarters didn't – you were consigned to three years in the junior secondary school, some of which were simply quite shocking.

There was a dead-weight pressing down upon schools in those days. As an adviser, my job in the early Seventies was to go around the schools to talk with staff about curriculum development. You'd go into some of them and find that the sole textbooks were *Holmes Comprehensive English* and *Holmes Comprehensive Arithmetic,* both stuffed full of dull and deadly exercises, and heads who were quite content to chug along in their cosy little rural backwaters, repeating the same old stuff year after year.

What we were seeking was an opening up of the curriculum so as to make the old topics livelier, more relevant, and to introduce fresh approaches to engage all pupils. The backwoodsmen would counter attack by claiming we wished to abandon the basics. Not so: the skills remain essential. But I also believe there are other ways of engaging pupils than simply relying on blind rote learning and punitive exercises. What we were trying to do was to explore ways of encouraging pupils to think, and not have to depend upon set rules. Do you know, I've been in a classroom where pupils were taught decimals by such prescriptions as 'you multiply by shifting the point towards the window'. Too bad if the next room they entered had the window on the other side of the room: they would end up by dividing!

I think that the real glory of the North-east education system has, historically, been the lad o' pairts. There's no doubt that the attention it gave to pushing the bright, hard-working lad on, up from his wee parish school and into success in the bursary competition and thus into university, was something to be proud of. As a result, the region has produced some first-class engineers, medical men, lawyers, scientists, men of letters. But all this was done at a cost – and it was the vast majority of 'ordinary' kids who suffered. You can't have an education service which exists for the select few and which deliberately turns the rest into failures. The education service must work for everyone; after all, any child only gets one crack at it.

Andrew Dick, born 1936, interviewed 2008: Buchanhaven

The new methods

It was the time of the 'new' methods, just after the 1965 'Primary Memorandum' came out. I was advised to read the book by a good friend, Helen Collier, sold my soul and impressed the interviewing committee, Lord Aberdeen included. But I was very much out of sympathy with the so-called new approaches and what it meant for the kind of solid traditional curriculum I had always stood by. I got the job at Lumphanan even

Our Scottish education served the bright, hard working minority pretty well. But it also generated a large number of casualties.

In days before the 'Memorandum.' Dominie John MacKellar, Luthermuir School, supervising the digging of the school garden, 1935.

I would give them the Three Rs, History, Geography and even French; they got spelling and grammar and Doric poetry by Charles Murray.

though it was obvious they were not over enthusiastic having to appoint a possible reactionary such as me.

I knew I was giving the children what the parents wanted, but that was going against the new creed. 'Burn the old books! Out with the times-tables! Get rid of spelling and grammar! No more long division or multiplication!' Now it was all about projects and self-expression and letting the children learn through discovery.

When my pupils went up to Aboyne for their secondary, I was informed how well they'd been prepared, unlike some of the other schools who had been converted to the new methods. I would give them the Three Rs, History, Geography and even French; they got spelling and grammar and Doric poetry by Charles Murray. Former pupils still fondly remember learning *The Puddock*, *The Whistle* and *It wisna his wyte* – though pupils from the Deep South weren't quite so keen! I'd fire off mental arithmetic questions at them each morning. Even though the class consisted of 33 pupils from P5, 6 and 7, and my role included being janitor, secretary and games master, I don't look back on it as being arduous. A pupil told me his sister was training to be a teacher and that I had no right to give homework. I thanked him for the information and said they were free not to do it, provided their parents came to see me and excluded their children from homework – but none ever did. We held Christmas and musical concerts, school sports, jumble sales and even took the senior pupils to a five-day holiday in the Highlands (Jimmy Sim as sergeant major). The parents were fantastic in their support.

But my position was being made impossible. I was the rebel and I was up against determined people in the shape of the Directorate. In 1976 I left - or was I pushed? I suppose I should have kept my mouth shut but, really, when I consider what was happening to education I despaired. A lot of good old teachers were alienated at that time, along with some younger ones. Over the following years I tried to run a croft, I swept chimneys, worked as a labourer, did a social work qualification, even cleaned floors at Asda.

Douglas Aberdein, born 1938, interviewed 2008: Lumphanan

Into digs at the age of 11: I'd had enough

Till then, all the children from Strathdon just went to Towie for their secondary. But I passed the 11-plus and went to Alford, with two others. This meant staying in digs. I stayed with the local butcher's van-man, Bob, and Mrs McIntosh. He was the van-man who drove up to deliver to the glen, so there was already a connection. During the week I stayed with the McIntoshes and went home for the weekends. I had to cycle the five miles up the glen on my old bike.

The digs cost a pound a week and the county paid for it. I didn't enjoy being away from home. You just had to go through with it; there was no option if you wanted a full secondary education. But it was a huge adjustment, especially for a young girl. My sister joined me after two years so at least I had company. But then the McIntoshes moved away and I had to find new digs, and I wasn't very happy in them, especially as my sister had to go to another family.

The school at Alford meant lessons and more lessons. The methods were all much the same: the blackboard, the teacher talking and writing on it, the pupils sitting there, listening quietly. And there were books and more books. We had lots of homework – the weekends would mean three hours of the stuff. I had to take all that home plus my suitcase on the carrier of the bike. In the winter-time it would be dark. I had a torch on

Elspeth Dey
Before she had to leave home to go to school. Elspeth at Strathdon School, 1951: centre, middle row with white ribbon.

Eventually I said, 'No more'. My father and I had a big battle over it, but I left.

the bike. I used to carry this load all the way in the dark up the glen by myself. That's how it had to be; you just had to get on with it by yourself. But there's many a night I would be cycling up that glen in tears and in the dark, anxious to get home.

I was at Alford for three years. Then I had to go on to Inverurie. If you wanted to go on to take your Highers that's where you had to go – and I was still only 14. I was there for two years but eventually I said, 'No more'. My father and I had a big battle over it, but I left.

I do regret it now, but I was fed up with having to live with other people and being shifted about. I was now going to a school 45 miles from my own home. There was all that cycling home at weekends. I'd had enough.

Elspeth Dey, born 1939, interviewed 2003: Glenbuchat

The born teacher

I passed the qualifying exam and got into Inverurie Academy. It just happened out of the blue one day as far as I was concerned. I wasn't aware of any anxiety or of gearing up for it. I just walked into school one day and it was there, on your desk. And on that rested your fate for the rest of your life.

My family had no aspirations for me whatsoever. My mother was one of 17; her mother had died at 47, whereupon my grandfather – an inveterate drunkard – just upped and left. Five of his children were still of an age when they needed care and for a while an aunt did her best to fill the breach; but in the end my mother had to be given up to an orphanage, Aberlour Orphanage. When she left there at 13, it was to go straight into domestic service.

My father left school even earlier, at 12, to work on the small family farm at Keith Hall. He was one of 10. He was fee'd at 14 and had a spell going from farm to farm. He then became a roadman and when the war came served in the Fire Brigade at Inverurie. After 1945, he entered the Loco Works where he spent

'My father left school at 12' – and became a roadman. Here he is one of the gang seeing to a bridge at Kemnay just before the war.

many years as a 'lifter', a position which required great strength.

So both my parents' lives had been dominated by physical labour. They were always amazed at my progress. Because they didn't really know what was going on, I got a free hand in what was happening; I'd come home and say, 'I'm staying on at school,' and they'd say, 'Are you sure you're going to able to do that?' But, equally, if I'd come home and said, 'I'm going to leave school tomorrow and become a shop assistant', they wouldn't have batted an eyelid.

There were no books in the house, not even a bible. Nothing. The only book I found when my mother died in the house was *Haste Ye Back*, the story of Aberlour Orphanage.

I couldn't really talk to her about what was happening at the school. What she did do – which was really generous of her – was to hear things, my Latin vocabulary, my French and so on. Even though she couldn't understand anything at all about it herself, she would listen and then take up my books and ask me questions about them. But, basically, she would just keep her distance; my parents were bewildered about what was going on, although they were always pleased to do anything to help. You know, my mother even went out and took a part-time job so that they could afford better to allow me to stay on at school. She hated it, but did it.

But education was just about getting on. It was nothing to do with enriching your mind or developing new horizons. Anything else would have been a luxury. The pieces of paper were more important than the content. Qualifications were the thing, the need to get them so you could get on. Get on!

The methodology was didactic. Stand in front of the class and copy this down from the blackboard. It was very traditional – but it did get results. There was a very harsh punishment regime: everybody quiet, everybody in individual desks, sitting there in serried ranks. We had a lot of very dedicated teachers, but they all had the same method: 'You will be absolutely quiet; you won't say a word and you will learn! We will tell what it's all about and you will write it down and you will get ink exercises once a week, which will be handed in and corrected, and you will be given marks out of 20'.

I wanted to be a teacher – this is a sad little story – and I wanted to be a teacher from the age of four. It's the only thing I ever wanted to do; there was something about this idea that you could tell people things. I had this Sunday school teacher I fell in love with

After working on the roads, Wilma's father became a lifter at the Inverurie Loco works. One of the works outing, early 1950s. He is second right, front row.

From pupil to teacher to lecturer. Wilma ended her career in the Environmental Studies Department, Northern College. She is one of this staff group, and can be just seen beneath the pillar on the right, 1991.

and I thought she was wonderful. She would gather us all around her and talk to us and tell us stories. That's what I wanted to do. I never wavered from that. Later, when I was watching all these teachers at Inverurie standing out in front and telling people the way it was, I wanted to be one of them, I wanted to be out there, teaching people about things.

I can look at the changes of the last 50 years from the teacher's point of view now. Teaching is a great deal harder, I think, than ever it was in my early days because, now, the pupils are a great deal more aware and more worldly than we were, and also because the systems in the school have encompassed a great deal more interaction. Although our system was very rigid and there was no room for the exchange of ideas, it was certainly easier upon the teacher doing it. I admire the way teachers nowadays try to involve the pupils in their own learning, but it does make it very much harder for the teachers and, in some ways, for the pupils, too, because they have to take more responsibility. We just had to learn and regurgitate and that was enough.

It suited me, this regime. But that kind of system, for those who were failing within it, must have been a daily hell, because if you can't learn something to the point of being able to regurgitate it properly, then that means you are going to get hammered all the time. School must have been a very poor experience in my day for many: at least nowadays, with more encouragement and interaction being used, they all have something to contribute. They are much more supported in their learning now, too. If you failed to learn then, there was no 'learning support'; if you failed, you failed, full stop.

I would go along with the picture to a certain extent that, in those days, everyone did learn the basics. Young people nowadays might be less secure in their spelling, their punctuation, their general knowledge and so on, but they have more social skills, more opinions about things. Mark you, I can find it alarming if I come across a piece of bad spelling or someone who doesn't know where Ecuador is on the map. But then I have to stand back and think, 'How important is it that we know these things?' I had a friend, a young mother, and she was saying that her son – he was 13 – didn't know the capitals and I said, 'Yes, but I bet he'll be able to find the capital of Venezuela in seconds on the web.'

My son's going to Holland and I'm not sure he even knows where Amsterdam is exactly, and I'm thinking, 'Should I tell him about Amsterdam?' But no, that would be the old fashioned way of doing it. No, he'll just find out about it by being there and he'll end up with more street knowledge than I'll ever have. It's a completely different mind-set now. 'I don't know these things – but I know how to find out about them.'

Wilma Machray, born 1939, interviewed 2001: Inverurie

> I admire the way teachers nowadays try to involve the pupils in their own learning, but it does make it very much harder in some ways.

The retired Head: it's not so easy now

I was a pupil at Kintore, 1945-52. I looked back at my own teachers and realised the kind that I wanted to be. It was the friendly ones, the ones that had shown a personal interest.

I went as head to Tough in 1968 and was very happy there. I also found that the 1965 'Memorandum' was revitalising primary teaching. It fitted in with my philosophy of the personal approach, with my ideas about child-led education. Now you could start talking about projects, about Environmental Studies, about centres of interest, instead of just academic subjects.

And then James Michie was appointed Director of Education. He blew in and whoosh! We got a new radio, we got a TV, we got proper lighting, a new coat of paint. All this helped us to get closer to the kids in our rural area. I was living out there among them; the parents began to rally round. It was a farming community. They gave you everything that you wanted. There were lots of parents meetings to discuss the new Memorandum.

There was a certain spirit flowing through it all then. It would have been impossible without James Michie's leadership. I loved listening to him. It was indicative of what was happening that we would all go and listen to him at in-service sessions, even on a Saturday morning. He fired everybody up. He'd get those eyebrows working and enthuse us all; he would tell us that he was right with us – and he was.

A brand new school. Pat Walker at the opening of Kellands, 1975, with colleagues Sandra McIvride and Emily Bonner.

'I miss the kids.' With the school five-a-side football team, 1982.

In 1971 I became Head at Hatton. The Seventies were a great time to be in teaching. We all seemed to be together: directors, teachers, parents, the SED. It was a disaster that later this spirit was allowed to ebb away. I met a young teacher just yesterday and she told me, 'I love the kids, but oh, all the paper work – it's killing us all!' That's why I got out. I found that I was spending my time either making up agendas for meetings, or writing the minutes of meetings, or laying out plans, or reports of plans. My approach had been to go into the classroom and work – with the kids.

It's not easy now! If a Pat Walker was to come into the profession 30 years on, and try to do it that way, he would just crack up. I meet the kids' parents in the street and they say, 'We never seem to meet the Head these days, he's always in the office'. My doors were always kept right open. I knew all the kids, all their parents, the families – even the grandparents by the end. But you can't make teachers like that – it's just me and the environment I grew up in at Kintore. That's the old tradition, of course, the teacher in the community. It's not me being selfless; it's me doing what satisfies me the most.

After my spell at Hatton, I served as HT at Kellands, Inverurie from 1975 to 2002. Now I'm retired. But I still talk to teachers, I still hear their complaints. Basically, they are only really happy when they are with the children. But there are all these other things they have to do, all those external pressures. Towards the end you could see a swing back to the way it was at the start. Academic attainment is the thing now too. There are so many endless tests. And the parents get agitated, 'Has he passed his Level B yet?' And it all adds up to another horrible batch of paper work.

And the inspections hanging over your head are another pressure. Teachers can crack up under the strain. The bad bits appear in the press right away. I remember one local head; he turned white overnight, his school got such a bad report in the P&J. It just finished him.

I'm glad to be getting out. I've done my bit. Let somebody else get on with it now. But I see the young ones come in and immediately they're rushing off to meetings. It seems to be a national disease – the police, the medics, the Social Work department all seem to be afflicted. It's on the farms, too: every cow has to be tagged; if you shift them into another field you have to submit a report about it.

But there are a couple of things I miss. I miss the children – that's for sure. And I

> It's not easy now! If a Pat Walker was to come into the profession 30 years on, and try to do it that way, he would just crack up.

miss having my own bunch of keys on me all the time. With them, I could drop into the school at any time; sometimes at the weekend I'd pop in and just walk around, look into the rooms, see what was on the walls. Or go into the gym and kick a ball around for a bit. Quite often in the evening, in the winter, I'd see a light on in the school and then I just had to go in and see what was going on, who else was there. I was always talking about the school. My wife used to tell me to shut up about it.

But with those keys in my pocket I could always know that it was my school – at any time, evenings, holidays or at the weekend. Really, it all comes back to being in your own community. At Tough the people would do things for you, for their school. The first week I was there, a farmer came up to me and, 'Ye'll be needin' some tatties, eh?' A sack would appear a couple of days later; and at Christmas, a tree would be tipped over the dyke. At sale time, something like a lamb would be donated for the raffle – you didn't have to ask, it just happened.

Pat Walker, born 1939, interviewed 2003: Hatton, Tough and Inverurie

The Qualifying exam: parting of the ways

I plagued that teacher. She was a farmer's wife who would come to school in the morning with the chicken's meat on her clothes because she'd been feeding the hens. She was a big woman who would sit on her desk with her feet up on a chair. She could strike the fear of death into us all, but I was a bit of a rebel and would fight against her. She'd put us into a circle and fire questions at us; if I spoke out of turn she'd put my face to the wall, with my feet in the wastepaper basket. But I refused to be frightened of her. I had a social conscience from an early age and I knew that what she was doing was unjust.

Somebody once dared me to run through the playground with no clothes on. So I did. Oh, that was bad news in New Byth! I was 11, in the big class now. The kids took away my clothes and I couldn't find them to put them on again. This was in the girls' playground, but they'd tipped off the boys. I felt

exhilarated; there was a row of fir trees and I ran in and out of them – I remember the prickling sensation up and down my body. Then Mrs Cruickshank came out! I was a hussy and all the rest of it. My mother was informed; she simply asked me, 'What on earth did you do that for?' I didn't really know. I think that Mrs Cruickshank was afraid there might be an outbreak of streaking in New Byth. She made me feel ashamed. Till then I had not been aware that I should look on my own body like that.

Mary Harvie
The scene of the crime. The row of trees at New Byth where a young Mary Harvie ran amok some 60 years ago.

Mrs Cruickshank was a well respected teacher in the community. She was an efficient teacher. I loved the books, being able to read, the world of imagination and learning. But I hated the discipline, the way others were being broken and disciplined and were taking it. We were all strapped. She would take the ruler and smack us over the hand, but it was the shaming that was the worst. She would put a label on you and that was to be seen as a threat. Maybe I was bright and energetic and didn't take easily to the restrictions of the time. I began to see myself as trouble and to act up to my reputation. I was boisterous and not amenable to discipline.

I got to the academy at Turriff by passing the 11-plus. Only three of us went from my year. Mostly, the village children went up to the secondary, housed in the 'Old School' up on top of the hill, where they got a more practically orientated course, with woodwork and home economics.

Going to Turriff meant a parting of the ways. I had to move away from my friends. I cried my eyes out and begged to be allowed to stay on at New Byth with the rest. It was my great-auntie Mary who talked me out of this. She insisted I was getting a wonderful opportunity – and she was right. A whole new world was being opened up to me. You began to speak differently, to learn foreign languages. You were aware that now you might become a teacher or a doctor. The very act of passing that exam at 11/12 had the power of changing your whole life.

To go to Turriff was definitely different. You had to catch the bus and dress up in these stockings with a liberty bodice to keep them in place. Frequently, I'd have the stockings off before the bus had pulled away. At first I hated it. Then I began to love it: I loved the curriculum, I loved the Academy. I got to know Jane Austen's novels, to take Science, to speak French and do Latin. I thought myself very smart to be doing these things. And Turriff proved to be a very good school.

Mary Harvie, born 1940, interviewed 2003: New Byth

With 'Iron Duke', 2012, the model train Richard Bennett's soldier father made for him during the war.

A Fifties education: I just took to it

My father was killed in action, near Arnhem, in 1944. All I had of him are a couple of letters, a few photos and a model train which he helped make, when he was at Army camp in Northumberland. It was called 'The Iron Duke'; I still have it. The story of the train is interesting. My father was sergeant of a company that had quite a few tradesmen in it. He organised an assembly line to make toys for Christmas for the men's children, then made a deal with the shops in the village to make some for sale. The price of a handmade engine like mine was five shillings.

After the war, things were very hard for a war widow like my mother. We had to move about a fair bit, staying with relatives or wherever she could get a post as a farm housekeeper. I had to shift about for my schools, one of them being Drainie, where Ramsay MacDonald had been both pupil and pupil teacher – not that much was made of

Drainie Public School 1950. Richard is the smart boy at the right, front row. The teacher is Miss Houston.

The father he never really knew. Richard with parents at Bishopmill, a year before his father was killed in action.

He gave me a second chance, but I failed once more — so whack, whack, whack!

Enjoying school and life. Richard aged six.

the fact that a British Prime Minister had ever been associated with the place.

Drainie had about 60 on its roll then and ran to three teachers. The head was Mr Charles Keith and he was a stern, tall and rather chalky figure, always smartly dressed and very conscious of his position. He was of his time and had no compunction in wielding the belt. This was imparted for poor work such as spelling mistakes as well as bad behaviour. I was something of a star pupil, but that didn't save me.

We had to learn a John Clare poem and recite it in class: *Little Trotty Wagtail.* I memorised it diligently, but when I came to say it out, Mr Keith took exception to the way I was intoning it. He gave me a second chance, but I failed once more – so whack, whack, whack! We just accepted that that was the way of it: the headmaster had the power of judgement and punishment and we were his obedient subjects.

It wasn't just a question of academic perfection; there was a moral dimension to our learning. On another occasion, we were asked to compose a story, and I did mine about going to Elgin on the bus with my friends. To spice my tale up a bit I invented a scene where we hid beneath the seats so as to avoid having to pay the fare. We read through it and when we came to the bit which described the crime – purely made up, remember – he gave me a huge crack across the side of my head: 'Absolutely disgraceful!'

Basically, the school served a community of farm children in the agricultural area around what was then HMS Fulmar, the predecessor to today's Lossiemouth RAF base. The school photos show the sort of social class we were. The range of dress on display is revealing. Most of the parents had made the effort to turn their children out as smartly as could be for the school photo and there's an array of ties, jackets and Fair Isle jumpers on display. But you'll also see some kids with matted, uncombed hair and candles of snot coming down from their noses. It wasn't so much a range of poverty that was being

Involved in all aspects of school life. Richard as a member of Elgin Academy rugby team, as hooker – first right back row.

displayed, but of care and pride.

We finally got a council house and moved to Alves. Alves was a bigger school for me. It had its own junior secondary department. The system was that at the age of 12 you sat the qualifying exam to determine whether you were academically fit to go on to Elgin Academy – and therefore enter a Highers course – or simply had to work out your school career at the one place. People talk of the proud democratic tradition of rural Scottish education and of how it has always enabled the able ones to get on and reach the academic heights. In my experience this lad o'pairts tradition – a myth really – is much exaggerated.

Of the 22 in my P7 class I was the only one who did go on to a senior secondary education. Yet there were some able children, ones who could have coped very well with the challenge of a Highers course, who simply stayed at Alves and left school with no academic qualifications.

Economic circumstances would have militated against their going on, but that couldn't have been the only factor. After all, I came from a poor background yet I did go on. Here, the determining factor wasn't just my ability: my mother was extremely ambitious for me and was prepared to make the necessary sacrifices and that made all the difference. I think the root problem for many was that they didn't prize education nearly as much as the myth has it. Socially, they seemed to have this ingrained assumption that three years of junior secondary and then out into the practical world of farming, apprenticeships, or housework was their inescapable destiny.

My mother, however, considered it a triumph that I should pass the exams to get into the academy. She would feed my huge appetite for reading by going to jumble sales and looking out good books for me. The Aberlour Orphanage sale – Jupp's Jumble Sale – was an eagerly awaited annual event and she'd get up early to take the bus and make sure she came back with one or two volumes of the classics that she'd managed to get for a few coppers, along with clothes and kitchen utensils.

I can't explain my early absorption in reading, except to say that right from the start it was something I took to. The school fed it; there were class libraries and there was the Boots Library in Elgin. I devoured everything: I was into Dickens at the age of 10, and the old classics such as *Lorna Doon*, the *Last of the Mohicans*. I also swallowed down the Billy Bunter stories and the *Wizard*, *Hotspur* and the *Rover*. In those days such comics carried real stories – can you imagine a young lad today opening up his weekly comic and being confronted with a spread of densely packed prose, unrelieved by any graphics? But that's what we read in those days and we loved it. We ran a trade in swapping so I could get through them all – Alf Tupper, Tough of the Track, Wilson, the lot. It was all genuinely imaginative, sharply written stuff and gave me a real feel for narrative structure and description.

I cannot complain about my personal experience. Later, I found everything I wanted at Elgin Academy and thoroughly enjoyed my years there. It gave me the academic satisfactions I craved and also a wealth of social involvement – friendships, sport, organisations, events. For me it was the complete educational experience. I loved the academy.

Richard Bennett, born 1942, interviewed 2011: Drainie and Alves.

A small rural school

I had the Geddeses, oh yes, I had the Geddeses. No-one could forget that pair! They were a remarkable pair of identical twins and enjoyed a formidable reputation in the district. They were in complete control ; you were left in no doubt about that from the very start. There was a difference: Mary took the younger group and she was actually quite kind. But at eight, through the curtain you went to Betty, the hard one. Her attitude seemed to be, 'Right here's this rabble my soft sister has handed on to me – I'll soon sort them out!'

What really sticks in my mind is I'm naturally left-handed. But Betty wasn't having any of that. I was the only left-hander in the class and that wouldn't do at all. To be left-handed was different, unnatural and not to be tolerated. If ever I tried to use my left hand she would batter it with a blackboard cleaner or a ruler until it had the desired effect.

It was a good grounding they gave us. There were lots of exercises, homework right from the word go. Everything had to be neat and tidy. You had to work on both sides of the page – 'waste not, want not'. Always, when you got a new jotter, it was your responsibility to keep it in the shape you got it in. By the time you got to the middle it would naturally be getting a bit scruffy and that's when they'd haul you over the coals and tell you how much you had let things slide.

Which is which? The identical twins, Betty and Mary Geddes, in wedding guest regalia. (Mary is on the right).

The concerts were very big. Once one finished it would be on to the next. As soon as you came back after the holidays you'd be told what the concert was and the parts would be allocated – a pixie, a soldier, a bear, whatever. Everybody had to take a part.

There was the concert, there was the Christmas party, there was the sports day. All big events that had to be prepared for thoroughly. The sports day was an inter-school event held down in Stonehaven. That's where you would come up against the big guns like

Fetteresso or Dunnottar. Muchalls had never won it, but in my P7, my last year there, we succeeded in bringing it back as our parting gift. The sisters prepared us for it. They would hold the tape for the races or the rope for the high jump; they would sort out the relay and the baton changing. They put you through your paces; they were very ambitious for their school.

Alan Blacklaws, born 1944, interviewed 2003: Bridge of Muchalls

'The concerts were very big': a typical line up from one of the annual shows put on by Mary and Betty Geddes.

Not a left-hander among them. The pupils at Muchalls, sitting up straight for the Miss Geddeses, early 1960s

Happy to be there. Bridge of Muchalls line-up, 1950s. Alan Blacklaws is sixth from left.

A dominie at 24: always on duty

I got the post of head teacher at Fetterangus in 1970, while I was still doing my probation. In those days the dominie was expected to inhabit the official school house, situated next to the school.

We now found ourselves occupying an impressive granite house into which our old Bucksburn semi would have fitted four times over. Downstairs, there was the lounge, sitting room, drawing room and a massive kitchen. Half way up the stairs, there was a bathroom and, at the top, four more bedrooms. I was occupying a mansion, I was 24 years of age and I'd been receiving £810 per annum. This wasn't enough in those days to earn the right to my own bank card or any overdraft facilities. But now I was the occupant of a huge house which I had to fill with furniture, so I approached my bank and told them

> I was occupying a mansion, I was 24 years of age and I'd been receiving £810 per annum.

of my promotion. 'Oh, a head teacher – congratulations! What can we do to help you, Mr Duncan?' I was now given my own bank card and offered a loan. My pay had risen by £240 but my status had gone up by even more. It meant something to be a dominie, even at the age of 24.

I finished at Robert Gordon's College on the Friday and was required to commence my new post on the Monday. No day off for flitting, no induction period, just straight in.

They're all yours! A young Roddy Duncan in charge of Fetterangus School, alongside colleague Mary Chapman, 1972.

Attendance compulsory! Roddy (third right) at the Fetterangus WRI party, 1970. His wife, Charlotte, is standing, ninth left.

When I got to the village that Friday evening it was to discover our furniture had been delivered and dumped into the garden. The house hadn't been lived in for several months and no one had thought to check it over for us. When Charlotte turned on a tap, the water came cascading down the kitchen walls. The pipes had been frozen and had burst. This meant we couldn't turn on any electricity. The priority was to get the furniture in before nightfall. That first night, we spent sleeping on a mattress on the floor in complete darkness. Thankfully, the P1-3 teacher, Mary Chapman, arrived with her husband, Harry, and brought with them a Tilley lamp.

In the village I was to be known as the dominie and the large school house was a statement of my position in the community – and there we were, scrabbling around on the floor in the dark!

In fact, we passed a very happy three years there. Fetterangus was off the beaten track, a village you passed by on the way to Peterhead and caught a glimpse of across the fields. It was a world on its own; some of the children hadn't ever ventured further than the mart at Maud. The majority on the role were children of parents who themselves had been at the school. It was a stable community.

They were great people in the village, but you were always under their gaze, always on duty. One Monday, I was going down the street and was stopped with the comment, 'Ah see ye wis daein yer washin yesterday, dominie!' Sunday! Everyone else in the village had been doing their washing but, evidently, the headmaster had to maintain different standards. Another weekend I'd gone to get some rhubarb from our patch and been accused of gardening on the Sabbath.

You had to be totally involved in the doings of the community. In those days the hall acted as the bar for the Gala. There was a huge queue to get to it and I was spotted by Eddie Gray, 'You'll hae a dram, dominie, won't ye?' As soon as I took it, a woman came up to me in triumph: 'Weel, dominie, ye've jist wan me half a croon.' 'How come?' 'Simple – I bet that ye wid tak a drink and I wis richt!'

But the support was unstinting. I was anxious to equip the school with new, up to date materials and the parents cheerfully raised the money each time. When I left, I was able to tell them that they had raised over £47 per head – and this was in the early 1970s.

That must be more than £600 by today's values.

In return you had to act as a leader of the community. There was no bank there and the minister resided over in Old Deer; there was no doctor, no vet. So I was the one who was required to witness form signing, to countersign the wills and the applications. Charlotte was expected to play the part of the dominie's wife even though she had a teaching post of her own, in Peterhead. She had to attend the WRI; there are photos of her in the line ups. We all went over to the Freemason's Arms in Strichen for the WRI party. The president came up and said, 'Well, dominie, you'll honour us with a speech tonight, won't you?' I knew next to nothing about the Rural and had to spend the three-course meal, frantically racking my brains for something to say to them all.

Looking back I realise how much I owed to Fetterangus. I had to cater for a class of 29 at four different age stages; they ranged from the P4 boy who couldn't read to the mature P7 girl, destined for university. I had to speak to parents, some of whom were twice my age, and win their confidence. I had to adapt to living in a small rural village and play a leading role in its affairs. I went there as a callow youth and emerged a seasoned professional. Yes, I have much to thank Fetterangus for.

Roddy Duncan, born 1946, interviewed 2011: Fetterangus

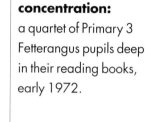

A study in concentration: a quartet of Primary 3 Fetterangus pupils deep in their reading books, early 1972.

Secondary education

Our secondary school was a bleak place. The staff were hostile to self-expression and displays of mirth or emotion were taboo. The system stamped on creativity and was imbued with the Calvinistic ethos that we were sinful and were born to suffer. And the school made sure we did.

The education was like our school meals: force-fed, cut-price, indigestible and certainly not nourishing. And so much was omitted. The history of Scotland, for example, told in vivid dramas till 1603, ceased forthwith at the Union of the Crowns. We weren't taught anything about our people's history, our land struggles, our tremendous body of literature or our proud legacy in innovation in all fields. Women were rendered all but invisible in our syllabus, though the anxiety of our female teachers to be approved by the rector was clearly visible to our impressionable eyes.

Right from primary school, it was all rote learning and our task was just to spew it all back. Having a critical attitude or thinking for ourselves about our course material would have been treated as insurrection. Having a good memory, I could deliver, so I became classified as a good pupil. This, in its turn, created a crushing pressure to continue to perform well. I found I could, but it was really a survival skill, not true education. In reality I was nothing but an excellent parrot.

Any child who did not get through the 11-plus was really doomed. There was a rigid caste system where the academic girls, for example, had the rights to a cupboard which served as our cloakroom – C-stream girls had not. And the strap was reserved mainly for

At least there were the holidays. Daphne – foreground – during the October tattie break, early 1950s, with siblings Iain, Jenny and Kathleen.

Wearing the school uniform. With sister Kathleen (left), 1958.

working class boys. This bred divisiveness and understandable bitterness towards the academic children, with bullying one of the lessons the teachers did impart well.

I remember the day Alison Mac came to school wearing red stockings, a colourful departure from the norm. At the assembly, after the dirge-like hymn – 'Courage brother, do not stumble' – the rector fixed his eye on the line of girls where Alison was standing

Secondary class line up, Aberlour, 1960. Daphne is standing far left; Janet Pickering is far right.

and pronounced, 'There are to be no coloured stockings in this school! There will be no witches here.'

Witches! He could have stepped right out of the Inquisition. And the harsh sound of his coldly administered beltings echoed down the corridors at regular intervals.

The fear of authority was palpable. My class had some rebellious spirits in it – but how mild were our transgressions compared to today. In Secondary 4, bored out of our skulls in yet another spare period, we would go into the maths room, which boasted a piano. One of us innocently struck up *Chopsticks*. The fearsome janitor – the rector's right-hand man – came roaring at us in wrath and said he would report us to the rector. When we stood quaking before him, he intoned menacingly, 'I must warn you girls that you are in serious danger of expulsion.' *Chopsticks* - Expulsion!

I think what we got at Aberlour then was an extreme version of the Scottish system. Perhaps in a way it had been moulded also by our rugged terrain, which had over centuries bred a dogged dourness: I remember one of the teachers would exhort us daily, 'Perseverence, laddie, perseverance.' And persevere we did. Decades later I still sit endless exams in my nightmares.

Daphne Francis, born 1946, interviewed 2008: Aberlour

The incomer to the Tin Academy

At the age of 10, my father became the exciseman at Cragganmore Distillery and I started the school at Ballindalloch. This was a completely different school from the one that I had left back in Sussex. It was a one-teacher school and had a roll of 17 or so. It consisted of one room, with no electricity or running water. It was lit by oil lamps and heated by a stove. The local postmistress would come in each morning to light it before we got to the school. The toilets were outside, at the end of the small playground. It was all rather primitive and that did strike me at the time; I'd come from a modern glass and concrete building at Telscombe Cliffs.

The building itself was a rather makeshift, metal affair, with a corrugated iron roof. Locally, it was named the Tin Academy. It was quite cosy inside. We always arrived before the teacher did, since she commuted from Grantown-on-Spey and her train didn't come in till 9.30. We would settle ourselves by the stove before she arrived; it was burning before we got there and had a fire guard around it on which we could put our gloves so that they were warm for playtime. No doubt the children of Ballindalloch are now bussed off to a centrally heated, electrically powered school, but we didn't feel any lack. The school had a happy atmosphere, a family feeling about it.

The ages covered the full primary range, so that there were children from five to 12, all in the one small room and all under the one teacher, Mrs Reid. I'm not quite sure how she went about organising us all, but she did it marvellously well. She seemed to know

The school consisted of one room, with no electricity or water. It was lit by oil lamps and heated by a stove.

An earlier return to Ballindalloch, 2005. Outside the former exciseman's house where she lived in the late 1950s. Janet is third left, her husband Mike and daughter Anna at her side. With them are her brother, David Northcroft, his son Mat, daughter-in-law Elaine and their three small daughters.

each one of us from inside out and to care for us. We did have to spend time working on our own while she was seeing to the other age groups, but it all seemed to work very well. She'd then come round and go over our work with us. There was never any disorder; it was all very controlled.

I remember how thoroughly we were taught the basic subjects. When I arrived at the school I'd been struggling with fractions, but now that I was getting individualised help I soon made good progress. At first, it was very difficult adjusting. My main problem was I couldn't pick up what the other children were saying; I remember the first day and how bewildering I found it all. And they all stared and stared at me; it was rare for them to see any outsiders. The main problem was their dialect. But Mrs Reid was very kind and understanding; she had a word with the rest of the children and things soon got better for me. But I do remember that at the end of that first day I was in tears; the culture shock had been so great.

In the end I became very settled there. I was soon a member of this family of children, and no doubt ready to join in the staring at any strange arrivals – if there had been any.

I remember that primary school very fondly indeed. In the two years I was there, I received a much better education than I had done in Sussex. This was partly a matter of size. In Telscombe I had been one of a class of over 30; the teachers seemed to me to have been strict and not to know us very well. But Mrs Reid seemed to value every one of us and to see the strengths in all of us. If it hadn't been for her, I doubt whether I would have got on so well or achieved university education later.

Janet Pickering, born 1946, interviewed 2004: Ballindalloch

The dyslexic: a complete frustration

My academic career was a total disaster. I found Mackie Academy a complete frustration: I knew I had the ability within me, but whenever I tried to express it on paper I got into a tangle, lost heart and became incoherent.

Then years later, sometime in the mid Eighties, watching TV one evening, I suddenly found myself face to face with what my problem had been. It was a programme on something termed 'dyslexia' and as it proceeded to go through all symptoms, I realised it was talking about me: the short-term memory problems, the day dreaming, the lack of focus, the ability to absorb odd bits of information – that was me. I now realise that the fault hadn't been some sort of stupidity but a medical problem, one that had a name and that I shared with thousands of other folk. But when I was at school there had been no recognition of what is now called 'special learning difficulties' and I'd been led to believe I was simply thick and incapable.

Can you imagine what it's like when you come to write something down only to find that you've gone straight to the second letter of the word and that immediately you've made that mistake it will earn the red pen? You want to cross it out and start again, but crossings out aren't really approved of and are seen as a sign of ineptitude. So the whole thing begins to break down and you give up, your confidence in shreds. Well, that's what I had to confront on a daily basis. Now the computer allows me to get round the problem; I can cut and paste and use the spell-checker and end up with the version I know was always there in my head, but then, with only a pen and a blank piece of paper and a teacher who insisted on judging me the same as everyone else, I had stood no chance.

I can honestly say that that programme, which I came on quite by chance, changed my life. Up till then I'd gone around with this weight of anger and frustration seething away inside me. Now I had something to blame, but it was no longer myself. That knowledge didn't make any difference to anything in the external world; but it made all the difference to me, inside. It gave me a new wave of confidence.

Martin Sim, born 1947, interviewed 2011: Stonehaven

> I'd been led to believe I was simply thick and incapable.

No longer afraid of the written word: Martin Sim as he is now, with wife Sheila, taken at his home town of Stonehaven.

The walk to school

Ready for the fancy dress parade at the village fete. Betty McCorkindale with parents, 1952. The outfit was home made, and the feathers came from the family hens.

When I was six, we moved to Riverside Cottage, Kirkside, by Banff. There was no school transport for me; mostly it was just a question of walking it. It would take me an hour; with my little legs those two miles were long enough. I was an only child and so I was by myself. My mother would come half the way with me and meet me half-way along, coming back. She had contracted polio and was a bit lame, so regularly walking the whole distance was out of the question for her.

I must have been petrified. I've been a fearful person all through my life. Three years ago I had time-line therapy and was taken back in my mind to those early days. I was asked to recognise when I had first experienced these feelings of fear, and I came out with 'when I was six'. I think it was those walks that started it all. I've developed arthritis in my neck now and I reckon it's because of all that time I spent walking along with my head turned to see if anyone was following me. You'd go along the river and through the woods. There was no tarmac road, only a rough track with bumps and stones.

I was attacked by a man when I was six. He tried to rape me. He offered me a lift on his bicycle and I accepted because, with my long journey, I thought it would offer me

Another walk safely behind her. Betty with class 1A at Banff Academy, 1953. She is front row (sitting), second from left.

some help. I was completely innocent. I was saved because my mum and I used to use a code whistle to each other as she came to meet me along the track. I heard her signal and I cried out, 'That's my mum!' Later he was caught. I wasn't the only one; he had a liking for young girls. But that one experience was quite enough to mark me.

My parents were keen for me to do well at school. Walking to school with my mum was how I learned my tables. We'd walk along together and chant out 'two times two is four; two times three is six' and so on as we went. I'll always remember that, the pair of us droning along through the wood.

Betty McCorkindale, born 1947, interviewed 2003: Banff

The tawse: I detested that dominie

I detested that dominie; I found him a coorse, cruel character, very free with the belt. I'll tell you what he did to me once. It was assembly and I found something to laugh at. He told me to come out and get three of the strap. I thought one stroke would be reasonable so when he came to hit me the second time, I withdrew my hand. But I needn't have bothered – he raised the belt and smashed it right across my face. That was in front of the whole school.

But I got my revenge. In my last week at school I waited till the lunch hour and then quickly toured round all the classrooms, opened the teachers' desks and removed their straps. I took them all to the woodwork room and cut them into ribbons and deposited the bits in the bin. I walked out of the school and never went back.

Four years later, I happened to be attending a pal's wedding. One of my old teachers was also present: Miss Robb. We got talking. 'Gavin', she said, 'tell me – was it you that removed all our straps and destroyed them?' 'Me, Miss Robb? Oh no, I'd never thought of that.' 'Well, Gavin, you owe me £14 – that's what a new strap cost me.' But I didn't pay up; I bought her a drink instead.

Gavin Sim, born 1949, interviewed 2011: Cuminestown

That dominie is not in the picture. Gavin Sim among the back row boys at Monquhitter School as an eight-year-old, 1957.

The embryonic journalist.
The four-year old Norman Harper ready for a family do.

I can remember the overall she wore, the shoes she had on, the lipstick she wore, the colour of her shoes, the colour of hair.

The journalist

The teacher who taught me for the first two years was Miss McDonald. I had never come across anyone quite like her before. I was just mesmerized by this figure that was standing there, up before the blackboard. I can remember the overall she wore, the shoes she had on, the lipstick she wore, the colour of her shoes, the colour of hair. She would have been in her late 20s, maybe. She'd been born and brought up in Alford, but you wouldn't know it from her accent because it was Received English. It was from Miss McDonald that I learned English, because before that, at home, there was only the Doric.

I met her once outside the classroom, because my uncle had a grocery in the village and he would come out in his van and go round all the farms. One Saturday, he offered to take me; one of the stops was the farm where Miss McDonald lived with her parents. She hopped into the back of the van, and I, being sat in the front seat, wasn't sure whether I should turn round and have a look. I've a vivid memory of listening to my uncle using her first name: 'Lil'. It had never occurred to me that she had a first name! It's still talked about in the family, that on the Monday afterwards, I'd hovered about after the bell had gone for playtime until Miss McDonald asked, 'Yes, Norman, what is it?' 'Please, Miss, my uncle called you Lil!' She just laughed and said, 'Well that might be because that's my name. But don't tell anyone else.' And I did keep the secret – you always did what the teacher told you to.

Round the lower part of the classroom were rows and rows of books. I remember going up to Miss McDonald and asking whether I could use them. 'Absolutely. Any time I'm not teaching and you've done your work, you must go and use the books.' I did so, frequently, and I think that's what started me off on the written word, certainly on a love of reading.

I would say we were diligent. Parents in the country still saw value in education. Consequently, you had the impression they were more on the side of the teacher than the pupil. It never occurred to me not to work hard at school, because the teachers made the atmosphere for learning so congenial.

Then in Primary 6/7, we went to Miss Walker. There had been this children's programme on BBC about some kids who ran their own newspaper. I thought this was fascinating and went up to Miss Walker to ask if there was any chance I could run our own class newspaper. It must have been mesmerizing for the teachers to see us all willingly producing all this written work. There were news stories, jokes, cartoon strips, fiction – and I was the editor, of course. I remember asking Miss Walker: 'We'd like to run a competition – but what can we do for prizes?' And I remember her, dipping into her own purse and handing over half-a-crown. So, we bought 10 packets of crisps, at threepence each, and every week we handed one out as a prize.

I sometimes wonder if primary teachers realize that they have an immense formative influence, not just on the seven years of primary education, but on their pupils' whole lives. Scarcely an hour goes by of my waking existence that doesn't refer back to what I learned at Alford Primary School. The skills I use, the social skills, the way I behave in

treating other people, in working hard, in simple things like that – abstract things, moral values, all sorts of things. Everything, in some way, I can trace back to my teachers at that school.

I've no detailed knowledge of how education is carried out now, but I can tell you what the results are. I've played a heavy role in training new journalists. I look at the test papers we set for trainee journalists, and I despair at how they are using the language – the grammar, spelling and punctuation – and I get the impression they don't see the personal need for these skills because that's what sub-editors are for, to take care of such things. But that's taking no pride in your own work. You wouldn't hire a mechanic who didn't know one end of an engine from another, so why have a journalist who doesn't know about grammar, punctuation and spelling? It's a question of attitude towards work, of having a philosophy of what an educated person is.

I don't mean to be disparaging about those who were teaching in the Seventies /Eighties, because I know this policy was handed down from on high, but I think it's fairly clear that the results of this education mean that the people who had their education then haven't had the same basic grounding my generation had.

The compensation is that they are much more at ease in social situations; they can relate to people a lot more. That's why we hire journalists who don't have the mechanics of the language, but who are brilliant at interviewing people, who can draw people out.

Oh dear! I would never have dreamed that I'd be sitting here in the 21st century and be speaking like some old fuddy-duddy! I once spoke to a lecturer from Glasgow who said he took everything people told him about dropping standards with a pinch of salt, because he found that what everyone claimed was that it was the year after they'd finished which was the year when standards began to drop. That's what the people who finished in '75 said about those who came later, and what people in '65 said about the generation of '75, and so on. So I suppose I'm guilty of that. I suppose if I was training someone whose education had finished in '85, he would claim that the rot set in 1986…

Norman Harper, born 1957, interviewed 2002: Alford

P6, Alford Primary School, 1967–1968. Back, from left: Edwin Smith, Donald Fleming, Billy McCombie, James Stewart, Alan Shand, Norman Harper, George McHattie, Ian Stewart. Middle, from left: Catherine Fordyce, Roy Penny, Kenny Morgan, (unknown), Bill Ledingham, Michael Robb, Graham Stuart, Jim Beattie, Ewen Coutts, June Wilson. Front, from left: Rosalind Davidson, Catherine Watt, Susan Raeburn, Maureen Bruce, Jackie Adam, Marion Bruce, Sandra Robertson, Hazel McWilliam, Angela Durno, Annie Mitchell.

The modern pupil gets around ... Mackie Academy ski trip to Quebec, 2004

... and Paris. Elgin Academy pupils on the Paris trip, 2007.

The teacher: I really enjoy it

I really enjoy teaching. I've always liked working with young people. I feel I have a natural rapport with them. I always make a point of showing them respect and I nearly always get it in return. I'm one of those people who can see the good in young people.

I enjoy the banter and the camaraderie of the staff room too. I'm aware that some people have the view that teaching nowadays must be hell, that kids no longer have the discipline, the interest, etc, etc. Certainly there's no longer the same sanctions, not with the belt abolished. But I would not like to use one: a smack is one thing, but to use a belt is to wield a weapon. It has to be accepted that children nowadays do have rights, that they will expect to be heard. I've no problems with that. I'm interested in what they have to say and I respect it. In my career, I've only ever encountered two pupils I have no time for, that I wouldn't give the time of day to. Some of the older teachers can feel a bit uncomfortable with the informality of today's classroom, but my view is that if you lose the human touch, then you lose everything. Certainly, it can be a hard profession: there will be days when you're just not feeling up to it, yet you have to go in and perform. Pupils just won't learn from teachers they don't like or respect.

Craig Sim, born 1972, interviewed 2006: Elgin

The school leaver

And now I'm on the brink of leaving school; I can only look back on it all with gratitude; I've enjoyed it all. But on Monday there's my final exam, then the signing of my Leaver's Certificate and that's that. I'm not sure that I really want to leave all this behind me and venture out into the real world. Mackie's been such a welcoming place.

I've been allowed to speak – something I've never been backward about! Being encouraged to voice our own ideas can only be a good thing, but I must admit that sometimes it can all go too far. We are made very aware of our rights in Modern Studies and Personal & Social Development and this can go to some pupils' heads. The idea is to empower us, but for some it becomes a matter of 'my entitlements' and 'you can't make me do that – I know my rights!' There's a poster on display which tells us, 'Under 18s; Know Your Rights!' and which lists all that we are entitled to under the European Union constitution. For example, there, you are told that nobody can force you to join a group, and that's a 'right' that gets thrown back in adults' faces sometimes. So ,when some pupils are told that if they join the concert band it will make them better players, the answer comes back, 'No, you can't make me go; I've a right not to.'

There's no longer an automatic respect for people in authority in the community. Young people are no longer willing to be allocated a particular box for them to fit into. Respect for the older generation is something that has to be earned. Nobody can assume they will be deferred to just because they happen to be a lawyer, a policeman or a teacher. One of the problems is that these people no longer live in their own communities in a way that makes them visible and playing a leading role. The teachers here at Mackie commute in from all over. In the past, the older person would be known to you, would be someone you'd see on the street, would know your parents, but not now.

Jenni Keenan, born 1992, interviewed 2010: Stonehaven

On the brink of leaving school; at Mackie Academy summer 2010.

Post school: the university student, at Stirling, summer 2011.

GOING TO THE KIRK

The church at Cuminestown where Gwen Haggart's father, John Nelson Hall, was minister during the Fifties and Sixties.

A music heard no more

I came out of teaching in my early 40s. I had been taking afternoon evening service as a lay reader up in Findochty. I'd been doing that kind of thing for year. On this evening I was being given a lift in the car of a fisherman; he turned and asked me straight, 'Why aren't you a minister?' I found I could give no answer.

I retired in 1995. With the small kirks, there's been so much erosion, so much amalgamation, no doubt about it. The lack of funding, aged congregations, aged buildings, the scramble for money to keep it going. When you think about the way things have gone over the years, the operative word I find is 'background'. Once, the background to their lives that people shared and could take for granted was solid – not now. People did refer to the church as a presence in their lives, as something that was there for them. We all went to Sunday School in the Thirties. I'll tell you why: the kirk was somewhere to go to break the monotony of the Sunday. People in the confines of

Although this shot of the Banchory West Church choir on a 1954 outing to Inverness might appear to be of a bygone era, the church itself is still a thriving one (see 'Tony Stephen'). Moira Jolly (see 'Going to School') is third from right, her mother beside her.

the croft, of the farm, were conditioned to go to the kirk for an hour or so on the Sunday morning as a relief, as a way of getting out and meeting people.

But no doubt about it, there has been a falling away. The background – and I come back to that word – is no longer there with the people. It's been like a music for them through the ages and now it's no longer heard. Yet I wouldn't go the length as to say we have become a non-Christian country so much as a-Christian. The knowledge, the understanding can no longer be regarded as a common possession. There's no doubt that Muslim is the more intense religion nowadays for those who adhere. It is a force which is observed as part of their daily life, as a form of behaviour. That's not the case for the church, not here in Scotland today.

Charles Birnie born 1925, interviewed 2004: Strichen

What can you put in its place?

I've been reading Richard Dawkin's latest attack on traditional religion in his *The God Delusion* where he suggests that religious faith is the product of a primitive mind and that we should be beyond that level of superstition by now. I don't think of myself as very Christian, but I do know how in the past religion was of value to people. It gave them something outside themselves, a source of meaning. It would help people come together; it was a binding force in the community. I was brought up in the church and my mother was a dedicated goer, but in adolescence I came to the conclusion that I could no longer accept its beliefs. I am more inclined to adopt a biological view of existence and to accept that we are here primarily to pass on our genes to the next generation. But I do feel that it is wrong to strip people of their faith if they sincerely hold it and you can't put anything in its place.

–*Taken from his book,* KICK THOSE SLEEPING DOGS, *Leopard Press, 2011*

Pierre Fouin born 1928, interviewed 2007: Glen Tanar

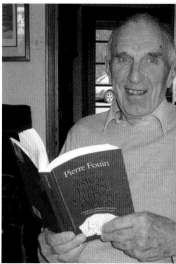

You just jumped

The church has played a large part in my life. I'm sad that young people no longer attend, that there's been such a falling off. But I can understand that for the younger generations traditional Christianity must pose a lot of hard questions. In my day you simply aimed to be a true believer, someone who followed the Book. We didn't look to question what was preached to us from the pulpit. But there's so much suffering in the world: take that abduction in Portugal of that little three-year-old girl – how do you explain that God is still loving and merciful when He allows something like that to happen? How do you tell a five-year-old that Jesus is 'up there' and when he looks up to the sky at night and sees a satellite whizzing around all lit up that, although it is up there, you can't expect it to see Jesus?

We were brought up in a disciplined environment. The minister held a position of great respect in the community. My father tells the story of when they were in the fields hard at it getting in the harvest on a fine day; they looked up and saw the minister

When the minister told you to fetch his peats then you just did it.

approaching: 'Oh, no – I ken fit's comin noo!', said my father. And sure enough, the minister wanted them to go off in their horse and cart to collect his peats for him from his lair. And that's just what they did, harvest or no harvest.

It's like my National Service: when the officer said 'Jump' you just did – and when the minister told you to fetch his peats then you just did it. And when he told you to follow Christ, you just jumped. I'm not sorry it's been that way for me. Discipline made me, and both the Forces and the Church have been part of that discipline. After all, the church is more than simply a place to go on a Sunday; like the Army, it's a way of life. The church is a centre for the whole community; becoming involved in it is joining you to others. To believe in the church is to believe in the human race. If it finally goes what is there to take its place?

William McRae born 1930, interviewed 2007: Peterhead

A Protesting Catholic

In 1954 my life changed completely. That's when I married Charlie Shaw and became a farmer's wife, over at Blairs, next to the Roman Catholic seminary. We had a lot to do with the seminary; not only did we rent our farm from them, but the Shaw family were practising Catholics and attended all the services in the college chapel. I'd been brought up in the Church of Scotland. When I got married I decided I would have to look into the matter of Catholic beliefs. I went for instruction to Father Stone in his room at the college and became a convert.

'A sense of relaxation and welcome.' Chatting with Cardinal O'Brien – then head of Blairs Seminary, 1980s. From left: Margaret Davidson, Charlie Shaw, Tom Davidson, Dorothy Shaw.

I've never regretted it. Back then, the liturgy was still in Latin and the rituals compared to the Church of Scotland were very strong. But there's also a great sense of relaxation and welcome; I found the whole experience very satisfying, both emotionally and spiritually. I loved the colour and atmosphere; it's a beautiful chapel and on a Sunday at mass, with the choir and the organ music sounding out and the light shining through the stain glass windows, well, you can never fail to feel uplifted.

People would come from far and near to enjoy those services. I also had a lot to do with the boys there. Lovely lads they were, so well mannered and keen to learn. Groups of them would come to the farm to be given instruction into the basics of agriculture and they were always so polite and attentive. I don't think it was only the biscuits I gave them that appealed.

My Catholic faith means a lot to me and I still attend mass regularly, though now at

'It's a beautiful chapel.'
Father Moran marries Jean and Steve, Blairs, 1984.

Banchory. But I would describe myself as a protesting Catholic rather than a slavish follower of all its dictates. For example, I can't accept its strict line on euthanasia, not when it's so simple to help those near the end and who are suffering so terribly, just to slip away. You go into an old folks' homes and see them all sitting there with their dead eyes, not able to recognise even their own flesh and blood and you have to wonder what is the point of it all. I'd hate the prospect myself of becoming a burden to those around me and I'd welcome the possibility of a merciful release.

I would think of myself as a flexible Catholic. I can support the church's stand on freely available contraception to each and every young girl who wants to play with fire, but I can also see that in many areas, where there is a great deal of poverty and overpopulation, then a relaxation of the teaching would only be sensible. On the other hand, we do need the church to hold the line in many areas of modern life. Today abortion appears to be freely available more or less on demand but, to me, there's no doubt the foetus in the womb is a human being in the making and that to abort it is murder.

Like a great many Catholics I've been grieved to see the problems that my church has been suffering over the last years. The scandals surrounding paedophilia have done much damage, no doubt about it. Human nature can be a terrible thing and the Catholic Church has not been able to keep some of its worst aspects at bay.

So there's plenty to protest about. I have discussions with my own priest from Banchory and am quite open about all these issues. He's a man of about 50, a lovely boy. But I do know what my faith has brought to me; there's plenty of life left in the old church yet. As I say, I've never regretted crossing over.

Dorothy Shaw born 1933, interviewed 2012: Blairs

A first Communion. Daughter Jean is on the right.

A Catholic wedding. Jean Shaw and Steve Barry, 1984, Blairs.

I doubt
whether
many of
them really
believed in
the whole
supernatural
paraphernalia

Top of the Form, BBC
Home Service. Ian
Campbell was captain
of the winning Mackie
Academy team in 1959.

A bit of ritual

In the rural North-east, people have supported their local church, not for reasons of piety so much as social cohesion. I doubt whether many of them have really believed in the whole supernatural paraphernalia like the virgin birth, but they've gone along on a Sunday because they have wanted to support 'their church'. Like the laird, the minister has been thought of as a useful social force, good for opening events or for starting off a celebratory meal with the grace. He has given such social events their necessary bit of ritual and ceremony. But this has nothing to do with God; rather with community organisation and stability.

Charlie Allan born 1939, interviewed 2006: Methlick

Son of the manse

The manse had status, but not the means to sustain it. It was a large house with multiple bedrooms, a reminder of an age when the minister stood high in the parish and had servants and the resources to support a way of life notably grander

Ian is on the far right,
with Joan Clark
(producer) and fellow
winners John Bone,
James Freeman,
Gordon Shanks and
David Stoney.

than the majority of his congregation. But by our time, my father was having to make do on very scarce resources. It was a cold unheated place – cold is a theme which seems to run through my life: even today friends will remark that mine is the only flat in Edinburgh where you have to remove the white wine from the fridge in order to chill it!

As a son of the manse, one was expected to behave and to dress in a certain way. Before going out into the street I would be inspected to see that I was neat and tidy. And, of course, church attendance was absolutely assumed. I grew up playing a role in the church; playing the organ, tolling the bell, helping count the offerings. I resented none of this; the church was simply an integral part of my life. And congregations were still plentiful.

Church attendance is still a regular feature of my weekly life. The church I go to is packed with young people. In my work, the 19th century Scottish novels I taught were full of instances where the rigidity of the Church repelled the young – I have been immersed in the topic of the dying church all through my teaching career. It's there in George Macdonald, in Robert Louis Stevenson and in Gibbon too. It's an abiding process of questioning and self-questioning which reaches out now as it did then.

My father did his very best for his congregation. He was very much respected in the community; he earned less than many of them, but was always ready to give more.

When I landed up at Mackie Academy and was asked, 'What do you play? Football? Cricket? Tennis? Rugby?' and I answered, 'No, but I do play the organ', I knew I was bound to be made fun of, that my social credit would be sunk. I was regarded as 'different'; and that was that. I was branded as bookish, so that when it came to Top of the Form and the need to select a captain I was a straightforward choice.

Ian Campbell born 1942, interviewed 2010: Inverbervie

> I have been immersed in the topic of the dying church all through my teaching career.

Daughter of the manse

Being brought up in a manse was never a gloomy or restricted thing. I must say, however, that when we entered our teens we did begin to become conscious of having to be different. In Edinburgh and in Dundee we had been just an ordinary family among others. It was totally different when we moved up to Aberdeenshire. There we encountered the concept of the 'manse family'. There were a certain number of people who had standing in the community – the banker, the doctor, the headmaster – and the minister was very much part of that.

In Cuminestown there was this sense of having to be 'daughters of the manse', that we had to behave in a certain way. My sister took to it with much more difficulty than me: she was a bit of a rebel. She wanted to look Bohemian, to wear make-up, to dress outrageously. Teenagers do that kind of thing nowadays and nobody takes much notice of it, but back then, well… My father would tell us, 'You've got to remember that the people in the village will look on us all as the "manse family"' She would rebel against that. I was never so adventurous, so I didn't get involved to the same extent. She would tell me, 'You are always the Good One.'

The manse had been built in 1749. It was huge and had two large gardens and a steading with hen houses and glebe land. No central heating and when the weather was cold you had to wear jumpers and boots even indoors. My father had some eccentricities and he suffered from rheumatics in his wrists. He would cut off the sleeves of his old jumpers and cardigans and wrap them round his wrists for added protection. He would

The minister's daughter, Gwen Haggart (Hall) in the manse garden, Cuminestown, 1960.

> When the people called we would be expected to collect their coats and later to hand round plates of scones and cakes.

also put them round the telephone earpiece so that it was nice and warm when he went to use it. Being poor we couldn't afford to light all the fires; in the depths of the winter, some of the rooms had frost on the inside of the windows which never seemed to thaw out.

There was always a lot of people coming and going at the manse, meetings to do with the parish and so on. This meant my mother would have to spend the whole day beforehand baking and that when the people called we would be expected to go and collect their coats and then later to hand round the plates of scones and cakes. When we were old enough we became helpers in the Sunday School; from the age of 14 I would be taking the little ones and telling Bible stories with their sand trays and cut-out figures. It never crossed my mind that I might not have to be doing this, that I might not believe in it all.

Our grandmother died when I was 10. She was one of the old school, who wouldn't even let you wash your hair on a Sunday. You were allowed to go for a walk, but not to play with a ball or a skipping rope on that day. You couldn't even cut your nails. I never really questioned it. I suppose we just loved our grandmother. After her death, things did relax a little, but our father still had some of the old attitudes. I remember when I went into Aberdeen to the university and my sister was starting at Gray's School of Art, we would take the bus home for the weekends. We were staying in digs and we'd be taking the whole week's washing home with us. That would be done on the Saturday – no washing machine! – but that meant we had to do the ironing on the Sunday before catching the bus back. Father wasn't comfortable with this and he would ask, 'Do you really have to do this on a Sunday?'

'Always something on.' Gwen's father, Reverend John Hall, in the late 1950s, at the annual church fair with the local MP, Patrick Woolridge-Gordon. Gwen's mother is first left.

Part of my present work is to be responsible for the development of the communication and speech skills of candidates for the ministry in the Church of Scotland. Not all of them are young by any means. Many of them are in their late 30s/40s, people who are feeling a call to a new direction to their lives. It's interesting to see the number of those who give up good careers to go into the ministry and find fulfilment there. At present we have an engineer who's been a university lecturer and been very innovative in the oil industry. He's also a man with four children who are still at home, so all this is a huge commitment for him. There are quite a lot of people like that, people who are able to bring new energies into the Church. The Church actually prefers entrants with some life experience. And now a lot of them are

women. I think most of them will make very good ministers.

I still see the Church as having a real social role. This is especially so since the General Assembly brought in the concept of the 'church without walls'. This holds that the church is not so much a building as a body of people who work within the community. Those parishes, which remain in the old ways, won't be the ones to survive, but if a church can see itself as reaching out into the community, then it will keep going in some form or other. We are now branching out into the 'ministry of all believers'. This holds that the church is no longer the sole preserve of some figurehead who does everything in the parish, but of a team. I know that in my father's time he and Mother were expected to do everything.

The good thing now is that the Church is aware of all beliefs, of all practices. It has taken on a multi-racial, multi-cultural dimension. It has hopefully become much more tolerant and accepting. Tolerance and respect: that's the way forward.

Gwen Haggart born 1943, interviewed 2004: Monquhitter Parish

But never on a Sunday. Gwen, third left, as member of the Turriff Academy hockey team, winners of the area shield, 1960.

A forgotten hero

Our minister, D. S. Garrow, was a super man who did such a lot for the village. You'd see him tootling around in his old Austin car, one of those big square box models. He was unmarried, but he was always very good to us children. You'd love to run a message for him, because you knew there would be a 'silver penny' at the

> **As an elder, my father insisted on going to the minister's funeral. There were only eight at the graveside.**

end of it – a half-crown as likely as not.

But he had a rather lonely ending of it. He ended up in a home and when he died he was buried up at Portsoy. There were very few at his funeral. My father hadn't been well, but as an elder he insisted on going up to it. He was so glad that he made the effort; there were only eight at the graveside.

Yet this was a man who had been at the centre of Woodhead life just a dozen years before, a minister who had done so much for the community. Then a few years ago I was raking through a junk shop in Turriff and I came across a clock. I looked at the plaque; it had been presented to 'the Reverend D. S. Garrow in appreciation'. I looked at it and thought, 'Well…'

George Philip born 1945, interviewed 2007: Fyvie

The Reverend Jean

I went to Glasgow University. In my second year I had the horrendous experience of failing an exam. My plan had been to take a degree in Modern Languages and then go on to become a teacher. I had made a deal with God, however, that if I was to go on and do an Honours degree, then I must do so with all my exams passed first time round. No matter that I sailed through the resit – I'd made my deal with God and so I determined that I was not meant to do Honours.

I graduated in 1968 with my ordinary Arts degree, but during that final year, when I did one subject in Divinity alongside my Arts subjects, I attended the General Assembly in Edinburgh to listen to the debates on whether the Church of Scotland should admit women to the ministry. I remember sitting there, up in the gallery, when this elderly man got up and waved his bendy bible: 'Moderator, there is no rush: we should send this back down to Presbyteries.' And suddenly, from nowhere it seemed, there popped into my brain the thought, 'Oh, no, you can't do that. If you don't agree to pass the motion today I won't be able to start my course in September.' This was the first time the notion of being a minister had really crossed my mind and here it was, apparently a fully formed intention.

Well, they did pass it. This was May. I went home to Kilmarnock and the following Sunday I accompanied Mum and Dad to our local church. At the end of the service I went up to the minister and said, 'Do you think you could give me a reference? I'm going to apply to be considered as candidate for the ministry.' I went to the manse that very afternoon and watched while he typed it. Until that spring I'd assumed I'd be spending the next year at Jordanhill, training to be a school teacher. God works in mysterious ways.

My family were fully supportive. When I went to the selection school there were three women in the group. We were subjected to all sorts of tests and interviews to prove our suitability. Then it was off to university again to do my BD degree. The course did me the world of good and matured my personal faith by making me question the sort of

Easter on the Glebe. Sharing an early morning service with the Reverend Grainger Stoddart, of St Peter's Church.

very fundamentalist beliefs I'd had up till then. It encouraged us to adopt a critical viewpoint and to be investigative in all we did.

After my Probationary year I had to start to apply for a charge of my own. There were plenty of vacancies, but I got plenty of rejections. A lot of congregations still seemed to be wrestling with the whole concept of a female minister. I'd go along to interview and have to field questions that were aimed at my gender. I was once asked what I thought would happen if I became pregnant, to which I replied, 'I would hope to be married before that happened and as I don't have a boyfriend at present I see that as a purely hypothetical question'. There were other worries for committees: how would I cope at a graveside when it was still the custom in many places for that to be an exclusively male event? Even, at one charge, the objection that the manse had a long drive and it would be a real concern to think of a young woman having to make her way up it on a dark winter's night.

Finally, there came the invitation from Peterculter. I came from Ayrshire and knew nothing about Culter or Deeside but, like Gideon, I was content to entrust myself to God and to follow this path. I can still recall the phone call from the Session Clerk and the disbelief that he couldn't quite keep out of his voice as he informed me, 'We would like you to be our sole nominee'. Here was a man old enough to be my father doing something that he'd never dreamed would be his lot: asking a 26-year-old woman to take the step towards becoming his minister.

So in January 1973, and after making more than 30 applications all over Scotland, I took up my post as minister of Kelman Memorial Church, Peterculter, in the Presbytery of Aberdeen. I remember waking up in the manse the next day and thinking, 'What have I done? I am the minister here.' But both I and the congregation were determined to make it work and I think we did.

To begin with, there was a certain amount of feeling our way together. There were some interesting cultural issues to navigate. After all, these were the Seventies and the era of the mini skirt – and I wore a mini skirt. And I never wore a clerical collar, because I felt that that was designed for male wear.

The people were warm, especially when you got to know them and they you. Apart from a seven-year spell in Forfar, I spent the larger part of my ministry life in Culter and now my retirement, too. It's my home; it's where my friends are. I also love Culter – I mean, just eight miles from the sea and on the edge of the hills and Deeside, who wouldn't?

I wasn't aware that any member of my congregation left on account of my

Jean Montgomerie
with her father, 1998.

'What have I done?' A very young Reverend Jean Montgomerie in the pulpit of Kelman Memorial Church, Peterculter.

appointment and gradually, as we got to know each other, they became my extended family. I'm grateful to them for their willingness to make things work. I suspect that some of them became quite proud of the fact that they had taken the bold step of appointing a woman, especially when I was asked to serve on various General Assembly committees and then became convener of its Board Ministry.

One of the things which frustrate me is when folks pronounce, 'The Church must modernise!' I don't think the average non-church person realises just how much the church has adapted over the years. What happens now is light years away from the sort of experience I had as a young girl back in Fifties Kilmarnock and that's as it should be, not because what was happening then was wrong, but because the church is an evolving organism. I used to claim that I could go into the pulpit and do a cartwheel and the outside world would never know about it, because it would never take the trouble to find out what is really happening inside churches these days.

Naturally, ministry has had its share of frustrations. We have moved into a more secular age, one in which people claim still to respect Christianity, but see no personal need for the Church. I've lost count of the number of times I've heard people tell me that it's quite possible to follow Christian practices without having any contact with the Church. Well, in my humble view, to maintain and to develop your faith then you need to be part of the Christian community, to be an active, worshipping part and not simply a vaguely approving onlooker. Christianity is not just a bundle of ethics; it's a relationship with the living God.

I also find it frustrating when people confuse the church as a building, as an institution, with the church as a community of believers. That's why, in my words of welcome to a congregation I would say, 'Welcome to worship' rather than 'Welcome to Church'.

It is my firm belief that if I hadn't committed myself to my faith, and to the ministry of the gospel, I would have had a much simpler life. But I chose the only possible way for me and that has brought great fulfilment.

Jean Montgomerie born 1946, interviewed 2011: Peterculter

Let us gather in the river

Our local minister was Robin Mitchell. He was a larger than life character. My parents would speak of the time when, having just arrived, he preached this hell-fire sermon warning his congregation of the dangers of drink. He cited with great approval the parable in which the wine was poured into the river Jordan. Just as everyone was looking askance at each other, wondering what kind of a killjoy minister they had been landed with, he then announced that they would all now sing, 'Let us gather in the river'!

Andy Hall born 1954, interviewed 2006: Maryculter

It was doing my head in

Going to church was simply part of what you did then. When I was at primary school I would go twice on a Sunday, morning and afternoon. I was taken into E&M's in Aberdeen for the purchase of my special Sunday outfit. I became a Sunday school teacher before I left for the university. The church wasn't just a place for worship; it also acted as a social centre. It was where I went to the Girls' Brigade each week, too.

Our family church was the Congregational. At this period the Close Brethren was powerful in Peterhead and this created divisions within the community. When I was in the later part of my time at the secondary school one of my closest friends was in the Brethren. I remember being very saddened to hear how there had been splits in her family over the doctrine, coming from parts of the Brethren, as I saw it, and I used to ask myself, 'What on earth has this to do with Christianity?'.

The sect leader was Jim Taylor and he seemed to have great satisfaction in issuing more and more restrictive edicts that were designed – as far as I could see it as a teenager who questioned things I didn't understand or agree with – to exert more and more control over his members. Some of the edicts that I can remember (but maybe these came to me in an exaggerated form) were that women should not cut their hair; women and men should only have sex in order to procreate and they shouldn't watch television or listen to the radio. It was all about power, really, and I felt had little to do with true Christianity.

There were specific aspects of the edicts which particularly upset me at the time and these related to the fact that members of the Close Brethren were advised – even told –

I vividly
remember a
situation
when a
particular
woman
I knew
didn't attend
the funeral
of her own
mother with
whom she
had been
very close

that they shouldn't eat or drink with others outside their group. I vividly remember a situation when a particular woman I knew didn't attend the funeral of her own mother with whom she had been very close and whom she used to visit daily, and all because, as I understood it, her mother hadn't been in the Brethren — but was, however, a respected Christian in either the Baptist or the Methodist church. A close friend of mine told me that on the morning of funeral, the woman in question appeared at the family home with home bakes for the post-funeral gathering, but wasn't able to go to the actual service — and this of one who had been a loving, caring mother to her — nor to support her widowed father in his hour of need.

It would seem that the sort of fishing community which Peterhead was, during my early years, encouraged closed-in attitudes to flourish. I remember when my own parents died and I had to go up to the town to talk over the funeral arrangements, that it was mentioned that Peterhead had something like 20-plus religious groupings — and all this in a relatively small community. I'm not sure why this should be so, this intensity of religious observance. Perhaps, historically, it was to do with the way in which fishing people might be considered a particular group of their own, the way in which they would travel up and down the east coast, following the fish, from Shetland down to Yarmouth, and mix with their own kind rather than outsiders. Maybe, too, the constant exposure to the dangers of the open sea and loss of life had encouraged a somewhat bleak and punitive attitude to religion — I don't know. I had always been brought up to believe that Christianity was meant to be underpinned by a value base that included loving thy neighbour, in being willing to forgive, about helping each other and valuing differences.

Of course, I'm speaking here of the way things were 30 years ago; I know that attitudes and ways of behaving have loosened up considerably since my time as a teenager there. When I left for Aberdeen University I began to lapse from the church. My parents had hoped that I would continue to be a practising member and that I would join the university Christianity Union. I remember a painful conversation with my mother. When I explained how disillusioned I'd become with the way that institutional religion was splitting the community and how big a gap it was opening up between what I considered true Christian values and how people were being asked to behave towards each other she said, 'You're just making excuses, Roseanne. You're using other people's interpretations as your excuse to opt out.' We had to agree to disagree at the time — though in later life I came to realise how true her words had been.

Another girl I became very friendly with when at university was also a Peterhead girl. She was a few years older than me. She had started university later because at the time of completing her Highers she was in the Close Brethren and at that time university wasn't permitted. Instead, she had to work in Peterhead for a few years until the religious edicts had become sufficiently liberal to allow women to go to university. She was, and still is, a very bright and able girl, one whom I considered myself to be very fortunate to make close friends with, then and for years to come.

My memory at that time was that it was only when Jim Taylor was exposed as a charlatan that she and girls like her could finally attend university. This simply confirmed for me, in my early twenties, that I could no longer relate to institutionalised religion. I'd enjoyed the services and the music and the togetherness of my childhood Sundays and also getting to understand the bible and its principles more fully, but I felt that formal religion could no longer play a part in my adult life. I felt that I had seen and experienced too much religious hypocrisy in my teenage years and early twenties. In the end it was doing my head in, so I felt that I simply had to walk away from the institutionalised religious scene at that time. But this didn't mean that I didn't consider myself to believe and do my best to uphold Christian principles and to attempt to live by these in my own day-to-day life. Quite the opposite.

Roseanne Fitzpatrick born 1955, interviewed 2011: Peterhead

Amidst God's nature

I'm optimistic about the future. That, I suppose, is largely due to my Christian faith: it gives me a progressive framework which I find I can fit my life into. It makes me feel that I'm going on a journey, that we are all tending towards a better place. The family had a pew at Maryculter Church, but nowadays we go to a charismatic, non-

denominational church in Aberdeen, one which, unlike so many of the old established churches, is full of young life and vibrant energy. I know it was a sadness to my father, to think that the latest generation of Irvine-Fortescues were no longer filling the old box pews at the local church, but I feel we have to go to the place which will nourish our faith.

I think that living here on the estate has supported my faith. Being outside, amidst God's nature, among the birds, the trees and the butterflies – that and working with the good earth, according to the basic rhythms of birth, growth and dying, well,

that daily experience is bound to bring me into a deeper harmony with God, bound to refresh the spirit. I also believe that my faith has guided my relationships with the folk around me. I was brought up to be always approachable, to welcome everyone into my life, from whatever background, and the realisation that we are all simply passing through this life, all of us, has deepened that.

'The good earth.'
The parklands at Kingcausie House, autumnal scenes.

Henry Irvine-Fortescue born 1958, interviewed 2010: Kingcausie House

The new ministers

I know that I have become something of a rarity among my generation – someone who still goes to the church and takes an active part in it. It no longer has the place in the community it used to have. When I was not long married, we met this pair of GPs from Inverurie and got talking about the decline in the significance of the church. What they said was striking: in their experience the doctor had now come to take on the pastoral role in people's lives that had once belonged to the minister. The minister might still go his rounds and call on people, but this had come to be seen as a social visit; it was the doctor that they would take their personal troubles to and seek guidance from. My own feelings about this can be summed up in one sentence: the church hasn't succeeded in involving itself in contemporary life and in people's most intimate concerns. It no longer carries much relevance beyond the purely ritualistic. Sunday has come to be just about the busiest day of the week – shopping, DIY, sporting events, entertainment, runs in the car – and no room for the church. It's become crowded out by the busyness of modern living.

Fiona Squires, born 1962, interviewed 2007: Newtonhill

Not a pulpit but the people

We lived on a farm just on the edge of the city, out at Bucksburn. Looking back, I appreciate this upbringing, hard though it seemed at the time. As a family we were always at work, outdoors and in the midst of the round of birth, life, sickness and death. Our early lives were firmly rooted in the basics of life.

But I never considered farming as my career. I wanted to work with people rather than animals. My own vocation came on me gradually; I never had any sudden Damascus moment of blinding revelation. We were always a church-going family, though Dad wasn't always keen to attend. He would welcome any excuse to get out of it and would find something more pressing to see to on the farm. I must admit that quite often I was happy enough to offer him my practical support. But our local church was Newhills, which had a dynamic minister, Norman McIvor. He was particularly strong on youth involvement and had gathered a striking bunch of helpers in that field. I was drawn to them and gradually got more and more involved.

Then, when I was 16, Dad was invited to become an elder and that brought him back into a fuller engagement with the church. His revival of faith pushed me along, too. I was working on a project and the issue of how you know you are a true Christian came up. The leader said, 'Well, do you believe that Christ died to save you? Yes? Then you are a Christian.' I listened and found myself thinking, 'Well, that's what I believe – so yes, I am a Christian'.

Norman McIvor had the inspiring idea that the church in his parish should work through teams of people, rather than just look to the minister to take the lead in everything. We had various socially directed projects, both in inner city Aberdeen and

Ready for school and the life ahead.
Tony Stephen at the family farm, Bucksburn, mid 1970s.

further afield. A group of us went over to California and worked in the poorer Hispanic neighbourhoods: building, painting, fitting out schools and orphanages.

So my Christianity has never been a remote or ethereal affair; to me it's an active faith, one that involves people and has a vigorous social dimension. It was while I was at the university that I finally realised that what I wanted to do with my life was to live as a committed Christian and to devote myself to the church's youth work. I applied to the Church of Scotland and was appointed to the position of youth leader here in Banchory, 16 years ago.

It was at university that my great passion for music and for making music also found an outlet. There had always been a great deal of music in our family home. I met up with some guys who were forming a group and had a gap for bass guitar, so I got hold of an instrument and went along to their practices. That's where I actually learned to play – by being a member of a band and having to. I was with them for a couple of years and then they broke up. Four of us went on to form a new group – the Dawntreaders – after the C.S. Lewis book.

This was a wonderful time, making up our own material, touring, playing to enthusiastic live audiences. Our aim was to produce harmonious, melodic music, but with something of the power and drive of rock, too. We like to think we created our own mix, had our own identity. Our stuff had a serious social concern, but the priority was always making good music. Our involvement was with the themes of relationships, of loss and love and justice. We had no pretensions towards changing the world.

Of course, the music scene of the time did associate itself with a certain lifestyle. We played clubs, went down to Glasgow, London, even toured in Europe and the USA. On the road there are always going to be a certain number of girl followers and the opportunity to become mixed up in a pretty free series of relationships. There are also drugs and plenty of alcohol. But I stayed apart from all that as much as I could. Yes, there were some around me who did indulge, but they respected my position. I took care never to be judgemental. My Christianity is based on people, not hard and fast rules about behaviour.

Music, of course, continues to be a part of what I do here in Banchory. But the work stretches out into all corners of life. I've been fortunate to work with people who have been ready to live out what they believe and to see that Christianity is an active force that is there for the whole week and not just for their Sunday best. As the youth worker, I've been able to tap into the energies and the idealism of some wonderful young people here in Banchory. My aim is not a big

Bass guitarist in action. Tony in his Dawntreaders years, 1990s.

The Dawntreaders. Tony is far right with, from left, Darren Alexander, Daniel Hawthorn, John Martin.

Sunday evening with the 'Cutting Edge Bible Study Group', Banchory West.

My Christianity is one that finds its meaning through action, out among people.

conversion but, rather, to encourage people to come to understand the Christian story through contact with those who are inspired by their faith to go out and help others.

I know that Banchory might be thought of as a rather well-off little commuter town, but there are still pockets of actual poverty and need and all the more wanting because they are in danger of being covered over by the prevailing affluence. And my experience is that human beings, wherever and whatever they are, have yearnings and needs quite regardless of the money in the bank or the car in the drive. Banchory is certainly not immune to the difficulties that are caused by family break up, by terminal illness, by fractured and lonely lives. My job is to seek these out and to try to bring practical help.

I've never seen my role as going round banging on people's doors with my bible. My Christianity is one that finds its meaning through action, out among people. Because of my background, I've managed to get young people involved in projects that bring practical assistance. Do something like that and the spiritual stuff will naturally grow from it. People often remark, 'Oh, it must be so hard trying to work with young folk these days. They just want to go their own way all the time'. Actually, I find it quite straightforward. It's the easiest thing in the world to interest people in the story of Jesus – it's the greatest story ever told, one with an immediate appeal. My purpose is to show that it is more than just a story.

The difficulty that most young people have is when they try to respond to the excitement of the Christian message by going along to a church and then find that all they are expected to do is to sit there and listen respectfully to what they are told from the pulpit. Jesus was a revolutionary, one who demands a real and active response. To follow him is to go out into the world and to change it for the better. So let's get these young people to take their energies out into, say, Tillydrone and sweep the streets and paint the walls and fetch the medicines. Get young people actually involved in working together, then they will come into contact with real role models they can follow and believe in.

This is why I'm not pessimistic about the future of the Church. I am fully aware that church attendances have been steeply falling over the last half century. But I would draw a clear distinction between the church as a physical institution and as a spiritual force at work within the wider world. If God is true and made real through personal relationships and community action, then we can remain confident that the Church in that sense will always prosper.

I don't mount the pulpit, because that would be to erect a barrier. Nor do I wear a dog collar or put on robes. When I was the youth leader I didn't find such a uniform helpful – and now I am minister I want to maintain that sense of openness and connection. When I was called to the full charge I made it clear that I had never seen myself as the traditional Church of Scotland minister who would have to be all things to all men. I would be looking to the members to work with me in offering the wider community a Christian witness. The last thing I want is to be thought of as a Sunday morning performer in robes and pulpit, or as the man in black going on endless rounds of ringing doorbells and sipping cups of tea in all the houses of the parish.

I see myself as an enabler rather than a centre stage performer – and, yes, that goes for my approach to the ministry as a whole.

Tony Stephen born 1969, interviewed 2012: Banchory

Explaining his position. Tony in discussion, 2012.

Sometimes I don't strike people as a minister

I had been brought up both in the church and with music sounding in my ears. For me, the two quickly became entwined. My father was an elder and I went to Sunday school. From an early age both my sister and I were sent to learn the piano at Miss Allan's, who was the church organist.

I disliked the exams you were expected to take for the grades and began to agitate to give up the whole thing. But Miss Allan's response was to put me on to *Jimmy Shand's Book of Waltzes* – and there were seven of them, 'Volume 1-7'. I think I almost preferred the Trinity College of Music pieces to that. But I persevered and I'm very glad I did. In some ways you could say that if it hadn't been for those piano lessons I wouldn't be in the position I am today. Miss Allan began to find the church organ duties too much and so she introduced me to them. My participation in the church services gradually led to other steps – taking prayers, helping out with services, and so the decision to train for the ministry.

Of course, there was far more to my vocation than the music. Mortlach church is a very beautiful building; I drank in all of that and learned about its history. The

Attending to parish business – or is it at a game of Solitaire?

> My task is to help others to discover their own values, perhaps by engaging them with life's most urgent questions.

atmosphere of the church spoke to me and enveloped me. That was one side; on the other I later worked with people and acted as a social worker and developed a deep interest in them and their problems.

As a young organist, I was surrounded by the liturgy and grew to appreciate its form and language. I also listened to the weekly sermons and found myself caught up in the questions they raised. I came to enjoy the challenge they represented, the impulse to dissect these nascent texts and to answer the question of why they still speak to us today – or do they really speak to us now? I learned never to take anything at face value, but to explore it, to get right down to its very depths of meaning. Do that and you will usually be rewarded by finding something that corresponds to our daily life, a message to stir the spirit and to refresh the soul.

In my opinion, there is nothing more dangerous to religious belief than the hard fundamental line, that they have all the answers and that the rest of humankind must be brought to follow it. The vital thing is to be open and ready to explore. The Church's texts might be ancient, but there is much to discover in them. I love to find out as much as I can of the history of faith and to grapple with issues of theology, to seek out fresh messages which help people to confront the difficult questions that assail their lives, to come to terms with their pain and to assuage their grief. My task as a minister is to leave people with questions rather than an easy answer, to give them the room and the stimulus to come, as I have, to make their own response. I have a suspicion of those who claim to have the sole solution to life's confusions, who tell the rest of us that they already are in possession of the one and only truth.

I believe very strongly in the pastoral side of my work and that this cannot be divorced from my preaching from the pulpit. I spend a lot of my time visiting, in getting to know people and understanding their needs. When I came here, to Kilry, the congregation averaged at about 20/30; now, after six months, it's up to over 80 – and I know that among them will be a proportion who found faith hard, who might even be agnostic or atheist, but they are welcome to share in the Church's quest. The Church offers worship, but also an opportunity to come together as a social act, to enjoy fellowship and also to feed the mind as well as refresh the spirit. Theology, philosophy, liturgy, the music, the richness of the

Ian Murray with two of his other enthusiasms: Lucy the dog taking a corner in a 1914 Stutz car.

words, all these join together in making for an experience that is different from the rest of
the week and can send the individual back into those other six days in a spirit of
refreshment. I am aware that the Church today is faced by much criticism. In some
respects I would say I am one of those critics. I am at one with those who say that the
Church can be dogmatic, can be exclusive. Sometimes I do not strike people as a minster
at all, but there is a deep conviction in what I do. My faith is that my task is to help others
to discover their own values, perhaps by engaging them with life's most urgent questions.

I can remember that when the careers adviser came to the school and asked us all what
we thought we might be doing with our lives, my response was, 'I want to become a
minister of the church'. I was 13 and already knew; the fact that my reply elicited a burst
of laughter from the rest of the class and a look of bafflement on the adviser's face didn't
deter me.

Ian Murray born 1970, interviewed 2012: Dufftown

Uganda, not South Africa

I've grown up in a committed Christian environment. God directs and informs my
whole life. It was 2003 that I was baptised into a full membership of the Church. It
was the commitment I was ready to make and mine alone. All of us in the family
have been given that freedom, to choose or not to choose God.

You see, as a Baptist minister, my father believes that you can offer people God, you
can tell them about His truth, but you can't force it upon them. That has applied to other
areas of life too; it's been my choice whether to wear make-up, which I don't, or what
clothes to wear or not. If I don't have a short skirt, then that has been my choice.

The missionary year. Rachel Adams in Uganda, 2009.

It's been my choice whether to wear make-up, which I don't, or what clothes to wear. If I don't have a short skirt, then that has been my choice

At the water pump, Uganda 2009.

I study the bible daily. I constantly find myself coming across new insights, but it's my own daily experience which confirms what I find there. I'll give you an example. As part of the selection process for my missionary work I had to attend the selection weekend down in Birmingham. We had to meet each other for the first time in this strange room and I was so nervous that I could hardly speak to anyone. That night I prayed to God for confidence. The next morning when we gathered for breakfast at the table I spilt honey everywhere. Well, that broke the ice; after that we all started laughing and helping each other to tidy up the mess and we discovered that we were going to get on really well. Was God answering my prayer?

Originally I had set my thoughts on going to South Africa for my missionary placement. Everything I heard about in the weeks leading up to the selection weekend seemed to be pointing that way – the news on TV, photos and pieces in magazines, in the press. We were told to go away into the garden and pray for guidance, then return and enter our choice on to a form. I went straight to the box next to 'South Africa', but at that point I heard a voice saying, 'No, not South Africa'. I took up my pen, but found it wouldn't write. I prayed a bit more and tried to listen to God. I returned to 'South Africa'; I tried to get my pen going by scribbling with it at the side, but same result, 'No, not South Africa'. And then 'Uganda' popped out of the page; I'd hardly heard of the place, but there it was, standing out on the page as if it was in bold lettering. Now I found I could write, so 'Uganda' it became. I am sure that was God's will acting on me.

I'm very excited by the prospect. I've already done some missionary work in Romania and that was a very positive experience. It hasn't yet been decided where in the country I am to go, but I do know that my work will be teaching English as a second language and also being out on the streets. It will be my task to go out and encounter the poor and the homeless. I will build bridges of friendship and carry the message of God's love across the bridge to them. But it won't be for me to try to force my faith on to them; I do realise that I can't simply walk into another country and start telling its people what they should do. On the other hand, I have been called there, so my work with them, on the streets and in the hospitals too, must have some purpose. It is to offer God to them; whether He is accepted or rejected is for the people themselves to decide.

Rachel Adams born 1990, interviewed 2008: Kinneff

It doesn't stop me believing

I am a practising Christian. I know that congregations in many places are diminishing rapidly, but at Fetteresso we have a vigorous one. A real effort has been made to open up the church to the young. A new minister has encouraged modern music into the church and there's a good going youth group; there are mother-baby groups and fashion shows. The whole atmosphere is a welcoming, inclusive one.

I know that my position is a minority one and that it's now quite unusual for a secondary school pupil to be an active church member. Many of my acquaintances tell me that modern society has banished the whole idea of God. I suspect that a lot of young people are like that because they don't want simply to follow what the older generation has told them and want to think things out for themselves. We talk about it; often they find it frustrating that, although I am a down-to-earth person, I still have room for God in my outlook.

To some extent I can understand that hostility. In my own family, my maternal

> It's now quite unusual for a secondary school pupil to be an active church member.

grandfather was a Protestant and he married a Catholic. My granny was told by her priest that if she went ahead with a marriage to 'that man' she wouldn't be allowed into the church again. So I can understand it if people view the Church as divisive and authoritarian.

All I can say is that things are changing and what I have experienced is fellowship and support. When my friend Sam had his car accident, we formed a great prayer chain; those

A minority position? Altries Church, Maryculter. Opened 1844, abandoned 1935 and now a ruin.

Still part of the North-east scene. St Cyrus Church, 2012.

in the church got busy with phone calls, with comforting talk and all-night vigils. He was in a car driven by his father, who hit a patch of black ice. Sam's so tall that he fell into the space between himself and his father and broke discs in his neck. His spinal cord was intact, but he was paralysed from the neck downwards. Some of his feeling is coming back and he's now reached the stage where he can feed himself and is looking forward to the time when he will be able to transfer himself from his bed to the wheelchair. There is hope; my experience is that faith is a force that we can draw upon at times of great need; without it we'd have been in a very dark place.

For me science and God can co-exist. I'm fascinated by Physics, but that doesn't stop me believing in God.

Jenni Keenan born 1992, interviewed 2010: Stonehaven

ALL MANNER OF FOLK: Part 2

Huntly, at the heart of all Strathbogie affairs: the Post Office staff on Coronation Day, 1911.

POST OFFICE

MONEY ORDER SAVINGS BANK
PARCEL POST TELEGRAPH
INSURANCE AND ANNUITY &
REVENUE STAMP BUSINESS

The local historian: a lot to be proud of

'Huntly is still Huntly.' Patrick Scott on the streets of the town where he has lived all his life.

Sixty years ago, the centre of Huntly looked much as it does today. It's all around that changes have taken place. There's so much new housing and, of course, the supermarkets.

One great difference is the traffic. When I was a boy, you were more likely to see horses than cars. Many tradesmen did their business by horse and cart. One of the dairies had a huge chestnut coloured horse I was frightened of. It towered above me. Mr George Dow was the milkman and he delivered a pint of milk each morning to my great-grandmother who lived just across the road from us. She was in the habit of giving this great beast a softie each morning. If ever she wasn't waiting at the door, the horse would bash the door with its great head; once it took the knob into his mouth and yanked it right off. Another milkman was a bittie over fond of the drink and at the end of his round he'd sit back with the reins loosely dangling and let the horse have its head. It would then gallop, hell for leather through the streets, anxious to get home to its feed, and people would stand back, pressed against the walls to keep it out of the way of its flaying hooves.

There were lots of factories in those days: woollen mills, meal mills, an agricultural implement works, the Gordon Cleaning Company and a large laundry. They all had hooters which sounded a bit like the war-time air raid sirens. They sounded at eight a.m. when the work began, at lunch time and at six p.m. when the toil for the day ceased. As a wee boy, I would stand at the window sill, looking out at the great crowds of men and women hurrying home from the laundry and from Stephen's woollen mill.

On Market Day, I would often see flocks of sheep and herds of cattle being driven through the town, to or from the mart. Sometimes a neighbour would knock at the door and shout: 'Mrs Scott, Mrs Scott! There's a herd o coos comin doon the road!' Gates would then have to be firmly shut lest a coo get into your gairden. The long beech hedges in East Park Street suffered a great deal from the munching cattle. The man who lived opposite us was a great gardener and was always quick to get out his pail and shovel. Often a neighbour would knock at his door and announce, 'There's horse's dirt alang George Street'. Straight away, he'd be off on his bike to collect his latest prize, which was placed in a box strapped to his pillion.

An agricultural centre: local farm servants congregate in the Square on a Saturday afternoon, 1910.

There were lots of little shops, especially grocers and confectioners. We patronised Gauld's of Bogie Street, known as 'Gallies'. Old Mr Gauld would come to our house in his pony and trap to take my mother's order for the week and later that same day he would return and deliver it. He invariably gave my sister, brother and me a sweetie each. You could get most things you needed made or repaired locally – furniture, clothes, shoes, leather goods, clocks and so on.

There was some class distinction, which determined which part of town you lived in. Tradesmen and professional people tended to live in the 'New Feus' – in streets such as Richmond Road and Gladstone Road. Nevertheless, everyone seemed to get on well together. Lots of things went on in the town. The Golf Club was a municipal one; there was football, cricket, bowls and tennis. The town had a brass band, which played at the corner of the Square during the summer. There was a Dramatic Society and an Operatic Society, which each year put on a Gilbert & Sullivan production. All the kirks had good-going choirs. Huntly had a noted composer, Ronald Center, who came to our primary class to give us singing lessons.

So there was a lot to be proud of, growing up in Huntly in those days. We certainly knew we were a cut above Keith. We had a name for the citizens of that place – 'Keith cyards' – Keith tinks!

I've been a Huntly man all my life and have become immersed in its history. The changes since my boyhood have been no greater than in other places. But the feel of being in an agricultural centre has been lost to some extent. When the Gordon Highlanders were disbanded there was real dismay in the town; a monument to the regiment was put up just beside the Gordon Schools. We still think of ourselves as the capital of the Gordon Country. When I go about the streets I'm often stopped: 'Ah, the very man I'm looking for!' This is followed up by some question of local history – 'Is it true there was once a cigarette factory in Huntly?' or 'What was the name of woman who kept a laundry in Church Street?' Yes, Huntly is still Huntly!

Patrick Scott, born 1937, interviewed 2009: Huntly

Patrick Scott is the author of several works on aspects of Huntly history including A History of Strathbogie *and* A History of Huntly Cricket Club.

'A lot to be proud of.' The Huntly Volunteers fire off a feu-de-joie in the Square to mark Queen Victoria's Diamond Jubilee, 1897.

The farmer's daughter 1

Always a reader and a story teller, Sybil at Ellon Academy, 1952.

There were seven of us: five brothers and one other sister. I was born upstairs in the best bedroom. My mother's aunt lived with us; I'm told that while my birth was taking place, she sat in the kitchen, wiving away, and when the doctor arrived, she said, 'Weel, doctor, if it's anither loon, ye can jist stapp it back far it cam frae!'

In those days when the doctor made a home visit you had to pay him. When I was young I suffered a lot with my ears. I'd been to hospital for an operation, but that hadn't cured me. I was put into a room with an elderly lady beside me; there'd been no books to read and you got a visitor once in the week. When I got home, I insisted, 'I'm niver iver gaen intae the hospital again.'

Well, there I was one Saturday morning out in the yard, chopping away at the sticks, when I saw this car draw in about. I heard my mother calling: 'The doctor's come to see you'. He came up to me: 'What a good little girl to be chopping the sticks for your mummy. You must be getting a lot of dust in your throat from all that – let's take a look, shall we? Just open up your mouth and we'll see'.

The farming background: Sybil Copland as a baby with her parents, lodgers and other family members, 1941, at the family farm, Fornety.

A few days later, I came down one morning, all dressed for school, but my mother took my hand and told me, 'You're nae gaein to skeel the day'. She led me through to the dining room where I saw the table laid out with a clean white sheet – and that's where I got my tonsils removed, by Dr Gordon, on the table of the dining room at Fornety farm. I was given a dose of chloroform and that was that. When I came round, my first meal was ice cream and jelly; I soon forgave my mother and thought the whole experience not too bad – certainly better than a week in the hospital.

Another doctor who came to the house was Dr Martin. Again it was a Saturday and again I was chopping away at the sticks. I saw this lovely red car coming in and I knew immediately it must be Dr Martin. He parked and went into the house. Then I heard the turkeys getting excited. All I could see of the car was this crowd of turkeys screeching and gobbling all around it and digging into its bodywork. Now, Dr Martin took great pride in keeping his car as shiny as possible and what the turkeys could see when they looked at it was their own reflection staring back at them. So there they were, pecking away at these strange other turkeys; there must have been 50 of them, all over the car, its roof and its body, scratching and furiously pecking away at the deep red paintwork. When the doctor came out he just about had a fit. My mother was furious at

me for not chasing them away and saving the doctor's car. But I hated those turkeys, fierce gobbling excitable creatures that they were.

From an early age I was expected to play my part in the work of the house and the farm. I'd be out in the fields helping at the hairst. I had to drive the tractor. The hairst was always a bit of rush to get safely gathered in before the next rain. I can remember being out under the light of the harvest moon, deep into October.

On Fridays, if it was holidays, it was quite a ritual for me to go into Aberdeen for the mart with my mother, and then to call in at the Co-op at the bottom of St Machar Drive, where my mother would hand in her order. When the shopping was delivered, it was my job to put it all by, safely stored in all the right places. This could be quite an intricate task since my mother seemed to have little cupboards and corners all over the place. I'd be anxious to get the job over so I could get at the *Beano* and the *Dandy*. We had this long dark corridor off the kitchen and that's where the matches had to go, in a cupboard there. But this Friday I couldn't be bothered walking all the way into the corridor to stow the big box of Swan Vestas away, so I just threw it into the lobby to be properly seen to later. The throw was quite a distance and as the box landed there was an almighty bang and the stink of burning. I waited till it had all died down, then I opened the lid of the box, only to discover all the matches had been spent. There they were, lying inside, still neatly laid out in their tight little rows, but the match heads were all back and useless. I quietly closed the lid on them and put the box into the cupboard where I should have taken them in the first place. I never said a word to anyone about what had happened.

Picnic at Bennachie.
Like many farmers, Sybil's parents took in summer lodgers from the city. This group shows her parents at the front with baby brother George. The visitors include Dr Mair and sons.

Sybil's parents
married at the Buffet,
Ellon, 1920.
The best man is
Alex Cruickshank and
the bridesmaid
Nan Barrack.

It was the job of the maid, Lucy, to lay and to light the fire, so there came the inevitable day when she called out, 'Mrs Barrack, I'm needin a new box o matches'. My mother went to the cupboard and handed the new box over to Lucy. The next shout was, 'Mrs Barrack, this box ye've gien me, it's nae eese.' 'Nonsense, Lucy, it's a bran noo box. Here lat me see.' When my mother took a look, she found all the match heads black and spent. I never let on what the truth was; to Lucy and my mother, the box of spent new matches for ever remained a big mystery.

The work seemed to be always there; there was aye another task to see to. If my mother ever saw me beginning to be at a loose end she would tell me, 'Jist gae doon to yer granny's an help her'. So I'd pop down to the cottage and granny would tell me, 'Cam awa, quinie, an clean these silver speens,' or 'Gie these dishes a wash,' or some small job like that, just to keep me busy and satisfy my parents I wasn't being idle.

I remember the day sweeties came off the ration. There was this shop in Ellon, Alzapiedi's, which made their own ice cream. This was wonderful stuff and folk would

Those turkeys!
Sybil's mother
keeps them quiet
with some feed.

come from miles around to buy a slider or a cone there. Well, when the sweeties came off the ration our mother gave us a half-crown each as a reward for all the hard work we'd been doing about the farm. She wanted us to be able to go into Ellon and get something really fine for ourselves; a real treat after all those year of rationing.

When my brother and I got to the shop, what should we see but this great long queue, out onto the pavement. I was worried there couldn't possibly be enough left to spend my half-crown on. But my turn to be served came and the racks of sweetie jars on the shelf still held enough to make my purchase. But what to buy with all this money and this new freedom? I decided in the end to go for something which would last a long time, so I bought some Dolly Mixtures – I reckoned that if I ate one a day they would last me the rest of the month.

We'd go visiting at the weekend. You'd be in some relative's house, sitting down to this great spread of home bakes, thinking you might be getting a bit of leisure at last; but then after everyone had finished at the table, my mother would turn to me: 'Now jist you gie a han wi the clearin awa,' – no respite even then. But I never resented it. Everyone else in the house was always busy too; work, the never-ending work of the farm and the farmhouse, was just accepted as part of life. We all had to pitch in. That's what's wrong today – the young people haven't got enough to do, not useful things, that is.

Sybil Copland, *née* Barrack, born 1939, interviewed 2008: Foveran

The story-teller: writing from memory

Freedom! A first bike, 1950s.

The houses down at Fittie were, by today's standards, quite primitive. I remember taking my daughter back to show her the place her mother had come from and I can still see the look of horror pass over her face that her mother, her own mother, had come from such a – to her – old slum. 'But where was the bathroom?' 'Bathroom! We never had such a thing back then. We just made do with a wooden lean-to toilet round the back'. The look of horror became a shudder.

My daughter should think herself lucky that she never had to use the outside lavvy my granny kept out at her croft at Logie Coldstone. It was called 'The Hoosie' and it stood out among a ruckle o stanes, like a sentry box. You'd go in and squat over the hole and then use a sheet or two of the squares of old *People's Friends* my grandfather had carefully cut up and hung on a nail. You never lingered long in there.

My childhood could be summed up in one word: Freedom! We were allowed to go out and play all day long. Ballater was such a secure little place where everyone looked out for each other and where tradition seemed to dictate where you would go and the games you would play.

Each time of the year brought its own pleasures. In the spring you'd revel in the return of the light evenings and the chance to get outside after tea. But the summer was the great time. We loved Gala Week when you had the fancy dress parade and the circus might come to the village. In the late summer, you'd see the royals arriving at the station to be driven up to Balmoral and that's when the shops would be at their brightest, all tricked out with tartan, and selling souvenirs. On the day of the Braemar Games, we'd all gather on a patch of grass at the bottom of the village, and watch the steady stream of cars driving by to the Games: the Daimlers and Bentleys and all the other posh models.

The autumn was the time for getting out among the trees and picking their various fruits. We'd climb up for the cherries off the geans, always sour, but we prized them nevertheless. The chestnut trees were higher and you'd have to throw a stick up among the branches to get the conkers to fall to the ground and then there would be the scramble to get hold of a real bosker. Halloween meant a neep scooped out at the kitchen table. You'd carefully carve out a mouth, complete with

Where tradition determined affairs. Bridge Street, Ballater, in Edwardian times.

a jagged set of teeth, pop your candle in and then you'd be ready to go around the nearby houses and do your turn. For that you'd hope to get an apple or maybe a handful of wine gums or a penny or two. The following week was Bonfire Night with tattie soup and treacle scones.

Out at Logie Coldstone.
Granny and Granda Davidson, 1940s.

For my father, Christmas was just another day on which he had to go out to work, but for me it meant a stocking at the end of the bed and the chance to thrust my hand in and pull out a slide or a brooch or a tangerine. And there would be a present or two, all handmade by my father in his shed – a cairtie, a dolly's cot, a sledge. Hogmanay meant First Foots at the door, with a lump of coal and a bottle and the cry as you opened the door of 'May yer lum aye reek wi ither fowks' coal!' There would be songs around the fire and someone would produce a moothie to get us all going. Mother would prepare a hen and there'd be broth and clootie dumpling. In the evening it would be board games and cards around the fireside, the whole family joining in.

I loved my time at Banchory Academy. My favourite subject was English and I was fortunate to have a truly inspirational teacher in Miss Henderson. I fell in love with the novels of Hardy: to me his descriptions of the land and of the seasons were sheer poetry. Miss Henderson lent me her own copies. I'd write essays for her and put all my new found words into them. 'Look, Mary,' she'd say, 'this is fine, but you don't have to dress everything up in all these fancy big words. It's far more effective if you just write from the heart'. I had to learn I couldn't outdo Keats.

I came quite late into my writing. Up till my retirement I was busy bringing up the children, looking after the home, getting on with my teaching career. I once entered a short story competition run by Bisset's bookshop in Aberdeen and came second. I was invited to the prize giving and that's when I encountered Jessie Kesson, who was presenting the awards. She spoke in this deep smoker's voice and had a cigarette in her hand, constantly. She gave me this advice: 'Mary, your story was fine, but fitever you dae, dinna write aboot stuff ye dinna ken! Aye write aboot fit is close to you, nae fit ye hae to mak up.'

My first real piece was about that old toilet out at Logie Coldstone. I was trying to show the truth about the 'good old days'. I loved going to visit my granny, but I hated having to go out and shut myself up in that dark, stinky old shed. To me, it was the epitome of all that has thankfully gone. I called it 'The Hoosie'.

Over the years I would sit down and dip back into my memories and the words came. At school we hadn't been allowed to use Scots, but I find that I prefer to do my work in it. It helps me to reach deep down into my memories of those times. It's my mither tongue.

I found my pen had the power to make the old scenes and characters come alive for me in a way that seemed to sum up a past way of life. I would put the pieces away into a drawer and sometimes I'd take them out to read to the kids at school, but mostly I was doing it for my own satisfaction.

But then my husband died suddenly and I found I needed something to help fill the awful gap, so I decided to take my writing seriously. I got my pieces together and took them to Minto of Inverurie to get published. They were sold out within six months. That gave me a great boost. I seemed to have struck a chord with people. I then got a second volume together and that went well too.

I'm now trying to extend my range. The third book is just out and is based upon local legends, *Through the Mists of Time*. My current project is a historical novel, *Bovaglie's Bairn*.

I enjoy writing; it acts as a release. I usually get down to it when the dark evenings come in November and that's me for the next six months. The past is important to me because that is where my roots lie. I found that when I was teaching I was preoccupied with reports, with pre-plans, with assessment sheets; now that I am retired my brain has been able to clean itself out and all the memories have come flooding back. So that's what I write about: as Jessie Kesson said, the things I ken, my life, my memories, my roots.

Mary Munro, born 1941, interviewed 2008: Ballater

The author: Mary as depicted on the back of her books.

Mary Munro has written a series of individual reminiscence and short story books: Deeside Reets *(2004);* Tales in the Mither Tongue *(2005) and* Through the Mists of Time *(2010).*

The councillor: only in it for themselves?

My abiding love is angling. From the age of eight I started fishing in the local rivers and by the time I was in my teens I'd become a real devotee. My first rod was a simple bamboo cane, with an old reel and a worm hooked on to the end, and off I went down to the Urie. Then, for my 11th birthday, I got my first proper rod and I was away.

I'd never call myself a brilliant fisherman, just a reasonably competent one. A few-salmon-a-season angler, that's me. But catching fish isn't really the point of the game. Angling offers so much more than that: you're out in the fresh air, usually in beautiful surroundings in the midst of nature and able to follow the moods of the weather and the passage of the seasons. You get so much peace when you have a rod in your hand. You can wander the river banks all day long and nobody will question what you're up to. I love the peace of it all, the soothing solitude that it gives you. I've seen me get up at the back of five, just when the dawn's arriving and then, with a rod in my hand, I can find myself watching an otter playing with its young, or see the heron perched on a stone, like me watching for a catch. You're away in your own world; if ever I've got something on my mind, then an hour at the riverside will usually solve it.

In fact, it was through angling I got into the Council in the first place. I was a member of the Angling Association. In 1974, local government reorganisation had now led to the replacing of the old Inverurie Town Council by the district and regional tiers of administration. Angling in Inverurie had always been run locally and for the public under a royal charter granted by Mary Queen of Scots in 1558. We were worried this situation might change.

Well, one day I bumped into Danny Gordon, a retired doctor from Ellon and an old bridge player. 'Aye, aye, Raymond, 'I hanna seen you for a whilie, but I've heard plenty

The future Provost in short trousers: Raymond Bisset with his grandparents, early 1950s.

Landing a 19-pounder, river Don, 1988.

from you'. 'How's that?', I asked him. 'Well, there's all these bloody letters you keep writing to the press about the fishing in Inverurie. Look, if you really believe in your cause then why not stand for the Council and do something about it, instead of all these damn bletherings'.

I went home to Heather and told her about my encounter; she encouraged me to stand and so I did. We were just on the point of getting married and I spent the honeymoon tramping along the banks of the Don, followed by a couple of weeks around the doors of Inverurie, trying to get signatures for my campaign. Privately I thought I had a bit of a cheek expecting folk to support me for the council on what was just a single issue campaign. On the night of the vote counting I didn't even bother to attend and just went home to my bed. When I got up the next morning, it was to the shock of my life: I'd hauled in more votes than the other three candidates combined. I think I'd fought such an active campaign, going around, knocking on doors, that people had felt like giving me my chance. Besides, it was clear that the future of the town's fishing rights struck a chord with folk. They saw that we were trying to preserve something that was local for the people, that we were fighting for Inverurie's historical rights.

I began in Gordon District as an ordinary Independent member; in 1988 I became Deputy Provost and then, from 1992 to 1996, I was the Provost. Following the reorganisation of local government I became Convenor of Aberdeenshire Council and then I was Provost from 2003 to 2007.

You can't say I've had many dull moments during that time. It's amazing what people expect you to do for them. Not long after I'd been elected, I was in the Gordon Arms enjoying a quiet drink when this chap came up to me: 'Is your name Bisset? Are you a Cooncillor?' When I told him I was, he said, 'Weel, in that case, maybe you widna mind organizin ma wedding fer me'. I had to explain as gently as I could that wedding functions weren't really part of my remit.

Then, for a spell, I would be awakened by the phone ringing at four in the morning. My parents were getting old by this time, so I would hurry down to the ringing phone, heart in mouth, thinking something must have happened to them, but no, it would be this old lady telling me,

The Prince and the Provost: Raymond and Charles at Ballater Station, 2002.

'It's ma drains again!' I'd tell her that the repair of drains lay outside my area of responsibility, but she would insist on reporting the matter to me.

I also got a phone call from a man in Lossiemouth: 'I'm lookin fer a hoose nearer Aberdeen and I'd like you tae git me ane.' I explained that I didn't actually allocate

houses to individuals, but that I would do my best to look into the general situation. He wasn't even in my area and what I didn't know then was that his own Moray Council had given up on his case. Anyway, he pestered and pestered me, refusing all explanations. Then, one evening when I was returning to my home in Keith Hall, I found this car there and a whole family in it. It was my friend from Lossiemouth, intending to camp out on my front drive till I got him a house. When I went inside, Heather told me they had already been knocking at the door, demanding hot water and so on. There was a baby in the car. I phoned up the police and they told me they couldn't really do anything about it, not just for an overnight stay, but that they would come along and have a word. When I got up the next morning and looked out, I was relieved to see that they'd gone. But that wasn't quite the end of the matter: a couple of days later I went out to my car to discover that a big boulder had been put thought the windscreen. On another occasion, this chap from Woodside came into my monthly surgery and demanded I find him a house – 'If nat, ma mates'll come roon an sort ye oot'.

An interesting job, being a councillor. As well as the problems, you have a lot of superb experiences, too, and meet many good people. I've spent a week in Berlin with the Gordon Highlanders, I've dined with the Queen, sitting next to her, at Balmoral; I've had lunch with her at Haddo House and alongside Prince Charles at the Castle Hotel, Huntly. I attended the British Piping Championship, where I acted as its chieftain; there were over 100 bands in action that day and I had to stand on a dais for their march past. I've been introduced to Gorbachev and to Archbishop Desmond Tutu – an amazing little man, one who seemed to fill the whole room as soon as he came into it with his gigantic charisma.

But it's the ordinary humdrum work that fills out your life as a councillor. Much of what you do is distinctly unglamorous – answering and writing letters, getting on the phone to administrative departments, chasing up queries concerning planning matters, housing, recreation facilities, getting involved in campaigns to raise money for a dialysis unit, going round schools trying to explain how the new budget arrangements are meant to work, and so on. People from all sides come to you for advice and ask you to write

I would be awakened by the phone ringing at four in the morning. This old lady telling me, 'It's ma drains again!'

All in the day's work. Being interviewed by Grampian TV, at Gordon Highlanders bi-centenary celebrations, Inverurie, 1994.

letters on their behalf; sometimes you find yourself acting as a sort of lawyer – the difference being that they may charge £250, whereas we do it for nothing. But every now and then you'll get a letter, perhaps in spidery handwriting from some old body you've managed to help, saying 'Thank you,' – and then it all becomes worthwhile.

You have to accept that to many, their own particular problem becomes the centre of their world and that they expect you to react accordingly. I remember this elderly woman who happened to meet my wife in the street and immediately assailed her with, 'Wis Raymond tellin ye aboot ma winders?' She had earlier come to me because some putty had fallen out of her window and here she was, assuming that I would have rushed home and told Heather all about it as the hot news of the day.

It's hard work – and has become much more so since I started out. Back in the early Seventies, Inverurie was run by its own local council which met once a month. But nowadays it's more or less a full time job: when I was Provost I would spend 70 hours a week at it, be on the go till 10 at night. There's not only all the work you do for individual constituents, there's the various functions you have to attend as the Council's representative and the speeches you have to offer them. People see your photograph at some plush dinner and assume it's yet another junket, that our lives are one long round of wining and dining and getting paid handsome expenses out of the public purse. There's still the feeling around that what was good enough in the old days of leisurely local councillors, discussing highly specific matters to do with such and such a street's drains, or making arrangements for the annual gala and enjoying their own wee bit of status in the local community, should still hold good – at least in terms of what we receive in return. Look at all the moans about councillors' expenses: I know there might be some abuse, but what really underlines the criticism is the attitude that we should do it all for nothing, that we should be happy to dig into our own pockets, as well as our time, for the honour of representing the public.

Many people will tell you, 'Ach, they're just in it for themselves'. Actually they are right about that – but not in the way they think. The vast majority of councillors, of whatever political party or none, are in it for what they get out of it: except that it's not money; it's human satisfaction. And I've certainly enjoyed lots of that.

Raymond Bisset, born 1942, interviewed 2009: Keith Hall

The fiddler: taking up the torch

Farming and the fiddle, that's my background. To begin with, I assumed I would follow my father and be a farmer. I felt that the countryside out at Tarland was my natural home.

But he was inclined to put me off: 'Why wid ye be aa day up to yer knees in skitter?' He was more inclined to encourage me to go on with my music, to go to the college and really work at it. I wouldn't be where I am today without my parents' support.

The first competition win, Kirriemuir, 1981.

I did have a natural feel for the fiddle right from the start. You hear some performances and that's all they are, a performance. Everything might be technically in order, but there's nothing that tugs at the heartstrings. The emotion of the piece has to be in your blood. One moment you can be playing something – a jig – and everybody's up dancing or sitting with their feet tapping; the next you switch into a haunting air and bring tears to the eyes. It's magical, to realise your playing can create a whole feeling like that.

But you don't always hit it; it all sounds easy and natural, but you have to work at it. If I haven't been playing for even a couple of days then my muscles will start to tighten up and I can no longer play with quite the same mastery of feeling. Your shoulder, your arm, have to be kept really supple if you are to express the emotion freely. Folk will say, 'Ach, but surely you winna be needin tae practise sae muckle noo – it aa sounds sae easy fer you'. But it's the other way round: to get into that easy flow, you have to work really hard beforehand.

The first time the fiddle came into my consciousness was this way: my grandparents stayed nearby and me and my brother would often be down there. Sometimes we'd stay overnight, in the old box bedroom: 'the Glory Hole'. Under the bed were old boxes with things like books and postcards in them. I used to love raking through it all.

One of the treasures was an old fiddle case and, inside it, a fiddle. I'd get in the way of taking it out and putting it beneath my chin and going through the actions of playing it. I must have seen performers on the TV, because I seemed to know exactly what to do.

The fiddle had lain there for years. It had come into the family as a present from one of my granny's uncles to her when she was newly married. This uncle had kept a butcher's shop down in Angus and one night he'd been in a pub and came across this old man who was wanting to sell the fiddle to raise money for more drink. He got it for 10 shillings. It turned out to be a wonderful investment: the fiddle was made in Paris in 1893 and is a very fine instrument indeed.

Well, I began to show a real interest in granny's old fiddle. It had been lying there, forgotten for years. At the start of her marriage she'd been keen to have a fiddle in the house, even though she didn't play herself, because in those days folk would still be in the way of popping in for an evening and getting up some songs for themselves. But those

Making it look easy. Paul in his natural habitat, at a fiddle session in an Aberdeenshire pub.

Paul with Rhea Martin, daughter of Lewis Grassic Gibbon, at the annual Lewis Grassic Gibbon Dinner, Arbuthnott, 2012.

Not much changed since the days of his parents. Tarland, where Paul still plays regularly in the Aberdeenshire Arms at the head of the Square.

It is here in the North-east that the traditional Scottish fiddle music reached its highest pitch. It's rooted in the agricultural heritage of our region.

days were now in the past and the old instrument was lying there neglected. I went to granny: 'Granny, I'd like to learn to play the fiddle'. Her reply was, 'Weel, in that case ye'd better hae it then'.

I got lessons at the school from Andy Linklater. Then my parents encouraged me to join the Banchory Strathspey & Reel. I was nine years old and at first I found it all a bit scary. I started off with the basic exercises and techniques, in the classical tradition. But you'd also come across the odd Scottish melody and I would look forward to that. My parents kept me at it: practice, practice. They would insist on an hour's practice each night, though on Christmas day I was let off with half an hour.

I compiled a cassette which came out when I was 20. That was the taking-off point for me. I began to aim at being one of the best soloists. I got in the way of analysing my playing so as to get hold of what made it truly Scottish. It was a slow process, but I kept plodding away and gradually I found myself more and more at the forefront.

My Scots fiddle tutors were, first, Angus Shaw from Banchory and then Douglas Lawrence, who was the most acclaimed pupil of Hector MacAndrew, so I'm part of a tradition that goes right the way back to the father of Scottish fiddle music, Neil Gow.

I see myself as picking up the torch of a great tradition. There's no shortage of good players around but, unfortunately, there's plenty of bad traditional fiddle playing. Although most can play well enough, they've slipped into a homogenised style of what now passes for the traditional but which, in fact, is a synthetic matter of bits and pieces taken from all over. The repertoire might be Scottish, but what you get is a treatment that is full of hell-for-leather reels and flashy fiddling, filled out with fancy tricks. It might be entertaining, but it lacks substance. Traditional Scottish fiddle music has now become a part of show business.

What makes the situation even more crucial for me is that it is here in the North-east that the traditional Scottish fiddle music reached its highest pitch. It's rooted in the agricultural heritage of our region: all the little farm communities where people would gather to play and to listen. My fear is that the North-east style will become more and more standardised. I also fear that the conditions which gave rise to our distinctive styles are going. If you go along to Tarland School nowadays what you will hear the kids in the playground speaking is no longer the old Doric, but a more generalised kind of Scottish English. Not nearly so many of them have a farming background now.

But my attitude is that if you are worried that something precious is going to disappear then you'd better do something about it. I perform; I bring out recordings; I tutor; I give talks; I've brought out DVDs. In the past, the fiddle was rooted in the region's everyday life and no special effort was required to keep it going. But now it is and that is what I aim to do – to keep the wonderful old tradition of North-east fiddle music alive and well, into our own age.

Paul Anderson, born 1970, interviewed 2006: Tarland

Paul Anderson is a prolific researcher, composer and performer of traditional fiddle music. His work may be heard on a number of CDs and at numerous folk and arts events throughout the North-east.

The ex-prisoner: I've learned so much

I was sentenced at the Glasgow High Court to three years, of which I served 18 months. I was sent to Barlinnie, a notoriously hard prison. It was all a real eye-opener. I found myself among hard men from Glasgow who would get really violent about the Rangers–Celtic thing; they would hurl abuse at each other and all that was quite foreign to me. These were men who would smash you in just over a silly little dispute on the pool table. When I arrived, I was all suited and booted up, whereas everyone else was casual in jeans, so I got some stick for that. Then the first week was spent in a cell where there was no toilet and you had to slop out. The food was disgusting.

That first week was very tough, but then I got moved into another hall where the regime was much more relaxed and you got the chance to take courses and get involved in various activities. It was a different world: the place was squeaky clean

'**A notoriously hard place.**' Barlinnie Prison, Glasgow.

and that's the way you had to keep it – if you didn't, you got put back, simple as that. There was a pool table plus your own toilet and sink, TV and kettle in your cell.

Then I got chosen to take part in the Listener Scheme that was run by the Samaritans.

'It did get easier.'
Prisoner in his cell,
Barlinnie.

This had been set up in response to the suicide rates in prison. If you are feeling suicidal, the last person you want to approach is an officer; if you confide in a fellow prisoner there was the risk you would affect him, so the Listeners were set up as a confidential service where you could act as sympathetic stranger who operated in strict secrecy. You took on a lot of responsibility. Normally Barlinnie is very strict; to move around from one part to another would mean an officer escort, but as a 'stranger' you got a security pass to enable you to go to whoever needed your help. You'd hear about problems that made you look at your own life differently; some of the despair you met with made you realise that your own situation wasn't really so bad after all.

I was teamed up with a guy from Aberdeen and we worked well together. You got the respect of the officers; to begin with, they treated us as if we were just another bunch of hard men from Glasgow up to every trick in the book, but they quickly came to realise we were what you would call normal human beings. The Governor gave us his backing. My last three months were in an open prison, but I gave up the first week of that because the Samaritans invited us to attend a course at Stirling, where we had to make a presentation on the work we were doing. We were the first Barlinnie prisoners allowed to get leave to do that kind of thing.

I got other things out of my prison experience. I also met someone from Torphins and we became really good friends and still are to this day. At school I'd never read a book; in prison I got through more than 20. I went to educational classes on computer and film review; I did some five open learning courses on business management and human resources. You can't imagine what that kind of opportunity to get out of the routine means to you in that situation.

I got privileges; the prison authorities had obviously decided I would benefit from the development opportunities they could give me. I worked at cleaning the chapel, regarded as a really cushy, once a week job. But the minister took to me and asked me to help organise a Christmas reception for some of the other prisoners. This meant we had to take the tree into the chapel, in the dark, and help prepare juice and sandwiches. I remember moving through the prison with the tree and our special passes. Then, after the reception, we were allowed to take a couple of cans of juice back to our cells and that's a rare privilege because, normally, cans are banned from cells because of the way they can be made into sharp edges. But there we were in our cell, drinking juice and thinking this is the life!

How I ever got into all this is still a bit of a mystery to me. I was really stupid, I know. It was one of these situations where you get caught up in doing something for a friend and then a friend of a friend. I had this flat in Aberdeen and I agreed to let someone drop a package there for me to keep for someone else to pick up. Other people were arrested; it was this girl from Wolverhampton who was picked up. She knew nothing about Aberdeen, so the police took her around in their car to try and jog her memory. All the tenements and the flats looked alike to her, but then she spotted the sunflower I had in my window and that was that.

At school I'd never read a book; in prison I got through more than 20.

But when I was released, I was able to get my old job back immediately. My boss knew I was a good worker and that what had happened was out of character. I've moved on to other jobs since but I've never been without one. I've always been honest and upfront about my past. I would like to think that I've now put my experiences behind me, that I've learned a lot about myself and can go on to make a success of things.

Prisoner #70351, born 1970s, interviewed 2007; Aberdeenshire

'A kettle and a TV.'
Barlinnie cell room.

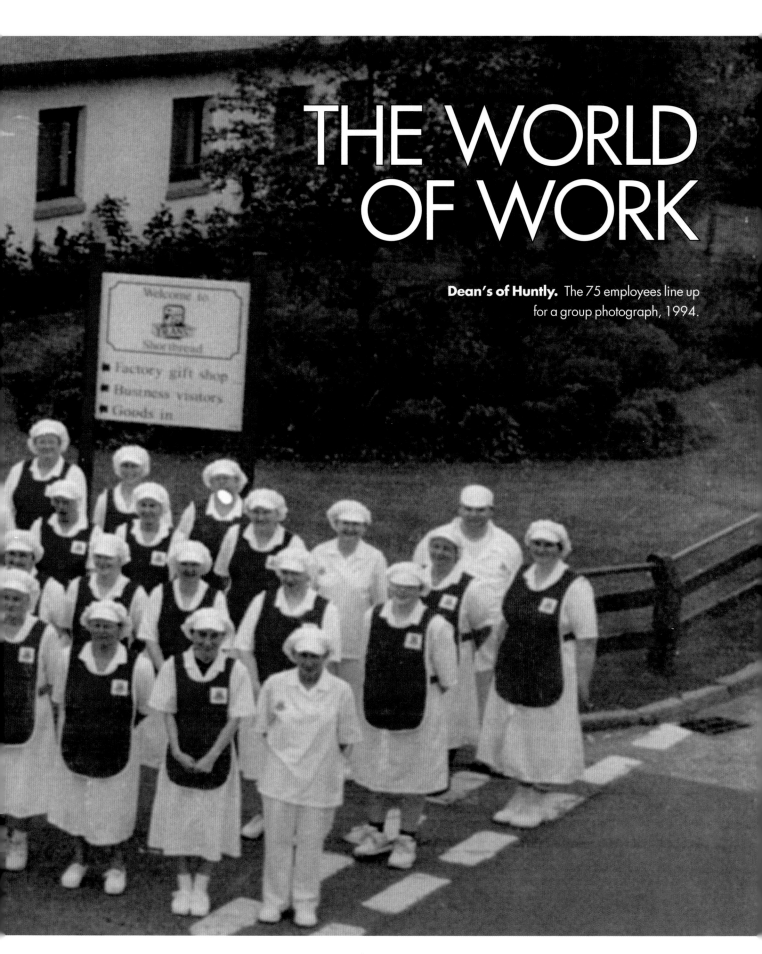

THE WORLD OF WORK

Dean's of Huntly. The 75 employees line up for a group photograph, 1994.

Welcome to
DEAN'S
Shortbread
■ Factory gift shop
■ Business visitors
■ Goods in

Inside the
van was just
like a shop
with clocks,
watches,
jewellery,
ladies' stuff
on display.

The travelling shop

My father acquired a grocer's shop in Alford. Over the years, he expanded it into the biggest retail business in the area. When he died at 87 in 1987, the paper carried the headline, 'Founder of North East Shopping Chain Dies'.

He started the first mobile drapery van in Aberdeenshire, in 1931. He had it fitted out with shelves and boxes which contained the more intimate items, such as ladies underwear. He started out with an old Model T Ford and then moved onto Chevrolets and Dodges. By the time the war came he had specially built shop-vans: for drapery, for groceries and furniture. By 1939 we had two grocery and two drapery vans, and a furniture removal van.

We prided ourselves on offering the community a complete service and on being a good employer. The staff were part of the family; some of them had come to us as boys. 'Wandering Willy' (Willie Murray) started at 14 and retired at 67. To have your own van and go out on the road was the ultimate. It was a responsible position, one which could only operate on the basis of complete trust.

He would get to know his area and its customers fully. The drapery vans would only visit a particular area every six months and would travel big distances. Others were doing the same, in their own line, from Alford. Back in the Fifties, there were 26 mobile vans doing their business between Alford and upper Strathdon. Few people had cars in those days and the van was a vital part of their daily lives and not only for the goods it brought. The regular van stopping at your farmyard acted as a social centre, bringing news and human contact. We prided ourselves on never letting the customer down. 'The customer is the most important person in the shop' – that was our motto.

We got a lot of our furniture from Lebus of London, in those days the largest furniture factory in the world. They'd send their catalogues up, we'd order and they would dispatch the stuff by rail or, later, pantechnicon. You'd send away your order on Monday and by Friday it would with you, up in Alford. You don't get

The start of it all.
Family, staff and vehicles line up outside their Alford store, 1929. A three-year-old James Gordon is centre stage while his father, J. A. Gordon, is third on his left.

service like that now.

We would go down to London every year, to the exhibitions. We were always looking for something that bit different. My father had great vision that way. He'd compare prices and go for value, but he also had an eye for what might catch on. At the back end of the war you could get a decent wardrobe, chest of drawers and dressing table for £10, the lot. You could furnish a whole house for £100. All good solid stuff.

We started to branch out with the mobile shops over to the west and up north. The big paper then was the *People's Journal*. We'd advertise in it and hire the hall in somewhere like Gairloch or Aultbea. Our routine was to load two furniture vans and a

drapery one and drive up. We'd be in the hall for three days and during that time the local crofters would come to see what we were about and place their orders. We had our own exhibition van: inside it was just like a shop with clocks, watches, jewellery, ladies' stuff on display. Another van would be fitted out to open up as a men's shop. We carried toys, too. On the West Coast you'd hear the men saying, 'You boys are costing us a lot of money, ye ken!'. They'd talk about the 'Gordon's bankie' they had to keep in the house for the stuff we sold each visit.

In my younger days I had a fancy to join a circus; the idea of being in a team, going from place to place, appealed to me. Well, I suppose the mobile vans became a bit like that. I loved being on the road, never going to bed in the same spot for more than a day or two at a time, always on the move. You'd spend the evening loading up; you had to get everything in its right place so you could lay your hand on it immediately the next day when you were hundreds of miles away. You'd leave early in the morning, in a convoy, arrive, bed down in our caravan and then spend the next morning preparing to open up in the afternoon. You knew the folk had been looking forward to you coming, that the women and the children would be coming in to inspect the latest clothes and all the furniture and to spend their pennies on a toy or two. You'd want to put on a bit of a show. It was like the circus coming to town. I recently met a gentleman in Poolewe who told me that he bought his very first toy and Dinky car from us and that they are still a prized possession.

But by the 1980s the business began to die. People were getting cars; the big warehouse shops and supermarkets became an attraction. Like everyone else, we had to wind up the van side of things. But we kept going back in Alford by adapting to the changing times. We'd always tried to keep ahead, on the lookout for any new lines that might work in Alford. I once went down to London and spotted these Doc Marten boots on sale. I came back: 'I've seen something that will really go in Alford!' We took a chance and bought in 200 pairs; they sold out in no time. Of course, you didn't always get it right; the saying, 'There's never been a good buyer who never made a bad buy,' holds true. But you have to be prepared to try something if you're going to keep the business moving.

James Gordon, born 1926, interviewed 2007: Alford

The Gordon's fleet, during its 1970s heyday. Willie Murray stands fourth left with K. Mackie next along. They both served over 50 years in the firm.

'**They would get to know their customers fully.'** K. Mackie with regular customer Mrs Cooper.

On guard: George Lawrie in his signalman's box, 1960s.

The Signalman

I started as a porter at Aboyne Station, then went over to the signal box at Lumphanan. The Deeside was a lovely line and it's a tragedy it was ever closed down, but I must admit there was a lot of overmanning. At Lumphanan there'd be a stationmaster, a clerk and two signalmen and all this for a very quiet station. You had some trade during the summer with the tourists and the day-trippers, but the winters would be very slow.

The freight traffic dried up when everything started being palletised and taken by road. Another thing that killed us was the working procedures. If a small window got cracked, an inspector would come out from Aberdeen to look at it, file his report and then a joiner would come out to measure, go back and come out again to make the repair. It was maybe a half-hour job, but it took three different days to sort it all out.

Most of my time was working for British Railways before the denationalisation came in. The pay wasn't great. But they looked after you; you got the uniform and you got free travel. We still have 16 passes a year to this day and can travel all over the country for free. Last month we were down in Bournemouth. Out of curiosity I popped into the station and asked how much the fare to Aberdeen would be. '£159.50 - each'!

We had to handle much more luggage on the trains in those days; nowadays most people see to their own, but then a lot of them would look for assistance. There'd be the ones who'd shout out, 'Porter, porter – my cases!' and then give you tuppence as a tip. The doctor, he was different. Whenever he had visitors coming off the train, he'd come to meet them and slip you a two-shilling coin. That's what I call a real gentleman.

In 1960 we suffered a great snowstorm. The minister was due to take the train down to Glasgow to make an important sermon. 'You and your railways', he complained. 'Well, there's one thing I noticed and that was you didn't come down to help shift the snow.' 'Oh, do you think a prayer would have helped?' 'No – but a shovel might.'

At a small country station the signalman was a Jack-of-all-trades really. I loved to look after the station garden; we took great pride in making it the very best on the line. We grew larkspur, lupins, French marigolds, all sorts, and from seed, too; I

Better than a prayer: George gets to work with shovel to clear the way, February 1960.

got great satisfaction from digging over the beds and getting the seeds in and then watching them come up. I'd spend hours raking the platforms and then I'd go up on to the bridge to the other platform and look down on it all and see not a mark or a weed and both platforms stretching out so smooth and so bonny. That's what gave me great pleasure: everything in its place and nothing out of it.

I enjoyed my work. When I can see that everything is just so, all fitting together, well, that gives me so much satisfaction. Things like that still do: I love to see a table all set out, with the knives, the forks and the spoon all in their proper position. It's the railwayman in me, I suppose.

They thought that the Deeside line would be saved from the cuts because of its royalty connection, but I knew it had to go. Too little business, too many employed to see to it. People talked about the tourists and it's true that Deeside is a lovely area and the scenery is second to none. On a summer day when the sun is out and the water is sparkling then plenty of folk would like to take the trip along the line, but there were plenty other days, when it would be dreich and grey with the trees dripping and the ferns hanging down and then nothing could be more depressing, I can tell you.

George Lawrie, born 1931, interviewed 2008: Lumphanan

'Scenery second to none.' Lumphanan Station, 1920s.

George with his brother and sister.

The Distillery Worker

I n 1955 I got married and four years later decided I had to leave farm work to get a job at the Glenlivet Distillery, where I worked for 17 years. The trade was expanding then and extra staff was being taken on, at better rates of pay than was possible as a farm worker.

I started off as a tunroom man and was there for four years. Then, for tuppence an hour extra pay, I became a stillman. Then for a further tuppence an hour I progressed to mashman, later becoming assistant brewer. Genlivet Distillers acquired Longmorn

A traditional craft.

The workforce at Aberlour Distillery in proud pose, 1921. Photograph supplied by Iris Wilson *(see 'Family')*; her grandfather, William Taylor, is second right, back row.

distillery and I moved there as assistant manager in 1976.

I think the secret of this area's eminence in whisky must be the fine soft water that comes off the hills. But much of the final quality is difficult to account for in a scientific sense. That was particularly true when I began back in '59. So much depended on the individual and here the handed down knowledge is vital to the process.

It's a craft. The workers didn't serve an apprenticeship or study for a diploma; they entered the distillery work, as young as 18, and worked their way up by observing and absorbing the way things were done until it became instinctive. When I started, the process had changed hardly at all since the 19th century; it was something you took in as a tradition, a way of life almost.

Regularly, we took production results and this was measured as the amount of gallons you could extract from each bushel of malt; if we managed to achieve 2.80 then that was reckoned a big production. But that's back in the Sixties and Seventies. Whisky production has changed hugely with the use of technology. They now get 3.00 plus gallons, as a matter of course. It's more of a factory style operation now, less of the old artistry. It's not so much how well the team has performed, as whether the machinery has been kept running efficiently. The gain is we now have a more stable product, but I can't help thinking something of the old character and variety has gone. But maybe I would say that – I'm getting old.

We had great pride in our distillery, not just the end product. but the way we went about our business. But I must admit that my greatest love was always the farm. Nothing could beat going into the byre on a winter's night and hearing the cows snuffling into their straw under the glow of the Tilley lamp and then, when they saw you, lifting up their heads in recognition that it was you and no one else. The whisky was fine but at the end of the day it's a product; the cattle were living beings that knew you and responded to you.

John Goodbrand, born 1932, interviewed 2008: Glenlivet and Longmorn

The Machine Operator

In the Broch in those days it was either the fish or a job at Consolidated Pneumatic – the Toolies – so when I became 16 went to see Mr Sherrin, one of the bosses. He told me, 'I've a jobbie fer sam young laddie, but I reckon you micht be ower sma for it'. 'Nae worries,' I said, 'I micht be wee, but I'm strang.' He took me into a store and showed me all the shelves with pieces of equipment laid out on them. 'Can you lift stuff aff thae shulves?' I showed him I could, so I got the job.

I liked the store, but I knew I'd never get anywhere there, so I took up an apprenticeship at the machines. The Toolies made compressors and it was my job as an apprentice to get to know all about their parts. The first day, I was put on a machine and told by the boss that I'd be expected to learn how to put up all the different machines on the floor. There were 20 of them; the men on the machines would show me what to do. I learned 19 of them, but the 20th was difficult because the man on it had been there for years and didn't fancy showing some new kid all his secrets. He wouldn't let me watch him; whenever he was about to set up his machine he'd send me off to get his fags. But then the labourer for that machine told me that he'd go and get the fags while I could hide and watch what happened. I managed it; the setter never suspected anything. When the boss came to see how I could set up the machine, he just smiled to himself. I succeeded; that wiped the smile off his face; he knew he was no longer the only one who could do it. And then the boss turned to him and congratulated him on being such a good teacher.

Alex Rennie, born 1934, interviewed 2008: Fraserburgh

A master of his work. Alex Rennie at his lathe.

The man on the 20th machine had been there for years and didn't fancy showing some new kid all his secrets.

Blowing his own trumpet. Alex at the centre of the 1953 CPT Christmas party.

A one-man band. In later life Alex has become a noted entertainer. This is the sleeve of one of his CD compilations.

You had to wear a white shirt, but everything else about the uniform was black. No trousers then — and how I could have done with some on those winter runs!

The bus conductress

I can still remember my badge number: 'LL1611'. You had to wear a white shirt, but everything else about the uniform was black: black skirt, black hat, black tie, black shoes, black jacket. No trousers then – and how I could have done with some on those winter runs!

I thoroughly enjoyed it. Everyone travelled by bus back then, because cars were only for the well off. The buses always seemed full, with folk chatting away and having a laugh with each other. Nowadays, they just seem to sit there in silence, lost in their own worlds, listening to their earphones or fiddling around with their mobiles.

Not all of the passengers were a pleasure, however. On the evening runs, some of them would come on with a good drink inside them and then they could get aggressive. I remember this regular who would get on at Aberdeen and then had to be let off at the Bridge of Muchalls. He was unsteady on his feet and we would have to get off and accompany him across the main road – and he always gave us a sixpence for our trouble. That wasn't so bad, but there was this other customer who was quite abusive. We'd tell him that he'd arrived at his stop and had to get off, even though it was still half a mile off – our little revenge!

But the majority were appreciative. Things were quite free and easy compared to all the rules and regulations now. If we were on the late Dundee return run we'd be going through Inverbervie at seven and we'd let the Bervie Chipper know we'd be wanting our order ready when we came back up, and there it would be, waiting and wrapped up for us at 11.45. There was one driver whose wife was keen on flower arranging and in the springtime he would stop the bus at this belt of trees just outside Laurencekirk and pick some sprigs of fresh green foliage to take back to her. The passengers just accepted this sort of delay – nobody thought of lodging a complaint back then.

On those long country runs, with just one or two passengers coming on at a stop, you had time to sit at the front and chat to the driver. I'd take my knitting bag on board and always had a jumper on the go.

The winters were harder then, but the motto was that the bus always had to get through. You'd pack a shovel and a couple of hessian sacks before you set off and if you got stuck you had to dig out a space under the wheels and hope the sacks would give a firm grip. But with the size of those wheels you often just had to wait for some farmer to come along with his tractor. Twice I was stuck overnight in the drifts – once on the Auchenblae run, the other time at the T-mast along the Slug. We didn't have any passengers on board – they'd seen the weather and decided to stay home, but the bus had to make the attempt. All we could do was sit it out while the lights got dimmer and dimmer and the heating weaker and weaker. The drivers always had a pack of cards handy, mostly to fill the gaps between runs at the depot, and we played two-handed games to while away the hours till we were rescued.

There was a limit of eight passengers permitted to stand, but often enough at busy periods we'd just ignore that and pack them all in like sardines. We didn't like to leave anyone standing at a country bus stop if we could possibly squeeze an extra body on

board. And we were quite obliging as to where people were taken on or set down. If someone stuck out his hand by the roadside then we'd pull up, stop or no stop.

One of the most memorable characters connected with the buses was this man Sandy. He was backward in some way and would spend all his days at the Stonehaven depot, watching the buses coming and going. Although I doubt whether he could read and write, he had a knack with figures and learned up all the times and registrations and had them off pat. Even the inspectors sometimes consulted him over a particular timing or vehicle and he always had the answer. It got to the stage where we'd say to him as we left on our runs, 'Sandy, will you make sure the kettle's on for when return?' – and he did, without fail.

Anne Stephen, born 1937, interviewed 2011: Stonehaven

Number 'LL1611': lining up with the rest of the Stonehaven bus depot crew, 1960s. Anne Stephen is second right.

The waitress

I left school on the Friday; a farmer was coming home from the mart in Aberdeen and came in past the house. He'd got my particulars from Greyfriars House on the list of school leavers and was looking for a servant. I'd never clapped eyes on him before – and there I was just turned 15, packed off to become a live-in servant, looking after a farm

Spotlessly turned out: Margaret Hay, Burnett Arms, Fifties.

house and three young children. I started work that very Sunday.

I just had to get on with it. I had to get up at seven each morning to mix the hens' meat and feed them. Then I had to make breakfast. There were stone floors to be scrubbed with cold water. Then I had to get the children ready for school. I was asked to do all the housework – no hoover, just duster and dustpan. It could be 11 at night before my work was done.

The children once broke three cups; I felt I had to replace them though it wasn't my fault. All this from the 30 shillings I got each week. Out of that I gave my mother £1 and then I had to spend four shillings weekly for butter from the farmer's wife. This left me six bob for myself. I got the Saturday afternoon and Sunday off every fortnight and a half day on the Wednesday. For a treat I'd go into Aberdeen on the bus and catch the shows at the Tivoli. You could get a ticket for the Gods for 1/6d; I remember watching Callum Kennedy and Johnny Victory on stage.

The job lasted one year. The farmer went broke and had to sell up. When the roup was held, my father came over and told me that he'd fixed up another post for me and that I'd be going to the Burnett Arms Hotel, Banchory. No consultation; I was simply told I had to go.

At the Burnett Arms I started off as a live-in housemaid. The hours were long but shorter than on the farm. I had to start at seven each morning, work till two and then start again in the evening, from seven till nine. My first task was to scrub the outside steps and then polish and hoover the entrance hall. All this had to be completed before the guests started to come down for breakfast; everything had to be nice and shining for

At the ready for the Masonic Lodge dinner. Margaret and sister Anne are in the team; the chef is Arthur Douglas.

them, always. My last task at night was to go round the bedrooms, turning down the beds and putting hot water bottles into them and then go downstairs again to make up their trays for the morning tea.

I had my own uniform and this consisted of a blue overall with a spotless white apron all around. You had to do your own washing and it was vital to keep it white and clean. For me it was an object of pride, to be smartly turned out and able to greet the guests

with a pleasant 'Good Morning'.

When the hotel had a big function on I would be asked to act as a waitress to help out. I mixed well with the clientele and so I was asked to become one of the full-time waitress team. You had to provide your own uniform and this was black dress, white cuffs, collar and apron, black stockings and black shoes. The aprons had to be changed fresh each day.

At a function the normal menu was starter, soup, sometimes a fish course, main course – often steak, beef or salmon – sweet, coffee and maybe biscuits and cheese to round things off. As well as waiting on table you would have help with the tidying up at the end. Weddings could be a nightmare with all that confetti to clean away.

The waitress duties depended on what table you had to serve. The top table would have the full silver service where the guests would first have their plates placed in front of them. Then the waitress would return with the main course laid out on a silver salver and she would have to serve each guest individually, using a spoon and fork. It was quite an art to balance the food safely, as the tray could be hot and heavy and often you had to use white cloths so as to save your arms from being burnt.

Margaret Hay, born 1939, interviewed 2011: Tillyfourie and Banchory

The wedding team.
From the left (back) Margaret and sister Anne; (front) housekeeper Miss Mathieson, Mrs Grant, sister Rosemary

The 'New' Vauxhall Victor.
1962 staff dance at the Royal Oak Hotel, Banff, of AW&H Davidson, Vauxhall agent. Bill and Aileen Allan are back row, third and fourth left.

The garage mechanic (male)

My first pay at the garage was £1.18 a week. That was as an apprentice, but even when I got married I was taking home less than £10 and that was in 1962. These days it's all about replacement parts, taking out units and slotting in new ones, but we were expected to repair and fine tune and tinker around. Now you can plug the car into the computer and it will tell you when everything is running properly, but we had to use a screw driver and our ears. Repairing and servicing cars back than was as much an art as a mechanical job, one that you had to develop a feel for.

You did this by following an experienced mechanic around and observing and listening. Discipline in the workplace was vital: if the foreman told you to jump you'd ask, 'And how high?' It was still the period of National Service and so the great majority of the men had been subjected to military discipline and had brought it back with them.

As an apprentice you had to serve your time and pick up all the dirtiest jobs. The worst I remember was seeing to a fish lorry that had broken down; it was a hot summer's day, the lorry was stinking to high heaven and I had to crawl underneath it with all that foul gunge dripping down into my face. Then there was the time a snow plough lorry broke down in the middle of the night and I had to go out to it the next day, dig my way through the piled up snow and get beneath it so as to fit a new prop shaft. There I was, fiddling about in the cold, surrounded by snow and worried that it was melting fast enough to lower the lorry down onto me and crush me to death.

But that's the sort of service you were expected to provide for our customers then. Vehicles were much less reliable and required much more attention than they do now.

Bill Allan, born 1940, interviewed 2011: Banff

The joiner and undertaker

My father came to Oldmeldrum in 1938 and set up a joinery business which I inherited. I never had to advertise my business. People just came to me, through hearsay; being a well-established local concern they trusted me and I could trust them.

It was my father who had built it up. He'd get his timber from John Fleming in Aberdeen. They were brilliant to us; when he was starting up and hadn't always got the ready cash, they would still supply the timber and tell him to pay when he could. That's how things were done then – trust and personal contact. I'd be in the office with my father and the reps would come along and I'd hear my father say, 'Sorry, Sandy, but I really can't give you the money right now,' and the reply would be, 'Don't worry – just give us a shout when you can'.

We didn't bombard customers with reminders: we'd have two big settling up dates – July and the year's end. We knew we could wait till then and not be let down. Nowadays it's different: impersonal, all done by computers and drawn up agreements. Often you find yourself doing business with people you can't put a face to, people that you've never met. In my day if there was a problem I'd sit down with the other person and sort something out between us – now it's letters and emails and secretaries on the phone.

It's not that people are less honest these days so much that they just don't deal with things on the old person-to-person basis. Once if somebody needed a job done he'd get

No job too small or too big. Loading the new bell tower which the Duguid firm prepared for Fyvie Castle, early 1990s.

The end of a long story. Norman Duguid takes a moment's thought on the final day roup of A. Duguid & Son, Oldmeldrum Joiners.

in touch with his local joiner – or plumber or builder or whatever – and discuss it with him; then he could leave it to you to do a satisfactory job. Now people get the *Yellow Pages* and phone up firms they know nothing about.

I'm retired and the business is now gone. I don't miss the joinery side of things, but I do the undertaking. There's a lot more to undertaking than simply putting on a dark suit and a serious face and parading alongside a coffin. It's a demanding role; you have to go to the family home and ring that doorbell knowing that when it opens you're going to be in the midst of a family who are struggling to come to terms with what has just happened to them. You have to take control, sit down and help them to see what has to be done.

My father passed on some good advice to me. 'If you want to survive in this business, just remember this: whether it's the funeral of a prince or a pauper, he aye belongs to somebody. Treat them with proper respect and you'll manage fine.' After all, you only get the one chance to make a proper job of a funeral; it's not like a door or a window when you can always go back and put it right.

I like to think that what I can bring to the situation is a human touch. Show them you are confident, that everything is going to be properly organised. Remember, you are going into their homes and talking with them about someone they've loved. The worst is when you have to deal with the death of a baby or of a young person who has been killed in a road accident, perhaps. You go in and you find all the generations there – the brothers and sisters, the parents, granny and grandad – in a state of shock and yet you've only got a day or two to do it all for them. That's hard.

Norman Duguid, born 1942, interviewed 2008: Oldmeldrum

The storeman

I left school as soon as I could. Two or three of the lads just above me had already left and they had jobs as message boys for local shops. I looked at them, saw the freedom they were getting and that they had money in their pockets, so I thought, 'that's a fine job!'. Now I know I should have stuck in at school, but at the time it seemed a good idea so I left and became a message boy for a local store.

I'd go round the customers on my bike, taking and delivering their orders. For many of them this was done on a daily basis; I'd be delivering butteries, butter, sugar, margarine, jam – the basics. In this way I came in contact with the wholesalers when I had to go there to replenish the shop's supplies. From the start I was fascinated by the kind of work a wholesale depot did. You'd go in and gaze up at these rows and rows of groceries; all the big names were represented – Heinz, Bachelors, Cross & Blackwell. You'd see lorries coming in from all parts with new supplies and you really felt you were in the thick of things.

In 1962 I got the post of storeman at Hutcheon's of Turriff, Ltd. I found it quite fascinating, all these men of the road riding the highways in their great lorries, going to

Sorting it all out.
The 25-year-old Alan Riddell, now at Caribonum, Turriff, where he went to work after his spell at W. D. Hutcheon.

the ends of the country to bring back all the goods of the day. I developed an interest in their lorries. You'd see wonderful vehicles, ranging from some ex-Army conversion jobs to the majestic eight-wheel Major Mk Vs. We had a guy who would sit at a table as the goods went out and he'd read out the orders: 'Six cases of beans. Ten packs of sugar. Five of peas,' and so on. Then HTL would deliver to all sorts of shops, large and small, throughout the North-east: you'd see our lorries setting off on a run that might take them to Dufftown, Huntly or down to Ellon, Methlick and Mintlaw. A wonderful spread of names and places.

A good life, both at work and away. Alan, third right, enjoying the table at Butlin's, Ayr.

In my summer holidays I'd go into the cab of one of the older drivers and join him on a trip, just to see the road and get a taste of these places whose names I'd seen on the sides of the lorries. I loved to ride the cabs with those men who knew all the tricks of the road. Sitting up there high in the cab you felt 'fair Erchie', a real king of the road. You got all the stories too. There was this guy who was to join the Merchant Navy and had to report to the pool in London. He went down on one of the lorries; the driver took him right into the city and then pulled up at a bus-stop, opened the cab door and told him, 'Here y'are then – Lunnen!' This to a young lad who'd never been out of Turriff before. When the driver was asked about it later, he remarked, 'Anly wye te larn'.

'We'll nae mak Turra the nicht' – but all part of Alan's romance of the road.

Once I joined a summer run down to Carlisle. It was just an ordinary trip, but I

> The drivers would swap stories of battling over Beattock Summit in the snow and how they would meet up in the Jungle Café.

remember sitting there with all the men in the big transport café on the edge of the town and watching all the lorries coming and going and seeing all the various places they'd come from and thinking, 'This is the life!'. The drivers had an annual dinner dance at the Royal Oak in Turriff and they would sit there with their drinks, arguing the pros and cons of the various lorries and roads. They would swap stories of battling over Beattock Summit in the snow and how they would meet up in the Jungle Café run by Mrs Honeybell on the old Shap road. Magic names, great adventures!

The firm was taken over by J.R. Rank. Joseph Rank himself came up to Turriff in his large chauffeur-driven Rolls, brandishing a big cigar, pointed at HTL and said, 'Yes, I'll buy that one,' and then floated his way up to the board room to conclude the deal. There was no immediate effect on us, but after a while the organisation changed. Other firms took over some of our work and eventually the whole operation was shunted off to Dundee and that was that.

Alan Riddell, born 1946, interviewed 2008: Turriff

The printer

I joined the *Montrose Review* in 1965. Newspapers had to run to an absolutely strict time table. You'd reckon on 1,300 copies an hour, so to get through it all the machine was going backwards and forwards, 'bouff, bouff!' hour after an hour.

Until computerisation came in, the printing process was in essence the one that had been in use since Caxton back in the Middle Ages. It was very much a hands-on, intensive labour business. When a run was on there was always an atmosphere in the works: people would get het up and shout and bicker with each other; the work was that intense. The process was full of possible pitfalls and yet we always had to produce the paper on time. Upstairs with three linotypes going all the time, 'thump, thump, thump', and three compositors, you'd hear constant shouts and arguments. Then the editor might suddenly appear and demand a last minute change. I've seen it happen that a big story had broken – a fire or a bad accident – and he'd come running in with: 'Get that story off the front page – we're going with this one now!' – and there could be as many as 1,000 copies already produced. Then you'd hear the moans and the curses. We were constantly battling the clock.

The real pressure would burst in on us on a Wednesday afternoon. That's when the newsagents would send in their boys to pick up their copies, hot off the press. The official deadline was supposed to be five o'clock, but from about four-thirty onwards you'd see them edging in, hoping to be the first off the block. And we'd have hundreds of fresh newspapers piling up all about us as they came pouring off the rotary presses.

Nowadays the *Review* and all the other papers are no longer printed in Montrose. The work was shifted to Forfar, then to Edinburgh and now it's all done in Sunderland. With computers and mobile phones it's no longer necessary to have the stuff printed near to

The best of printers in the best of hands. John and his beloved Heidelburg, 1987.

where the reporters are; they can simply file their story and send it off down the line, electronically. The old works closed on 14 January 2000. One Wednesday afternoon shortly afterwards I asked if I could go and have a last look. Rather grudgingly, they let me in and I wandered about. Wednesday afternoons had been our very busiest time, and the works would have been full of noise and frantic activity – and here it was completely still. The big presses that would have thumping and whirling around were standing idle; it was an eerie, eerie sight; a ghost works.

The machine I felt most for was the Heidelberg. This was German built, a really smooth and efficient printer that we bought new in 1960. Now it was to be broken up for scrap. 'You can't do that!', I protested and so got permission to find a home for it. In the end, the National Museum of Scotland in Edinburgh agreed to take it. I was given the task of supervising its departure. It was sad to see it go, but I had saved the *Montrose Review* Heidelberg – a machine which I knew inside out and in a way that nobody else could.

The work was demanding, but I was proud of my craft. I'd go into a newsagent and see folk buying their latest copy of the *Review* and catch them looking at the front page, all nicely set out and cleanly printed off, and I'd think to myself, 'I printed that'.

John Smith, born 1947, interviewed 2012: Montrose

62 awards 25.
Bill Tyrie, former foreman at the *Montrose Review* Press and employee there 1927–89, presents John Smith with a watch to mark his quarter of a century at the company. John went on the complete 33 years there.

The hairdresser

My father had his own business in Aberdeen: 'Jon, Hairdresser and Parfumeur'. He also had salon in Stonehaven. But in 1961 he dropped dead with a heart attack, leaving me and my mother to carry on as best we could.

It was a difficult time. By the Sixties the baby boomers were coming of age and they were beginning to dominate the scene. The move was towards new styles, towards the cut and blow dry; there were the moptops inspired by the Beatles. The era of the old barber in a long grey coat with a pair of scissors and clippers in his hand, who would sit you down and proceed to give you a short back and sides, completed by a clart of Brylcream, was still with us, but the younger generation were asking for something more fashionable, more individualistic.

We decided to sell up in Aberdeen and concentrate on Stonehaven. When Dad died I started going into the shop to help; it was a natural development for me to train as a hairdresser when I left school. I attended the course at Aberdeen College. I received a thorough training.

Hair cutting can never be a matter of pure manual skill. We were taught that a good haircut is like a cat's fur — it should just blend, no steps, just blend. Nature doesn't work to straight lines, but to a graduation, a blend. Whichever way you stroke the cat's fur it'll always be smooth and that's what a good haircut should be too.

So much of the business is a matter not simply of technique, but of insight, instinct and flair. Psychology plays a huge part. You have to build up a partnership of confidence between you and your client. People will come in and tell you they are fed up with their old style and want a complete new makeover. But really they only want to freshen up what they already have. They ask for advice and claim they aren't really sure what they want — but deep down they are. The important thing is to extract what they really desire out of them, not to impose something new and alien on them. You'll start and they'll tell you, 'Oh, but my fringe usually sits that way — let's keep to that,' and then, 'Oh, I didn't mean you to uncover my ears!' What they are after is reassurance and a new slant, that's all.

The family business.
Martin Sim's father, in his mid-teens at W. Gellatley, Tobacconist & Hairdresser, Allardice Street, Stonehaven, where he began his career.

Our aim is to remain a trusted, reliable local salon. After all, in a small place like Stonehaven you'll see your clients walking around the street and I want to know that they are happy with the service we've given them. And that's what the great majority really want: a nice, comfortable style which they've developed over the years and which they know suits them, and a salon they know will deliver it to them every time. The odd customer will always be demanding something ultra-fashionable, but in many cases I fear they are chasing a ghost and will never be truly at rest with their hair and their appearance.

Chatting to the customer? I'm always happy to do that, but I know that some prefer

silence. I usually try out some kind of comment on the weather, or a piece of latest news and if that doesn't go anywhere than I'll let the customer sit in peace. But hairdressing is a sociable industry, isn't it? You've got to like people and enjoy interacting with them. Occasionally you're told deeply personal matters. There was the guy who, out of the blue, said, 'My wife's just gone off with someone else'. And then went on, 'I never knew there was anything up – though I did know the other party – a woman!' Now, that's something you wouldn't have heard when I started out. And more recently I had the woman who informed us that she couldn't really look ahead to many more appointments, as she'd just been diagnosed with terminal cancer. When you hear something like that you can't just go into the, 'Oh well – and where are you going for your holidays this year?' routine.

All you can do is listen and be sympathetic. It's a privilege to be trusted with such sensitive matters and you must never forget it. It's an extension of the fact that the person is already entrusting themselves to you by allowing you to handle their heads and take a pair of scissors to it. I suppose it's rather like going to the doctor. And just as most of us feel easier with a doctor who's had some experience of life, I think the hairdresser with a certain amount of maturity is at an advantage. The younger hairdressers may be up with the latest styles and hip talk, but it's us older ones who can enter into what, in the end, life's all about.

And now the day's approaching when I'm going to have to give the business up. Neither of my own sons is at all interested in taking it on, so I'll have to sell it. I'm just not sure how I will feel when I turn the key for the final time and later walk past and see a different name above the door. All I know is that I've had a wonderful time, meeting and serving such a fine cross-section of Stonehaven folk. I'm grateful to them all.

Martin Sim, born 1947, interviewed 2011: Stonehaven

The builder's apprentice

I'd planned to be a motor mechanic, but when I told this to the youth employment officer, he just said, 'Forget it. Your maths is nowhere good enough'. I went home and told my father. 'Right you'll have to be a joiner. I'll have a word with Brem King and get you started there'. The word came back, 'You start on Monday morning, first thing'. What happened when I reported for duty is something I'll never get out of my head. I went up to Brem King and said, 'Mr King, I'm Colin McLennan and I'm to start work with you. What's the rate?' And he just looked at me and replied, 'Flat oot, laddie, flat oot! That's fit the rate's to be, flat oot!' Brem King ruled with a rod of iron. He made me get a 'proper' haircut; he disapproved of my tastes in music. Once when I was on the site listening to my transistor, he just took his sledge-hammer and put an end to both music and radio. My school education didn't amount to much, but you could say I've enjoyed the University of Life.

Colin McLellan, born 1948, interviewed 2004: Newtonhill

> I went up to Brem King and said, 'What's the rate?' He just looked at me and replied, 'Flat oot, laddie, flat oot!

The demolition man

In the 1970s, I branched out into demolition work. The old school at Cuminestown was being demolished and this local boy had bought all the slates off the roof. He got over a pair of slaters from Fyvie, but they couldn't get the nails out. Well, there was a dance at the Commercial Hotel that night and I met up with him there and he told me his story. 'Div ye still wunt the slates?', I asked him. 'Ach, I'm nae needin them noo.' 'Weel', I said, 'in that case I'll tak them – will £150 dae?'

I'd never taken a slate off in my life. There was this young lad at the dance I knew. I went up to him: 'Frannie, cam doon the morning an we'll hae a go at thae slates'. It was a two-storey building, so I went up into the loft. I found all the nails from the slates were sticking out inside it, an inch deep. I got Frannie to go inside while I clambered up onto the roof; he knocked out the nails and I was able to collect them all, everything single one of them.

Do you ken what I made from all those slates? Well, I had folk queuing up to buy them at ten bob each. I made £5,000 that first week and it was all in cash, too! 'God,' I thought to myself, this is easy money.' So I continued with the work and set up my own business.

Every day is different and you're your own boss. You get plenty of challenges, plenty wee adventures. I was up in Inverness doing a job at the mart there. I stayed in a caravan on the site. I managed to sell a lot of the salvage and had the cash in my pocket. So there I was that night, on the street waiting for my mate outside the pub. A couple of police came by; 'Move along there', they ordered. 'Bit I'm jist waitin fer ma pal.' They seemed to take exception to that and grabbed me and searched me. They came across the £480 in notes from that day's job. 'Where did that come from?', they demanded. 'Ye ken fine fa it came frae – ma back pooch,' I told them. Well, they didn't like that and proceeded to give me a real thrashing. Then they handcuffed me and hauled me off to spend the night in the cells. The next day I was woken up, given a cup of tea and a bacon roll and released. My £480 was returned to me. It was explained that they had thought I must have been a drug dealer with all that cash in my pocket, but now they realised I was an upright citizen and were letting me go. No charges; my money back.

Even so I decided I wouldn't be telling my wife what had happened. But a couple of days later I got a phone call from her. 'Now, what on earth have you been up to?' 'Naethin,' I told her. 'Well, how do you explain this bill I've just received from the Inverness Constabulary? It's for £25, bed and breakfast.' Well, that had been a dear bacon roll and cup of tea, I can tell you. The only good thing was that the cell was warmer than my caravan.

Gavin Sim, born 1949, interviewed 2012: Cuminestown

> I had folk queuing up to buy slates at ten bob each. I made £5,000 that first week and it was all in cash, too!

The butcher

The main skill you need as a butcher is common sense and flexibility. When I started out at Kemnay it was all beef. People used to buy roast beef on the bone; now it's all boneless. That's a reflection of how people now live. They no longer take the time to cook whole foods; they want something quick and convenient. Look how popular beef burgers have become. That's because they're cheap, easy to prepare, easy to eat. A well-made burger is a good food, but people go to their supermarket and fill up with branded stuff; if they went to their local butcher they'd get a quality product which is much more nutritious and tasty than something out of a packet.

Another change is the tendency to do a bulk shop. In my young day there were no codes, no sell-by dates. People tended to get in their food fresh each day. But now with freezers and the family car to take the load home in, they buy packaged food to last them the week.

The younger generation has become cut off from the real sources of food. They think milk is something you pick up in a carton at the supermarket. When I was young you'd be aware of each bit of the countryside holding its own dairy farm; you'd see the cattle being led in for milking twice a day, across the fields. I could count half dozen dairy farms around Dunecht, all within a

Now for all that DIY! Jim Collie on his last day in his shop, April 2010.

Typical butcher's shop, Inverurie 1980s

Adults may want meat and two veg, but the kids prefer chicken dippers or pizzas and that's what the whole family ends up with.

10-minute radius. Now there are none.

The old kitchen skills have disappeared too. My mother, like most housewives then, would spend hours cooking and baking, so you'd see her handling basic food products like eggs and flour. In the summer she'd get in extra eggs and store them in a stone jar so as to tide her over the winter. Can you imagine telling a modern wife that come July she should be looking ahead in that way, ready for winter. The way food has become a globalised industry means that nowadays we all expect any food to be available all year round and in plentiful supply.

The traditional North-east meal is seen less and less often. People have too much money and they buy in readymade stuff which they pop into the micro-wave. That's not cooking. Now, my mother would always make things from scratch, with care and with knowledge. She couldn't throw it into the bin if it didn't work out and go to the freezer for a pizza. You couldn't afford to do anything but make the best out of what you had in the house – which wouldn't be very much.

That's why there are fewer butcher shops now. It depends on the family background. If they come from a home where the wife ruled the kitchen and used recipes handed down from her own mother, then they are much more likely to want to carry on that practice. But in the great majority of homes nowadays the woman's out working all day and hasn't the time. In a lot of cases the family eats what the kids want. The adults may want meat and two veg, but the kids prefer chicken dippers or pizzas and that's what the whole family ends up with.

So shopping and eating habits have changed a lot in my 45 years. The years in the shop were enjoyable – lots of people, coming in from all walks of life, plenty laughs, good gossip. I found out that what really counts in life is common sense. Look, you can spend your whole life chasing after the latest gadgets, but if you've got warmth and comfort you won't go far wrong – that and good food.

Jim Collie, born 1950, interviewed 2010: Kemnay

The painter decorator

To an outsider, painting and decorating can appear to be monotonous stuff, but we've always gone for varied work like sign writing and fancy finishes. It's not all slapping on emulsion, you know. A lot of skill and experience goes into what we do, but I doubt whether the public appreciates it. Decorating is something they think they can do themselves. People who wouldn't dream of engaging with a plumbing or electrician's job assume they can go off to B&Q, return with tins of paint and rolls of wallpaper and just get on with it.

The best customer is the little old wifie who doesn't feel up to DIY and who is quite welcoming, partly because she appreciates your skill, partly because of the company you give her. The older the customer, the more likely you are to be given a nice cup of tea and a fancy piece. She'll news away while you're getting on with the job. I never mind that; I'm happy to chat and be friendly.

They regard laying out money on bringing you in as a fair investment, whereas younger couples, moving into the new schemes going up all over the North-east, find the cost of their mortgages is such they are loath to hire in someone when they can tackle a spot of DIY.

Being in my line of business has its sensitivities. I'm being invited into people's homes and for me that's a matter of trust. People are forever asking me, 'Fit's so-an-so's hoose like? Fit kin o furniture div they hae?' But I never tell them; a customer has the right to expect confidentiality in return for putting their trust in you. Often they'll give you the run of their homes while they are away. Some regular customers, at the end of a job, just tell me to hold on to a key for the next time. You'd be amazed at the number of keys I hold here; I could burgle half the homes in the town.

But I think we've lost something. Call it the work ethic or a sense of personal responsibility, but all I know is that you can no longer rely on some of the values I grew up with. Take the matter of apprentices. I no longer take any on and part of the reason is that they were becoming less and less reliable. I've had some real disasters: one of them, I remember, only lasted the week. He'd come along, assuring me he was willing to stick in and learn, so I started him off with the sort of tasks I was given in my early days – rubbing down surfaces, doing the spoots, watching and picking up what the full range of jobs in being a painter decorator was all about. He completed one week; come the following Monday no apprentice! Then in mid-morning his mother appeared to inform me that her Jonny wouldn't be coming back and that he was resting in bed after all his labours. He hadn't realised that being an apprentice would demand doing such hard, boring jobs like rubbing and mixing; he'd been looking forward to getting on with wallpapering and gloss finishes. That kind of drudgery wasn't for him.

Duncan Naysmith, born 1951, interviewed 2011: Inverurie

The bakery director

Mum had been brought up on a farm and had all the domestic skills. She was excellent in the kitchen, knew all the old recipes and was an expert baker. The business grew up quite naturally, from simple beginnings. Dad had a long association with the Huntly Pipe Band, which began in 1948 with my grandfather as one of its founder members.

You'd be amazed at the number of keys I hold here; I could burgle half the homes in the town.

Helen Dean stepping out with some more homemade bakes from the house where it all began, 1990.

The Dean family have also been staunch supporters of the Huntly Pipe Band. Bill Dean senior leads the way at the Braemar Gathering 2002.

As the band developed it started branching out and began to undertake trips to play at folk festivals in the likes of France and Belgium. We also hosted exchange visits. The band began to look for ways of raising funds and Mum started to bake for it. We'd go off to play at places like Tomintoul and Grantown. Mum would accompany them and go into the hotels and offer her shortbread.

Gradually the little side-line began to take off. Mum found herself under pressure to bake more and more. All she had was a small kitchen in an ordinary council house. She had a sink, a Belling cooker and, over her head, there'd be the pulley laden with washing drying out. I always tell the story of how us children would go into the kitchen where Mum might have to make up 30 batches of mixture and we'd fight to be the one to run our fingers round the empty mixing bowls and lick them clean.

Lots of other women then would have had the same kind of upbringing and skills, but it was Mum who had the enterprise to take it forward. Banks didn't lend out money in those days to working class people like ourselves, so she went into business with help through her step-brother, John, who provided the initial cash to take over an old grocer's shop and convert it into a bakery.

Mum had a really difficult first year; the work was non-stop; at the end of it Mum and Dad had a profit of £10! They were on the verge of giving up. The breakthrough came at the Keith Show. They took a stand and were visited by the Mace group distributors. They got talking and by the end of the day my mother found she'd been engaged to supply the Mace group.

There was still plenty of hard work ahead. We'd spend the weekends driving up and down the A96 to lots of small shops, trying to persuade them to place an order. I remember how elated Dad was whenever he made his first sale into a new store, and could bring the good news back to the car – and then on to the next one.

Who would do that kind of thing now, I wonder? There they were slogging away, going around trying to persuade shopkeepers in places like Mosstodlich and Kennethmont to take in some of their shortbread and still having to get on with the business of bringing up a family and Dad still holding down a job with the Council. I suppose a lot of what you might call north-east character went into that – the work ethic, sense of trust, stubbornness, pride.

When I left school the business was still quite small, with a turnover of less than £100,000, so I had no thought of moving into it. I served my time as an apprentice sheet metal worker and then had four or five years of fond memories in a job I really enjoyed.

But in the mid-Eighties there was a downturn in the business sector and I took the decision to return to Huntly to go into the family bakery. I did this reluctantly: I was leaving a well-paid job doing work I loved and here I was back in small town Huntly, in a bakery, wearing aprons and working in an alien environment with 20 part-time ladies. It was no longer sheet metal; now it was mixing butter and flour, or chugging round the country in the firm's delivery van.

But I got involved. When I look back over the last 20 years and compare where I am

now to where I started, well I can scarcely believe it. I've learned so much, and not just about business, but about people and about myself. It's been a real privilege to learn how to engage with others, how to work in a team and how to lead, about the finance and the communication processes which all that has involved.

Our target turnover is now £10,000,000. We employ 135 staff, including both part and full time. A bit of a jump from the first days of my mother, and her part-time helpers, Jenny Hay and Betty Keith, and a profit of £10 for the year.

So you can see how proud I am that we've managed to grow in such a global environment, that we've managed to market something that's thoroughly local in origin and character. None of this stops me from having my own 'Abit' moments —you know, those times when everything seems to be going too well and you find yourself saying, 'Abit… 'I'm a North-east loon after all. I worry that the next generation won't have the same strong basis as we did, the same pride and passion for what we can do here in our own North-east. I understand the struggles that went with it, what you had to do to adapt and to grow. That was my education.

Bill Dean, born 1964, interviewed 2008: Huntly

Fifteen years on... and the company has grown into an internationally renowned enterprise. Bill and Helen Dean with Bill Dean junior on the right, 2005.

'The culmination of all I've worked for.'
Marianne Bell's Emporium, 2012.

The garden centre director

The family business has been in quarrying and construction. My father and his brothers owned a quarry at Blackhills of Tyrie. Sand and gravel. The business has been a success, a real family business too. I started working for it when I was 12. I got a Saturday job in the office, handling phone calls, taking in orders, advising reps, sending out radio messages to the lorry drivers. It was a real job, an eight-hour day for £5 pay. You had to be on top of the business and all its products.

So my background was work ethic and management of money. My parents supplied the school clothes, but if I wanted anything more fashionable then I had to save up for it myself. You were taught never to borrow money and always to pay your bills as you went along. No credit cards. It was still the custom that each 31 December people would come into the office to settle any outstanding bills; the attitude was, don't go into a new year with any unpaid bills hanging over your head. I've seen men coming in, opening up their jackets and taking out a wad of notes and then peeling off the correct number. It was a point of honour to keep a clean slate.

I'd set my heart on a garden centre business and we bought this plot of land alongside the A96. It's a seven-day a week business. I've three daughters and they're all involved in it; we keep up the tradition of the family business. My youngest one – a 12-year old, the same age as I started out – comes in during the school holidays to help with the dishes. That's where you start, on the ground floor and then work your way up, isn't it?

Kellockbank Country Emporium is the culmination of all I've worked for. In my father's business I was familiar with concrete products for the garden and that led me to an interest in gardening goods in general. Besides, I'd always enjoyed serving the public; I'm a people person. Twenty years ago there were few centres like this, but I knew from my own family experience how much we'd enjoyed going out on a Sunday drive and popping into somewhere to look around the goods and take some refreshment. Kellockbank is a development of that idea. It's a product of recent social trends where people have their own cars and more leisure time. We particularly appeal to the older generation and to women. People are now retiring younger, living and keeping their health longer. In my childhood, in a farming community you used to stop work at 65 and were dead before you were 70; now I've got people in their 80s as regulars.

We act as a meeting point. People no longer do as much home entertaining as they used to. In the past, families would do a lot of visiting relatives and whenever they called by they'd get a scone and a cup of tea. Well, we can fill that gap; people arrange to meet here, enjoy a chat and a lunch or an afternoon tea together and then go on their way back to their busy lives.

I've never found that my gender has been a disadvantage in business. As a young girl my contribution was taken seriously and I never gave the fact that I was female a thought. But habits die hard: occasionally people will call in and ask for 'Mr Bell'. There can still be the assumption that because this is a family business I must be under my husband.

I think women running their own business is a growing trend. I've a friend who manages the old family building business in Peterhead; she took it over when her father died of cancer and there she is, competing with other firms and making a real go of it. Then there's another woman I know who has her own fleet of haulage lorries. Her father had a lorry and she'd grown up longing to drive it and it grew from there.

But to me, what I do doesn't seem at all unusual, certainly not unnatural. I was brought up on hard work, on enterprise, and on taking responsibility and pitching in – whether you were male or female.

Marianne Bell, born 1969, interviewed 2011: Tyrie and Kellockbank

> I was brought up on hard work, taking responsibility and pitching in – whether you were male or female.

The apprentice cooper

When I was on the brink of leaving school my father approached the manager at Glenfiddich Distillery: 'Have you got a job for my boy?' On the Monday morning I found myself being marched down to the distillery's cooperage, handed a pair of dungarees and sweeping brush and told to get on with it. This was a complete shock to me; but at that time everyone believed it was important to get a good trade and to serve an apprenticeship, so I was delivered up to Dufftown's main industry.

From the start I loathed it. It actually got worse, over those four long years. To begin with I was put under the wing of an older man, Andy Sherratt, working out his final year before retirement. The day he did go is etched on my mind. A small ceremony was held, and, as the young apprentice and thus representative of the future, I was asked to say a few words as he was handed his retiral gift. It was a cheap Timex watch and that was his reward after

50 years of faithful service, years in which he'd built up a store of ill health from the job. He was a, lovely gentle man and a faithful worker and this was his reward. I found the whole event unbearably sad; I was determined that wouldn't be my fate.

Of course, the work did have its moments. One of them came when the distillery was celebrating its centenary and a group of VIPs was being shown round to watch us all busy

Before the four-year incarceration. Ian Murray in the garden with his sister, Dufftown, late 1970s

'I never want to be in his shoes': Ian Murray as the young apprentice, handing over the retirement gift to Andy Sherratt, his journeyman at Glenfiddich, 1986. Duncan Stewart, distillery manager is left, and George Dykes, cooperage manager, is on the right.

at our work. One of the party was Malcolm Riffkind, Secretary of State for Scotland. My task that day was to paint the ends of some casks. So as he approached I put on a great show of busily slapping on emulsion when, swoosh! – a great dollop of bright yellow landed on Mr Riffkind's dark suit.

One job, which came round every fortnight, was to accompany Andy into the warehouses to check for leaking casks and to put a patch of putty over it. Andy told me to be sure to take a biro pen with me – a vital piece of equipment. Vital, all right, because I was shown that what you had to do was to empty the casing of the pen by extracting the tube of ink inside and then you could use it as a straw to suck the whisky out. In this way you'd be given the opportunity to sample some lovely malts. But, he strictly instructed me, 'Never let oan that you hae a pen wi you'.

There was this day when we were there in the warehouse – the exciseman, the cooper, myself and two other young lads – and the manager appeared. He was carrying a pad of A4 notepaper. He looked at it, then turned to us: 'Would any of you have a pen on you – I seem to have forgotten mine?' Eager to please, the two young warehousemen cried out, 'Yes, Mr Stewart, I've got one here'. He took them, held them up to the light and then said, 'Aye, aye, you'd better come with me'.

All around me I could see what the work was doing to people. I could see how it would wear you out so that at 65 you'd end up with elbows gone, stiff and swollen joints, rotten lungs from a lifetime of breathing in thick dust, and quite possibly cirrhosis of the liver from the availability of over-proof whisky.

Three days after I'd completed my time at Glenfiddich, I went home, into the back garden, and made a little funeral pyre. Onto it I heaped my piece bag, my tupperware box, my notebook, my leather boots with their steel toecaps and my dungarees. The centenary bottle of malt which we'd all been given as a memento I used to light the flames and my completion certificate was used to top up the fire. I'd always been responsive to the ceremonial and so I found the whole event deeply satisfying – and completely liberating. I was ready for my new life.

Note: after leaving the cooperage, Ian studied for the ministry – *see 'Church Going'*.

Ian Murray, born 1970, interviewed 2011: Dufftown

The garage mechanic (female)

I'd always seen myself as going into Dad's garage business. He tried to persuade me otherwise; when I started off he'd give me the most horrible jobs to scunner me. If a car came in and the oil hadn't been changed for ages, he'd take the sump off and hand it over to me to clean. The oil would have set like jelly, but I managed it. I had to clean cars and he'd check them over for even the slightest fault in my work. But none of this put me off; the garage was the world I'd grown up in. I started going into the garage when I was five to watch Dad at work. I was fascinated by the way he could take an engine to bits and then put it all together again.

He gave me a hard apprenticeship. 'Remember I'm not your dad here; I'm your boss and you're just another member of my staff.' He'd bawl me out and sometimes I'd find it difficult not to burst into tears. But we always managed to sort out our problems; our attitude was that if a difficulty arose then you had to sort it out on the spot and not let it fester away. I just had to get on with it. I know that being female is still a rarity in the garage business, but I'd rather be in a workshop with men; women can be so bitchy, always talking about one another behind their backs. My aunt works in a kitchen and she's forever coming home with stories of tears and taking sides.

I love being hands-on, finding out how things work. I enjoy the customers, striking up a rapport with them. We're a local garage and customers keep coming back, year after year. One of them moved to London, but he still gets his annual service done by us when he comes up each year. These are people who tell us they appreciate coming to a small country garage where they know they can get service they trust. Some of the larger garages will fix a problem by simply getting in a new part. We know that our reputation depends on treating our customers as we would like to be treated ourselves.

Sometimes I get prejudice as a female in what's usually a male environment. Once this man came into the garage, an older man, and Dad was off somewhere. 'Fa's the boss?' 'He's not here just now; perhaps I can help'. 'Na, na, there's nae yis in tellin a lassie like you. Fat wid you ken aboot it?' I noticed that his wheel sump was leaking and advised him that it would have to come off. In the end he accepted that I was 'probably' right. But you'll still get times when I've answered the phone and the customer comes in later with, 'I was speaking to the girl in the office...'

I get great satisfaction out of being able to fix things. There's a fair variety: the mornings might be spent on routine MOT work, but in the afternoon we'll get down to a big job like putting in a new gear box. We get a lot of passing trade with breakdowns on the A90. And Cammachmore's a nice small community to work in: I like the place, I like the customers – and I love my job.

Laura Ironside, born 1979, interviewed 2007: Cammachmore

> He gave me a hard apprenticeship. 'Remember I'm not your dad here; I'm your boss and you're just another member of my staff.'

John Ironside & Daughter: Laura with her father, Bridgecroft Garage, Cammachmore 2012

LIFE AT THE BIG HOUSE

An historical pedigree: Some present day descendants of the world famous Aberdeen Angus breed, which had its origins on the estate of Ballindalloch Castle, seen in the background.

The chauffeur's daughter

I was born at Edgehill, Milltimber. My father was chauffeur to Sir Thomas and Lady Helen Jaffrey. It was a lovely house, a wonderful place to grow up at. Milltimber was right out in the country then. The house had a beautiful walled garden, lots of wooded areas, quite an acreage altogether. There was a pair of cottages, one for the head gardener and the other one, where we lived.

Sir Thomas was a lovely man. He'd started out as a Buchan farm servant's son and always remained a plain down-to-earth character. He had a good brain, went into the banking business and rose to the very top of it.

My father had to go down to London to take delivery of the big Rolls-Royce. He had to wear a tailor-made uniform. Oddly enough, this was made up for him at Lawson's in Market Street, Aberdeen, a tick shop. When I was a youngster I would deliver the papers to the house, papers like the *Financial Times*, and on the first of each month, Sir Thomas would invite me into the drawing room, take out his wallet and present me with a crisp 10-shilling note. Often he would make a little joke, 'Actually, Dorothy, I'm a bit hard up this month, so you'll have to take the money on tick'. Then he'd ask, 'You do know what "tick" is don't you? No? Well I'm very pleased to hear it'.

Sir Thomas had no family of his own and so he looked on us as something of a replacement. He was very tolerant of all our ways; we'd run around the garden, climb up

Raising money for charity. The day of the pig raffle at Edgehill House. The eight-year-old Dorothy Shaw and the adopted daughter stand left surrounded by local Milltimber girls.

Edgehill House in its heyday. Sir Thomas and Lady Helen Jaffrey with their adopted daughter in the foreground.

on the high walls to pinch apples from the trees. His wife, Lady Helen, was a bit grander, but he was always the farm loon come in from Buchan. He always took an interest in what we were doing. He would invite me into the drawing room to play the piano for him. My mother set great store by my music and struggled to pay for me to go into Culter each Saturday for my regular lesson at a lady there. But I didn't really practise diligently, so my playing was nothing special. However, there I was seated at the grand

The chauffer's daughter gets married to Charlie Shaw, 1954.

All grown up.
Dorothy at Charlie
Alexander Transport
ball, Douglas Hotel,
Aberdeen, 1951.

piano in this splendid drawing room, with Sir Thomas smiling and praising my poor efforts and me thinking how this was really something.

Sir Thomas did a lot for charity. He would open up the house and its grounds for sales for organisations like the Red Cross. Local girls would be invited in to make up a choir and they would hold concerts in the great hall, with its sweeping staircase at the back.

Just before the war they adopted a Jewish refugee girl and she became a real friend to us all, especially me as I was about the same age. We would often play together and she'd invite me into the house. I can remember going up into the boudoir and sitting at the dressing table in front of the mirror and trying out Lady Helen's make-up.

A high spot was the time when Winston Churchill came to Aberdeen to receive the freedom of the city just after the war. It had been arranged that he would come out to Edgehill after the ceremony for his lunch and so my father had to go into Aberdeen in the Rolls-Royce and pick him up at the Music Hall and convey him and his wife out to the house. While he was there Sir Winston planted a tree in the garden and made a little speech. The tree is still there, 60 years on, and has a plaque to commemorate the event.

All in a good cause.
Dorothy's father and
Mrs Hendry, the
doctor's wife, handle
a basket at an Edgehill
House fund-raising
event, while
Lady Helen Jaffrey
presides.

Towards the end of his life, Sir Thomas had to take to a wheelchair and hire private nurses to look after him. They would wheel him out to sit in front of the house and he was always pleased to see any of us passing by and to ask how we were getting on. He was such a nice, genuine old man – a real gentleman.

Dorothy Shaw, born 1933, interviewed 2012: Edgehill House, Milltimber

> It seems weird now to think back on those years, but it seemed the most natural thing in the world to look after the Big House.

The start of it all. Estate worker Peter the Painter greets Mrs Nicol on her arrival at Ballogie House, 1946. Colonel Nicol is on the right; the pipes are being played by the head keeper.

A lovely gentleman

We came here in 1956 when my husband got the job of dairying at the Ballogie House Home Farm. This was under Colonel Nicol, who owned the big house and all the estate. In those days they employed a whole heap of people to run the house and its grounds. There were estate boys, three gardeners, servants for the house – kitchen maids, chamber maids, table maids, a butler, two cooks – and, outside, there were keepers and a chauffeur too.

I started work on the day of the Aboyne Games, August 1956. Since he was the president of the games the Colonel gave us all a glass of sherry. The years just flew past. You weren't in it for the money, but for the satisfaction. You took pride in seeing that everything was just so – it seems weird now to think back on all those years, but then it seemed the most natural thing in the world to look after the Big House.

Colonel Nicol was a magic employer, always very courteous and so thoughtful and kind. He let you get on with the task in hand and trusted you to do it properly. By the end he was calling me 'Isobel', but to begin with matters were very formal. I can remember how on the last day of the month all the men would have to line up in the office to receive their wages and they would be

Isobel as she is today, taken at her cottage garden in Ballogie.

called forward one by one: 'Harper,' 'McRobbie'. How times have changed!

At the end I was the only one left of all that big team of maids and gardeners and servants. Over the years, as they left, they weren't replaced and so gradually the staff just dwindled away. The house was a big place, difficult to keep up and so cold too. It was pulled down in 1984 and rebuilt to a more convenient, modern style. It had been an old three-storey building, situated at the end of a long drive with immaculately kept grounds all around. When we had the three gardeners the vases in the house could be kept full of fresh flowers just about 10 months of the year. I would swear that you'd never see such beautiful gladioli as we had then at Ballogie House.

The Colonel had come out of the Army in 1946. He'd had a public school background, but once he came to Ballogie House he devoted himself to the area. He believed in serving us all. He was the biggest employer in the area and a very fair one too. He was a councillor and he was forever jumping into his Land Rover to dash off to save some small country school or other. To begin with he was very strict in his manner and Army-like in his bearing. I think some of the local folk were a bit frightened of him. He'd go into the shop and bark out his orders and the people behind the counter would be intimidated.

But once he got settled in and we all got used to him he mellowed and became a well-liked as well as a respected pillar of the community. I certainly grew to like him very much and I think he must have liked me too – after all we stayed together for all those years.

I responded to the structure, to the regular routine of working in a big house. You'd

Playing a full part in the community.
Mrs Nicol cuts the birthday cake at an anniversary gathering of the Ballogie WRI. She was responsible for setting up the Institute branch in 1948. Isobel McRobbie is back row, centre.

He lived well into his 90s: A shot of Colonel Nicol during his final years.

go in in the morning and know exactly what was set out for you to do: dining room, sitting room, fires to be cleaned out and laid, grates to be black leaded, shoes to be cleaned, all laid out in a row. It was a real country house with dogs and plenty of wet and muddy feet coming and going, so there was no shortage of things to be kept in good order.

After Mrs Nicol died I saw the Colonel every day. She used to give me detailed instructions, but he just left me to work things out for myself. He proved to be easy pleased and eager for a chat as well; he wanted a bit of company, you see. It was a sad day when he died. Although he was 96, it came as something of a shock. He'd been ill, but seemed to be getting over it and we all thought the danger had passed.

No, I'll never forget that day. I went in as usual and set about my tasks but after a while I found myself thinking, 'My goodness, he's awfu quiet today'. Usually you'd hear him at his shower and shifting around, but that day, nothing. I went in and there he was laid out all cold, just lying there. I couldn't believe it – after half a century together, he'd gone. We all felt we'd lost something that had been central to our lives.

Isobel McRobbie, born 1935, interviewed 2011: Ballogie House

Outsiders don't understand

Game-keeping has always been in the family. My eldest son never wanted to do anything else. The minute he got his holidays he would go up to Glenbuchat to his grandfather – my father – and then, the night before the new term started, he'd come back down again for the school. He just couldn't wait to get into the game-keeping. For us, it has never been just an occupation; it's a whole way of life.

It wasn't a lonely life, ever. There was a burn that ran past the house and in the summer-time we played there for hours at a time. We lived beside the Lodge and there were always people coming and going. In the season we would go to the church with the laird; then my sister and I would be dressed up in navy nap-coats and Fair Isle berets on our heads.

The laird was very important in the community. He provided employment, but he also gave the community activities. At the end of the season he would hold a gathering; everyone would come and do a party-piece. Mum was a singer and she would sing; Dad was a fiddler and he had his own band. He'd play for the dancing. The Laird would lay on a great spread. The Laird's Social was a great event which everyone looked forward to.

The laird actually lived elsewhere, but he always came on the 12th August for the season and would be among us for three months or so. He brought a pair of Jersey cows with him so that he would have his own supply of high quality milk. My mother used to milk them and make butter and cheese from their milk.

Outsiders don't understand the estate system, but it's been very good to us. The owners look after their employees and they look after the countryside. But things are

The last photograph: Elspeth Dey attended Balloch School until its closure in 1948. This shot shows the entire roll at that date. Elspeth sits front centre, her sister Ann to her left. The teacher is Mrs Fraser.

All ready for the day's shooting. An interwar scene, Glenbuchat House, where Elspeth Dey's father (Webster) was head gamekeeper during her childhood. Colonel Milne and Mrs Milne are shown; the young girl is their daughter, Jessie B.

Fifty-five years later. Elspeth outside her Kingussie home, 2003, with Kathleen Northcroft, left.

different now. My son is the head keeper at Coignafearn, over towards Inverness. At one time that estate had about 30 workers but now it's down to two under-keepers and a ghillie. He's got 40,000 acres to look after. And they don't go about on ponies any more – it's all quad-bikes and argocats.

Elspeth Dey, born 1939, interviewed 2003: Glenbuchat Lodge

A certain social grace

The farming community was quite hierarchical. That was accepted as long as the laird was a good laird, that is someone who wouldn't turn people off the land and who would only sell to the sitting tenant. There was a certain obsequiousness towards Lord Aberdeen, but then people genuinely liked him. Whenever the community needed his support he was always there for it. All rather paternalistic – but so what!

On neutral ground the relations are quite democratic; generally, the North-east farmer will assume he has the right to speak to anyone, that no one has the right to order him about. In the pub, at the church, at the cricket ground, then matters will be pretty egalitarian. On the other hand, the classes do keep behind their lines of demarcation in a domestic sense. There will hardly be any threshold crossing, no invitations to private parties or to a meal. If they fraternise in that sense at all, then it will be at some semi-public event like the Christmas party or a retirement do in the hall. Similarly, the laird wouldn't countenance his daughter or son marrying down the social scale, and hardly any

The laird certainly took his turn on the roster to clean and look after the public toilet.

farmer would have been happy about his daughter marrying the ploughman.

Of course, the traditional laird as a species can appear to be as thick as dumplings. They've been brought up with their own priorities – hunting, fishing, balls, the 'season'. What the laird does bring to the community is a certain social grace: he's good at glad-handing; he can be relied upon, along with his good lady, to open things, to present prizes, to deliver the odd little speech of welcome or of farewell. They have this social ease and confidence, this aura of being to the manner born. Lord Aberdeen does all that very well. If the community wants anything from him in the way of visible support or presence, he'll be there. When Aberdeenshire closed down all those local toilets a few years back, we drew up a rota to look after and to clean ours in Methlick and he certainly took his turn on it.

Charlie Allan, born 1939, interviewed 2006: Methlick

What! still here, Burnett?

Hard times:
The main road at Carpenter's Croft, Boyndlie, February 1942.

M y father looked after the Home Farm, Boyndlie. Its owner, the local laird and of the Ogilvie-Forbes family, lived in the Big House. My father was on a wage to look after the farm and mother had certain 'feudal' duties as well.

If I met the laird out on the pathway, I was never quite sure what I had to do. If he didn't look at you, then that was easy – you just went quietly by; but if he did, then you had to wait for his grunt in your direction and then you would say, 'Good morning, sir,' and tug the forelock.

Father was brought up in a little lodge on the estate. He'd gone to the little school at Boyndlie. He had educated himself mostly. He was a member of the library; he'd read all kinds of books. He'd read to us as kids. Nowadays there's no doubt he would have gone to university,

> If I met the laird out on the pathway, I was never quite sure what I had to do.

After a spell in London, he returned and he got a job dutch-hoeing the avenues. How frustrating he found that, I don't know. He never talked about it. It was a kind of taboo subject, something a father doesn't mention to his son – a bit like sex. But after a while, the post of grieve came up and the old man applied for it. This was in the middle of the summer, at the time when the Ogilvy-Forbes all decamped to Ventnor in the Isle of Wight for the yachting. My father had to attend an interview for the post. So he made his way down to Ventnor, was shown in to meet auld John Charles Matthias Ogilvy-Forbes, who looked up from his *Times* and said, 'Ah, Burnett, so you want to be… ah… want to… ah … now tell me, does your wife make her own bread?' The answer was 'no', but my father had the presence of mind to say, 'But she's an excellent cook and does a lot of baking'. 'Ah, very good…' And that was that. No next question, only the face peering up from behind the paper after a minute or so: 'What! you still here, Burnett? Better get back up and start on the work'.

The next laird was always wanting another housekeeper – he was forever finding fault

with the one he had. He used my father as a sounding board: if he was thinking of a particular applicant, he would seek out my old man's advice – and often enough it would be, 'Steer clear of that one!' The most succinct application that my father ever saw was, 'Dear Sir – will I do?'

Rent day was a great occasion: a roll call would be held every quarter; the estate factor would come out from Aberdeen and my mother would have to feed him. They all had bottled beer and I got the job of barman – Cruickshank's of Fraserburgh would send over a crate. 'The Rents' were tense affairs: it wasn't just a question of handing over the cash or signing a cheque. Serious negotiating had to be done – you might ask for a new roof for the byre, for example.

There was a strong personal flavour to it all. When people would look at Sir George Arthur Drostan Ogilvy-Forbes, they wouldn't see him simply as 'the landlord'. He was something more than that. He would turn up at concerts, grace the WRI with his presence, would cut a ribbon to open a new room at the school. It was a paternalistic society. The estate asked you for service but, in return, it would look after you. When my father retired, they were given a cottage for a while, and when they went into sheltered accommodation, the estate sent them a cheque for £1,000.

The estate is now a company and so the personal touch has gone from it. It's now the Boyndlie Estates Company. The house I grew up in is now rented out.

Bill Burnett born 1940, interviewed 2003: Boyndlie

The jewel in Banffshire's crown

There has been some sort of edifice at Ballindalloch since 1467 and this present building dates back to 1546. My family has occupied it continuously since then; we are one of the very few castles still lived in by the original family.

My father inherited the estate in 1950. I was an only child, so I was literally the last in the line and always knew that one day I would have to take over the responsibility of the

castle and the estate. It has left me with a lifelong sense of responsibility to and for the castle and its surrounding estates.

I was brought up by a governess in the castle here till I was 14. I owe such a lot to her. She lived in, and after breakfast each morning we'd go upstairs and there would be academic lessons till lunch time. The afternoons were devoted to crafts. She was a tiny woman, the daughter of a Free Church minister from Tobermoray, and she taught me everything. Her standpoint was always, 'Remember wherever you go, make me proud of you. If somebody's playing the piano, make sure you can play it too; if somebody is playing cards or billiards, then you must be able to, too; if somebody is painting, then so must you. In everything you are called upon to do, make sure that you are a credit to me and to your parents.

A continuing tradition:

Lady Macpherson Grant, author of cookbooks and head of the ancestral home, in the dining room which was once the great hall of her 16th century castle.

If you are bad at something, no matter – but you must make the effort.' So I grew up able to turn my hand at anything and everything. We did knitting, we crocheted, we did painting, music, collage work. The lesson of Robert the Bruce and the spider was impressed upon me: 'never ever give up!'

My father – like nearly all men of his class at that time – didn't consider any great need to educate me beyond the basics, along with the skills of a household head and future hostess. He always maintained that after my formal education was over I'd go abroad for a spell, learn some French, some Italian, go on courses and then return home to marry, have children and run the household. Any notion of having to work for my living was quite foreign to his way of thinking.

Well, I did go on courses, hundreds of them, but then I got offered a job. I was thrilled. I remember ringing him up from London and telling him, 'Dad, Dad, I've got a job!' Silence at the other end and then, 'But darling – daughters don't take jobs, do they? They marry and have children!'

I'd taken a course in flower arranging and had really been enthused by it. I got a job in London with Constance Spry, the renowned expert in the field. I had to go to Covent Garden at four of a morning to select my flowers and then I'd be off to arrange them in places like No 10 Downing Street, St James's Palace and Canterbury Cathedral. In the end, I was running my very own business.

What really stands out for me all these years later is the East Enders in the market. There weren't many people like me going around at four in the morning and having to

bargain over flowers as her job. I never did master a Cockney accent. But they took me in and made me welcome. I knew I was fully accepted when I arrived one morning and this stall holder cried out, 'Ere comes our bonny wee lassie from Scotland!'

During my early childhood we lived in some style. It was still the days when a family like ours was expected to run a large domestic staff and we were served by butlers and maids. I always remember that my father was taking his shoes or his boots off every 10 minutes just to give George the boot boy something to do. And he was simply one of a whole retinue of staff – butler, maids, cooks. We had 10 gardeners then; now we are down to one. Then there were all the outside staff: the gamekeepers, the ghillies, estate staff, a clerk of works.

My parents had the great foresight to renovate the castle in 1965. Until then there'd been no proper central heating or electric supply. Every time you tried to switch on a light it would make a fizzing noise. And when it rained you would have to rush around with buckets to catch the latest leak. The castle was a complete nightmare to live in. So my parents had to make the momentous decision which lots of similar landowners were facing at that time: either to let the castle slide gently into a total ruin, or call in the builders and go for a complete renovation.

Most buildings like this one have had to be become charitable trusts or given over to the National Trust, but we are anxious to keep ours in the family. I've always been absolutely determined that this should be so; that's where that sense of duty which was planted in me right from the start, comes in. I am the 22nd generation and with three children and seven grandchildren there is every prospect the line will be able to continue.

That we've managed to pull things round is due to Oliver, my husband, who worked in the city and knows his way around finance. My parents were of the traditional laird stock, content to live as Laird and Lady and not give a thought to commercialisation

I always remember that my father was taking his shoes or his boots off every 10 minutes just to give George the boot boy something to do.

An honour for the whole county:
Lady Clare with the honorary degree which, in 2010, was awarded by the University of Aberdeen in recognition of her work within and for Banffshire.

whatsoever. They were of their generation, one which considered their estate for living in and for entertaining guests. People would come up with their dogs, their servants, their rods and their guns, live on the estate, be our guests and that would be that. My parents looked to live off the rents from the farms on the estate, but that was hopelessly insufficient.

We had to change all that. With his banking background, Oliver realised that substantial growth in the income stream was needed to pay the salary and maintenance bills at a time when farm rents were falling behind in relative terms. The first thing we did was to start letting out the fishing and shooting rights. Then we went in for corporate entertainment. We began to make the estate work for us. We rented out cottages as holiday homes. We renovated 65 houses altogether, put bathrooms and electricity into them. Later we laid out a golf course and we now have a windfarm, too. Thirty years later there is no doubt that the strategy has worked, and that our cherished home also functions as a successful business.

But what it has also meant is that the days of leisure have gone forever. Corporate entertainment has forced me to become a cookery expert. To begin with I suddenly found myself having to do all the food preparation by myself, and for important guests too – chief executives, industrialists, ambassadors and the like – and I'd never even had a lesson in my life! I went to the library and took out books on the subject and in this way I taught myself how to cook. In those days I was still young and carefree and could simply throw myself into our new situation.

Now I'm in the position where I actually write cook books. They've been a success and I think the reason for that is partly because I had to learn from scratch and to make my recipes as simple as possible. After all, you have to improvise your ingredients when the nearest delicatessen is miles away. You can't just pick up an avocado when that requires a 90-mile round trip to Inverness. But if that was needed to keep the castle going, then that's what I had to learn to do.

If I'd been born 25 years earlier, my life would have been so different: I'd have had staff to do everything for me and my role would have been that of the Lady of the Castle, not cook, interior decorator, flower arranger, accountant and all the rest of it. But do you know, I'm glad things have turned out the way they have. I would have missed so much if I'd simply been a lady of leisure or a gracious hostess. I'm sometimes asked: would I prefer to have been born with the proverbial silver spoon or been given the castle with no money and the task of keeping it going. And every time I reply, it's the latter. It's been a wonderful challenge.

Of course, I haven't done any of this unaided. Oliver, my husband, has been a rock. When he married me he was taking on not only the individual; he was also taking on the castle, the county, Scotland – and my dogs! And then there are a number of angels who have kept things going - housekeepers, cooks, gardeners, all manner of staff and helpers.

By 'the county' I mean Banffshire, whatever the politicians might have done to the map. If anyone ever refers to my address as Moray, I tell them, 'Excuse me, but I think

Her other role:
As Lord Lieutenant of Banffshire, Clare Russell and husband Oliver accompany the Duke of Rothesay on his visit to Glenlivet Distillery.

you must mean Banffshire.' Banffshire is a wonderful county, one that has been cherished by my family for over five centuries.

So there is plenty for the visitor to enjoy in our part of the world. Tourism is vital to the economic future of Scotland and we are at the heart of it. Personally, I am delighted that Ballindalloch Castle is open to the public; a Grade 1 listed building such as ours, in such a fabulous setting, well, it should be enjoyed by everyone. The fact that we are constantly open to the scrutiny of the public acts as a stimulus to us all: the gardener and the housekeeper are proud to have their displays and their shining silver and brass remarked on by our visitors. Ballindalloch belongs to Scotland and I am its steward, not just an owner.

I think of myself as an ambassador for Banffshire and for Scotland. In 2002 I was invited by Her Majesty the Queen to become the Lord Lieutenant of Banffshire – a very great honour; it's a great privilege to serve Her Majesty and the county in this way. I am the 11th Lord Lieutenant (and first lady Lord Lieutenant) of Banffshire. What this means is that I am Her Majesty's personal representative in the county. If there's a royal visit, then I have to organise everything, from the moment they step across the county border to the moment they depart. The landing of the helicopters, the people to be presented, the police, the sniffer dogs, all the security – it all falls to me. And for the rest of the time I have the honour to give out medals and awards, deliver Her Majesty's messages of congratulations on diamond weddings and 100th birthdays, liaise with the Armed Forces, the TA, the local cadet force and the British Legion, make arrangements for wreath-laying on Remembrance Sunday, open places and events, make speeches, host garden parties and be involved in several charitable organisations – the list is endless.

I don't actually enjoy public speaking; it's just something I have to do. But then, think of all the wonderful variety of local people I get the opportunity to meet and to talk to. The armed forces, the scouts, the girl guides, the schools, Women Rural Institutes, Rotary clubs – I love going out and meeting them all. That's why, on 3 June 2012, we will be inviting all the people of Banffshire, all 46,000 of them, to come to the castle to mark the Queen's Diamond Jubilee. It's to celebrate Her Majesty's reign and it's to celebrate the county of Banffshire and its wonderful people.

'It rained a little at times, and the thermometer may have been on the low side for June, but for most of the day the sun shone on the crowd of over 5,000 Banffshire folk who joined Lord Lieutenant Clare Russell, her husband Oliver, and the Deputy Lieutenants of the county to celebrate the Queen's Diamond Jubilee at Ballindalloch Castle…' —PRESS RELEASE

Lady Clare Macpherson-Grant Russell, born 1944,
interviewed 2011: Ballindalloch Castle

Lady Clare is also responsible for a number of books, including
I LOVE FOOD, I LOVE FOOD2 *and* I LOVE BANFFSHIRE

One of a dying breed

In 1956 my father was asked by Lord Stonehaven to come and be his head gamekeeper at Rickarton House. He was a well-known and respected gamekeeper. He was a crack shot and would win prize after prize at shows and at clay pigeon shoots throughout the North-east. He was also an expert angler and back in 1922 he'd once taken a record catch at Findhorn when he'd landed 15 salmon in the one day.

So people would come out and take in what he had to tell them about gamekeeping and country life in general. To me it was a real privilege to follow him around and to meet all the interesting folk who came to see him and to notice how much they respected him. After all, the gamie was a figure of authority, the man who had command of the whole shoot. I must admit I got a bit of a thrill to be the gamekeeper's daughter on days like that. He bred labradors, though it was always the spaniels that were his great passion. I'd love to mix in with his dogs and to run little messages for him when he was out at a shoot.

In those days it wasn't corporate shoots, but invited guests, people who always made time to stop and chat and who knew what they were at. To go to the Big House first thing on the morning of a big shoot with all the dogs excited around you and my father rushing about seeing that all the cartridges were to hand and enough to last the day, and then all the guests coming in looking forward to the event – well that was really exciting.

He took his job very seriously and had great pride in the standards he maintained. He

The figure of authority:
John 'Jock' Millar poses for a retirement picture, 1967, after 52 years in gamekeeping.

always used to say that he was one of a dying breed, that once he and his kind had gone, the estates would find it difficult to persuade any of the next generation to be on call 24 hours a day, seven days a week as he was. He remembered when he first started out and received 14 shillings a week as his pay. And when he died at the age of 69 the local press ran stories with headlines like, *Top Scots Gamie Dies*. He'd devoted his whole working life to his profession, all 52 years of it.

Lena Burr, *née* Millar, born 1946, interviewed 2012: Rickarton

The keeper of the Castle

Except for spells at prep school and later Eton, I spent practically the whole of my childhood at Kincardine Castle. Now all this might sound like a rather exclusive, privileged upbringing and in some ways it was, but you should bear in mind that values such as the work ethic and social responsibility were drummed into us right from the start. It's true that I've inherited a fine Deeside castle as my home, and some 3,000 acres to go with it, but I've been brought up to accept that with privilege comes responsibility, that the family has not only to sustain the estate, but use it for the benefit of our local community.

Take the issue of affordable housing. After the war, the Government made a great push for council house building. This estate gave land to the local council for its housing – and when I say 'gave' I mean exactly that – a gift. The stated intention in the deed is that this was for the provision of rented houses for working people. It came as a blow to find, a generation later, these houses being sold off at a discount for the purchasers to make a handsome capital gain. There are about 70 houses on the estate and the bulk of these are leased at modest rents in order to try to provide housing to meet local need. Kincardine Estate is actually responsible for providing three-and-a-half times as many affordable

I've been brought up to accept that with privilege comes responsibility; not only to sustain the estate, but use it for the benefit of our community.

The keeper of Kincardine Castle: Andrew Bradford.

rented houses as the local authority does in this area — 50 against their 13.

The castle has 70/71 rooms in all. On a wet day we used to send the children off with the challenge of counting them all and they never came back with the same answer; their estimations would vary between 60 and 80.

I took it over in 1979. For me, the estate was simply my life; I'd always assumed that I was there to work for it, for the common weal. From an early age I'd been involved in tasks to do with the farming and with the house; I became an estate labourer from almost the time I could walk and had imbibed the values of hard work, prudence, thrift and careful planning. And now if I see the gutters need clearing I'll simply get the ladders out and climb up to do it myself. That's probably how I will meet my end: falling to my death with some wet leaves in my hand, trying to keep Kincardine Castle weather proof and going to the very end.

So I had this sort of double life: nannies, a nursery and then boarding school on the one hand; stooking, wood cutting, carting stuff about, splitting logs, that kind of hard labour, on the other. Both seemed entirely natural to me; I never thought of myself as enjoying an indulged upbringing. In fact, much of it was quite Spartan. The castle did have central heating, but it was very central and didn't extend to the bedrooms. You'd squeeze the toothpaste and find it was frozen stiff and that you had to stand on the tube to get any out. I got into the way of leaving some on my brush each evening, when it was a little bit less cold, for the morning. You'd find the wash basin all frozen up. But none of this struck me as extraordinary; it was winter and that's what happened.

Nor did we have much in the way of toys either. I remember a sort of rattle made up of shells on a string and a teddy or two and some blocks of green mahogany which had to serve as our Lego. Kincardine Castle had one television set, but this was situated in the servants' quarters, so we saw little of it. My parents appeared to have a Luddite attitude towards modern technology: there wasn't even a fridge and in the summer you'd be drinking milk from the cows, which had a sharp, even rancid, flavour.

In any case, we were outdoor children and would always regard our natural habitat as the grounds of the house, not its interior. Building huts, damming burns, bonfires, walking through the woods, climbing trees, careering around on bikes — that's what we'd spend our days doing. We would have to be summoned in for mealtimes by the ringing of a bell. I had a great deal of freedom. At the age of four, I came upon a bull which had broken out from his field and was wandering about; I slipped my finger into the ring on its nose and led it home. I had no fears; the environment was my friend and my playground.

On paper I am a very wealthy man, I know, but that is on paper; in terms of actual disposable income I don't have a heck of a lot. I'm aware of inheriting a situation which has been steadily in decline from the grandeur of the pre-First World War days of multiple servants; my parents' lives were marked by going from an era of servants to one of none at all.

I don't know if you're following *Downton Abbey* on TV on Sunday nights, but if you

are, you'll get a glimpse of how far the world of the Big House has changed. Now, Kincardine Castle has never been as big scale as they are, but a lot of it is quite evocative. You'll note how formal and class conscious that old world was – and that these qualities lingered on among the servants longer than they did upstairs. Downstairs, in the programme, they are painfully aware of rank, of where they should sit at table, of how they should address each other, and how they should be uniformed.

But after the First World War that world of service and protocol began to be eroded and that's the period my parents lived through. So, if I say we didn't feel particularly rich, it was because of my consciousness that a Big House like ours was becoming more and more difficult to sustain – and the loss of servants was a mark of that. My parents' existence here was characterised by the remorseless dropping off in the number of staff they could afford to keep on and the sheer day-to-day struggle to keep a large, expensive and impractical house going.

When, in the early 1980s, we moved here to take my parents' place, there were no servants left. This was a fantastic decline from earlier times, times which were still within living memory. For my own interest I've been tracking these changes by consulting old house plans and documents. I've looked out the floor plans of Kincardine Castle for the 1890s, for example. To my surprise I've discovered that this whole place was erected to accommodate my great-grandmother and her family – but that meant no more than her two children and four sets of guests at any one time.

So this grand edifice of 70 rooms was put up for four family members plus four couples as guests. The amount of rooms can be explained by the number of servants it was considered necessary to have. Look at the titles of some of those rooms: there's a beer store – important because till quite late on, part of the wages were in beer and that would

The aurora borealis lights up the castle's northern skies.

date back to the period when water was less pure – a wine cellar, kitchen, scullery, butler's pantry, and so on. Downstairs would have been a whole separate world of people and of their equipment – ranges, hot plates, fires, ovens, sinks, larders. There was the cook's pantry, there was Mrs Pickering's Personal Store – Mrs Pickering was my grandmother and she would have kept that room for the safe storage of vital items like candles and soaps. Then there was the flower room for the flowers that were taken in from the garden and used to decorate the house, there was the brushing hall for the cleaning of shoes and boots, and also outdoor clothes. There were no washing machines in those days, so muddy clothes were dried and the mud brushed off by hand. There was not only the footman's room, but also the stranger's footman's room – to cater for guests who would bring their own staff with them. There was the housekeeper's hall, the servants' hall, the butler's hall, the male servants' bathroom – and so on and so on.

The house had to be so extensive to accommodate this vast substructure of servants and equipment, because that is what used to be considered essential for any self-respecting country house. It was the norm for the period. Indeed, it is estimated that in Britain more people were employed in service by the end of the 19th century than in the whole of the shipbuilding, coal and iron industries combined – and that's in the days when the country did have such things.

In some ways, you could say that the Big House filled the gap left by the absence of any social welfare system. It provided a secure roof, food, clothing, companionship. Of course, the staff had to work pretty hard, but in return they were looked after.

When we took over at the end of the Seventies things were at very low ebb. Inflation was 25%, marginal tax rates stood at 97%, staff was expensive, overheads were rocketing; the whole enterprise was collapsing. It's no wonder that in the decades after the Second World War many old houses were abandoned and deroofed. But I never considered doing anything but try to keep going. I remember once this German visitor drew up before the house in his vintage 1920s Bentley, looked us up and down, and then exclaimed, 'Mein Gott, you don't actually live in dat house, do you?' Whereupon I replied, 'You don't actually drive that thing, do you?' His response was simply, 'Touché'.

Kincardine Castle is like a well-crafted, rare old car: thoroughly expensive, not at all practical, but beautiful and a privilege to own. We had two options, essentially: to attempt to preserve the house as an anachronistic museum piece or to make a living concern out of it – to keep it mothballed in the garage or drive the hell out of it, in fact. Well, if you owned a Bentley, isn't that the only thing to do with it?

So we open the house for corporate groups. That can be very exciting. I've put on gourmet dinners and had Gordon Ramsey preparing the meal in the kitchen; I've had the great joy of listening to Clio Gould playing her Stradivarius in my drawing room; I've walked round the grounds with members of the CIA and an Arabian oil expert. My eyes have been opened up to a range of experiences – and I haven't had to leave my own hearth to enjoy them.

I'm a working part of the estate community. The tenants and the workers become

The Great Hall – one of the castle's 70 rooms.

members of an extended family, people I have grown up with, worked alongside and shared the ups and downs of life with. In the summer our old gardener died and he'd been with us 49 years; before him his wife's father had been gardener; they had three children who all worked on the estate and we've also employed some of their children. So, in my lifetime a whole network of family members and four generations have worked for us. We knew them not simply as employees, but as friends; it was a great honour to be asked to speak at his funeral.

I'm involved in conservation. Here at Kincardine, that means two aspects, the first of which is building. The second is ecology. I have inherited these precious buildings and it is my duty to attempt to keep them going. But that can't mean no change at all; you can't just keep them as a museum: they must respond to changing circumstances. Today, that must mean looking at our energy usage. Now, if you look out the window at the back you'll see a new building project and that houses our new woodchip burning plant. My next move is to explore the possibility of erecting a single wind turbine and that promises to provide a balanced energy programme for the whole estate.

So alongside our inherited properties, I have an ambition to develop Kincardine into an exemplary example of good modern energy practices. Now we can offer our visitors tours of the boiler house, as well as the great hall and the gardens. All this is aimed at ensuring that the estate will have a sustainable future and that the best of its past will be there for future generations to enjoy – and to live in. I don't see myself as the permanent owner of Kincardine Castle, but as someone who is passing through and who happens to have been entrusted with its stewardship for a certain length of time, that's all.

Andrew Bradford, born 1955, interviewed 2011: Kincardine Castle, Kincardine O'Neil

Andrew Bradford has written a book about his estate:
A LITTLE BIT OF PARADISE: THE STORY OF A KINCARDINESHIRE ESTATE.

Henry Irvine-Fortescue, his mother Margaret, and wife Hazel and two children at the front entrance, Kingcausie, June 2011.

Maintain, protect, improve

I'm aware that my upbringing has been different from most. But I must say that running an estate of this size and kind does have its difficulties; it's a privilege, but with it has come responsibilities. In my father's day there were some 12 or 13 employees: gardener, a couple of gamekeeper ghillies, a pair of foresters, a whole lot of farm staff. Now we're down to two men on the farm plus me. I do pretty well anything and everything. I don't run Kingcausie as a sporting estate; my father had little interest in the shooting side of things and nor do I.

Growing up in the big house was a great adventure. I did most of my schooling as a day boy at Robert Gordon's College. This meant that we could return to the estate out in the country each evening and enjoy its freedoms. We got up to all sorts – tree houses, dens, cycling along the local lanes, generally exploring. Our parents gave us a lot of leeway. There was an old car on the estate and we were allowed to knock about in it. By the time I was 10, I was careering along the private roads of the estate and picking up basic mechanics. My parents would invite people out for tea and they'd bring their children with them and there they would be, sipping their tea and looking out of the window and suddenly catching sight of us flashing past in this old beaten up Beetle car. My parents just let us rip; they accepted knocks and bruises as part of the growing process and trusted us to learn from our mishaps.

I personally feel very close to my ancestors and what they have bequeathed me. I'm aware of my duty to conserve the best of what has gone before and to keep developing the estate in their name. When I look out and see a tree which is 300 years old and know that it was planted and nurtured by one of them, I feel very much in touch with Kingcausie as a living inheritance. I can even identify the ancestor who was responsible. Take the front field and its fine woodland pasture; I can consult old maps and match it against James Irvine who, around 1700 when the trees were planted, was in charge.

So I have a very personal feel for the whole estate and what has gone before. I can look at each corner of it and associate it with my family's efforts to build it up over the years. When I look at a bit of the landscape round here, I see all the people who've gone before. I've always enjoyed drystane walls and rejoice that Kingcausie has some particularly fine examples – and that's because they were constructed in the 1820s, just after the Napoleonic Wars. I can think of the men who built those walls and the pride they took in their craftsmanship. I myself like to be hands-on, to get my hands dirty; I like humping boulders back into their walls where the cattle have knocked them out – not just a repair job, but an act of homage.

I like the earth. My father always used to say that it was more important to maintain the land and not the house. He never spent much either on it or on himself; the money all went into the cottages, the roads, the farmland, the estate as a whole. He hadn't a lot of time for fancy airs and graces and for high living. I subscribe to the same philosophy. I've seen my role over the last 30 years as renovating the properties and bringing them up to a reasonable modern standard. This has been a massive undertaking. Most of the farm cottages were built in the 1820s and 30s and have required work on damp coursing, on

the roofs and on putting right the nail sickness.

I also feel that Kingcausie is now in better shape than when I took it over. I was horrified when at the Western Peripheral Route hearings a landscape expert came along and branded us as 'an estate in decline'. Well, if you adopt some kind of National Trust cosmetic viewpoint and expect Kingcausie to maintain its smooth lawns and have a retinue of gardeners lovingly manicuring the approaches, then that maybe appears to be case. But that is to adopt a false historic reference point. In fact, Kingcausie is a good solid example of an estate which has adapted to modern circumstances. It's a living, working, productive farm, with well modernised properties that offer warm and comfortable living conditions. I am proud to have contributed to that.

We were brought up to expect to work for the estate. My childhood was full of chores. There were always baskets of broad beans from the kitchen garden to be podded, or baskets of rasps to be picked, or the lawns to be mowed. Oh yes, those lawns! In my boyhood I seemed to be forever going up and down with the mower; I had quite enough of that to last a lifetime and now that's the one thing I simply refuse to do. I much prefer to do something that will last, like going out with the chainsaw and cutting down the

A living inheritance:
Henry Irvine-Fortescue, with his mother, wife and two children outside Kingcausie, winter 2009.

Henry showing members of the Buchan Field Club around, June 2011.

I've expanded the herd from 80 to 200 breeding cattle and upgraded the machinery; I've tried to shift us from a basic dog-and-stick approach to a modern, efficient farm.

overhanging branches of a birch, so I can make room for a new specimen – something that will be there in 20 years' time.

My great-grandfather had this saying: 'I can't do the things I want to do because of the things I ought to do, and I can't do the things I ought to do because of the things that must be done, and I can't do the things that must be done because I'm not strong enough and the day isn't long enough'.' I can't do everything I'd like to do for Kingcausie, but I can ensure that my generation has played its part in ensuring its longer term future. The trick is to realise you can't do it all and to have the wisdom to select what the priorities are, here and now.

I suppose you could say my approach has been a mixture of the practical and the romantic. I do hanker back to the time when things were a little bit more straightforward, to when society was, shall we say, rather more cohesive, more inclusive than it has since become. My mind-set is still that of the paternalistic laird, one who follows in the footsteps of my father and cares for the welfare and the property of the workers – his people. It's the right way – but it's not the economic way.

But Kingcausie is a survivor. I adhere to the old family motto, which is 'Sub sole, sub umbra, virens – under the sun and under the shade I will flourish'. I do believe in that. Our badge is the holly, an evergreen, which, come whatever time of year, whatever conditions, will continue to grow. I also have a strong Christian faith and I believe in the provenance of God. And in each generation there's been at least one of us who has held on to the same faith.

I've now been running the farm for 10 years; I've expanded the cattle herd from 80 to 200 breeding cattle. I've upgraded the machinery; I've tried to shift us from a basic dog-and-stick approach to a properly modern, efficient farm. My vision has been to maintain, to protect, to improve. That's my mantra for Kingcausie: maintain, protect, improve.

The next huge mountain to climb is the state of the main part of the house. It's got such a lot that needs doing to it, after years of neglect. For us the question has to be confronted: we want to live in the old house and breathe new life into its fabric, but how much money and effort will that take? And with the Aberdeen by-pass planned to roar past our front door, would it be worth doing anything at all?

The house is B-listed. I had the Aberdeenshire Council conservation officer out here and she said 'No' to just about everything I was planning to do. I came to the conclusion that she simply wanted time to stand still and wouldn't be content until we were living under candlelight and emptying our chamber pots out of the upstairs window each morning. Of course, I want to preserve what is, after all, my own family house – but there has to be some allowance made for the way in which a house must adapt and be developed. If not, then people will simply be forced to abandon their property and so the nation's heritage will be lost completely. She declared, 'Do you realise that even the very wallpaper is part of the B-listing?' And here we were looking at all that paper which was peeling off the wall with the damp and which had mould growing beneath it. Yes, it's wonderful old 1852 wallpaper and very handsome to look at, but then she doesn't have to

attempt to live with it as a modern family.

Any civilisation has made progress by allowing the latest generation to take over what the past ones have done and to build upon that. Development and adaptation – that's the human story through the ages. I'm concerned to fulfil the stewardship of Kingcausie, but consider that I can only do that if I'm allowed to have room in which to breathe fresh life into the place, not sit in it like the custodian of some old museum, watching it decay gently about my ears.

Henry Irvine-Fortescue, born 1958, interviewed 2010: Kingcausie House, Maryculter

In good shape.
Kingcausie House from the west.

ALL MANNER OF FOLK: Part 3

League Winners: Morag Pirie, front row, second left, as a member of the league winning Aberdeen University football team.

The motorcyclist: the first lady biker

I got my motorbike when I was 18 and still living at home. I got a job at Stonehaven and it seemed a natural step to get a bike of my own so I could travel the three miles back and forth to my work. There was no question of my father permitting me to stay in lodgings. His attitude was that I was too young to be allowed to leave home, not at 18! In fact, he wouldn't even permit me to wear make-up. When I had the job at Delanzio's shop, I remember Mrs Delanzio remarked that I never wore lipstick. 'Oh, no, my father would never stand for that,' I told her. But she insisted I try some. I was careful, when I got off the bus at the road end, to scrape it all off before I dared show my face through the door. 'You jist tak that muck aff yer face!', that's what he would have told me. And his word was law.

I saved up the money and went into Cheyne's in Aberdeen and bought this little ASA Bantam, which I christened Bumper. The registration number was GRG 624. I was, as far as I could tell, the very first female motorcyclist in the North-east. In 1956, the Stonehaven photographer Freddie Stephen came up to the farm and took a series of shots of me and my bike. The story appeared in this magazine, the *Scottish Clubman,* and it was made out that I was something of a dizzy young girl, at a loss mechanically. That wasn't true: I could find my way around the mechanics and I could change my own spark plugs.

But there's no doubt a lady motorcyclist was out of the ordinary. People would stop and stare as I rode past and lorry drivers would toot and wave at me. The bike was my pride and joy; I'd spend hours tinkering around on it and cleaning it up till it was sparkling.

I loved that bike, but in the end it proved itself to be a liability. It was a reliable machine. But the wheels were small and narrow and on the winter roads there was always the danger of losing control. I came off one morning when I skidded on the brae into Stonehaven in the ice. Then I had a second tumble and that was it. My father at last saw the sense of me leaving home and getting digs in Stonehaven. At 21, free at last to come and go as I pleased, and to wear lipstick.

SCOTTISH · CLUBMAN   6ᴰ

ANNE HAS THE RIGHT IDEA IN HEAD GEAR

(See Story on Page 8)

THANK YOU !

This being the first issue of the eighth year of publication of the " Scottish Clubman," we take this opportunity of extending heartiest thanks to our advertisers and readers for their faithful support.

The North-east's first lady biker: *The Scottish Clubman* chooses Anne Stephen as their cover girl, 1956.

Anne Stephen, born 1937, interviewed 2011: Muchalls

A BIKE BEFORE A BOY FRIEND, ANY DAY!

A Country Cameo in

Words and Pictures

Devised by

A. J. STEPHEN

1 *Meet 19-year-old Miss Anne Ingram, of Stonehaven, and "Bumper" the Bantam — "Suppose you've guessed, we're off for a run."*

2 *First, fix the headgear—"My helmet's been a 'must' since I started motorcycling over a year ago."*

3 *All set—"Saved for a bike since I left school at 15. 'Bumper's' my first, helped by a 'sub' from Dad. Mum doesn't like 'em."*

4 *"Bumper" stopped for no reason!— "Heart's in the right place, but maintenance isn't so hot. I wonder...?"*

5 *Let's see what's wrong—"Could be the head? 'Bumper's', I mean!"*

6 *Oooh! So that's the trouble—"To think I cleaned that plug only yesterday!"*

7 *Tools away, all set again—"My, what a day for a run. Better 'n bus-conducting every day. Wish we had two-wheeled buses!"*

8 *Off we go—"Did you ever see a happier couple? Boy friends— Bah!"*

Far from being 'a dizzy young girl' – but that is how the magazine portrayed Anne.

No TVs or play stations – but always plenty to do. Ian Cameron (back row, left) with gang of friends, late 1940s. Beside him stand Johnny Simpson and Alistair McGregor; in front are Fiona, Rosie and Charles.

A young Ian with his mother and Major, the dog, Albert Road, Ballater.

The mineralogist: learning how to keek

For me, Ballater is God's own country. As a local historian, I want to share its wonders with the outside world. My own training and work as an engineer, coupled with a fascination for geology, led me to set up my own company, Castle Plant (Deeside) Ltd, and this digging of holes taught me that there is no such thing as 'a stone', only a variety of minerals. The search for local minerals has held my curiosity ever since.

On one occasion I volunteered to take a party of oilmen up to Loch Builg. Their objective was to reach the summit of Ben Avon and I was to pick them up in my 4x4 when they came back off the hill. When they appeared, I asked them 'What did you see up there?' 'Not a lot', came the reply. 'But you were at the top of Ben Avon!'. 'Oh well, it was rather misty; we didn't really see anything'. 'But what about the birds, the animals, the burns, the rock beneath your feet?' They'd never learned how to 'keek', how to open their eyes to the wonder of what is all around, and beneath, them. Their sole purpose had been to bag another Munro.

You see, I was brought up to keek. We didn't have TVs or playstations when I was a boy. But what we did have was Ballater and the hills and the River Dee. We got to know every tree, every type of bird's nest, the tracks of otter, deer and wildcat. We would hunt the riverbanks for oyster catchers, dippers, red shanks and the colonies of sand martins that made their nests in the sand banks. We got to know every rock and every pool. We knew the dates of the great spates and where the river had left its victims after every flood; amongst the logs and trees we found carcasses of deer and sheep.

Ballater in the Forties and Fifties: what a playground! The magic of it all for me was the bustle and mix of soldiers, training for war, and the North American loggers, clearing all our hills of trees for pit props and defences for the Channel beaches. Between civilian Newfoundlanders and Canadian Forestry Corps loggers, the train loads into Ballater soon brought 1,200 men to live in our midst.

To a young lad like me, those men took on the stature of heroes. I was especially taken with the Newfoundlanders. At that time, their island was quite independent of Canada, an untamed place where they'd use hard-packed snow to get the trees out on tractor-drawn sledges. To them, the Deeside hills and its timber presented few challenges. They built and lived in log cabins in the woods.

I started school in 1943 and have clear memories of how the Canadian Forestry Corps soldiers would pay us a visit each month when their rations arrived from across the Atlantic. They would drive up in their big 6x6 truck and enter the school, carrying tea chests, full of goodies. They came into the classroom, these big weather-beaten men in their smart Army uniforms, with webbed belts and high-lacing boots. They'd address our teacher as 'Ma'am' and take off their caps. Then they'd take their tea chests up and down between our rows of little desks and invite us to dig deep. Each pupil was allowed two handfuls – of chocolate bars, of oranges, biscuits, sweeties and tins of meat and fish. Our mothers would tell us, 'Never mind the sweeties – ging for the salmon!'

When you see that sort of generosity, accompanied by such gracious, easy manners, it leaves an unforgettable impression. To me, these loggers were gods. I was fascinated by

Men with the stature of heroes. Newfoundlander logging camp, Ballater, 1940s.

Before the developments: Craigendarroch Hotel, 1960s.

'God's own country': Ian outside his home, 'Abergairn', Ballater, 2012.

their machinery. The huge six-wheel trucks, the bulldozers, the caterpillar tractors which could crawl up the steepest hills and return, dragging behind them the huge bundles of whole trees. They had a huge influence on me, one that never left, and led me into a lifetime's association with heavy, and mostly North American, plant.

Between times, Ballater has gone through difficult periods. It had been founded in the late 1700s as accommodation for visitors partaking of the mineral waters on Panannich Hill, but from the arrival of the railway in the 1860s, it became more and more dependent on the line. Everything came by rail: mail, newspapers, fish fresh from Aberdeen fish market, coal, cows and passengers. Ballater was an LNER company town, but nobody took much notice of that until Dr Beeching closed it down in the 1960s.

Prosperity departed with the line: shops closed, development waned, and Ballater School was downgraded to Primary only – and to add to our misery they abolished our Town Council. But then in 1982, Ron Alison, an engineer with Kildonan Investments, came to the village with news of the time-share chalet holidays he'd seen abroad. Just at that time, the Craigendarroch Hotel came on the market and Ron realised this would make a wonderful site to introduce time-share holidays to Deeside. They approached our little company and asked if we would like to get involved. And so began a long association with Craigendarroch.

The next eight years were spent excavating, pouring foundations for 93 chalets, and landscaping. With the chalets came the sale of 50 x 93 time-share weeks and the potential all-year-round occupancy. Today, 30 years on, the enterprise is in the hands of the Hilton International group and is still a major attraction for tourists and by far the largest local employer.

The off-shoot is that Carigendarroch visitors bring business to the shops and the pubs and have helped Ballater gain its reputation for first-class restaurants. Ballater has been resurrected.

I've been very fortunate the way my life has worked out. I've been able to combine my career with machinery with an environment I feel it has been privileged to enjoy. I talk of the bedrock as 'the bones of Scotland'. I was sitting with a geologist friend on a hillside one day when the rocks beneath us started to make cracking noises; there was very little movement, just this loud hissing. At times like that I feel a contact with the forces beneath us, with an ancient volcanic energy. For me, the stones are still alive.

Machines, landscape, words, history, geology, Ballater, the Dee – it's just what I do.

Ian Cameron, born 1938, interviewed 2011: Ballater

Ian Cameron has written a number of works about Ballater including Plant and Roots, *2008, and* Albert Road, *2010.*

Joel with his Alford Academy Gospel Choir, Music Hall, Aberdeen, when they won their Category.

The newcomer

I was born in 1962 in a place called Luanshya, in the copperbelt of Zambia. My father was a miner; I was one of 10 children. The whole town was based on copper; Zambia is very rich in the mineral and lots of British companies worked there. But Zambia became independent in 1964 and, later, a policy of Zambianisation was introduced. Till then, the mine had been managed by the British ex-pats while the Zambians acted as the workers. The British lived in large houses, situated above the mines where the prevailing winds blew all the sulphur-dioxide which the smelting process emitted into the atmosphere, away from their homes and on to the workers' quarters.

Before independence there had been a form of apartheid in operation. For example, there were separate shopping zones and there was very little social mixing.

I started school when I was 10. It wasn't really till the 1970s that a proper system of education was being introduced. The aim was to give a basic education to everyone, but hold a sort of elimination from then on so that only the brighter ones could go the whole way up the secondary stage.

Zambia has given us a rich musical background. I come from a very religious family, one that tries to follow the word of God. So church music and gospel choirs have played an important part in my upbringing, as well as all the traditional songs of the country. I'm quite musical myself. I play the guitar, though not to professional standard. I've a good ear and harmonising is a strong point. In fact, I started the Alford School Choir a couple of years after I arrived here, in 1994. I'd go to the local church and feel that the music was in need of being jazzed up a bit. We started off with a small group and have gradually built it up from there. We now have 40, something I'm rather proud of. We're always being invited to sing at church services and at school concerts.

We started off with songs in English, but I've now taught them some 10 Zambian songs which they sing in Bemba – one of the main languages of the country. They sing unaccompanied and do all the proper actions, too. It's true that Zambians might be a

From the Sandé family album.
Joel with Emeli, Lucy and Diane, over the years.

little more rhythmic naturally, but my pupils here have managed to get into the spirit of the Zambian music very well.

Maybe the way in which singing in groups comes naturally to a Zambian is because there is still a close family life there, with the emphasis on the whole extended family joining in activities and interacting. Here, you can live in a street for years and not get to know your neighbours; but there, it's impossible to be alone for long: cousins, second cousins, uncles and aunts are constantly dropping in. I must admit I do miss that here. We have a saying in Zambia that 'It takes a village to bring up a child' and we live by that, at least out in the rural areas. And we also value older folk; grandparents are looked up to for the wisdom they can bring to the young.

How I came to Britain in the first place is this: I was picked out as a bright pupil and was then taken up and sponsored by the mining company, the Zambia Consolidated Copper Mines Ltd. I passed through the system of national tests at every stage and did my A Levels. You know, I did well right the way through the Zambian educational system – I like to think that if I'd been born in this country and able to enjoy the opportunities of young people here, why, I reckon I could have risen to become an astronaut!

In the event, I had to settle for an Engineering degree at Sunderland Polytechnic - now 'University'; the system was that the mining company would sponsor you for that and then would look to you to give them at least two years 'payback' by returning to work for them.

It was in Sunderland that I met Diane. She was also a student, at that time studying the Primary Education course. But, after her first year, it became clear she couldn't continue with it: music was an integral part of her course and she just couldn't manage it. So I bought her guitar and that's how we met. She did continue, but converted to a Combined Arts course.

Our relationship blossomed and we ended up by getting married. My intention at this stage was to return to Zambia. I graduated in 1988 and went, taking my new wife with me. But it was the very worst time to introduce someone from the UK to my native country. It was in the thick of a severe economic slump, with copper prices hitting rock bottom, and the shops were empty. I think, however, we could have settled but for the fact that Diane contracted malaria. She had to come back home; I had to stay on and do my two years of 'payback'.

By 1990, I had returned to join her. We were living in her home county of Cumbria, at Ulverston. It was difficult for me to find a suitable job. I was qualified to land a post at places like Selafield or the Vickers yard at Barrow, but because of the security concerns you had to have five years' residence. And by now, with the birth of Emeli and then Lucy, I had a family.

Diane's family accepted me. Obviously I wasn't quite what they might have been expecting for their daughter's husband and there were a few shaky moments to begin with – not so much because they had any hostility towards me, but rather because they were worried about the difficulties we might encounter as a mixed race couple. But in

the end, all was well. In fact, Diane's father left me something in his will; I was told that this was a very special favour and that I must have become his favourite son-in-law for that to happen.

Then Emeli started at the Infant school and they wanted governors, so that's what I became. One of my colleagues there asked me about my background. I told him about my degree and my two years in a responsible position in Zambia. 'Have you ever thought of teaching?', he replied – and that got me thinking. As a qualified engineer I was asked to visit some of the local schools to have a look at the Technical lessons as a 'Neighbourhood Engineer'. I remember being at this High School in a Technical class and discovering that the teacher seemed to have little confidence in what he was trying to do. I just knew I could do better than that.

So Diane and I talked it over. I'd been thinking of Aberdeen for some time because of the opportunities there might be in the oil industry there. So I decided to enrol in the PGCE course at Northern College.

A fortnight before the graduation, I found out that I'd been appointed to Alford. I knew nothing about this Alford, so I got on my bike at the weekend and cycled out from Aberdeen to have a look. One of my colleagues at the school later told me what happened. I parked my bike and took a walk along the main street. Apparently, people were coming to the windows to take a look at this strange black man that had suddenly landed in their midst. Everything went very quiet; you could have heard a pin drop.

The Head, Bobby Graham, made me welcome; so did the rest of the staff. I can't say I've ever encountered any serious problems in my 20 years here. The worst has been some boys running up and calling me 'Frank Bruno' and then running away – but that's been about it. As for me, I felt confident enough: I now had a post and the demoralising business of being unemployed was over. I had my qualifications; I'd been in charge of a 68-workforce back in Zambia. I knew I could do it.

Now I feel very much at home in Alford. I keep thinking that if I were to drop dead

Joel as Principal of Technology, leading his Alford Academy team to success in the North-east Young Engineers and Science Club award, 2012.

'Thank you for everything.'
Emeli Sandé's million-selling disc, presented to Alford Academy, December 2012.

tomorrow I'd be well mourned: the Gospel Choir would perform, my old pupils would turn out, the villagers would gather. I feel known, feel accepted. I can walk down the street and meet people I can chat to. And one of the very best aspects has been when former pupils come back and tell me how they are getting on.

I knew that Emeli had a special talent right from the start, though I can't say I ever realised just how famous she would become. And she was always strong academically. At Standard Grade she got straight '1s'; at Highers it was four 'A's and a 'B'. She went to Glasgow University to do Medicine there; it was only in her fourth year, and with no resits behind her, that she was becoming so involved with the music that she decided to convert to do an intercalated degree in Neuro-science.

She was a member of my Gospel Choir. When she was 12, she entered the Inverurie Talent Show and although she didn't win, she returned three years later with a group and won. She always had this very mature voice; when she was only a young girl, and if you hadn't seen her, you'd think it was a grown woman singing.

We took her down to London, to a rapology contest, organised by the radio station, Choice FM. What she was offering was a bit different from the rest and although she didn't win she got the whole audience joining in. She made an impact: 'Where is she from?', they were asking. 'What, from a small village in Aberdeenshire? Wow!' It was a good experience for her; up here audiences had been so reserved; down in London they were so street-wise, so outgoing, and it was a challenge for Emeli. Our thinking was, 'Right, she's conquered Inverurie, now let's conquer London!'

Then she entered a talent competition run by the BBC, called 'Lowdown' with Trevor Nelson, and this time she did win. People were now taking notice; record companies were actually coming up to Alford to try to sign her up. She left school and took a year out to take stock. Nothing happened, so she decided to take up her university place. Then, in her third year at Glasgow, she started to write songs; one of them, *Diamond Rings*, became a hit and that was a breakthrough.

Emeli had always written her own material. We bought her a piano when she was 13 and she quickly learned to play at it, experimenting with her own material. She did have a few lessons, but never embarked on a formal course. Everything that she did was her own natural way. She was always singing about the house. I had a grandmother who would go into a trance and sing with her eyes closed to the rest of the world, oblivious of anyone else, and do this for a whole hour or more. Well, that's what Emeli would do. When she started on a song, she would go on and on, deep into the night. You'd hear her in her room at two am; you'd knock and tell her, 'Emeli, do you realise what time it is?' and she would reply, 'Yes, yes – just a minute or two more!'

Of course, it was a great honour for her to be chosen to sing at the Opening Ceremony for the Olympics. She did well and we were in the audience too, but it was all a bit nerve racking. She had told us that at the rehearsal the day before something had gone wrong with the technology. The earpiece, which was to count her in as the dancers were performing, hadn't worked and she had a blank and lost the words. So when we watched her live we were fearful that the same thing might happen again – in front of all those millions of viewers. We were proud to hear her sing, but we were also crossing our fingers and counting down the verses: 'Well, that's verse one safely through; verse two; verse three…' *Abide With Me* is a hymn for the dead, so at the end there was a moment's silence and we were the only ones cheering – with sheer relief.

We do realise how far Emeli has come and how so many people appreciate what she is doing. She now has such a hectic way of life, touring all over the world, with TV appearances, recording, media interviews. When she comes home to Alford she just collapses for a day or two and sleeps right through into the afternoon. The first day she was here, just before Christmas, we didn't dare disturb her; she slept right up to three in the afternoon.

Then she paid a visit to the school. It was priceless. The children had been told to expect a special visitor, which they assumed would be Santa, so when the door opened and Emeli walked in the whole place just erupted. You watch the video and all you can hear are shrieks and cheers that go on and on. Once she got some silence, she told them all that this is where she had made her own debut, in that very hall, on the stage in a nativity play as Mary, aged five. As she put it, 'This is where my musical journey started'. She then told them she wanted to give something back to the school; she would present her first million-selling disc, *Our Version of Events*, to Alford Academy as a token of her gratitude for all the school had done for her. She then sang for them all and invited them all to join in, which they did.

Alford has been a good place for my two girls to grow up in. It is peaceful and secure. And it's given them opportunities. Lucy was able to develop her football here and almost reached the Scottish team. They both had a fine education at the academy and got degrees. Lucy graduated First class Honours in Law at RGU.

We like to think that Diane and I have managed to give them both a solid, sensible upbringing, too. It was wonderful to have them both in the house before Christmas. Just like the old days – and making sure that they both still helped with the washing up!

Joel Sandé, born 1962, interviewed 2013: Alford

> At the end there was a moment's silence and we were the only ones cheering – with sheer relief.

The female referee

The family home was in Parkhill, about three miles from Bridge of Don and out in the country. I've played football for as long as I can remember. We had a large garden and Dad marked out a pitch for us, with goals. We each had our own football, a good quality hard white plastic one, and we inscribed our names on them. At the primary school, at lunchtime, we all played in the playground together, boys with the girls, all mixing in. I usually played in goals while my twin sister, Heather, was striker. Usually, it was just the pair of us that played football along with the boys; the other girls tended to be in their own groups, skipping or simply chatting.

To us, sporting activity was a natural part of our lives. At home it was expected that as

'Always part of our lives.' Morag Pirie, as a Primary 7 pupil, among the Gala trophy winners, Dyce, 1987.

The footballing sisters: with Heather, 1997.

Officiating at the Scottish Women's Cup Final, 2001.

long as the weather was all right, we would be out, kicking about the garden or going off to play with some of the children who lived in the farm down the road. We did play on the Nintendo, but if Mum saw me sitting at it indoors during the day she would tolerate it for maybe half an hour and then it would be, 'Come on, you can't waste the day sitting indoors all the time. You've got a lovely big garden to play in – outside!' Not that we needed much encouragement: outdoors was our natural environment.

When I got to university I joined the ladies' team there and loved it. I was still a goalkeeper; although I'm not really the size and the build for it, I could always throw myself around and learned how to judge the angles and when to come out and when to stay on my line. I was quite brave, a bit stupid and pretty agile. Then, when I was in my third year, I saw an advert for a new team in the city and I joined them. So now I was playing maybe three times a week and football began to take over my life. I must admit it did affect my studies; in the end I just scraped through.

My football world was expanding. A member of the team turned out to be the newly-appointed football development officer for the city and one day she told me that she was involved in a tournament for young people; 'Would I like to help?' I went along and loved it. Now I was attending coaching classes and finding out as much as I could about the game.

Unbeknown to me, our local postie was in the gym working out and he noticed I was part of the football course there. He got into a chat with me; 'Have you ever thought of going along to the referee classes?' Now at this point I had no thought that I might end up reffing big matches or any adult male games, but I was mad keen about the game; if nothing else, the classes would improve my knowledge of the game.

The development of my refereeing just seemed to flow naturally from all that. I had had no particular ambition to break ground as a female referee; it all came along as the logical next step. I started out by being asked to help at tournaments for juveniles, girls and seven-a-side to begin with and then broadening out to boys and then into the youth development leagues. What started as fun began to take a hold of me. Brian Christie, the president of the association, came up to me: 'Morag you're doing well – we've been keeping an eye on you. Now you need to tackle the men!'

So what has seemed like a huge pioneering step really came about as part of growing involvement in the game I'd always thoroughly enjoyed. I went onto the Sunday leagues, then the juniors and finally the seniors. I was running the line at matches and watching some of the men in the middle and thinking to myself, ' I reckon I can do that too. Why not?'

My first Highland League match was at Christie Park: Huntly v Wick. There was a presentation to me in the pavilion before the start and the media took an interest. Since then, I've been in the middle for many other Highland League fixtures; I've also done the same in a range of UEFA tournaments all over Europe.

The sort of comments I used to attract have now largely passed. I don't think there'll be a repeat of the time when a manager claimed I should be at home making dinner for

BORN TO BE WILD

LOCHSIDE TRAGEDY

ROSE WITH A THORN

DIADORA

THE REF'S A WOMAN!

my man after he's been to his football. You just have to shrug off comments like that. On the field it's the same; I'm just on auto-pilot, so if I see two guys squaring up to each other then I'll just wade in and deal with it. Mark you, if I saw the same pair fighting in Union Street then that might be a different matter!

Morag Pirie, born 1975, interviewed 2008: Parkhill

Front page news: cover girl for the *Leopard* magazine issue of November, 2005.

The folk singer

My family lived in the Blackhills of Tyrie, on a croft. In those days the crofts formed a whole community in their own right and it was one which my family had deep roots in. We still live there, just across the way from my first home. The crofts have changed a lot over the years. Most of them have been modernised and extended; their original land is now used for recreation, not farming.

Unless you have hundreds of acres, you can't make farming pay nowadays. It's all amalgamation into big combines; the traditional farm community has gone. Gordon Easton is a neighbour; some of his songs tell of the changes to the land and its folk, mourning for something precious that's passed away.

In the family line.
The young Barbara-Ann Burnett with Uncle James Park, who played the fiddle.

Dad talks of the little local shops and the smiddy or the soutar, places that would act as community gathering places, but they've all gone now.

The thing that seems to have gone is the old sense of community. Dad [now passed away – February 2008] often speaks of the days when our house would act as a gathering place for everyone round about. This was when his mother was alive. She would make sure that anyone who came by would be invited in and given tea and home bakes. He speaks of the threshing mill and how all the neighbours would congregate to play their part in working it. They'd work through the morning, then at lunch time they'd gather round the big table in the farm kitchen for their dinner, then work on into the evening. It was a real community undertaking. Now, the combine takes care of it all.

One of my friends at the Folk Club is Bill Buchan, who writes his own material, in the Doric. One of his songs is called *Buchan Parks* and tells of all the parks that now lie teem and neglected. But you can't simply call it a lament: rather it's a commemoration for a past way of life that had its attractions, but which was also very hard. We mustn't look back through rose-coloured spectacles, but we have to recognise there were values worth holding onto. Individual concerns have taken over from the old shared experiences. We live in different sorts of communities nowadays; we network over a wide area of acquaintances and no longer do so much face to face.

All that has changed even in my short lifetime. When I was a child Hogmanay was still a great event in the household. Our house would be full of folk who dropped in and had their supper. We'd watch the TV together and chat and sing. There'd be some kind of concert featured, with a ceilidh atmosphere and songs we could all join in. Then the bells would come and there'd be toasts and more chat. Now people either spend Hogmanay behind closed doors with one or two specially invited friends, or go off to some public gathering in the town.

The whole community has changed. There's been a lot of new people moving in and they seem to have come from the towns or from down south, in search of a quiet country lifestyle. You drive past and exchange a wave, but otherwise little in the way of real chat or invites into people's homes. Mostly, they are commuters who drive off to Peterhead or Fraserburgh each morning for their work, or to the supermarket for their weekly shop, come home, shut the door and get on with their own affairs.

Dad talks of the little local shops and the smiddy or the soutar, places that would act as community gathering places, but they've all gone now. There's no longer these local forums for people to meet up in and exchange the latest news. Now we tend to fit into networks that are held together not by the area we live in, but by our jobs or our interests. And even here, there can be a lack of actual human contact. Often, if I want to get in touch with someone, it'll be by text or email; we talk to each other via cyberspace.

The pace of change is unrelenting. At the school where I teach, the other day we were discussing council services and I was trying to build up a picture of their range by setting out titles around a 'telephone dial'. I asked this group of 12-year olds what a telephone dial was and was met with blank faces. For them a phone is a digital arrangement; to get a number you press keys. The idea of putting your finger into a dial, and having to move it round for each number, seemed to them bizarre. A hand went up

and a girl informed us that she had actually seen such a thing – in a museum! I nearly died: I'm only 27 and already the way we used to make phone calls when I was their age had become a bygone practice.

Song, verse and the Doric were all around me as a child. Granda on my mum's side sang bothy ballads and I would listen to him; Dad was into local history; Mum sang; my uncle played the fiddle, and just down the road, Gordon Easton was a huge influence. Music was a community thing, which had its roots in the days when people would drop in on each other's houses and pass an evening playing their instruments, or swapping songs. As I grew older I was encouraged to enter festivals, but I was never taught formally. It's embedded in the environment I grew up in.

People are interested in the music, but they also are in it for the camaraderie. All of us who perform get on well together and we convey our enjoyment to the audiences. Some folk clubs can be a bit rigid, but with us it's more open, and people feel free to join in and improvise. What we're doing is reproduce the spirit of the old days, when people would gather in each other's homes and improvise an evening of music together.

My repertoire stretches to about 40 songs. Some people go for the lyrics, but for me it's the rhythm or the tune, or whether the piece has a haunting melody or a strong chorus. In my repertoire I've bothy ballads such as the *Twa Recruiting Sergeants*, *The Barnyards of Delgatie* and *Mormond Braes*. Some of my songs go back to the old fisher days – the *Fisher's Wife* and the *Fisher Lassies*. I've also picked up some ballads such as the *Beggar Man*, which has the story of when James VI was going off on his wanderings around the country.

A lot of the material refers to a past age, but people are still producing new material. Bill Buchan, for example, is doing that. A recent song he's written is the *Immigrant*, prompted by the amount of people who have recently been pouring into Fraserburgh from Poland and Lithuania to work at the fish. This has created some social tension, so he turns the situation around by asking his listeners to imagine how they would fare as immigrants to these other societies.

Performing keeps me busy. I get a lot of invitations, which I find difficult to turn down. I can find myself doing maybe three a month: there's the Folk Club, old folks' homes, village events in aid of local funds. I perform all over north Aberdeenshire.

Barbara-Ann Burnett, born 1979, interviewed 2006: Tyrie

ON-SHORE AND OFF-SHORE: LIFE ALONG THE COAST

The harbour might be emptier than ever nowadays, but the memories and the pride are still there. Crowds gather for the Johnshaven Fish Festival, 1997.

'No trip when you didn't have to put your teeth into it.'
A small boat sets out in stormy seas in search of salmon, Newtonhill, Fifties. It is skippered by Colin McLennan's father *(see 'Family')*.

Skill and hard hard graft

I come from a line of fisher people. But now that's all finished. Once, the harbour was packed full of boats ; now the place is just deserted. The last decommissioning scheme, four years ago, just about ended it all.

I feel sad about it, but then how can you stop what's called progress? Oil is now the currency of the whole world, more important than fish ever was. For people of my generation, it's sad to see the decline of a proud industry – the empty harbour, the boat yards and the ice factories standing idle – but it has to be admitted that the coming of the oil has been something of a godsend. In some ways things are better than ever; this generation is more fortunate than mine was in its working conditions. We would go to sea for a couple of weeks, punish ourselves to get a reasonable catch, return exhausted, land our haul and then get maybe two days at home before beginning the whole cycle all over again. Now the men go offshore for two weeks, live in good conditions on their rigs, come back home and get two weeks rest before they have to go off again.

But I can't say I envy them. Since I can remember, I'd set my mind on the sea. It's a hard life and full of uncertainties and dangers. To my generation, fishing was our way of life and we accepted it all. Of course, it was tough business; I can't recall a trip when you didn't have to put your teeth into it; the boat never filled up with fish automatically. It was always a job that demanded hard work and proper skills, but if you put everything into it then you would get your reward – eventually. There've always been boats that did well and those that didn't; it's a matter of how much skill and character the crew show.

Skill and hard, hard graft, that's what fishing's all about. For me, I enjoyed the challenge of it all. You certainly never got bored, never had time to be. The work is constant; it goes on night and day. Your mind was always fully occupied, with the thought of what you were going to get and what you had just hauled in – or not hauled in. Then you would speculate on how much your catch might fetch in the market and what that would mean to the crew.

No, work on the oilrigs can't compete with that kind of satisfaction. Like a lot of old fishermen I've done spells on the guard ships which look after the rigs and I found it completely predictable, boring work. You just sit there waiting and nothing happens. To enjoy that kind of work means you must be tired of living. You go out for 12 days and it feels like 12 months. At the fishing, every day is different; at the rigs you just wonder what the days are all about.

The great thing about fishing is the feeling of expectancy: you never can be sure what's around the corner, what the next haul might bring you. You tend to believe the next one's going to be the really big one – and it comes off just often enough to keep you going. So despite all the broken sleep, the irregular meals, the constant soakings and all the other hardships, you keep at it. Look at any retired old fisherman and you'll see someone that doesn't look his age; they're still fit and active, interested in life. Compare them to someone who's worked at a desk all his days and you'll see someone who's stooped, who shuffles about and has a dullness in his eye. All that danger and challenge must be good for you, I reckon.

The great thing about fishing is the feeling of expectancy: you never can be sure what's around the corner.

I became a skipper in my early 20s; my first boat was a 75-foot seiner. We went all over the North Sea. We were after cod and plaice and to get them we had to take long trips, eight to ten days. The most important thing was to know where to cast the nets. You had to recognise the signs. The thing to look out for was to spot where the fish were feeding and the direction they were moving in. Where there's feeding, that's where you'll find fishing. It's all about the food chain: big fish follow small fish and we have to follow them. Fishing, despite all our aids, can never be an exact science; you need to develop a feel for it, an instinct for where the fish like to feed and the parts of the sea they would never go to. Really, you have to develop the ability to think like a fish. You take into account what's happened on previous trips; you keep an ear open for what others have been doing. You have to be careful here: chasing fish is like prospecting for gold: if you get a strike then you keep quiet about it. When you're talking on the radio to another boat you have to be alert to the exact tone of voice, to catch out those who claim they're getting nothing, but sounding quite happy about it. You have to learn what genuine disappointment sounds like over the radio when you can't see the speaker face to face.

Don't get me wrong: it's competitive, but we stop short of cutting each other's throats. You will try to be helpful to another boat – but only after you've given yourself a day or two's start on them. You learn who to trust and who to watch out for – the kind of skipper who'll be telling you he's having a hard time of it and then, when you get back,

'Never sure what's round the corner.' The Buckie fleet set sail for the open sea, *Campania* leading the way. A 1920s picture, when the Moray Firth ports had the greatest number of fishing vessels in Scotland.

you find he's landed a big one. It's all part of the job. After all, fishing's not like farming where the crop is confined to your own piece of land and you can freely help your neighbour with advice and machinery.

Oh yes, it's dangerous at sea, no doubt about it! It's so easy to fall over the side, to get snarled up in the ropes and take a tumble, or be swept over by a wave. You have to keep a constant eye on the size of the sea, on the state of the gear, on the crew. I was always afraid of a sudden accident; you get to care deeply about your men. That's one of the great privileges about being at sea, the companionship that develops when men have to live and work together and are dependent on each other's efforts. If somebody gets hurt or receives bad news from home, then the whole crew hurts with him. In other jobs you go your various ways home at five o'clock each day, but not us: you're living together, eating together, sleeping near each other, pulling together the whole time. You are a real team, a family.

It's very sad now to see the empty harbour and to think back to those busy days when it was full of boats, and all the businesses – the yards, the fish processing, the net factories, the supply firms – were in full cry. And we had the railway, too; fish trains would leave each evening for Billingsgate, loaded with the fish we'd caught. Now there's nothing.

But there's no point in mourning. We had the fish; they have the oil. You can't be stuck in the past. If I had to speak to the young today I would tell them this: I would like to be one of you. If I had to go back to the conditions of my teenage years, back to that fisher cottage, passing away the evening in front of a fire with no TV, no central heating, no carpets on the floor, knowing what I know now and enjoying the comforts of today, then I just couldn't do it. There's an old saying: 'Ye canna pit the clock back!' It's true.

A Fisher loon, born 1930s, interviewed 2008: Moray Firth

Sold down the river Lossie

The Thomsons weren't one of the original local families; they were in one of the immigrant waves attracted by the building of the harbour in the 1820s. These were people who brought with them a fierce work ethos, a desire to exploit the great riches of the sea as efficiently as possible. They refused to be stuck in any traditional ways; their attitude was, 'We're maybe doing all right – but we can do even better!'

Change has been a constant in our lives and we accept, even welcome, it. However, the great changes which Britain's entry into the European Common Market brought have been more than we should be expected to bear. The brute fact of the matter is the fishing communities of this country were sold out as the entry price for the United Kingdom's membership. In 1972, the then Prime Minister, Edward Heath, gave away Britain's fishing industry in his rush to sign up to the EEC. The Common Fisheries Policy allowed all countries equal access to the fish of the North Sea. Britain had more than enough to satisfy its own needs, but there could never be sufficient for all the other

member states. The result has been continual cuts in quota and endless regulations. Boats have been compulsorily decommissioned and in many cases those that were left have faced bankruptcy, unable to pay the crews or to service their bank loans.

We saw what would happen at the very start. At Lossiemouth, we blockaded the port in protest and campaigned as hard as we could against Government policy, but all to no avail. A proud industry and a precious way of life have been destroyed. Lossiemouth harbour is now a ghost place; it once used to be a scene packed with masts and activity; now it's just a pleasure marina for the rich and for the holiday-maker.

We understood there would have to be changes over the years and all we asked for was the opportunity to work with the Government to seek the best way forward and to continue our trade, not as it had always been, but within the framework of a progressive industry. But we weren't given the chance.

It's a far cry from what I grew up with back in the Forties and the Fifties. Lossiemouth was a thriving place then. Most of the young men have now gone off to the oil industry. They're still out at sea, but on rigs and supply vessels. You'll find Lossiemouth men all over the world – in Algeria, the Gulf of Mexico, Nigeria, anywhere the oil is. As for Lossiemouth, the place seems to be doing all right; you don't see any great hardship. But I wonder where the work actually is and how the money is really made. In my day you knew where people worked; you could see them going to it of a morning, all dressed up in working clothes; they were heading for a definite place – a workshop, a yard, the harbour, a factory. These were places with a real smell and a recognisable noise that was located at some local site you could go to and observe what was happening. Now the money seems to be spun out of thin air; the old traditional industries where people produced things and despatched them off on trains and in lorries to sell to the rest of the world, well, they've just disappeared. These days, how the economy works in this country is a mystery to me.

OFFSHORE AND ONSHORE: Life along the coast

John in mid career
when he was skipper of
the prolific *St Kilda*
and prominent
in fishermen's
organisations.
Here he is conferring
with Pete Lewis on
the wheelhouse.

I went to the local school; it was a tough place. We were grounded in the Three Rs and we were taught how to behave. But all we thought about was going off to sea. Not many of us were interested in the prospect of staying on and doing our Highers. My own father had been one of 12: eight surviving sons and eight fishermen. I only ever wanted to be a fisherman. I wanted that from the first time my parents told me I was to stay away from the harbour; they knew that if I went down there and took in the sights and smell of the place I'd think of nothing else – and they didn't want that. They would warn me of the hardships, the dangers, the ups and downs of the fishing life.

When you first went to sea, you went as a boy fresh out of the local school, but you very quickly learned how to be a man. You were driven hard; you were expected to pull your weight, to make your contribution, to be a member of the team. Right from the start, you would be taught to read the sea, to read the coastline. The skipper would be quite demanding, asking you to identify the various foghorns, the lighthouses, the ins and outs of the coastline. I have a great admiration for the older men I started out with; they were hard and tough but they were fair and they would look after you, see that you started right.

I started out on my uncle's boat. My mother had my woollens knitted and laid out for me. She had tried her best to dissuade me from going, but my older brother had already gone and she knew I would follow. She'd implored him to stick to a shore job, to be safe, but he would have none of it. When he went she wept for a while, but when I got to 15 she told me, 'I'm not going to cry for you; I know you'll just go whatever I say about it!' So she had already knitted my woollen mittens, my stockings, my jersey, everything needed to keep me protected and warm. Then I was sent off with a prayer and a bible and that was that.

I never regretted it. What an adventure it all was! The first day at sea I was as sick as a dog, the second I recovered, the third I felt fine and I never had any more trouble after that. I found I was in my element, doing the thing I was born to do.

For me fishing has always been a noble calling, one I was proud to serve. But I do realise that historically we've been looked down upon, seen as a sort of inferior people. The city of Elgin has always tended to regard itself as a more civilised place than its neighbouring fishing port. It's always angered me when outsiders look at us and assume, 'Oh, just a fisherman – well, anybody can do that. What is there in that?' Well, I'll tell you what there is – there's courage, and skill and judgement. There's a co-ordination of hand and eye and a steadiness of nerve and a willingness to work together. It's not just a matter of training either; you have to show ingenuity, a constant capacity to adapt to the situation and to devise fresh ways of confronting an ever-changing challenge.

My most satisfying thought as a lifelong fisherman is that I always got my men home safely, but the stark truth is that if you're not prepared to take the risk then you'll never make a living. You have to ask yourself: what is a risk? It's never just 'taking a chance'. At sea a risk is a calculation, one that's based on your experience, your reading of the situation, the evidence that's around you in the form of weather, sea, the state of the crew,

Lossiemouth now,
given over to weekend
pleasure craft.
A retired John Thomson
points out the changes.

the likely whereabouts of the fish. A good skipper will have to calculate his ability to lead his men into and out of the situation. He needs confidence in his ability to command the trust of the crew.

What makes a good fisherman isn't just all the practical skills, or even the knowledge that experience yields. There's the matter of character, of the fibre of the man. He has to have drive, he has to carry ambition within his spirit, and by this I don't mean simply the wish to catch more and more: I mean the will to do it well, to do it to the utmost of what

> **I wanted to be a fisherman from the first time my parents told me I was to stay away from the harbour.**

your trade can point you to. The good skipper is the one who is always striving to progress, to build on the legacy of past methods and past equipment and to drive onward to better and better ways. And of course, such a skipper has to be able to lead his men into these new waters; he has to earn their trust, not just morally, but as the one who knows what he is doing, has conviction in where he is leading them to. For that reason the skipper should never ever ask his men to do something he is not prepared to do himself. He is a member of the crew first, their skipper second.

The crew, the industry as a whole, was held together by this great sense of mutual loyalty. Men would go to sea together who knew each other inside out, men who came from the same kind of background and who would return onshore to similar kinds of homes, to families they were intent on bringing up along the same path of hard work, of team effort, of honesty and trust. That, I'm heart sorry to tell you, has largely evaporated. It's not that people are any less now, it's that the circumstances have eaten away at their souls. Look, how can a skipper keep the following of his men when he has to navigate a way through all the quotas, the regulations, the risk assessment provisions, the calculation of days allowed at sea, of everything that the present day throws at his freedom, to act in the best interests of his men?

That is my heritage and it is one which makes me all the more angered by what I see around me. There's a sickness which runs through the whole New Labour project. The basic ethic of the fishing community, where one lives for all and where people share and help each other is naturally socialistic, but good old fashioned basic socialism. It isn't this individualistic consumer society which has been politically pursued over the last 10 years. New Labour has tried to sever our bond with our past. We were always forward looking, but we thought to take our deeply-rooted morality with us. It was a question of, 'Life is getting better, so let's work together to make sure everyone has a share in its fruits.' We now live in isolation from each other. We are also cut off from the past that used to be held in trust for us by the leaders of the community – 'New' Labour, you see!

When I was learning my trade as a young skipper, we had a strong sense of living together in the one community. We were like the miners in that respect. We all lived along the same street, we worked together, we shared our leisure time together. When we wanted to find out the latest news and ponder what it meant, we'd make to the harbour and listen to what we were told there. We could rely not only on the content, but the wisdom with which it would be handed over to us. The news came slowly and was seriously considered. Now we live in an instant media world where the news flashes around us, in our cars, in our homes and we have no need to share it in that old considered way. So we no longer work together, share together, go to worship together, shop and seek our recreation in the same local places. Like the mining communities, ours has been broken up and treated as of little worth. Materially we might not have suffered so very much, but, spiritually, we are the poorer.

John Thomson, born 1935, interviewed 2009: Lossiemouth

The oil, the sea and overfishing

I stayed in a little village next to Buckie: Portessie. Portessie was all about fish; practically everyone in the village either went to sea or did something connected with the sea. I had a great boyhood there; the beach was just across the road and we were never off it. We'd search for crabs, look in the pools, do some beach combing, make rafts.

I was the Dux at Portessie, but I had little interest in continuing my studies. I saw all my chums just ahead of me leaving school, joining a boat, getting real money and that's what I saw for myself, too.

I started in the usual way, as cook. Now, that's a silly way of going about it, even though it was the norm. To be thrown into cooking for a crew of hungry grown men was neither fair on them or on you. Later on the system changed and young entrants were given training as apprentice deck hands. I began my so-called training down in the galley surrounded by tatties and bread and fish. And I was violently sick. It wasn't just the pitch of the sea; it was the confinement and the smell of fumes. The crew wouldn't have been so keen on their grub if they'd known how much of it landed on the floor and had to be scooped up again.

I was two years in the galley and then I was on deck. In those days everything had to be done by hand. You'd haul the nets in; you'd gut the fish into the baskets. We used to wear woollen mittens for handling the nets; I tell you the introduction of plastic gloves was a great innovation! For protection we had our thigh-length boots, sou'wester and oilskins. Everything had to be done at speed; the quicker you could clear the decks the better for the condition of the fish. So between hauls we'd be hard at it, gutting and icing and packing them into boxes.

Crews were usually five or six and that produced another problem: being in such a confined space with the same small group meant there was no escape from the stories you'd heard over and over. In such circumstances any little habit or turn of phrase can

Everything
had to be
done at
speed; so
between
hauls we'd be
hard at it,
gutting and
icing and
packing them
into boxes.

Bill Cowie's very first boat...
Sea Harvest BCK 44.

grate, believe me. Tempers would get frayed. For entertainment we had books and cards and that's about it.

I was fortunate: my father had a boat and I inherited it. I was a skipper at 24. The skipper has a fantastic amount of responsibility; the success of a trip can depend upon the decisions he makes and the skill and experience he can bring to bear. He'll consult the charts and decide where the boat is to go. That's a decision which is part experience, part good judgement, but also a hunch, an instinct. You'll take the boat into a new area, cast the nets and hope. You'll be looking at the faces of the crew when the nets are raised; if they're empty or they come up in shreds because you've hit a rough bottom, then all you can do is say to yourself, 'Oh shit, got that one wrong!' But if the nets come up full then you're a big hero and you feel that there's nothing to beat the life at sea.

The decline set in in the Nineties. There's no doubt that we were sacrificed by the Heath government for the sake of the UK entry into the Common Market. Afterwards you'd get French and Spanish boats coming right into the Butt of Lewis.

And then, as my career progressed, the technology changed drastically. We now had the ability to go out further and further, to catch more and more on any one trip. And that was our downfall: we began to overfish and the fishermen got greedier and greedier. That's just human nature and you'll encounter it in any walk of life. Fishing became an industry and began to behave like an industry, with the emphasis on higher and higher amounts of production – until the basic resource on which it all depended, the fish in the sea, became exhausted.

The Seventies and the Eighties were very good. It was only then that the stocks began to dwindle. Rules and regulations came in; there were quotas. We were now only getting a fraction of the previous catches. Crews became smaller in order to cut costs; it was harder to make a decent living.

I finished with it in 1992 and then I went onto the stand-by boats for the oilrigs. I finally retired in 1998. Since then Buckie has changed and changed. Once you'd walk down the harbour and find a hive of activity. In the mornings there'd be the fish market. You'd see boat after boat taking on its ice and boxes, seeing to its nets. There were all kinds of services on the go – chandlers, seafoods, ship painting, the full range of fishing gear and all the shipbuilding and the repair yards. Now all you'll come across are a few dog walkers. The crews that are left often come from abroad, from Latvia, Russia, the Philippines. Minimum wages most of them. A chap I know, and who fishes out of Fraserburgh, tells me he can't recruit locals any more.

There hasn't been a proper fish auction here for more than eight years. Buckie is now down to just a few clammers and they don't land very much. When I was going into the industry there would have been something like 800 fishermen in Buckie; now it must be fewer than 50.

What's happened are two things: overfishing which has led to quotas and to decommissioning on the one hand and, on the other, the rise of the oil industry. In the past, most local lads would have gone into the fishing; now they go off to work in the oil.

... And his final boat: *UL 95.*

In fact, Buckie is still doing well, maybe better than ever. Certainly living standards are higher. I go along to my golf club and all the talk in the bar afterwards is of how so and so is now working in Brazil, in Russia, the Far East. Buckie folk are scattered world-wide, using their old seafaring skills in the service of the new industry.

The collapse of the fishing industry is very sad, of course it is, But although it's tragic to be part of a way of life that's had its day, you need to keep Buckie's situation in perspective. A few years ago I went to visit relatives in Canada. We made a tour of the Nova Scotia coast. We went round all the old ports and what we found was that their position was just as bad as ours. The old cod fleets were all rusting and tied up. Some keep going with lobsters, but for a lot of them it's only the tourism that keeps them alive. Overfishing and an over efficient technology have killed us off, no matter where in the world we are.

No one saw the speed and the extent of our downfall. When I started out in the Fifties I had no idea that things would end up like this. But then I didn't foresee the oil coming in to take its place – nor that Buckie could lose its fishing and, not only survive, but become better off than ever.

William Cowie, born 1940, interviewed 2008: Portessie

The fisher folk are my tribe

My parents were fisher folk: my father came from Cullen, my mother from Portknockie. He was an engineer who died in the war, when I was less than one year old. He was on the *SS Nisus*, which went down with all hands on board.

Mother was one of six sons and five daughters, ruled by a wee matriarch who was all of the size of a tuppeny bit. They were Brethren at the time when the movement was quite fanatical. I remember the time I got hold of this tiny pack of playing cards, from a Christmas cracker, and they were straightaway thrown onto the fire. The Deil's cards, you see.

My grandmother ruled her family with a rod of iron. The six sons all went to sea. They weren't allowed a radio, because that was a means of introducing sinful material from the outside world, such as dance music and comedy. They had a little portable set,

> The women
> would wrap
> clouties
> round their
> fingers.
> These were
> to keep the
> salt out of
> the chaps
> and the nicks
> they'd get,
> all down
> their hands.

which they hid away so that at 11 each Sunday one of them could sneak outside and listen to the Shipping Forecast.

As a religion, the ways of the Brethren seem punitive and harsh. But it did give clear guidelines. Do this and the Good Lord will look after you; if not, then you only have yourself to blame. All the preaching was of hell and damnation; the God of Love never came into it. This fitted in with a way of life that was hard and dangerous. Loss at sea or a bad catch could be better accepted if it was to be explained as God's will.

As a widow, my mother was forced to work. She would follow the herring each season down the East coast from Shetland to Yarmouth. Gutting was back-breaking labour; vicious work. The women had to stay in sheds and sleep on straw mattresses. I had to go with her because there was no one to look after me at home. I remember going up to Shetland and seeing the shore, silver with herring just after the boats had come in. The first money I ever earned was up there: Mum was packing the herring into barrels and I was with her. This boat came in and a man came up to me and asked, 'Can you pull a rope?' When the crane got hoisted up, hauling the baskets of herring to land them, I pulled on the rope so that they could swing it over onto the side of the quay and then tip it out. I did it for three hours and was given ten shillings for it. I was nine and suddenly I felt rich. I also had blisters all over my hands.

The work for the women was non-stop. If the boat came in at three in the morning, the horn went and they had to jump to it. They would put on their oilskins and wrap clouties round their fingers. These were to keep the salt out of the chaps and the nicks they'd get, all down their hands. The barrels were heavily salted and the sting on the fingers could be excruciating. They would take a basket and tip the fish into a sloping trough, where the women would work all down one side doing the gutting, fish after fish, hour after hour. The gutted fish would then be taken and packed into barrels, head to tail, in layers all the way up, and with each layer protected by salt. All the bending over and the constant effort to keep up with the work made for a crippling time of it.

Then some Russian would appear in a furry hat, go over to a barrel and reach down into its middle to get his sample. He'd brush the salt off it, take a good look and then, if everything was to his liking, he would buy. At the end of the season, each woman would be given a firkin of herring for herself. There would be a party with herring and a great pile of tatties put in the middle of a table and some lemonade for the kids and maybe a beer for the men.

In the summer, I would have to follow the herring along with my mother. As the season ran for about four months, I had to go to school wherever she was. I enjoyed the school in Shetland, because you got hot chocolate instead of the wee bottle of milk in the mornings; the school at Yarmouth I remember because of how far ahead I was of the rest of the class there. I'd finish the work well ahead of the Yarmouth lads and then be allowed to read a comic while they caught up.

My upbringing was a strict one. For us, the Swinging Sixties never arrived; as far as we were concerned they were a London thing and didn't creep up this far north.

Working hard, keeping to the rules, getting on, respecting adults – it was all ingrained into us, all those values which have now become lost.

That sounds rather grim, but on the credit side there was a real sense of community. People trusted one another and helped one another. They kept their doors open and they looked out for each other. After I lost my father, every Friday there would come a knock at the door and there would be a neighbour with a plate of frying fish: 'Boat's in – jist tak this tae yer mither'.

Although I've grown away from it all, I still see myself as a member of a definite group. As a son of the Moray Firth I have an identity that clings to me yet. I can be walking down the street back in Portknockie and I'll still catch one old woman telling the other, 'See hum? That's Louisa's Jack.' I was once standing in the baker's and a local came up to me and asked me straight, 'An far are ye?' As soon as I told him I was 'Louisa's Jack', and he was able to say, 'Louisa's Jack – ach that's fine!', I knew I'd be allowed to take my place in the queue as one of their own. It's a very closed-in place, conscious of who belongs and who doesn't. My loyalty was to the fish. In the Moray Firth there were two separate and distinct tribes – the farming folk and the fishing folk - and I know which one I came from. My people had it hard, they could lose their lives at any moment, or could return from two weeks at sea without anything to show for it. If the fishing failed then they went hungry. But the farmers, though they'd moan about conditions, always had the produce of the land to live on. They might grumble about the rain and all the while the tatties would continue to grow. But if the catch failed, the mortgage on the boat still had to be met at the end of the month, just the same. It's no wonder that the fisher folk developed something of a siege mentality. They had to look to themselves for their strength. They didn't have the subsidies to help them along; they've never had the luxury of driving around in their cars down to the mart of a Friday to complain about their level of government hand-out.

Jack Findlay, born 1940, interviewed 2007: Portknockie

Walking down the street, back in Portknockie.
A view of Church Street.

Daughter of the sea. An infant Celia Craig with her father, at home in Gourdon, 1945.

The salt of the earth – and sea

My father was a man of the sea, as his family had been before him. Fishing in Gourdon was very much a family affair. My granny would 'sheel' mussels and bait a line for my grandfather. This was an intricate and time-consuming procedure. She had to take the long line and attach the bait (mussels) to the 1,200 hooks spaced at regular intervals along its length. The women would have to shell sufficient to supply all these, sometimes two or three mussels per hook; in all over 2,000 might be required.

Once the line was hauled in with all the fish on it, it would be 'raivelled' – all tangled and disordered; it then had to be 'redded' and any damaged hooks replaced. So fishing was something the women of the house had to get involved in as part of their daily lives. My mother baited my father's line for many years and employed a woman to shell the mussels. The sea and the tasks associated with it were all around me during my childhood.

My childhood in Gourdon was a very happy period. Ours was a self-sufficient world, with everything a young child could want for that time. We ran around Selbie Place, a new post-war Council housing estate, and made up stories to act out, from Cowboys and Indians to the Three Musketeers. Other days we would have a carpet which became a magic carpet out on the grass at the front of the house. My father had cold frames in the garden where he was nurturing plants; I remember the agony of having to go in to tell him what I had done when I broke a pane during my play. In the back garden we had my father's old Navy hammock, a tent and a swing. I learned to swim (taught by my father) in the harbour at a special spot which lay just to the north towards Inverbervie, called the Sandy Hole-y. Sometimes my cousin and I swam in the harbour. After your dook, you ran along in your dookers to Granny's house in Arbuthnott Street and changed there. She'd give us a 'shivery bite' – probably a piece and jam, or a biscuit. We had everything a child could want.

Life was fun for the children in Gourdon, but my father's life at sea was hard enough. He would have to get up very early to make sure he would catch the tide. You'd hear him getting up at three in the morning; you'd hear his feet about the kitchen and the clatter of his spoon as he stirred the brose. He was always needing gloves – mittens. He suffered from cold hands and to haul in the lines in winter would be a perishing job. When he came back, his gloves would be carefully sorted into pairs, smoothed out, washed and put by the fire to dry. My mother was constantly knitting them for him; people would speak of my father and his mittens as 'the glove factory'.

It was inshore fishing he did. The boat (a shapely Fifie skiff, *Trustful ME 132*) was around 30-foot, with maybe two or three of a crew. In the winter they fished for haddock, cod, whiting, flukes – gorgeous to eat and straight from the sea to our table. In the summer they went to the creels, fishing for crabs (partans) and lobsters. It could be a dangerous life, too.

I went out with him one summer. This was after my stint in Canada as a lecturer

When Gourdon still had a thriving fish market. Salesman Willie Heath in action.

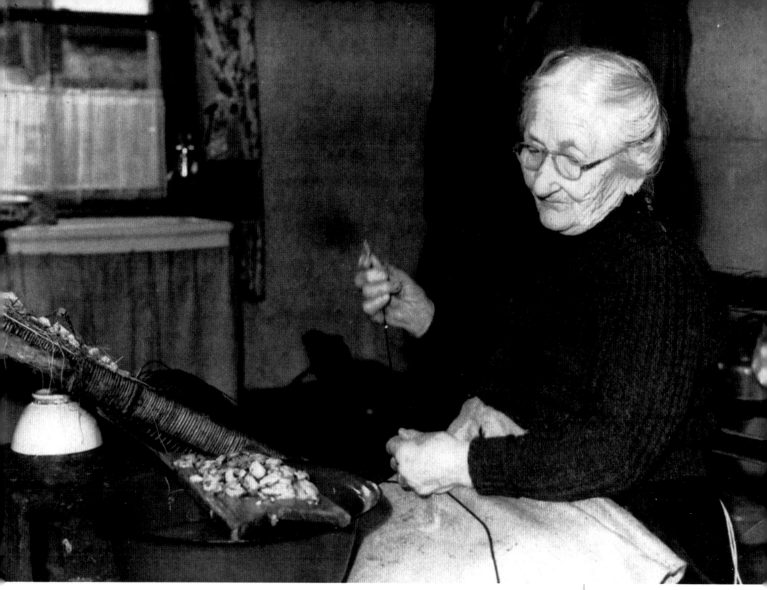

when I felt I needed a bit of grounding. I worked the creels with him. You'd go out on an early July morning and into the sun's path as it rose over the North Sea. It was a memorable golden time, like sailing into the very sun itself, all bathed in the glow of it. A pure joy. And there was still shellfish and, indeed, white fish to be had then; the depletion hadn't yet set in.

For me, the fishing folk of Gourdon were the salt of the earth. Growing up among them and being of one blood with them gave me a strong sense of what was basic and true in life – the elemental, if you like. That's why I developed such a marked sense of people, myself included, belonging to the land and to the sea. The poem *Scotland* by Alexander Gray sums up my feelings here:

'This is my country
The land that begat me
These windy spaces
Are surely my own.
And those who here toil
In the sweat of their faces
Are flesh of my flesh
And bone of my bone.'

Catch of the day:
Gourdon harbour,
1960s.

Celia Craig, born 1943, interviewed 2008: Gourdon

I enjoyed all
the harmless
banter
with the
fishermen
and engineers
from
the harbour
community
and the fact
that I could
soon hold
my own.

Nae guid'll cam o' a quine on board!

My background is completely Peterhead and its fishing. When my parents came together, Dad decided not to go into the fishing. The industry was going through one of its downward cycles so he got a trade. He ended up as a master plumber and builder.

I was part of a loving, supportive and very happy family life. I was, I admit, something of a tomboy and a bit of a rebel. I loved to keep the company of my dad and my grandfather. My dad had, as a side-line hobby, his own cobble and we'd go out, of a summer's evening, for a spot of line and net fishing, for salmon. I've got a photo of me, half covered by a big sou'wester, rod in one hand and, from the other, a salmon, just about bigger than me. Dad and a friend rented fishing rights from Rattray Head lighthouse all the stretch down to where the St Fergus gas plant now is and we'd take the cobble, load it with nets and catch sea trout. The usual trip was for me, my dad, Granda and some other friends, to make a cup of tea and eat sandwiches in an old caravan on shore and then set off. Once we'd made our catch, we'd haul the nets up onto the beach and I'd help to pick the fish out of them, load them into boxes so that Dad could then drive down to Aberdeen and sell them. I loved the adventure and companionship of it all.

So, after school of a summer's evening, down to the shore, run over the sand dunes, into the caravan for a tea and then out into the boat with these men – that was my way of life right up till when I went to university. I remember once this old man sitting on the harbour wall, uttering this warning as we were about to set off: 'Noo, Tom, there's nae guid gaen to sea wi a quine aboard. Nae guid'll cam o that!' I was already well into equality, so I answered, 'Well, if my brother can do it, so can I'. And then we came back all loaded up with a huge catch and I took great delight in going up to him and saying, 'Some bad omen going to sea with this quine on-board has turned out to be!'

I would describe my family background as a fairly traditional Peterhead fishing community one: hard working, very much hands on, with pride in how well you do the task, thrifty, honest and reliable. Dad was deeply involved with the fishing community and for many years was on the Harbour Board. He acted as its chairman at one point and played a leading role in securing the extension to the harbour. He was awarded an OBE for his services to the community. I was very proud of him always, but this recognition made me especially so.

**The fishing
background.**
A busy harbour scene,
Peterhead, 1950s.

It was quite a male orientated upbringing. My holiday and weekend jobs at school were in Dad's office. Most of the clientele was from the fishing industry and you had to develop a tough skin to cope. In the plumbing trade there are plenty of terms which carry certain connotations – 'nipples', 'female ends', 'joining parts' and so on; the men

would come in and quite innocently (or perhaps not so innocently) ask me if I had any of these services available and would I be able to supply them. I enjoyed all this harmless banter with the fishermen and engineers from the harbour community and the fact that I could soon hold my own. There was never any malice in what they said to me, just a bit of cheeky mischief really, towards a young female who also happened to be the daughter of the boss.

Roseanne Fitzpatrick, born 1955, interviewed 2011: Peterhead

No messing about with my mother

My mother came from six of a family and had grown up in a typical Peterhead fisher house, which was built gable end to the sea, with two rooms downstairs and a half attic upstairs. Her granny bade round the corner; at the age of 14 she was going out with her with the creel. They would catch the bus to Rora, five miles from the town, and there they would go round all the farm cottages and houses, selling their fish from door to door. When she told me all this years later, I remarked, 'God, you must have been glad when the creel was teemed and you could have a light journey back'. 'Not at all,' she replied. 'It was heavier coming back.' None of the farmhouses used cash, but would barter some of their produce for the fish. So they would come back

At the age of 14 she was going out with her granny with the creel.

**'Fisher Jessie',
Peterhead.**

The statue
commemorates
travelling fishwives like
Iain Bruce's granny.

PHOTOGRAPH: **IAIN MACAULAY**

laden with neeps and tatties and cheese, or with a 10 dozen eggs, held together by binder tow that would cut into her skin.

My mother had to act as both man and wife in the house. She was a big, strong woman. I can't say she was always very good to me; she had an awful temper. But I've never held any resentment towards her: I realise that things were tough for her and that she had to do all sorts of things to keep us all going.

There was no messing about with my mother. She was from a hard, hard line of fisher folk. From my earliest memories onwards I saw the sea and the harbour as my natural environment. I can mind the days I would go down to the small pier in the North Harbour – it's gone now to make way for the new fish market – and fishing the whole day long off it; or wandering along the beach, looking in all the rock pools for bait to go fishing with. I mind too my uncle coming home carrying a great big bag of clear polystyrene full of prawns. In those days prawns were regarded as mush and often ended up by being tipped over the side, but about once a month we could look forward to a boiling of prawns.

Between the ages of four and eight I would spend the summers up in Shetland when my mother went up there for the fish gutting season. There we had to bide in a herring gutting shed, which was a rough open place with a half partition to make sleeping quarters, and a coal range for heat and cooking. In my first year there I would be left to play about the yards, but the grown-ups would be getting up to all kinds of shenanigans, with wild parties, plenty of drink and some pretty free sex.

Everything about me, at the fish and at home was hard. The fisher folk have a lot of smeddum; their way of life teaches them to get on with it. Mother had an indomitable spirit; she was so strong. And there were good times, too. When I was up in Shetland there would be times when the Norwegian whalers would come by and there would be huge booze-ups. They would cook whale steak on the range and, a little loon of only four, I would get to stand on the horse-hair mattress and sing Jim Reeves songs to them all: 'Railroad, steam boat, grand canal…'

None of these experiences undermined me. My attitude is that I simply carry around a bigger jersey than most and that this is what I can draw around me to keep me fine and warm. There were never any warm greetings or friendly chatter about the doings of the day in our household. Just a 'Fit like?' and then sit down to the TV in the dark. Later on, there might be a, 'Onybody fer a cup o tea?' Apart from that, silence – except when my mother burst out in one of her temper rages. I mind one day my sister had been winding her up; normally my mother was a big, slow-moving woman, but on this occasion she was lightning fast. Like a flash she reached over her shoulder to the poker by the fire and brought her arm over so that it was flung across the room. It embedded itself in the door as my sister rushed out to make her escape.

But you've got to remember my mother was a single parent, that she was in constant pain with her back after all those early years trudging around with a great creel of fish strapped to it and that she was forced to take up anything, or to do anything, which would

put bread on the table. She would be up in Shetland spending the summer at the gutting and come away with £10 plus coal and tatties. No wonder she was short-tempered and hard on me at times. When I raised all this with some other folk who'd been with her in those days, they cut me short with the comment, 'Look, Iain, in those days people had to do what they had to do to get the sark on their back and sheen on their feet!' There were to be no reproaches as far as they were concerned; they accepted that that is the way it was.

Iain Bruce, born 1958, interviewed 2006: Peterhead

Oil, the new frontier

In 1982, at the age of 18, I became an employee in the burgeoning oil industry. I worked for a well established electrical company in Aberdeen who provided support to the oil industry. I was immediately sent off-shore, even though I was still serving my time as an apprentice. I moved from rig to rig platform; it wasn't uncommon to be on two or three different installations in one month.

My first trip was on a semi-submersible called *Bideford Dolphin*. I had to work 18-hour days, including night shifts in the engine room. You'd be there with the three other caterpillar engines hammering away and you attempting to rewind the one broken one. The heat, the noise, was indescribable. But I was now earning what seemed like a fortune

A calm day out on the rigs.
Eric McNeil, oil rig electrician, early 1980s.

after being on £25 a week.

There was a spirit off-shore in those early days: get on and do the job! It was still pretty raw and makeshift. On many a job, I had to share a small room with three other men, a double bunk on each wall and a door leading into the toilet off it. This was shared with the four occupants of the room on the other side of the wall, so that meant eight men to the one toilet. At night, you'd be stuck in this small cramped space, with three older men who'd be smoking and snoring and farting away. Not comfortable, but the community spirit was great. On average there would probably have been 50 to 60 personnel on a semi-submersible such as *Bideford Dolphin*; the pranks and banter were fantastic. I revelled in it.

And we were a great melting pot too – Yanks, English, Scots, Aussies, all working, eating and joking together. In those days the American work culture was prevalent. To the Texan oil men it was a case of us being 'white blacks' – people to be bossed about and whipped on. It was 'Our way – or the Highway!' And safety was not so much of an issue – not in those days before Piper Alpha changed everything. You'd see a roustabout or rough-neck with a couple of fingers missing from a mistake when spinning the chains to join the drill pipes together, or carrying a hand crushed when loading the drill strings up to the drilling deck. They would treat them almost as a badge of honour. In fact, spinning the chains was banned just as I was beginning my career off-shore and I only witnessed it taking place a few times, so I guess the movement towards safer working practices was just starting, as the North Sea began to phase out the gung-ho ex-pat Yanks.

Out there, you were right on your own. You could get to use the radio phone, at about £12 a minute, but that meant half the North Sea listening in to your messages to your nearest and dearest. These were the days before mobiles and emailing, so letters were still very important to us all and you'd wait with some excitement to see if you were going to receive one today. I was just a young guy, off shore for up to a month at a time, so a letter from home was a big thing. My girlfriend was a fantastic letter writer; you'd get 18 pages at a time and I used to devour them all. It was all a bit like those war films where you see them out at the front line getting a precious letter from back home. And the entertainment was limited – I must have watched the video of *Dirty Harry* ten times in one month.

For this particular job I had to work 18-hour nightshifts, stuck in the engine room. At times it was very rough out there, I can tell you. The platforms were fixed into the sea bed and therefore were mostly stable, but those semi-submersibles were only held in place by anchors so that they could be moved around to explore for new wells. We used to ride the waves and toss about. But all that was part of the adventure of it all; it was the job of the submersibles to travel from spot to spot looking for more of the precious 'black gold', so we felt we were at the cutting edge of it all. Although the oil industry was already well established, for me, as a young lad, I felt we were the explorers, out there at the very frontier, opening up fresh fields for the benefit of this great new industry. The culture was very much that of the pioneers, the men who were prepared to go anywhere

and do what had to be done. The Yanks were driving us on with a 'Get it done! Get it done!' 'Push! Push! Push!'

So there I was, on our small craft, like Captain Kirk boldly going where no man had gone before, even though many had; but I was a bit of a romantic and loved every minute of it. I made it into my own adventure; it was a great escape from the many problems I was facing at home at that time. We had to work a minimum of 12-hour shifts, but in those early days it was more common to put in 15 to 18 hours. The idea was to maximise working time. Get that thing fixed, keep production going, do what you have to do. Back then, I would have climbed anywhere, crawled into any small space. There was little thought of safety harnesses or erecting scaffolding. At times you just grabbed whatever was at hand and up you went. I've seen me climbing 30 feet up cable racks and then shinning out on a ventilation duct just to get at a light fitting. There was much more gung-ho and 'Just watch me do it!'

Now things have turned round completely and we're encouraged to think in terms of health and safety at all times. You can't make a move without some sort of risk assessment being carried out. To some degree it's gone too far the other way and procedures and paper work have come to bog everyone down and to stifle our initiative. It's certainly taken a lot of the fun and sense of adventure out of life on the rigs.

The companies are rightly scared of being sued in our modern day litigation culture – but the fact that everyone is so busy trying to cover their backs has at times had an adverse effect on the industry. It's my personal belief that eyes are better fixed on the job than on reams of paper work. I think it's fair to say that back when I started, injuries were probably seen as inevitable and accepted as a part of what we were – not that it's right to hurt anyone, but that was the mentality of the industry at that time. The standing joke amongst the lads at that time was, 'Safety is paramount – as long as it doesn't affect

Management began to furnish rooms with TV sets and DVD players; people stopped gathering together and stayed in their rooms. This was seen as a ploy to divide and conquer the workforce

production'. I'd say that the industry is now generally a lot safer, but strangely a more stressful and a less fun environment to work in. But then, maybe I'm just getting older.

Nowadays, the platforms are huge complex structures, and during construction, 'hook-ups', floating hotels, which can house 500 guys, with bridges, were used to take them from their living quarters out to the working areas. To begin with there were no TVs in the rooms, only this large common lounge where everyone would congregate. Then management began to furnish rooms with individual TV sets and DVD players; people stopped gathering together and stayed in their own rooms. This was seen as a deliberate ploy by management to divide and conquer the workforce and stifle any momentum towards challenging pay or working conditions. Unfortunately, that put an end to much of our social life too. In those early days guys would gather together; someone would bring a guitar; songs would spring up; there'd be jam sessions. Games of chess or dominoes would start up; people would mingle and exchange stories and jokes. Huge card schools would start up, where, at times, hundreds of pounds could change hands. It wouldn't be uncommon for someone to lose all their wages before they even got home off the rig. Much of that social element has now tapered off.

Things were much more primitive then in our basic living conditions. But I was young, I was innocent, I was without dependents; I was carefree. I revelled in the incidents; the dangers were part of the adventure. I reckon I became a bit of an adrenalin junkie; I just loved the buzz of it all. If the gaffer had told me to jump off the side and swim round the rig to fix a light, then I would have probably just done it.

But then along came Piper Alpha and it was never the same. It devastated us all and made us realise we were no longer invincible. I lost two good friends and knew a few more lads who were very badly injured. A whole new safety regime came into play; the original gung-ho spirit began to be replaced with a more safety-conscious approach. The pioneering Yanks began to depart as the British knowledge base built up and a calmer, more considered ethos took over.

Out off-shore you'd bump into all sorts. Some of the characters were inspirational. I would also have to say that the generosity of the off-shore lads is second to none with regard to raising money for charity. I have raised hundreds of pounds in a few hours on many occasions and millions of pounds have been raised and donated over the years. I even wrote a few poems over the years about my off-shore experiences. You'd find yourself working with some of the greatest guys on earth – or out at sea – but also one or two of the meanest ones. You had to be on your guard; you had to develop a long memory. There were guys I would do anything for; there were others I couldn't turn my back on for one second. Above all, you had to keep your end up; you had to show you were a force to be reckoned with.

But there was a huge camaraderie, too, on the big construction hook-up jobs where the flotels were used. I have heard stories of half a dozen guys jammed into one small cabin getting mellow. Then the stories would start; someone would get a guitar out, people would swap songs and tales and jokes, or play cards. It was just like being round the camp fire. There were a few close calls for those lads involved as there were regular raids by the company safety men trying to catch them out. There were smoke detectors in the rooms, so they'd stuff socks over them and afterwards spray the room with deodorant. The aroma might escape and be smelt down the corridors, so they'd also put towels under the doors and spray them with deodorant, and open the toilet door so as to get the fan extractor going.

'Stuck in this cramped space', but still able to snatch a few minutes of relaxation.

There were some real characters that were noted for various exploits. There was this guy Jimmy Varbitski, a cable joiner from Glasgow, who had the ability to lift up a pint glass and bite a lump out of it, just like that. There was this legendary little guy, Wee Donny. His party trick was to curl himself up into a suitcase and get his mate to appear in a bar carrying the case, put it up on the bar and join the rest of us for a drink. Suddenly the case would burst open, Donny would come leaping out, sing a song, crack a joke or two and receive the applause of everyone in the bar, plus a few drinks to boot. The drinking culture associated with the 'Bears' (rig workers) was huge and every night in Aberdeen was a weekend; we worked hard and we partied hard. On more than one occasion I boarded a train to get from Aberdeen to Portlethen, only to find myself in Glasgow, where the party continued for another few days.

There were all sorts of pranks. One was to hide a fish in a locker until it stank the room out; another was to short-make a bed; you did this by taking the bottom sheet and folding it so that when the guy got into his bed he found he couldn't put his legs more than half way down. More than once I'd go to bed and find it full of nuts and bolts. Other times I was stitched up good and proper as reprisal for one of my own pranks and would find my boots filled with hand cleaner, or my training shoes nailed down to a piece of wood. My favourite revenge prank was to gently rub fibre glass insulation all over the bed sheets of someone who had got me; this made for a particularly itchy and uncomfortable night's sleep and a nice rash to boot. Once, they took all my gear out of my locker, sewed it all together and replaced it. The result was that when I went to pull a fresh tee-shirt out of my drawer, the rest of my wardrobe came tugging out after it. The hours that must have been put into that sewing were incredible.

Any new recruit to a rig had to be properly initiated. He'd be sitting after a hard day's shift, completely at peace, and the rest of us would start chatting among ourselves about the 90-mile gale that was forecast and how there would be 70-foot, no, 90-foot waves. We could see the new guy turning yellow, so we'd turn to him and say, 'Don't worry – there's a fair chance we won't capsize'. Then we'd advise him to go to bed in his life jacket 'just to be on the safe side'. Now, a life jacket was a large cumbersome affair, guaranteed to give the wearer an uncomfortable night. To show the way, we would go to our beds in our life jackets, too, but once behind the curtains we'd remove them, while he would toss and turn, wrestling with his huge Titanic-style life jacket all night up in his bunk, waiting for the storm that would never come. In the morning we'd greet him, all innocence, with the hope that he'd had a comfortable sleep.

Another prank was to ask the new guy to go to the store and fetch a 'long stand for painting'. He'd go there, be told to wait and wait while the storeman 'prepared' his long stand – for hour after hour, until the storeman asked him, 'Well, have you had a long enough stand yet?' It's amazing how gullible some guys were: over the years I've seen people go for buckets of steam, tartan paint, sky hooks, fused hacksaws and the famous key to the V door, a door which exists only in name, so that much fun was made of the victim's going round various departments trying to locate this elusive key. Then there was the guy who didn't eat for three days, because the lads had wound him up that he had to pay for his food and he had no money with him.

Little of that would be permitted nowadays. Any whiff of a prank and there would have to be an enquiry. Everyone's become so safety minded. Why, these days on some installations if you're caught descending a staircase without holding onto the handrail, it's been known for people to be packed off for counselling. A far cry from those early days of missing fingers!

Eric McNeil, born 1964, interviewed 2012: Muchalls and the North Sea

From Buckie to Baku

My old man had his own fishing boat; it was assumed that I'd be following into the family trade. I must admit I was never keen on the prospect of a life out on the North Sea as a fisherman. Every summer holiday while I was still at school my father would take me out as part of his crew, and I hated it all. It was a dawn to dusk operation, hauling in the nets every three hours, and no rest. After one week of that routine, I'd just be aching for my bed. On board there was always this sense of pressure, to get the nets in, to make sure the chance of a good catch wasn't spoilt. And then you only got about three days ashore between trips and I'd see my father constantly on the phone, trying to organise supplies, to fix up repairs, and then it would be time to set off once more. That way of life didn't appeal at all.

So I decided to stick in at school and make sure I got some qualifications. My father always assumed I would be going to sea. When he saw me night after night, diligently doing my homework, he would be picking away at me, 'Cam on, jist pack that bag awa. You dinna need aa that stuff, nae fan you'll be joinin me oot at sea'. But I kept at it, passed my exams, and have never really looked back.

When I left school I applied to BP for one of their four-year apprenticeships, as an instrument technician. This is a key job on the oil platforms, where there is so much to control and to keep accurately measured – flow, pressure, density, etc., etc. I've been with the company ever since.

But the first year was a long one. The idea was to take us through the whole repertoire of tool-handling skills, so you'd pass hours working with screwdrivers, files, hacksaws, lathes, milling machines. The aim was to give you complete mastery over any tool that you might encounter; it was very much a hands-on, practical first year. The

You'd pass hours working with screwdrivers, files, hacksaws, lathes, milling machines. The aim was to give you complete mastery over any tool that you might encounter.

second one was more technical and took us into the underlying theory.

Then came the placements and for the next two years I found myself being posted to all over the country – Lincoln, Cardiff, York. You'd be one month among the nodding donkeys in Lincolnshire, the next out on a rig in the Forties. We went off in groups and were given money to stay in hotels – but, boys being boys, we would get hold of the local paper and look out something cheap and cheerful and then regard what was left over as our beer allowance.

I enjoyed the variety and the sense of adventure of it all. I'd go back to Portsoy between times and find guys still sitting in the same place in the same pub where I'd left them and wonder what on earth they could have been doing, compared to my experiences.

I now work in Azerbaijan, out among the rigs which are opening up the vast fields that lie beneath the Caspian Sea. There are about 200 of us working and living on board the rig: about a quarter expats, the rest the locals. The aim is to get them up to the point when they can be running the whole show, so a lot of my work is to train them up. The

It could almost be New York:
George Smith against the background of modern day Baku, Azerbaijan.

Out on the Caspian Sea: George's oil rig, operated by BP.

rig is 100 kilometres off-shore; there are millions of barrels still there to be exploited and now that BP has built a pipe line to the West, the production is just racing ahead. It's a bit different from the early days in Baku 100 years ago, when they would send guys down on ropes to dig a hole and bring the oil up that way.

Baku, the capital, has become a modern bustling city of some 3,000,000, with high rise blocks sprouting up everywhere. I first went out there nine years ago and all you'd see on the streets were these old beat up Ladas; now it's Range Rovers and X5s. One rich local business man recently lashed out millions on his birthday party, flying in Lady Gaga to entertain his guests.

I like the life out there. The winters aren't usually too cold, while the summers are scorching – and I do like the heat. We work 12-hour shifts and in our spare time a lot of us make for the upper deck and lay out our sun loungers. Not too glamorous though; all you are aware of is guys in their underwear and the smell of sun screen in the air – but also lots and lots of lovely warmth.

It makes a welcome change from those rigs in the North Sea. So many of them are now past their best and have become rusty old hulks where you have to scrape the muck and the rust off before you can get at anything. And, of course, the North Sea can be mighty rough, while the Caspian, though a bit windy, rarely kicks up nasty.

I've found BP a good company to work for; they look after you and you are rewarded for hard work. Of course, the company took a big knock over the Deep Sea Horizon spillage in the Gulf of Mexico, but it's bounced back and the lessons have been learned.

I get home every four weeks: four on, four off. I like that pattern. The earlier two-weeks system meant that you tended to spend the first week home adjusting, especially to the different sleeping patterns, then the second thinking of where you would have to be the next week – back at work. Four weeks home gives you the chance to get the DIY done and to put your golf back into order. I must admit I'm addicted to the game and would like to get my handicap down to single figures.

And with modern technology you can get back into your own home at the push of a laptop button. I'll often Skype back three times a day to catch up with what the family is doing. If something's been on the go at school, I'll quickly hear about it from the kids. I can watch my wife cooking the supper and follow her around the kitchen as she does it. I find that if the frustrations have been building up offshore, then I can soon escape back to my own home and a bit of Buckie sanity.

Whereas you would have once said that practically all the young men around here were connected to the sea, now you can still say the same – but it'll be the oil and gas industry. I could go to a wedding or down the pub 15 years ago, and find that all the chat at the table was about haddocks, quotas and the cost of diesel and feel completely out of it. It's now all about drilling holes for oil – and I still feel out of it. On my rig out in Azerbaijan there are about six of us from Buckie. The locals think that this Buckie must be a big city and can't understand why we don't have a football team to match Man U.

What I have inherited from the fishing background is the work ethic and a sense of team work. Dad was always busy; although he was the skipper, you'd always see him on the deck, lending a hand. The attitude was, 'I'm here so let's get on with it'. I must admit it's a fairly masculine culture out on the rigs, with lots of swearing, shouts and also winding each other up. I find it quite difficult to keep swear words out of my daily vocabulary when I'm back home; the problem is that on the rigs some people won't listen to you until you start throwing a few f-words in their direction.

Every trip will have its flashpoints and then the frustrations build up until you blow a gasket and let them have it. I think the occasional blow-out can relieve the situation and that everyone understands that. The usual thing is that the next day everyone gets on with it; we're all big boys and don't have to sulk. The one thing I detest on board is the moaner, the one who's always whingeing and looking on the black side. Humour, a bit of banter, respect for each other, being positive, getting on with the job, having the proper professional standards – these are the qualities that get you through. Where you come from is unimportant: I've worked all over the UK and when I'm on the rigs I've had to mix with all sorts and that's been no bother. It's the personal qualities that count, not some kind of geographical label.

So I'm quite happy with the way that my career has worked out. Once I was the only male member of the family not to be going out to sea as a fisherman. I could go to my granny's, and among all the chat of haddocks and the next haul, feel something of a stranger. But now I've become the conventional one, so many have followed on into the oil industry.

George Smith, born 1975, interviewed 2012: Portsoy and Azerbaijan

LIFE IN THE COMMUNITY

A royal spread. Muchalls Village Hall, June 2012, celebrating the Diamond Jubilee. Facing the camera are Mat, David and Kathleen Northcroft plus Janet Pickering.

Fun and games in the village

Once you'd come to Cuminestown on a Sunday afternoon and see the bowls, the tennis and the croquet all on the go.

Now there's only the football

My great love became tennis. I started with an old racquet of my mother's. The strings were dead, but it got me going. Then in the war when most of the young men were away, I'd go to the courts with this school pal and we'd play for hours and hours, with the courts to ourselves. He was a very clever lad who could aye beat me at lessons, but never at the tennis.

For a long time the village had a really good tennis club. I was its president from 1962 till 1988. We had two well-kept courts with a traditional wooden clubhouse. We entered the Buchan League and the first season were bottom with only three points. From then on we worked at it, till in the end we were in the top division and won the title five years in a row.

Ushering in a sporting era: Cumminestown notables gather for the opening of the village playing fields, 1933.

What's become of all that now? Well, the courts are deserted, the posts have been yanked up and the court is covered in weeds. Once you'd come to Cuminestown on a Sunday afternoon and see the bowls, the tennis and the croquet all on the go at the same time, alongside the football. Everything would be in proper order: the tennis players in crisp white shorts, the bowlers in smart black and white. Visiting teams used to tell us they looked forward to coming to Cuminestown; everything would be so neat and tidy and the hospitality would be first class. Now there's only the football.

The young just don't support village activities in the way they used to, nor do they go out and play sport from morning to night as we all did; the old guard retire and are difficult to replace and so the rot sets in. Very sad.

Ally Irvine, born 1926, interviewed 2008: Cuminestown

The start of another packed season: The Monquhitter Bowling Club, Cuminestown, 1956–57.

Isobel McRobbie
with her prize-winning
clootie dumpling, 1995.

Highlight of the month

It was in 1948, a couple of years after her arrival at Ballogie House, that Mrs Nicol started up our Women's Rural Institute. It quickly became a very thriving branch – shows, drama, talks, the lot. We used to sweep the board at all the competitions, coming home with every prize imaginable – singing, knitting, jam and jellies, baking. We held talks and demonstrations. Our members would come in from all the farms round about; for many, in our scattered rural district, the WRI was the highlight of the month.

Look, here's an extract from a typical year's programme, 1962/63. This'll show you the kind of things we got up to at our monthly rural:

July 25: 'My face is my fortune'. Demonstration by Mrs Duncan, Finzean, Beauty Councillor; competition: Victorian Posy'.

August 22: 'What wondrous things our hands can do!' demonstration by Mrs Coutts, Banchory. Followed by Quiz and Competition for a waist apron.

September 26: 'Better be safe than sorry'. Talk on First Aid in the Home by Mr Leslie. Demonstration of Jewellery Making by Miss M. A. Davie; Quiz and Competition on 'Making up a First Aid box using no more than 12 items'.

October 24: 'Skill to do comes of doing'. Demonstration on Toy Making by Miss Smith, Kincardine O'Neil. Bring and Buy sale. Competition – Home made doll, costing no more than 1/6.

November 28: 'That taste of the kitchen is better than the smell'. Demonstration by Rural Gas Co. Entertainment by members of Ballogie WRI. Competition: Cheese Supper Dish.

January 23: 'A haggis on a horn speen/ A tattie when the ither's deen'. Burns Supper Open Night.

The ladies of the Ballogie WRI, 1960s. Isobel is front left; Mrs Nicol sitting opposite.

But lifestyles changed, television spread to every home, farming households became fewer and we began to go down. Once we had 48 members; eight years ago that had faded away to eight and we had to fold up.

Isobel McRobbie, interviewed 2011: Ballogie

The mighty Dauntless

Don't tell me you haven't heard of the Dauntless! This was the Junior side which had been such a force in the Kincardineshire League – and the only team to bear that proud name in the whole history of world football.

Practically every boy in the village was crazy about football. I played from morning to night, everywhere we could. A lot of it was good old fashioned tanner ba' football. We'd look out a stretch of road where there weren't many windows, roll out an old tennis ball and away we'd go. Everyone pitched in, so to get anywhere you had to develop close possession skills. People will laugh at this, but I assure you that what Messi does for Barcelona nowadays and evokes such wonder for his ability to weave his way through a packed midfield, well, we had young lads who could get hold of that old tennis ball and go ping-ping-ping, all the way from one goal to the other.

My grandmother lived at the front where you'd find a nice long stretch of pavement, ideal for me to practise my skills on. Even when there was nobody else around I'd still be at it, throwing up a tennis ball and letting it roll off her roof, trying to trap it and knock it backwards and forwards against her house, honing my skills. When I had to run messages I'd always take a ball with me, dribbling it along the street. If there was no ball handy then I would just use a stone.

You'd go along to Wairds Park and stand behind the goals and watch the adults at their practice, hoping against hope that sooner or later you'd be invited to join in. Then, if you were good enough, you hoped to graduate to the Junior side squad, and be a regular member of their training sessions.

The Dauntless's great rivals were Gourdon Selbie. My second appearance for the team

Another win for the Dauntless.
The team taken before the 1954 match with RAF Edzell, which resulted in a 2–0 victory. Standing next to Major Scott in the back row is Aileen Law crowned 'Football Queen' the night before, and then Dr A. West of Robert Gordon's Technical College, who cut the tape.

A ground fit for the team. The committee at the opening of the reconditioned pitch, Wairds Park, Johnshaven, August 1954. The man centre front row is Major George Scott.

'Fa ech'm': The name is Clark Simpson, proud member of the Dauntless.

was against them, away. I remember running along the right touchline and catching this Gourdon wifie asking another, 'Fa ech'm?' – literally, 'who owns him?', meaning 'What's his name?' Lineage was very important, you see; you were representing your community, so people were keen to establish your family credentials, even if you were only a fresh faced 15-year-old from the neighbouring village.

We were expected to show high standards of sportsmanship. That began in the street; there was an implicit understanding that if people didn't play fair, then the game would simply fall to bits. When I came to play among the men I need have no fears that I'd be hacked down or have my jersey pulled. There wasn't even any swearing, not back then. Winning was important, but playing the game properly even more so.

Clark Simpson, born 1935, interviewed 2011: Johnshaven

Dry drapper with a view

I started as a Brownie and 50 years later ended up as County Commissioner for Gordon. My philosophy is that if you have enjoyed something, then you should be prepared to put something back into it – and I certainly loved my time in the movement.

I would thoroughly recommend it. It broadens the outlook and involves the young female in such a wide range of activities and group work. We were brought up on a regime of open air adventure, when you'd go into a field, pitch your tent, light a fire, dig out a latrine and get down to cooking. Well, that sort of free-and-easy approach is no

longer possible, not in our era of health and safety regulations. No site will take you on nowadays unless you bring proper cookers with you and it can provide you with flushing toilets.

So maybe the Guides no longer gives that old sense of pioneering adventure. But we have to accept that today's girl grows up in a modern age where high-tech mobile phones and Wi-Fi connections are the norm. I certainly enjoyed the old days when you could all pile onto the back of a lorry, drive off with your gear, and land up in some farmer's field in the back of beyond. These days you have to seek permission from the Guides Association, fill in bits of paper and carry out a risk assessment. You can't just turn up on a fine evening and say, 'Let's go to the park and have a game of rounders'. You'd have to think about whether you have the appropriate 'walking safety level' in place.

Now that's the sort of thing that encourages old stagers to grumble. They see the present Guide going around in all sorts of uniform – trousers or skirts as they like, and a range of tops and hoods. But this freedom of dress is only a sensible moving with the times. The essence of the Guides isn't in appearance, but in team work and purposeful activity – and they are still very much there.

But you can't help looking back on those more innocent times with a sense of gratitude for what they gave us. We used to take a group out to Switzerland each year for a camp up in the mountains. This was the time when the Kinky Cottage scandal was on the go and I can remember the delight with which the girls christened their quarters their very own 'Kinky Chalet'. There was a dry toilet, overlooking the most gorgeous views of the Alps. I remember one of the Strathdon girls emerging from it one fine morning, looking around and then pronouncing to us all, 'Ye ken this – there's nae mony fowk fa can boast of a view like this fram their ane dry-drapper!'. Happy days…

In 1992, I was to be presented with the Laurel Award – the highest there is for services to the guiding movement. It was a wonderful surprise. But my true reward for all those years has been the sense of fellowship and sheer fun they have given me. There are still a huge number of good-hearted young girls who respond to the ideals of the movement. Guiding has given me such a lot and it's good to know it's continuing to do that for the younger generation.

Heather Bisset, born 1937, interviewed 2012: Keith Hall

Heather Bisset receiving the Laurel Award from Captain Farquharson, Lord Lieutenant of Aberdeenshire, 1992.

I certainly enjoyed the days when you could all pile onto the back of a lorry, and land up in a field in the back of beyond.

Spot the real minister! It is the Reverend David Whyte (back row, first right) with his Keig Church Dramatic Group and his production of the Brian Rix farce *See How they Run*, 1957. The 'Reverend' Ian Law is two places along from him.

The travelling players

Keig was a very active church. Most of the community from round about went to it. My own father was an Elder and he would have been most disappointed if the family pew didn't have someone in it on a Sunday. I would go along to the Sunday school in the early morning and then go into the church and wait for the full service to begin. We just accepted that that is what you had to do.

The minister ran a dramatics club and we'd put on plays. Some of them were quite elaborate productions; one of them was the Brian Rix farce, *See How They Run*. We put it on at Tullynessle, Alford and Glenbuchat, as well as Keig itself. Then, when the minister left and took over a parish near Forfar, we went down and put it on there. We thought of ourselves as real travelling players!

Ian Law, born 1939, interviewed 2007: Keig

St Ninian's Park to Auchenblae Golf Club

Right from the start I was mad keen on the game. We'd all play in the street at Alford; you'd see a dozen of us going at it with a tennis ball any evening. I used to practise in the barn on the farm by myself. Again it was a tennis ball – a proper football was out of the question; it cost far too much.

Representing his country. Kenny Morgan in the dark strip keeping a watchful eye at St Ninian's Park, 1954.

Although Denis Law was there for the last of the trial matches, he never did get selected.

I got picked for the Scottish Schoolboys. This was the time of Denis Law. Although he was there for the last of the trial matches, he never did get selected. So despite the huge number of full caps he has, I can claim to have one that he never got – a Schools' cap! In those days he was just a little skinny lad with a pair of granny specs; you could never have guessed that he'd go on to be the greatest footballer ever to play for Scotland.

But there I was, a lad from the North-east going off to represent my country at St Ninian's Park in Cardiff. My gym teacher came down with me on the train; I'd never been further afield than a visit to my auntie in Edinburgh till then. The match was played before a 20,000 crowd. I've got a cutting which shows me alongside a Welsh player and you can see the background thick with spectators.

I suppose I must have been a bit nervous and visited the toilet a few times, but as a young lad you take it all for granted; you just run on to the pitch and play. We played the match on a frozen pitch. We'd come all the way for it, so there was no way it was going to be put off. We just had to get on with it. But football was like that then. We never discussed tactics or worked out special plans; we were simply handed our jerseys in the dressing room and told to go out and play.

After I'd represented Scotland, Huddersfield FC got in touch. They were keen to have me down, along with Denis Law. The manager and a scout came to the school and talked with the Head. I was summonsed to his room afterwards. Mr Ritchie just looked at me and shook his head: 'Huddersfield?', he said, 'Oh, I don't think so! A country loon, down into the big city - no, no.' He told me I should just bide where I was and work my way up more gradually. By and by another club would come for me – but they never did.

So my football career was all in the North-east. I had 10 years at Keith in the Highland League. My position was right-half. We never made much out of the game. The most I was on was £3 a game, with a bonus of £1 for a win and ten bob for a draw. I remember playing Caley in the match where they needed to beat us to clinch the league and we took them, 2-0. As we were coming off, their Alan Presley asked, 'Tell me you lads, are you on a big bonus for this game?' He was amazed when we told him it was just

Receiving his Scotland cap at the Alford School prize-giving from the rector's wife, Mrs Ritchie. Ian Law (see above) is also in the group, back row, second right.

With the Keith team that won the Highland League Qualifying Cup, 1962. Kenny is standing first left.

the normal pound. They'd been on £20.

But I enjoyed the career I managed to have. My great asset was my work rate. I always worked hard at the game and never let anyone down.

I started working at the golf course in 1989. I enjoy the job, always have. I was on holiday earlier this year and the wife said, 'I've got a fortnight, so I assume you'll be taking a fortnight too'. 'Oh no,' I said, 'a week will do me.'

There's only me, so I have to do everything. That's the way I like it. I start at 4.30 each morning; I can't wait to get started. Mondays are spent going round the course, cutting the greens and the tees. Tuesday it's the turn of the fairways; Wednesday it's back to the greens and shifting the holes. Thursdays I concentrate on the rough; Friday back to the greens. The grass never stops growing and I never stop cutting it.

The best time of all is five o'clock on a summer's morning when you can hear the birds singing and it's just you and the grass.

I didn't get any training. Nowadays I'd need letters after my name, but for me it was just a question of common sense and learning on the job. When I first started I thought that all I had to do was act as a grass cutter, but there's a bit more to it than that, as I've found out. One of my biggest tasks is to look for the first sign of disease and stamp on it as quickly as possible.

A well maintained course. Auchenblae Golf Club where Kenny was for many years the groundsman.

My other big problem is rabbits, but I manage to put down a little something for them and that does the trick. Getting rid of the mould and the rabbits, that's what a greenkeeper does.

Kenny Morgan, born 1939, interviewed 2006: Auchenblae

Fintry Burns supper, 1956. Janet is there, far left, representing the school pupils; the *Immortal Memory* is to be proposed by George Gill, the man smiling next to her.

The whole community joined in

The school acted as a social centre for the area. There was a Parents' Committee and they'd organise fund raising – mostly for parties and trips. We had an annual picnic outing in a coach to Banff Links and the open air pool at Tarlair – which must be the coldest place on earth! I can remember the odd sensation of feeling the water go up and down as the tide came in.

These outings were great events, which the whole community joined in. Work on the farms stopped and the farm servants were given the day off. We had races, sprints, egg-and-spoon, the sack race. The grocers in Turriff supplied picnic bags – sticky buns, sausage rolls and a huge urn of tea.

In the winter there'd be the Christmas party with Santa calling by. You'd get a gift of a toy. Then there was a Burns Supper; there were sales and whist drives to raise funds. The children would go along, but that usually meant just watching the adults, or talking to the other children at the sides – not always enthralling entertainment!

Janet Byth, born 1944, interviewed 2011: Fintry

The whole community joined in. The Fintry outing to Banff Links, 1954. Janet Byth is peeping over the left shoulder of the tall girl, centre; her father is the tall man at the back; her mother is crouching at the end of the second row, left.

A magic experience

I've been researching its history and it all seems to be shrouded in mystery. All this adds to the mystique, the feeling that the Stonehaven Fireballs are lost in the mists of ancient time. For myself, the appeal probably lies in the fact that I'm a natural pyrotechnic! I can recall being taken as a wee boy down to the High Street in the Old Town one Hogmanay and being allowed to gaze down on the procession from an upstairs window. I can still feel that awe and excitement as I stared through a small pane of glass down onto the flares and the sparks flying below.

That picture has never left me. So, when back in the 1970s, there was an appeal for fresh blood, I went along – and now, 34 years later, I'm still at it! It's such a brilliant, stunning spectacle. To the bystander it's exciting enough, but to those of us who are the actual swingers, the drama is almost overwhelming. Even before it begins and we're waiting for the time to light up, the anticipation sends your heart thumping. And then the procession starts and it's a great mish-mash of noise, light and sensations. The fire whirls about your head; the sparks fly and leave a glowing trail behind you and the shouts of the crowd press in all about.

Then there's the blast of heat against your face and the contrast between that and the cold fresh winter air. You're alone, swinging your own fireball, but you're also one of a team, a procession of flaming torches, marching along the High Street, trying not to lose your strength until the harbour is reached, trying to judge your steps so that you don't crush up against the ones ahead or get bumped by those behind. Oh, it's a magic, magic experience, I can tell you!

'That picture has never left me.' Stonehaven Old Town Hogmanay, as viewed from an upstairs window.

Martin Sim, born 1947, interviewed 2011: Stonehaven

'We went to the beach.' Children gather on the shore at Gardenstown.

Childhood games: life-long lessons

We'd get up to all sorts. Breakfast done, it would be outdoors, joining up with your pals and finding something to do around the village. There's no way any of us would have stayed inside; that would have seemed against nature.

A great thing was our dens. These would be in one of the sheddies you'd find in backyards. My granny had one and that became our great hideaway. We'd shelter in it from the rain; we'd eat meals in it; we'd take a flask of soup and buy a piece from the baker. We'd go around doors, begging, 'Onythin fer oor sheddie?' Often we'd come away with some old rug, a cushion or a lamp. That sheddie was our very own headquarters.

We also went onto the beach. We'd take buckets and collect buckies in them. The Gardenstown barber ran a shell fish business as a sideline, so we'd take our buckies to him and maybe get a shilling or two. Dad would take us on a fishing expedition at weekends. There was a place called the Tor with trees and burns, a great hunting ground for brown trout.

Another great game was 'Hunt the Fox'. We'd divide ourselves into two teams; one of them would count to 100 while the other would go off and find hiding places, anywhere, all over the village. The seekers would shout out, 'Hunt the fox!' and the hidden ones would reply with the name of another animal – 'Koala bear!' or 'Jaguar!' or something of the ilk. They would also be moving around, so the whole thing became a sort of cat and mouse game.

Keeping up the old games.
Playtime at Rayne North School, 2003, [taken from *Leopard* magazine, September 2003]

We played all the traditional street games such as 'kick the can' and 'beddies'. A lot of people claim that these activities are now dead, but I visit rural schools quite often and can assure you that in the playground you'll still see the old skipping and ball games – and you'll hear the old songs and chants such as 'A sailor went to sea-sea-sea'. Kids still want to be outside, playing and singing. But I doubt whether they get the same chances at home. The school playground is a secure environment, but a lot of parents are now scared to let their children roam wild and free. Traffic, fear of being molested by some stranger – all that has damped things down. And then there's the lure of the computer and the TV in the bedroom and all the rest of it.

That's a great shame; we got such a lot out of our childhood games and I don't just mean fun. Looking back, I can see we not only had great fun, but also learned a lot about life – how to work and play together, how to arrive at a decision and how to compromise; how to make up rules and the discipline of sticking to them.

We had an evening social just before Christmas where we'd go up on the stage and sing our hearts out for the adults. The local baker supplied sausage rolls and bradies; the ladies would appear with big trays loaded with sandwiches and cups of tea. In the summer there'd be the Sunday school picnic, an event for the whole village. There'd be events for everyone – granny sprints, three-legged races, egg-and-spoon – the lot. The men would hold a tug of war and there'd be great games of rounders. You'd get prizes too: tins of bubbles, a small bat and ball. Our favourite place was Turriff Den; we'd set off in a coach waving little flags and yelling our goodbyes. The adults turned up later in cars. The urn and biscuits were brought out as soon as we arrived and then later there'd be the big spread with wifies coming and going with their kettles and sandwiches and bradies and ice cream.

My father had an act we all looked forward to every year. He'd don an old oilskin coat and sellotape sweeties to it until it was almost completely covered, and then set off on a run with us children chasing and shouting after him, trying to pull the sweeties off. He'd dart and dive and stop and start until eventually he'd let himself be caught and then we'd all roll and clamber over him, grabbing at the sweets.

Irene Watt, born 1957, interviewed 2011: Gardenstown

Moving with the times

A big night out – Fifties style

Our main place to go was Dufftown. On a Saturday evening three buses would come down from Tomintoul and pick us up. For entertainment the big draw was the cinema. The second house showing would begin at eight; afterwards the last bus back would be at 10.30 and that left you just enough time to get a bag of chips from the chipper in the Square. I saw some wonderful films. The first one was *The Phantom of the Opera*, great stuff! I can remember Harry Lime and *The Third Man* and *2,000 Women*.

Then there would be the Friday night hop, which started at nine in the hall. To attend that a group of six of us would hire a car. We'd go to dances at Inveraven, Cabrach and all around. The bands were quite up to date and played quicksteps and all the rest of the numbers of the day. There was no real trouble; the bobby would show up at some point and stand at the door just to show his presence. I didn't go to pubs all that much. If you had a girlfriend then you tended to steer clear of them. My wife was never in a pub before we got married; it was something that respectable unmarried women just didn't do.

John Goodbrand, born 1932, interviewed 2008: Glenlivet

> There was no real trouble; the bobby would show up and stand at the door just to show his presence.

The morning after the big night out. Dufftown in the 1950s.

Keeping up with the latest fashions: Alan Robertson with the Royal Teens, 1968.

I had a pair of platform sole boots with two-inch heels, coloured brown, but edged by cream soles; they cost a whole week's wages.

Jolson and a smart white suit

After the Academy, I landed this job in Aberdeen as a quantity surveyor – for the princely salary of £7.1.8 a month! But I also had a second career. While I was at Inverurie Academy the school was trying to build its own swimming pool and the rector, the famous Dr Dixon, came up with a great fund-raising scheme. The idea was to give each pupil £1 and ask them to go off and come up with some enterprise into which they could invest the pound and bring back the proceeds to the swimming pool fund.

Well, four of us decided we would form our own band and run dances. A couple could play the guitar and I'd taken piano lessons as a boy. When I played from sheet music I was nothing exceptional; I couldn't read the music fast enough to do anything other than play mechanically – but I discovered that if I simply heard a piece, I could play it by ear. We held an event in the Kirk Hall and away we went. It was all pretty primitive, but we did raise money.

There was this band advertising for an organ player, 'preferably with own organ'. I got the job – by virtue of having my own organ, I'm sure! The band was called 'The Out' and we'd play in the Students' Union and a few local pubs. But anything we got had to pay for fuel, or HP on the instruments. The guy who ran the band – an Englishman called Ken Whitcomb – drove us around in this old clapped-out Bedford van and when it finally gave up the ghost, he went out in search of something that would really make us unique. He found it – a 1933 Rolls-Royce hearse which gobbled up four miles to the gallon.

I was with them for six months; great fun, but hardly remunerative. Then one Saturday night we were appearing in the Union when in came this band, 'The Royal Teens'. They were just about the best known of the Aberdeen bands of their day, but their keyboard player was on the brink of leaving, so I was invited to take over.

The stuff we played was the pop music of the day. This was the heyday of British pop, with the Beatles, the Rolling Stones and all the rest of them. I'd grown up with this; as a boy I managed to save up and buy my own transistor. I'd go to bed on a Sunday night and listen to the run-down of the week's Hit Parade, which was from 11 o'clock to midnight. And here I was playing it in a band!

Then I left to join an Inverurie-based band, the 'Billy Steele Combo'. But Billy retired and we had to rename ourselves; we became 'Jolson' and this became the most successful of my bands. At weekends we'd travel all over the north of Scotland appearing in local halls, and for good fees, too. You'd go to some sleepy wee place like Strathpeffer and you'd be setting up your gear in this great empty hall thinking to yourself, 'We'll never be able to fill this, not out here!' Then at eight o'clock, ten buses would draw up and folk come pouring out. You'd find yourself appearing in front of 700 young folk who'd come in from all the villages round about.

We had to be image conscious and that meant keeping up with the very latest fashions. Every now and then we'd go down to Glasgow to view the latest trends, and buy the stuff that hadn't come to the North-east yet – like platform sole boots. I had a pair with two-inch heels, coloured brown, but edged by cream soles; they cost a whole week's wages.

When I was getting married, I told my mother I wanted to wear a smart white suit – the height of trendiness then – and she had a fit. It was made clear that if I went ahead the whole family would be in danger of breaking up. I wore a traditional suit after all. I've got this photo of us taken in 1973 in this flamboyant sheepskin jacket – actually there was a practical reason for that: no heater in the van! I'd wear tartan trousers. We had our own loyal female following; you'd see the same groupies turning up at gig after gig, standing at the front, screaming for us.

Mostly, things passed off well, but there were some notable punch-ups. These were usually sparked off by rivalry between lads from different places competing for the same females. One of the worst places was Mintlaw Station on a Saturday night. Every time we played there, it seemed to result in a battlefield. The stage was only a couple of feet above the floor, so they erected a cage of steel railings around us as protection. So there we were, earnestly playing all the latest romantic love numbers, behind our tubular steel bars, and just a few feet away blokes would be shouting and throwing punches at each other.

Jolson were at their peak from 1973 to 1978. The market for our kind of band collapsed quite abruptly when the licensing laws changed. When we started, drinking up time was 10, so we'd start off in front of 50 teenagers who were too young to be in a pub. Suddenly, just after 10, the doors would fly open, crowds would pour in and that would give us a good 90 minutes. But then closing time became 11 and that killed us.

But it wasn't quite the end. In 1993 we got together again for a charity do in Inverurie Town Hall and that went really well. We made this an annual event for the following nine years; you'd get 400 in for two nights – proceeds all to charity. Over 10 years we raised £70,000.

Alan Robertson, born 1948, interviewed 2011: Kintore and on tour

That sheepskin jacket. Alan with his fellow Jolsons, 1973. From the left: Brian Hosie, Jim Walker, Johnny Smith and Alan Robertson.

Lulu in her fish-n-chip days, in the late 1960s.

Now if you want to mount an event at the Town Hall you'll be restricted to 150: then Health and Safety didn't exist; upwards of 600 heaving bodies could be crowding in.

How else to meet the opposite sex?

Growing up in the Sixties and Seventies I was part of the local dance culture. There'd be three dance events: ballroom dancing for the older set in Wyness Hall, old time dancing in the Railway Hall and modern dancing in the Town Hall. Being young I tended to regard the Town Hall as my natural habitat. That's where you'd hear music from the hits of the day and find girls dancing round their handbags, with the blokes prowling around and eyeing up the talent.

I started going when I was 14. My older sister would be given the task of 'looking after me', but as soon as we were out of the door she'd slap on the lipstick, tell me to 'get lost' and agree on a meeting time at the end of the evening.

Like all the rest I grew my hair long. We'd all get our hair cut at the local barber, Louis Cassie. He was one of the old school and would just sit you in the chair, get out his electric clippers and 'zzzip…' – before you knew it you'd been scalped. He had two assistants and the younger one, Shorty Stewart, would enquire, 'And how would you like it today?' He would always have the longest queue among us young ones. A bout of politeness would break out as Louis's chair became vacant: 'Na, na, efter you – nae hurry!', we'd assure the older customers and usher them towards the short-back-and-sides chair. If you did succeed in getting Shorty, you'd point to a photo of a model on the wall and ask for that, or tell him, 'Jist like John Lennon'.

You tried to give a dance to a number of lassies before you settled on the one who took your fancy for the last half hour. These Inverurie dances were big events. The promoter, Bapa Ewan, operated on a large scale and he'd run buses in from places like Kemnay, Huntly, New Deer and Mintlaw, so that all sorts of folk would come pouring into the town. Now if you want to mount an event at the Town Hall you'll be restricted to 150: then Health and Safety didn't exist; upwards of 600 heaving bodies could be crowding in. In the other two venues some decorum still existed with the two sexes sitting lined up on opposite sides, but the Town Hall was a bit of a cattle market.

The whole thing was quite rushed too; the buses had to be away at 11.45 because of the Sabbath. The strategy was to look out a girl from an outlying place, see her onto the bus and then search out an Inverurie lassie to take home. Two for the price of one! In any generation you'll always get one or two spoiling for a fight, so a punch up could break out at any moment. Usually it was territorial, with an Inverurie girl being bothered by a Mintlaw, Huntly or a Kemnay lad – and that could be the flashpoint. Tribal warfare!

But there was a code: fights had to be settled on a one-to-one basis, with a circle gathering round and ensuring a fair fist fight. The police would bring a Black Maria and park it outside, but that was really a matter of offering a physical presence rather than hauling people off to the cells. They preferred to sit there, smoking and watching the girls.

Those Saturday dances were big events. Big names were brought in – the Yardbirds, the Hollies, Lulu. I remember Lulu coming up as a new 16-year old star with the hit 'Shout!' a few months behind her, and there she was, doing her stuff, and then queuing up with the rest of us to get her chips from Squealer Smith's chipper.

Going to the dances was a necessity. How else could you ever meet the opposite sex in those days? We had a Dansette at home. I was into the Beatles, but my sister preferred ballad merchants like Englebert Humperdinck. My mother would sing along, but my father never did approve. 'Switch aff that noise!', he'd tell us.

Duncan Naysmith, born 1951, interviewed 2011: Inverurie

The real bee's knees

The Sixties and Seventies was the time when young people began to enjoy their own pop music and styles of dress. We didn't miss out on that in Keig. Mum and Dad bought a gramophone and my brother and I would go into Alford to buy records for it. The first one we got was *Seven Drunken Nights* by the Dubliners. We listened to it over and over again.

As teenagers we'd bike into Alford, to the Double O club, run by a teacher at the Academy. There you would play badminton, darts and snooker. We'd listen to the music of the day. There was never any trouble and no alcohol, just juice. On Saturdays the church would hold its youth club and that was very popular. The evening was split in two, the first half devoted to games and the second to dancing to the record player.

Fashion was a big thing. I was lucky because I could get into Aberdeen and buy really eye-catching, trendy gear. I always liked to go for something different and then come back to the village and show it off. There were two 'in' shops: Robert Rae and Alex's. I remember going into Robert Rae's and spotting this white canvas jacket. It had no collar, the belt was inside and it was flared. 'This is the real bee's knees,' I told myself. I took it home and Mum sewed fringes on it. That night I went to the dance in Alford in this spectacular white jacket with fringes up and down and all around. I had a pair of black trousers to set it off. It did the trick; everyone gathered around and admired it. I felt great, really different.

Alistair Black, born 1954, interviewed 2007: Keig

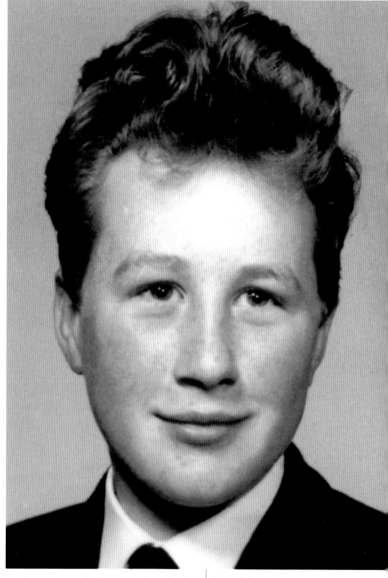

'Fashion was the thing.'
A 12-year-old Alistair Black sporting an Elvis hairstyle, 1966.

Roseanne Fitzpatrick in the 1950s…

Always in fashion …in the 1970s

A real fashionista

I'd regularly go into Aberdeen to look out the latest styles. I went in for the minis and the maxis and heavy make-up: white face, heavy purple eye-shadow, painted nails. Later, at university, I was into the hippy look – hooped earrings, long skirts: a real fashionista. I revelled in the changing scene and how, as a young person, we could express ourselves and be different from our mothers.

Drugs were coming on the scene, but never as far as I was concerned. The first time I personally encountered any was at a party in New York. We were sitting in a circle and I was offered a drag on some marihuana. 'Smoke?' the guy to my left said. 'No thanks, I don't smoke,' I replied. He looked at me as if I was completely naïve, which I suppose I was.

I did more drinking under age than I've ever done since. We'd go to this pub in St Fergus that would serve young people, cycling there and back. But when I was newly turned 17 I passed my driving test and could borrow my father's car. I remember one night coming home after a party with too much alcohol inside me and mounting a

… in the 1990s…

pavement and thinking to myself, 'This is stupid!'

It was the same with sex. Although I had a succession of boyfriends, I had strict boundaries. In my second year at university I was at my own 21st birthday party, drank a bit too much, and started flirting with this guy who owned a Porsche. He invited me back to his flat and then tried to come on too strong. When I told him, 'No! That's as far as it goes,' he accused me of leading him on. I ended up walking back to my own flat and leaving him to it.

So although I enjoyed the social scene of the Seventies and Eighties and was a bit of a rebel, I retained a definite set of traditional ethics. I followed the fashions and loved the music, but I did have the benefit of a very stable and loving family background to guide me. You can take the girl out of Peterhead, but you can't take Peterhead out of the girl!

Roseanne Fitzpatrick, born 1955, interviewed 2011

...and in 2011.

Raves were all the rage

We took the Ardennan over in 1991. Now, I'd gone to dances when I was young, to discos at Fraserburgh or Rosehearty and on the bus down to 'Flicks' at Brechin. These were sociable events – a whole set of us going off together to enjoy the music and the atmosphere. But in the early Nineties raves were all the rage and we had to cater for them at our night club. I'd never been in a circle where drugs were used – they were considered sleazy, not for the mainstream. But I was aware that drugs were now part of the rave scene, so I called on the Police for their advice. They paid us a visit and addressed the staff. They told us what we should be looking out for.

Some of the ravers would come already under the influence. It seemed to be part of the culture, just like their music was. This was heavy beat stuff that gave a continual 'boom, boom!' We had machines that released clouds of smoke from behind the speakers so as to create the required atmosphere. You'd see these ravers dancing and jumping about all by themselves in the midst of the smoky haze and you'd hear this 'boom, boom' going on till two in the morning. They never caused much trouble; drugs seemed to pacify them and you never had any of the punch-ups that could be the case at the old village hall dances. Generally, they just seemed content to get lost in their own world and do their own thing.

We lived in a flat upstairs and you'd see the cot with our daughter vibrating on the floor to the beat. To this day she claims to have a special relationship with dance music. 'I've got rhythm inside me,' she'll say. But it was all very noisy and tiring and the drugs weren't to our taste, so we turned our attention to more old-fashioned disco nights, playing the old hits and generating something of a party atmosphere. They went well; some nights we'd get 250 in on a Saturday.

Marianne Bell, born 1969, interviewed 2011: Inverurie

> We lived in a flat upstairs and you'd see the cot with our daughter vibrating on the floor to the beat.

Desk work beneath the traffic accident map at Banff, 1963.

The new recruits. Aberdeen City Police Training School, 1947. Stanley Rothney is second row, third right.

Pillars of the Community

The bobby: common sense, that's the thing

Common sense, that's the thing! Get to know your community and get in among them; that's how it works. Once you've identified the villains, make a thorough nuisance of yourself to them. Most people are reasonable folk, but there will be one or two who've no intention of being like that. These are the ones you have to be prepared to get in among, no nonsense. I remember when years later, I was at a function; I got speaking to one of the band and he told me, 'You were the one that kept me out of trouble'. He told me that as a young lad he'd got into all kinds of scrapes. But each time something went wrong in the neighbourhood, I'd be round to the door asking awkward

questions as to whereabouts and so on. I wouldn't have any definite evidence, but I knew how to make my presence felt. Then, he told me, once I'd left, his mother would lay into him and give him a hell of a bawling out. Eventually he got worn down. He remembered the time came when he was on the brink of doing something wrong he just drew back and said to himself, 'It's nae worth it – Rothney'll jist be roon ma door and git me intae anither row!'

I was quite ready to give lads like that the odd skelp round the lug; nowadays that would be regarded as assault, but then you knew that if they went home and complained,

Bobbies on parade.
Coronation Day, 1953, Banff Low Street. Superintendent Mowat at the head and Chief Constable Strath at the rear. Stanley is fourth from front row on right.

What the police patrolled in then: Stanley with a Ford W8 Pilot model, Banff, 1960s.

their parents would be giving them another and twice as sore, too. You've got to keep the initiative; you've got to earn the respect of your community by showing that no-one is going to fool you. The prevention of crime must always be the prime aim – nip things in the bud, keep your ears and eyes open. At Methlick I made a point of going every day to the smiddy. This was a natural focal point in any rural community then, a place where the farm workers would call by to get their horses shod and have to wait while it was being done and pass the time by exchanging gossip: who'd been behaving oddly, whether any strangers had been seen about the place and so on. You'd read the local papers and find out where that week's dance was being held, because you knew that was another place where the single young men, the ones more likely to get into trouble, would congregate. You'd go and drop in, just to see what was going on. Then, when they were leaving, as likely as not, you'd get someone for biking without lights.

You had to be ready to mix it. In those days recruits to the police had to be big men, not the kind of baby-faced young graduate types they often go in for these days. I remember Peter Scott out at New Pitsligo. There were a lot of quarry workers out there then and at the weekend dances they would often get into fights. Peter was quite prepared to haul a troublemaker out to give him a good thrashing. Then on the Monday morning when all the quarry workers were at their slabs working away, the news would go down the line, that 'so-and-so had bin given a richt seein tae by the bobby'. Usually the culprit, because of embarrassment, would keep his mouth shut.

I finally ended up at Peterculter as Section Sergeant. My area covered much of Lower Deeside. We'd be on the go from nine in the morning till two the next morning and beyond. You'd make sure you and your men would be out there in the community, seeing and being seen. We'd go round at night, shaking the door handles; some regarded that a menial task, but to me it was keeping an eye on things. It took us into places we wouldn't otherwise have got to know, up closes, into back yards. And the villains would also see you out and about and know to steer clear of your patch. When they got in their cars and came out from the city looking for easy prey, they would drive through Peterculter and on to places like Alford – 'Cos thae bluidy bobbies at Peterculter are aye on the go.' I always like to think it was the best run section in the Force – certainly the cream of the crop.

Peterculter in those days was still very much a distinct community. My work depended on inside knowledge and local contacts. The big crime during my time there was the day the Savings Bank was robbed. My wife suggested it was high time we got

Down memory lane, Culter Police Station, 2012. Stanley is with old colleagues, Bert Stewart at the front; Gordon Argo, Bill Mitchell, Jimmy Simpson behind.

round to stocking up the deep-freeze, so I decided I'd go off with her over the lunch hour to do it. When I got back I was greeted by the office girl: 'Far hae ye bin? The bank's bin robbed! Ye'll be for it noo – ye shid hae bin here, sergeant. They're aa oot here frae Aberdeen, wi the dogs an aathin!' I went out to the carpark and found that the place was swarming with police who'd poured in from all over.

But I managed to clear the whole thing up and have the villains under arrest by 7.30 that same evening. While the other police were milling around like headless chickens, a worker from the mill came to the station and asked to have a word with me – alone. 'I heard the bank's bin robbed,' he said. 'Weel I think I've some idea as tae faa's deen it.' He told me that just as he was going on to his two o'clock shift, he heard from this other lad that he'd been flagged down by this other worker and offered a fiver to drive him into Aberdeen. 'That's funny, I thought, he wis tappin me fer some cash jist yesterday an noo he's flush wi fivers.' He didn't know the man well; he'd come from the south on casual work at the mill.

Well, I went straight to the mill office and started to ask questions. I got an address in Aberdeen: Bridge Street. I went back to the station and told Littlejohn, my youngest constable, 'Come on Sandy – tak nae notice o aa this – we're aff tae Aberdeen'. By 7.30 the case had been cleaned up. We got to the Bridge Street address and found it was a seedy lodging house; at the side of the bed where this man slept we found a suitcase. When I opened it all the money was stacked up inside! My local connections certainly paid off, as I'd cleared up the crime – and I never did have to account for my lunchtime absence.

Working with the enthusiastic team at Culter was the most fulfilling of all my days as a North-east bobby. Sadly, Culter Police Station is now no more. It's been disposed of to a developer who intends to raze it to the ground and replace it with a block of flats. However, a trip down memory lane was afforded to the survivors of my old section before the work commenced. And it's pleasing to know that the coat of arms of Aberdeen County commemorating the opening of the building in 1895 is to be salvaged and incorporated into the new structure. At least future inhabitants in Culter will be kept aware of where their area's very own bobbies kept law and order.

Stanley Rothney, born 1923, interviewed 2007: Peterculter

The villains would drive through Peterculter and on to places like Alford – 'Cos thae bluidy bobbies at Peterculter are aye on the go.'

The country store

I t was a real country store which sold everything: groceries, of course, but also fireworks, paraffin, kettles, household utensils, toys, stationery, cards, wool for knitting, buttons – the lot. Sometimes the train drivers would pop in for fags and butteries; the train would just sit there with the signal down while they ran down the road and into the shop.

The vast majority of customers were completely honest. But not all of them – I had this assistant and she said, 'Fit why dis Mrs So-and-so kip nippin through tae the back? Ah'm sure she mist be efter nickin stuff'. I didn't like to confront the woman direct, so I

R&G Mowat, General Merchants, 1977

Changing face of village shopping.
The bakery at Newtonhill all set for a delivery, 1899.

told her to give me the wink the next time she saw this happen. Well, the woman came in, did her shopping and came to the till with her basket. After putting her stuff through she announced, 'I think that's a'thin, Mrs Mowat'. But I kept an eye on her and, sure enough, I saw her pop round the back, quickly put her hand up and pop this tin of salmon into her bag. So as she made to leave the shop I said, 'Excuse me, bit I canna help noticin that ye'll be havin salmon fer tea'. 'Pardon?', she said. 'I said, ye'll be haein salmon fer yer tea, bit ye've nae paid fer it.' 'Oh!', she said, as bold as anything, 'I dinna fancy it efter aa – I'll jist pit it back'.

On another occasion there was this wee girl in the shop with her mother and I caught her putting a chocolate bar into her pocket. I informed the mother, who apologised and ordered her to put it back. 'Ach!', the girl came out with, 'I didna want yer bluidy Fry's Chocolate Cream onywye,' and threw it in my face.

Everyone knew everyone else then and being in the heart of the village we saw all its life pass by. There was this man from just down the road who would roll home drunk night after night and his wife would batter him for it. She'd lay into him – but she was always careful to take off his specs and put them in his pocket before she started! Then there was this other man who lived at the bottom of the hill. One night he came home roaring drunk, so his wife just came up to meet him, tipped him up, grabbed him by the legs and pulled him down the street on his backside.

Then there was this woman who always went round with heavy make-up and long painted nails. Her husband was away a lot at his work, but she never had any shortage of stand-ins: you'd see her take them round the back and attend to them there.

It was a satisfying life, running the village's shop in the Seventies and Eighties, before Newtonhill became so large and the supermarkets took over. We lived upstairs and that meant you were never really away from the business. It was quite common for people to come to the door at night and ask us 'to oblige them'. Sometimes you'd feel like throwing the stuff at them, especially when you knew that all they were after was some item that they'd forgotten when they were at their regular shopping in Stonehaven or Aberdeen.

We sold a lot of stuff loose then; now everything is pre-packaged. We sold sherry and some customers would come into the shop with their own bottle and ask us to fill it for them, which we did from a large container with a tap on its top. Kiddies would come in and select four ounces of sweeties from a jar. Back then nobody had even heard of pasta or pizzas or Chinese food. Nobody took yogurt for their pudding. People would still come in for their two ounces of corned beef, half-pound of onions and a few tatties to make stovies. No readymade meals, sell-by dates or bar codes back then.

Taking over the village shop: Gertie Mowat arrives in Newtonhill, late 1960s.

Gertie Mowat, born 1926, interviewed 2011: Newtonhill

The doctor: who would you rather be?

Dr Brodie Brown was my model. In the days when he was our family doctor at Glen Tanar, there'd been little in the way of effective ammunition; what he did was to show a personal interest in each and every patient. He might not have much in the way of really effective treatment to offer, but what he could give was a feeling of confidence and reassurance. He would make the patient feel important and that often worked as much as anything else could.

When I first came into practice in 1958 at Culter, I was now in a generation that worked with antibiotics and acted as if personality was of less importance. The old guard were still there and there had been some big figures among them: Dr Philip at Huntly, Taylor at Peterhead, Gordon at Ellon, Park at Banchory, Gill at Inverbervie, all big men, great personalities. If they told you you were going to get better, then you believed them. Our generation would probably shoot some antibiotics at the problem and hope for the best. I remember old Dr Horne out at Portlethen. He was one

of the old school of family doctors and he once warned me, 'Don't do what I did. I gave too much. If I was out at night and spotted a chink of light at a bedroom window I would be at the door, wondering if they needed me. It was that which gave me my coronary'.

The graduate: Pierre Fouin on graduation with his parents, 1954.

Not the only one: among his fellow M.B.ChB graduates, Pierre is before the space between the windows, two down.

Half-way through the course. Pierre Fouin attends the 1951 Medical Ball. He is third row up, fourth left; the future Mrs Fouin stands second row, dead centre.

I've mixed feelings about the way things have turned out. There's been a tremendous improvement in general living standards. When I began you'd see some real poverty. But I'm not sure people are any happier as a result. I remember going into this old couple's house, really no more than a tin but-an-ben. But she told me, 'We hae a pottie soup an the fire, an we've oor auld age pension and we manage te pit a shillin a week by fer Christmas. Doctor, there's naethin comin o'er us!' They had very little – except contentment and that can be everything.

Towards the end of my career, and with the oil boom in full swing, I'd be going into big houses with all the latest gear on display. But you'd find a bored wife who never saw her husband because he was away at the office making the money. These were people who had nothing in their lives but work and material goods. Now who would you rather be? The levels of neurosis in society are as high as ever. When I started, Cults and Culter were still real communities, places where people knew each other and looked out for each other. You don't see so much of that now; people are more inclined to lead separate lives.

Pierre Fouin, born 1928, interviewed 2007: GP, Cults and Peterculter 1958-90

See also his KICK THOSE SLEEPING DOGS, *Leopard Press, 2011*

These people had nothing in their lives but work and material goods. Now who would you rather be?

Robbie Gordon helps a customer to choose, 1960. The German vases on the top shelf have now become valued collectors' items.

The rep: too much for the poor lassie

O ne of the travellers to my jeweller's shop was Mr Smith of Dunningham & Co., Aberdeen. He would take the early morning bus from the city, giving the driver a florin to be dropped at our door. At lunch he'd go to the Haughton Hotel, where he always took Scotch broth and rice pudding, which he especially liked because the hotel kept a small herd of cows in the field down the village and made its puddings with double cream. He would have his post-lunch walk around the village. Then back to our workshop and a session of stories and gossip till time for the four o'clock bus came round.

One of his favourite stories was of a visit to a business in Fraserburgh which offered ear-piercings. It was lunchtime and a line of five fisher girls were seated waiting to get their ears done – nothing fancy, just a needle and a cork. As he'd completed his own business, Mr Smith was seated there, watching what was going on. Well, the first girl went up, had her ear done, no bother, and resumed her seat. Then the second and then the third, the same: no fuss, no bother. But when the fourth got up for her turn, the other girls just upped and fled, shrieking with laughter. There, on the fourth seat was a puddle – the waiting and the thought of the needle had been too much for the girl.

Robbie Gordon, born 1933, interviewed 2007: Alford

The escapee – keeping up the record

A fter Stirling Hill we moved into a block at Peterhead Prison. They had room to spare since most of the warders were away at the war. There were two residential blocks at the prison: one, 'Block E', for civilians like ourselves and the other for the warders.

Off inside once more. Johnny Ramensky being led away after yet another escape bid.

This was the period when the famous Jonny Ramensky was a prisoner. He was a fantastic, almost mythical, guy, an amazingly skilled safe breaker, but quite harmless as far as any violence was concerned. Because of his skills and his gentle disposition he was given a fair amount of freedom. I remember once when we were locked out of our house, he simply shinned up a drainpipe, popped inside and by the time we reached our third floor, there he was opening the door and welcoming us in. He was jealous of his reputation as someone who couldn't be beaten; if anyone elsewhere made a successful breakout, he would immediately stage his own escape, just to keep up his record for the greatest number of escapes. He would usually be content just to spend a little while outside and then be recaptured – without any struggle.

There was a café – the Mayfair – near us in King Street, run by the Buchan family. One of the Buchan boys had been in the Special Forces with Jonny Ramensky, so every time he staged one of his escapes, Jonny would simply go to the café, take a meal and then

allow the family to phone the bobbies to come and get him. He was very good with the kids. The prisoners got supplies of fruit which we couldn't obtain during the rationing and the prisoners would hand out oranges and apples to the children. Many of them acted as gardeners and scaffies to the district. My little brother had a wee barrow and he would go around with them – all perfectly safe.

Heather Bisset, born 1937, interviewed 2012: Peterhead

Savings Bank – correct to last halfpenny

I'd always loved working with figures. There were no calculators then and it all had to be done in your head; I just found it so satisfying to add up a column and see it come out right.

The big day at the bank was each November 20: that's when all the year's balances had to be checked. My boss was James George Sutherland, a real stickler for accuracy; everything had to work out, right down to the very last halfpenny. He was unmarried, a member of the Brethren. To him the bank was himself. He insisted that it was all done, column by column, and that we stay there till midnight if necessary until they all agreed. One year the solicitor, who had an office up the stairs, lent us one of these new-fangled calculating machines, one where you entered the numbers and then pulled a lever to get the total. I really thought that that year would be a breeze and that we'd be able to get home early. We used the machine – and it worked! But Mr Sutherland insisted we go over the figures again, this time manually, as we always did – just to check that this new-

Everything
was much
more formal
then; smart
clothes had
to be worn
and that
meant black
skirt, white
blouse.
Trousers
weren't
permitted.

fangled machine had got everything right.

We were the team, just him and me, adding, adding, everything in our heads. But when I married, I was forced to quit my job. Company policy: no married women – and this was 1962! Everything was much more formal then; smart clothes had to be worn and that meant black skirt, white blouse. Trousers weren't permitted. Strict confidentiality had to be observed. Mum used to tease me: 'I see Mr. So-and-so wis in the bank the'day – wis he puttin in or takin oot?' It was a standard joke; she knew I had to keep my lips sealed. After all, we were a local branch handling hundreds of individual accounts in a small place where everyone knew everyone and in an age when people just didn't talk about their personal finances any more than they would have done about their sex lives.

Our customers were very regular and paid in most weeks some amount or other, even if it was no more than half-a-crown. There was a real savings culture then. I'd go to Bill's garage each Monday to collect the savings the employees had made; they enlisted in a scheme where each week a fixed amount was taken off their wages. People didn't have cheque accounts then and nothing like standing orders. They dealt in cash and I'd cycle over and collect it and take it back to the bank. The thought that I might be mugged simply never occurred to me – nor did it need to.

I remember going round doors to take in a fixed amount from people. It might only be two shillings, but it was regarded as important to save and never to get into debt as it was to keep your house clean or bring up your children properly. The habit of savings began in the school; you could pay in so much a week to the teacher and the school would take it to the bank. I would say it was a more honest society then; people only got what they could pay for. Now you see people going around with all sorts of new fancy stuff and you think, how on earth could they afford that? Of course, the answer is credit, but back in a place like Macduff in the 1960s, credit meant debt, and that was to be avoided – like divorce and living together unmarried!

My first pay was £3.4.6 for the week. I went out and bought my mother a small glass trophy cup. And that little glass trophy still sits over there in my own cabinet as a reminder of those far off days.

Aileen Allan, born 1943, interviewed 2011: Macduff

Post mistress: more than just a business

I had the conservatory at the back of the house fitted out with shelves and a small counter built. I began with the basics – papers and sweeties – and gradually extended the stock. I never assumed I would make a living out of the business; my aim is to keep it going as a service to the community.

I'm realistic about what I can and can't do. Apart from cigarettes and confectionary, I can't afford to get my stuff from the wholesale – I just can't buy in the bulk. If I were to

take in 24 cans of Coke, I'd find by the time I got to the last one, its sell-by date would have long passed. So I listen to what the customers want and then pop off to Tesco's to buy the stuff there and then sell it on in my shop.

It's impossible to compete with the supermarkets. They hold the range of goods I can't begin to match. But I'm here and on the spot and not everyone has a car at the door ready to whisk them off to town for some item or other – not with fuel the price it is! I accept that for many folk my shop is simply a backup – although I can get a bit miffed when they come in with, 'I was in Elgin today and I forgot to get such-and-such; thank goodness you've got it!' I smile nicely, but inside I'll be muttering to myself, 'I know, I know – but please don't rub it in!'

Not long ago they were talking of closing down the post office. This woman came out and interrogated me. What really upset me was she seemed to be only interested in figures, not people. The fact that if I closed people would have to go seven miles to post their parcels and buy their stamps didn't appear to concern her one bit. When she told me that they were thinking of closing me down, she seemed taken aback that I was near to tears. To her a post office was all about profit and loss.

In the end, they decided to leave us be, but the whole exercise was an upsetting experience. You see, I like to think that I'm offering a service to the community. Because I combine the post office with my shop, I can open all the hours of the day. Oh, sometimes I can find myself thinking when the bell rings and I'm doing something in the house at the back, 'Oh no, not again – I could do with a bit of peace and quiet!' But, really, I enjoy the whole business. We act as a real focal point for Archiestown: there's no school, no church; the hotel's really for the visitors; there's no doctor's surgery, so we are the place that people drop into, bump into other folk and catch up on what's going on. We sell calendars for local organisations, hampers for the playgroup and raffle tickets; we keep sponsorship forms, like the recent Movember one for prostate cancer; parents come by with their bairns for sweeties. Really, all that's going on in Archiestown passes through these doors.

Doreen Aldridge, born 1945, interviewed 2011: Archiestown

Ready to serve – and to have a chat. Doreen Aldridge at her counter, 2011

Always a friendly presence: Allan Riddell, Turriff, mid 1950s.

The postie: daily visitor, trusted friend

I suppose it was a natural development that I became a postie. Growing up and living in Turriff, I've always enjoyed being in the thick of the community, joining its organisations and going in for activities. In those days all the boys I knew here in Turriff did much the same – the BBs, the Air Training Corps and the Royal Observer Corps, going away to camps, learning how to handle situations, to accept discipline, to grow up. We were the baby boom generation, just after the war, and the town was teeming with young lads just like myself.

When I started my postie career in the Seventies, what we were delivering was appreciated: letters from distant relatives, cards to mark a birthday, helping folk keep in touch. Now people simply phone or email and the PO is all about what it calls 'household deliveries' – in other words, flyers, brochures, special offers, all the junk mail under the sun. Now people just groan when they get a handful of junk instead of real mail, but the postie still has to walk up the path to the door to deliver it.

In those days there was a more leisurely approach, more freedom to stop and pass a word about the weather, the price of barley, family birthdays and how the children were getting really big now. Nice human stuff. People were pleased to see you; they knew you were bringing them news of the outside world and little bits of local gossip. You'd get fly cups and even the odd meal. There was one farm, the other side of New Deer, where I'd get the most marvellous fly cup, complete with home bakes. The tea would always be ready for me and a seat at the table. Another customer would give me a dozen eggs every Friday. Then there was the old biddy who would come out and beg me to get her 20 fags from the shop a couple of miles away and when I brought them to her would say, 'Ach, postie, ye've saved ma life!' You'd go to a school and get roped in to watch the kids rehearsing for their show. 'Time for a cup of tea?', they'd say. You'd be delivering a pile of birthday cards and the man would come out and say, 'They're fer ma Jeannie; she's 60 today. Aye postie, ye'll hae tae cam in an gie her a hug!'

On his rounds, Allan and van, 1990s.

You'd deliver the card which marked a birth or a wedding, but then you had to take the ones which offered sympathy on a death. I always found that a difficult task; I never liked just to dump them through the door, so what I did was to hand them over personally and tell them I was sorry to hear of their loss.

I felt I was part of people's lives. I remember one home had a late baby, 'definitely the last', and she was christened 'Joy' because the family were overjoyed at her safe delivery. She was a bonny wee bairn and I was able to see her grow up through the years, delivering the cards to her on each of her birthdays till she was 20 and it was time for me to retire.

You saw the seasons through, shared comment on the changing weather. You'd see the

Among his mates.
Allan (second left)
at Butlin's, Ayr, 1964.

ploughing, the sowing, the growing and the reaping, hear all the ups and downs of country life. I saw the last of the reapers and the break-up of the small farms. By the time I'd finished, the wee parks had been swept up into big prairies where huge combines did all the harvesting. The farms used to have a group of four or five cottar houses around them, each with a farm worker's family living; by the end, farming had become industrialised, the old cottar homes had been bought up and renovated by incomers.

I enjoyed my time as a country postie. To most I became a daily visitor, a trusted friend. It was a job which made me feel good about the warmth and generosity of folk, here in the North-east, and of human nature in general.

Allan Riddell, born 1946, interviewed 2008: Turriff

Scotland's last handloom weaver

Luthermuir began as a weaving village, but by the time I was growing up, the trade had almost disappeared. Almost, but not quite. Luthermuir still had one workshop in operation when I was a girl and this was run by Willie Taylor. He was really someone left over from the past.

He kept his looms in a shed at the back of his house and that's where he did his work, day after day. He made beautiful table cloths and napkins, place mats and hand towels.

To begin with he'd pack his goods into a suitcase, catch the bus into Montrose and go round knocking at doors to try and sell his wares. One of his problems was that the quality of his stuff was such that they would last a lifetime and so do him out of future sales. But he did build up a reputation and when the Edzell base opened, the Americans became good customers; they recognised the sheer quality of the work, all offered at ridiculously low prices.

I was fascinated to see how his feet and hands worked together – such speed and such a

'The last weaver'.
Willie Taylor
demonstrates his work,
1980s.

'He was a lover of traditional music.' The environment in which Willie thrived is represented by this shot of a village hall dance of the 1930s. Janette Anderson's mother is back row, first left.

His favourite blooms. Janette presents Willie with a bouquet of chrysanthemums on his 90th birthday.

rhythm! He was the friendliest soul imaginable and he'd welcome anyone into his workshop for a chat. You'd see him sitting, bent over his machine, throwing his shuttle backwards and forwards and working the wooden pedals up and down with his feet. He'd be there all day long, with just the light of one bulb dangling from a flex and a paraffin heater for warmth. He'd go into the woods for bits and pieces of stick to keep his wooden looms going and he had an old bicycle wheel for his thread-winding machine. As weights to keep the ends of his thread in place, he'd attach things to them like old can openers. It was amazing to see how he produced such lovely cloths from such a basic workshop.

He'd sing to himself as he worked. He was a great lover of traditional Scots songs and airs and could play the fiddle almost as well as he could weave. Saturday night was the occasion for a get-together at his house. Early in the evening you'd hear him playing his fiddle to the dance music on the wireless. When the pub closed, folk would go back to Willie's house and there'd be stories and songs and fiddle music and lots of laughter.

He used to grow the most marvellous chrysanthemums; when the first frosts arrived, he'd cut the flowers and go round the village distributing them. By the time of his 90th birthday he was in a nursing home in Laurencekirk. I'd been down in Blackpool on holiday and came upon this back street shop that was selling lovely bunches of chrysanthemums, so I immediately thought of Willie. On the last day of the holiday I bought a bunch, flew back with them, went into to see Willie and presented him with them. He was delighted.

Janette Anderson, born 1947, interviewed 2011: Luthermuir

The railway signalman

In 1958 my father became signalman at Udny Station on the Buchan line, at that time still busy and thriving. It gave employment to a station master, John Munro; porter, Lewis Gray; junior clerk, Sam Reid, and two signalmen: my father, John Nicol, and James Duncan Scott, known to everyone as Peter. As well as the two signal boxes, there was the main station building housing a ticket office and waiting room and across the line was a smaller waiting room for those travelling to Ellon and beyond.

The station was very important to the farming community and surrounding villages: trains reversed through a large goods shed, unloading their vans onto a platform inside. A railway lorry then collected and delivered supplies every day to neighbouring shops. Alongside this shed was a huge store for Bibby's, the cattlefeed company, for distribution of its products to the farms. Every day, several fish trains steamed up and down to Fraserburgh and Peterhead. There was also the daily Cross & Blackwell train, taking up as many as 30 vans of empty tins to the factory at Peterhead and then returning full of peas and beans. The station also had sidings where empty wagons were shunted and left by one train to be picked up by another. I remember days were spent loading seed tatties brought in by tractor and cart, to be collected and transported to England.

Getting in the day's water: Eleanor Fordyce's mother, Mrs Gray, carrying the two pails of water, just delivered by the Ellon train, as she had to do right into the 1960s.

And of course there were the passenger trains, which for my family was the only means of escape from the village. How I loved these trains! Every Saturday morning my mother and I travelled to Aberdeen for my music lesson with Miss Harper in Burns Road. Every summer we ventured even further afield with a visit to my aunt in Cirencester, beside Gloucester. We could afford this as my father received a number of free rail passes for all three of us. But even more wonderful, as far as I was concerned, we went to school in Ellon by train. There were about a dozen of us from round about who boarded the train at Udny Station. A similar number, collected by minibus from Pitmedden and Udny Green, got on at Logierieve. The station at Ellon was about a 15-minute walk from the school, so we had the added perk of arriving late and, joy of joy, being allowed to leave early.

We lived in Station Cottages, which was

Udny Station, with Mrs Gray's enamel pails waiting to catch the train for Ellon.

a block of four flats with external stone stairs leading to the top two. The main drawback with the house was the water, which with a high lead content was undrinkable. It seems ridiculous now, that even in the 1960s, we had our drinking water delivered by train to the station, from Ellon. My father collected the large enamel containers every morning.

311

The station master's retiral: John Munro collects his watch from Jock Abel, who was signalman at Newmachar; Eleanor's father is far right.

My life as a child revolved very much around trains and I've never lost my love of them. Empty carriages sat in sidings which came right up to our door. I would climb into the old-fashioned single compartments, some of which were quite lavish, with ornate fittings, moquette upholstery and framed pictures of places I'd never seen. I did my homework there, read, or just pretended to be going somewhere. The signal box, too, became a second home, delivering my father's fly cup being the excuse to be among the bells and levers. It could also be a peaceful place to indulge my passion for books, between trains, my father himself reading when he could. I had to skedaddle quick if an inspector was on an incoming train and likely to visit the signal box.

So it was devastating when the Beeching Axe fell and brought to an end a century of the Buchan Line. The last diesel passenger train came to a halt at Udny Station on the 2nd October, 1965. The signal box closed the following June. It was acquired by a farmer near Newmachar and used as a porch.

It was the end of a way of life. Now the line is a walkway – but oh, the sadness at no longer hearing the hiss and shriek of steam, or the toot of a diesel coming under the bridge!

Eleanor Fordyce, born 1948, interviewed 2012: Udny Station

The landlord: local worthies at the bar

I n 1982, my parents took over the Fife Arms Hotel. On a Thursday morning, the old age pensioners would all go to the post office for their pensions and then repair to our hotel to spend some of it on refreshment. Dad would offer them a nip at half price – a sort of Pensioners' Happy Hour! One of them, Tommy Broon, was a great taker of snuff and he'd stand at the bar sniffing up quantities of it. One day my father took a working lunch while he served his customers; he put down his plate of haddock and chips, turned

to see to an order, only to be disturbed by this great spluttering noise. Tommy had sneezed the contents of his snuff tin all over Dad's lunch!

Another regular was Teet a'Bootie, who would come all the way down from Glenlivet for a convivial night at the bar. He wore an onion net drawn tight over his head and when he was advanced in his inebriation he would let fly a volley of German swear words, picked up during the war. One evening he got so drunk that Dad had to tell him, 'No more drink; time to go home!' But none of the taxi drivers in the village would touch him, so Dad had to get our car, throw him in the back and drive him all the way up to Glenlivet. He decided to call in at the Croft Inn on the way back to drop something off, so the return journey was delayed, but not by more than 10 minutes or so. He got back – and the first thing he saw was Teet a'Bootie sitting at the bar with another drink in his hand. He'd persuaded someone to take him back to Dufftown, entered the pub and settled himself down with a drink, all in the half hour or so it had taken Dad to return.

Ian Murray, born 1970, interviewed 2011: Dufftown

Keeping the bar in order.
Ian Murray's father at the Fife Arms Hotel, on the day on which they opened, 1962.

ALL MANNER
OF FOLK:
Part 4

A well deserved recognition. Neil Simpson holds his son Kyle
and receives the plaudits from Aberdeen and Manchester United
teams before his testimonial match, 2012.

Two of the four generations who have owned and run the Watson Ironmongery in Inverurie. Here is great-grandfather John McIntyre Watson, right, and grandfather James John, 1890s.

The local businessman

I'm the fourth generation of Inverurie ironmongers, whose earliest records go back to 1839. In those days an ironmonger's in an agricultural centre like Inverurie was a sort of Johnny-cum-aathing, a veritable emporium. That's what I was brought up on.

I had an enclosed Inverurie upbringing. We were a tight little family, ruled by the business. My father was a workaholic. The only time we ever really saw him was when he came home for the evening meal on a Sunday. It was the family custom to go to church of a morning and afterwards he'd slip back to the shop for more work. In the evening, he would come back and we'd all sit down for a big dinner. Then we'd all retire to the lounge where a fire was lit to warm up a room that was kept closed for the rest of the week. This is where the piano was. My sister or my mother would play hymns. I had my boy soprano voice and Mother a fine alto. Father would boom away with his bass; together we made great harmonies. He would have a big tumbler of whisky, resting on the piano top, and between hymns he'd take a sip.

He was severe man, very Victorian: not a father to handle his children. He never hit us; he had the Look which demanded obedience. Yet he was a physically insignificant wee man. He loved to sing and lead us in our four-point harmonies. A lot of it was sentimental Victorian claptrap, but the memory can still bring a tear to the eye.

He practised thrift to the point of meanness. He'd never buy notepaper: he'd take old envelopes, cut them open and fold them back. He would steam off unfranked stamps so as to get the good of them. Staff were strictly enjoined never to cut string off a parcel: they had to carefully untie it and store it in the string drawer. When he got his first pair of National Health specs, he wouldn't have them on unless he needed them for a specific purpose; to have them on all the time was to run the risk of wearing them out prematurely. I used to joke that when I got my first pair of National Health specs, he'd make me take them off if I wasn't looking at anything specific.

I was always going to join the family business. The only son of three generations of ironmongers – no choice but to embrace the family destiny. This meant going away to Arbroath – you didn't serve your apprenticeship with your own family.

I hated every minute of my apprenticeship, but I buckled down to it. My real aspiration had always been to become a church minster, but it was not to be. Maybe I'm too much of a sinner! There has always been a consciousness of God in my life. I'm too much out in the hills, revelling in the beauties of nature not to know that there must be a supreme creator. I remember climbing up Scafell Pike, standing on its peak, and looking round beneath the huge skies, drinking in the views and just knowing that there has to be a God behind all of this world.

Celebrating the Diamond Jubilee, 1897.

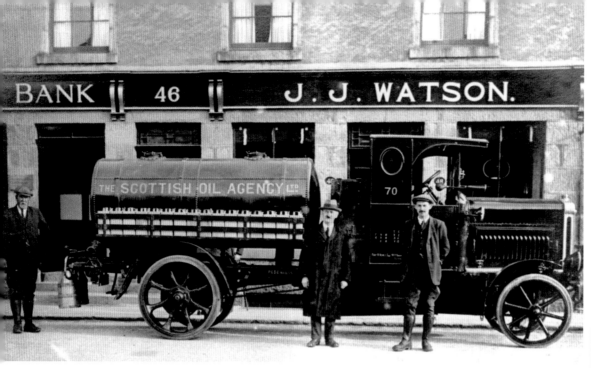

Delivering the goods, 1915 style. The driver is Mr Cowe, and the two colleagues are Mr Nicol and Mr Bruce.

After Arbroath and a year in Glasgow, I got the chance of a job at James Gray's of Edinburgh, a top ironmonger's, and was there a year when came the phone call: 'Your father's in hospital; you must come home'. The next day, I found myself standing at his bedside, gazing down at this strangely shrunken figure. So that was that: I was home for good, to take over the family business.

I'd never thought I'd be settling down to life in the little town I'd been brought up in, not at the age of 23 anyway. The prospect daunted me, but one morning I was walking up the Market Place, when I stopped: 'Is that a skylark singing, I can hear?' I listened some more. The thought that I could hear an actual lark in full voice in the middle of my own town gave me a thrill, a sudden sense of joy. From that moment I was in love with the place and have never wanted to leave.

'Everything had to fetched.' Father James Adam Watson serving a customer, 1940s.

There I was plunged into it, responsible for keeping the old family business afloat. The shop was well established, but desperately old fashioned. Nothing was on display; everything was either behind the counter or in store. You'd enter the shop and be confronted with a big zinc counter with tiles on its top and the shopkeeper standing firmly behind it.

I had to make it a more inviting place. The first thing I did was to get rid of that counter and the sense of a barrier between customer and shop. I was blessed with my staff. They've been people I've known and trusted and grown old beside. Some of them had come to the store as school leavers and then stayed on and on.

The business changed over the years. With people able to travel out to stores in their cars, everyone began to sell anything and everything. Along came Tesco, B&Q, and all the rest of the big general purpose stores, and the habit of driving out to them as a pleasure trip, to browse among the goods and pick up a bargain or two. Once my staff could name 90% of the people who came

Opening up the shop: 1977.

Playing a part in Inverurie life. James John Watson (front row with dog) at the opening of the town's bowling green, May 1896. His father was a founder member and he himself twice served as president.

into the shop, could chat with them about their families or what was happening in the town. People would shop locally and on foot. Now there's little of that old loyalty left; people prefer the anonymity of the big out-of-town store and the one-stop shop where they can go once a week, load it all into the car and then drive home.

In the end, it was the regulations and the paper work that got to me. The Health and Safety people took exception to many of the features of our old shop. They didn't like the low ceilings; they tut-tutted over the uneven floor; they demanded we cement over all the old flags in the cellars. They didn't like the tools we sold and the fact they were uncovered.

The last few years after Bert, my long-time partner and friend, had retired were a hard grind. I'd see him strolling at ease around the place. Then I had a stroke of luck. I came across this guy who was looking for premises in the town centre; 'Did I know, by any chance, of any property that might be coming up? 'Yes', I said, 'mine!' And that was that.

'Mike, it's done! I'm standing up on Bennachie instead of Bennachie standing on me. I'm free!'

I hated my shop life, but I must admit it gave me a good living. It gave me independence, the chance to run the show and be my own boss. And then suddenly it was all over. Three signatures in a lawyer's office, that's all it took: 161 years blown away! I remember going up Bennachie and standing there, taking out my phone and calling Mike Hay, my oldest pal: 'Mike, it's done! I'm standing up on Bennachie instead of Bennachie standing on me. I'm free!' It was a huge sense of release; I thought there might be a tear or two, but no. None of my kids had been interested in carrying it on and I knew how they felt. I hadn't wanted the business in the first place either. I sometimes dream I'm back in the shop, but then I wake up – and feel relief.

Stuart Watson, born 1943, interviewed 2011: Inverurie

Continuing the family role: Stuart Watson, President of Garioch Rugby Club, 1995.

The government administrator

I owe a lot to my early schooling at the local primary school in Tyrie. It not only gave me a thorough grounding in the basic academic subjects, but also inculcated the values which have stood me in such good stead throughout my life and career: respect for others, doing things properly, by working till you get them right – and don't let yourself down by being slapdash. That's what the school drummed into me and that's certainly what I got from my home life, too.

My father was a forward thinking man, who had wanted to be a doctor. But his father died when he was only 17 and he had had to take over the family farm. He liked nothing better than to engage in discussion about equality and human rights (although, of course, that sort of terminology was never used in those days) and he encouraged me to think about these issues from a very early age. No doubt about it, life was tough back then, but 'doing the right thing' was always at the forefront of my upbringing.

My mother had real drive and determination. Failure just wasn't an option in her book. But she went to her grave, disappointed I hadn't become a teacher. She'd inherited the typical North-east outlook that considered school teaching as the real mark of success for the 'clever' rural girl. In later years, if ever I mentioned anything whatever about the job I was doing, she would remain unimpressed, harbouring her unfilled ambition that I should have been a teacher.

But I have an aunt who is now 92 and she told me, when I was appointed CVO (for my role in the Queen's Golden Jubilee) and then CBE (for services to the Home Office): 'Your mother would have been so proud'. When I said, 'Do you really think so?', she replied, 'Oh, Mary-Helen, I remember her telling me that she always knew you'd do well'. But, of course, my mother would never have told me that – another North-east characteristic: be sparing with the praise, lest you get too above yourself.

I always knew an academic career was never going to be for me. Although I could pass exams, I never really envisaged myself as a teacher; indeed I would have been dreadful in that role. As I grew up, I was always enthralled by the apparent successes of folk who had ventured away from the area. I was always a bit restless, but I had no clear idea of what I really wanted to do.

To my parents' huge disappointment, I announced that I wanted to go to London to seek something different. I had seen this advert in the paper for the Civil Service: Clerical Officers. I kept the advert in my pocket and showed it to my mother. She disapproved completely; my father's attitude was, 'Well, if that's what you want, but you won't like it'.

So I found my way to the address in Saville Row mentioned in the advertisement. I got there on the very last day. I remember it all clearly. I got there at five minutes to four and found my way to the woman who was taking in the forms. I handed mine over and remarked, 'I hope I've filled it in right'. She looked at it and then looked up and said something that changed my whole life: 'Oh, but you're applying for the Clerical Officer grade. With these qualifications you should be going for the Executive Officer level'. 'What's that?' I'd never heard of such a person. 'Well, you get more money – and you get to be a boss.' But it was now just on four and the office was due to close. She was

Home values.
Mary-Helen Bayne playing at the family farm, Tyrie, early 1950s.

So there I was, with my strong Doric accent, facing these people and with absolutely no idea that I should be daunted by the experience.

Twice invested: receiving the CVO for her work as Head of the Golden Jubilee Office, 2002.

helpful: 'Look, I'll go and get an official application form right now and you can fill it in while I'm putting on my coat.'

She must have been my guardian angel. What I didn't know was that in those days only 12 new recruits were appointed to the Executive Officer class each year. In some ways my naivety helped me. I had to face an interview in front of a panel of five public school educated Oxbridge graduates, all of whom had attained senior positions in the Civil Service – I who had never been interviewed in my life. So there I was, with my strong Doric accent, facing these people and with absolutely no idea that I should be daunted by the experience.

Anyway, I got the appointment. That was the beginning of what turned out to be the most fantastic career I could ever have wished for. I was very fortunate and extremely privileged to have held a series of posts, ones which gave me the opportunity to meet and to work with so many interesting and high profile people, including the Queen, HRH The Prince of Wales and other members of the Royal Family, heads of state from overseas countries, and cabinet ministers of the governments of the day. When I retired, I was presented with a book of messages. One entry that always makes me smile is from Tony Blair, telling me how proud he was when I told him that I thought his accent was 'almost Scottish'.

I can't deny that there haven't been times when I've caught myself thinking: 'Here I am at the top table (so to speak), contributing to policies that would affect the whole of the UK and me just a quine frae Tyrie – and damn proud of it too!' You see, throughout my whole career, the drive I inherited from my mother, and the values of respect and fairness, which were drummed into me at home and at Tyrie School, have guided me along the way. My attitude has always been that there was nothing that couldn't be resolved if you applied hard work, honesty and good old fashioned common sense. I firmly believe that we are all products of our experience and my North-east background has been the greatest force behind me throughout.

...and the CBE for services to the Home Office, 2007.

Any regrets? Just the one big one: that neither of my parents lived to see me receive my honours from the Queen. To have them present at my investitures at Buckingham Palace would have been wonderful. But I did wear my mother's engagement ring on both occasions, so maybe they were there in spirit.

That was all then, and now I have come back to the North-east on my retirement. I'm returning, if you like, to my roots with my husband. We're both very happy to be back and thoroughly enjoying spending time with friends and the family: my brother, my niece and nephew and our twin great-nephews (our 'grandsons'). The boys have given us a totally new lease of life and they have a wonderfully uncanny way of putting everything into perspective.

As for this area of the North-east, it still has its own unique charm. But the demise of the fishing industry, the mechanisation of farming, and the soul-destroying damage to the landscape at the hands of local politicians have brought huge changes to the rural communities of my youth. There's still a lot of young talent here, but I fear it's being haemorrhaged at a greater rate than ever before – hardly surprising given the wealth of opportunities, not just in the oil industry, but also further afield. In the past, many of these young people would have been happy and proud to return after training or further education to reinvest in the place where they started, but I suspect that cycle is now a broken one.

Mary-Helen Bayne, born 1948, interviewed 2007: Tyrie

The farmer's daughter (2)

Being a farmer's daughter back then was an enjoyable upbringing. When you were at the school you knew that as soon as you'd got home it was change of clothes, a quick piece, then out to the work and that was just fine. You'd be thinking about getting home and out into the open air. That's where you wanted to be.

We all had our tasks to do. There were open fires to be fed, so the weekend task was to saw up sticks, then barrow them into the stick shed. Then there were the chickens to feed and the eggs to be gathered in and washed. The cockerel would chase you and the hens would come and peck at your bare legs, but you just had to do it.

The cattle had to be fed and that meant neeps, straw, draff from the distillery, bruised corn. It was great to get through the set task and know you were making a contribution. You had to hash the neeps and barrow them; you had to shovel the draff as it came on the lorry from the distillery. Keeping the cattle fed was a non-stop business. Then you had to muck out the byres. At harvest time and at haymaking, we'd all be out working as a team. We'd set ourselves a target and worked till we'd met it. I remember one night when we knew the rain was coming on, we baled and baled till we'd got everything safely in, and that took till two o'clock in the morning.

We all became quite attached to the animals on the farm. The collie dogs were great favourites and then there were the prematurely born lambs, which we'd take into the house and bed down in front of the Raeburn on some straw in a cardboard box. They were too weak even to suck from a teat, so you had to mix up some cow's milk and a drop of whisky and spoon it gently into their mouths till they could build up enough strength to feed themselves from a bottle.

It could be hard snow in the winter, but the beasts still had to be fed. The sheep would be outside and you had to take the hay to their troughs to make sure the ewes would have their strength kept up for the lambing. The only thing that gave me difficulty was my

Happy to be a farmer's daughter.
Moira Ross, aged 11.

A happy family.
From left, John, Moira, June, Norma and mother.

'We all had to play our part': bringing in the bales, early 1960s. From left: June, mother, John, Moira, Norma, Sandy.

hands. I just couldn't work in gloves, so they'd get all chapped, sometimes till the blood came. Mum would stick plasters on and rub in Germolene, but it didn't solve the problem. I just had to get on with it.

The diet was good wholesome food, everything homemade and plenty of it. It never varied. Sundays would start off with porridge and toast. Lunchtime it would be beef and broth, boiling beef with suey through it. Do you know what suey is? Well, you'd take some oatmeal, a little lard with bree from the soup and and tie it all together in a muslin cloth, which is tied up and cooked all through the soup, and then served up with beef and tatties. Delicious! Then for pudding, there'd be fruit and custard. Teatime meant cold beef and egg, along with oatcakes and cheese. But there'd also be a fly in the afternoon, complete with home bakes.

Monday was similar, with second-day soup and so on. Teatime was porridge and a boiled egg, or maybe poached egg and macaroni. Tuesday was stovies, using up the rest of the boiled beef. It was also home-baking day. As a kid, I'd love to eat the bits of oatcake that were left over after it was trimmed to fit the girdle. I remember once I was so eager to get at it, that I stuck my fingers in while Mum was still cutting with the knife and I got a cut finger for my pains. Tuesday was also when the grocer's and the butcher's vans would call, so at night you'd get a fried egg and sausages, or bacon for Dad.

Wednesday was bradie and tatties. Thursday back to porridge and boiled egg. Friday was the day Dad would be away at the mart, so we had corned beef and white sauce; then at night, if he'd brought back some fish, Mum would make fish and chips; if not, it would be fried egg and chips. Saturday was mince and tatties with a dumpling. Tea time would be something like sausage and egg, or bacon and egg for Mum and Dad.

You were never hungry. When you came in from the school you'd get a slice of bread and jam to keep you going till supper time. Mum would make our own jam and marmalade too: berries and rhubarb. The only time we got any food that wasn't homemade was a bag of chips at the Aboyne Games, on the Tuesday night when we all

went there for the amusements.

Our parents made sure there was still time for some family fun. We'd play games like snakes and ladders, and draughts in front of the Raeburn. Dad put up a swing for us on the big tree at the back door and we'd spend hours on that. Then we'd put some music on the gramophone and dance in the kitchen. Mum would join in, but sometimes she was just sitting there, getting on with the mending and the darning. The atmosphere in the house was always warm and caring.

When the Sixties came we'd all watch *Top of the Pops* – Dad and all. He was very keen on Abba – *Dancing Queen* and all that. I was into Elvis, and my sister, Cliff Richard. During the winter months we'd all sit and watch *Top of the Pops* and then it was out to water the cattle. Sunday was the quiet day. Dad would feed the cattle and then drive into Alford to get the Sunday papers. A read of them, then dinner, then his 40 winks. We'd settle down to watch a film on TV; we all loved the cowboy films. But at four o'clock it was time to see to the beasts again; I've seen Dad hanging on for the end of the film and then have to rush out to them.

When I was 16, I started going to the local dances. My sister and I'd have to wash the cement floors of the milk house, the lobby, the scullery and toilet, and then it was time for the rollers and the best dress, bought at the draper's in Alford, getting ready for the big night out. Those dances were just brilliant; the dances nowadays don't get a look in.

There was the great night at the Muggarthaugh Hotel when the competition for the Harvest King and Queen was held. Six couples were picked out and we all had to hold the floor and carry on dancing. Gradually, all the others were eliminated and my dance partner and I were the only pair left – I was the Harvest Queen. Ann Brand presented

The young nurse.
Moira at the Foresterhill
Nurses Home, 1982.

the cup. Then two weeks later, at Millbank Hall, I was chosen as the Beauty Queen. But that was the end of my successes in that particular direction.

But in 1970 Mum died. It was ovarian cancer. To begin with, it was thought she simply had flu, but when it was never getting better the doctor arranged tests in Aberdeen. The cancer was too advanced to do much about it. That's when we discovered that ovarian cancer was running through the family like a curse, being passed down from generation to generation. Her two sisters also died of it. Dr Marion Hall, the famous gynaecologist in Aberdeen, undertook an investigation and built up a family tree. She showed us that the cancer was setting in 10 years earlier with each generation; that's the way the genetic predisposition was working. My mother and her two sisters had all died of it before they reached 50. She took us in and explained the situation. The advice was to get our ovaries removed, and that's what I and my cousins all did – except for one who refused. She died of it at the age of 51. So, although this meant I could never have children, it was a wise move.

Father just kept going. It was hard, but that's the kind of man he was; he refused to be defeated. He set to with his own cooking, his own washing. But when he got to 65, he decided it was time to sell up. I was there on the day of the roup. A sad, sad day! It was heartbreaking to stand by and see all the machinery being auctioned off, to watch the cattle going off to new owners, and to think that my childhood home was passing into the hands of strangers. He got a house in Elrick and lived there in his retirement quite happily. He loved pottering around in his garden.

He was a well built man, always friendly, always cheerful. He always took pride in his appearance. You look at a wedding photograph and you'll see him well turned out in formal suit, with a bowler on his head. When we were young our task was to see his boots were kept absolutely shining. You'd work away at them and then show them to Mum: 'Nae shinin enough!', she'd say. 'Gae an gie them anither buff.'

When I was 21, I went into nursing. It was hard work, but I enjoyed it. There was such a great spirit among us all; we had a lot of laughs. With the geriatrics, there were bedpans to be washed out and rubber sheets to lay out on the beds; there were the ablution runs after the meals and the toilet runs and the washing of the faces and the hands to be seen to. A constant round.

A quarter of a century later and still nursing. Moira with colleague Rizi, 2007.

I think the nurses of today have a much easier time of it For us it was hard physical labour: lifting, stooping, bending over patients, fetching back and forth. Nonstop – a bit like the farm really. As a farmer's daughter, I'd been brought up on this kind of hard work and team spirit and that's why I think I adapted to nursing so well. I reckon it was the country girls who made the better nursing recruits because of their farming background, where you just had to muck in, and where you saw life in the raw and learned to get through it all without being shocked or complaining.

I ended up in the Eye Unit and that's where I met my husband. He'd suffered an agricultural accident. So there I was, the farmer's daughter who married a farmer. I still take an interest in the latest developments. It's so high-tech now. Farms run to hundreds of acres, yet the labour force is down to one or two at a time. The work's as hard as ever. There's so many acres to see to, and so few to do it, that making tight targets and ensuring that the work gets done within a strict timeframe is the only way a farm can operate at a profit.

I've always kept up my interest in what was going on the farm and I do even yet. I still read the *Farmer's Weekly* and the *Scottish Farmer*. Farming's something that gets into your blood and it's certainly been in mine. I'm still a farmer's daughter at heart.

Moira Ross, born 1948, interviewed 2011: Craigevar

> Father just kept going. It was hard, but that's the kind of man he was; he refused to be defeated.

The international footballer

I'm very much a North-east lad. My granda was a farm worker and we stayed with him in a wee place, out near Alford. To get to Cluny Primary School I had to cycle three miles there, three miles back; from the age of six, I'd be doing the journey all by myself, no bother. People tell me that's where I must have got my energy from.

I'd spend hours by myself kicking a ball against the wall of the house. I'd throw it up onto the roof and it would catch the guttering as it came down and send it in different directions and I would bring it under control.

Then, in 1970, the World Cup in Mexico was shown on TV; there were some great names like Pele and Petrov and Charlton and they inspired me. The Commonwealth Games were held at Edinburgh and I was also able to watch them on the TV; seeing all the athletes doing their stuff filled me with enthusiasm. I'd go running the one-and-a-half miles to the end of the road and back again as fast as I could, pretending I was a great athlete.

Sadly, my granda died of cancer. In 1971 we moved to Newmachar. It was only when I arrived at Newmachar Primary School at the age of nine that I began to realise I might actually be quite good at football. Until then, I'd had nobody to measure myself against. I'd simply been one of those wee boys, taking part in any old kick-about I could find. I'd take a ball with me wherever I went. I used to get hold of a sock and stuff it with anything I could find, so I could kick it about in the house. I'd get a balloon and practice keepy-ups, silly wee games all by myself.

I can't say I was ever a keen scholar; football was always at the centre of my attention. I'd sit at the desk dreaming about playing for Aberdeen, alongside my hero, Joe Harper. And when I did come to make my debut for the club, I found myself doing exactly that.

A North-east loon on his grandfather's farm, near Cluny.

In fact, I passed the ball to Joe and he scored! Ambition achieved – maybe I should have retired on the spot.

Opportunities for proper games were limited for a country boy like me, but at Newmachar we managed to have kick-abouts morning, noon and night: we played before school went in; we played at lunch times, we played at break times and we played after school and after tea as well. We played on the park in the village, with the swings as one goal and the wall the other; there was a roundabout in the middle, which we learned to negotiate. It was all-comers, back and forwards, matches that ended with scores like 21-20.

I think one of the reasons Scottish football doesn't seem to have the same talents nowadays is that kids no longer play out in all conditions and in mixed age groups like we did. When you're simply part of a great crowd of kids and with no ref or organised tactics, you just had to learn how to look after yourself. We were always doing things with the ball to improve our basic skills: if there weren't enough for full size game, we'd play headers, or one-touch, or three goals-and-in.

At Bankhead Academy, I managed to work my way into the team. From that point on everything seemed to fall into place. There were some good players in that school side and some of them were going into town to play for Middlefield Boys' Club; they suggested I join them. Middlefield was a well structured set-up with a successful team. Then I got picked for the Aberdeen Select, with Lenny Taylor and Bobby Clark as the coaches.

So I had my foot in the door at Pittodrie. But scouts from other sides were coming along and I was invited down to a number of top English clubs. Then Lenny Taylor told me, 'Just to let you know, Aberdeen want to sign you'. I was still at school. The next day the Middlesbrough scout came on the scene with, 'Look, we know that Aberdeen are showing an interest, but we really want you. We'll fly you down tomorrow and you can spend three days with us'. I was torn, but the president at Middlefield advised me to give it a try. I flew down, was picked up at the airport, and found myself playing for their reserves that same night. It was against Barnsley and we won four-nil.

Middlesbrough were actually a bit naughty. When I got off the plane back at Dyce, the Middlesbrough scout and the Middlefield president met me. They kept me at the airport for two hours, trying to persuade me to put pen to paper. I was still only 15 and, really, a signature at that age required a parental consent, but there they were at the airport

The rising star.
As Middlefield Boys
Club captain,
Neil Simpson receives
the British Under-16
Championship
Trophy, 1976.

A team of winners.
Sir Alec Ferguson
rejoices with his
Aberdeen team after
once more becoming
League Champions in
1985. Neil – with
bottle – is in the back
row, left.

with the form telling me to sign up. They got an ex-Aberdeen player, Jimmy Wilson, to come along and add to the pressure by telling me that local lads never did well at Aberdeen, because the supporters would always be on my back. I remember sitting there, getting pressurised by the whole situation; there were these three men going on at me and I wasn't used to arguing with adults.

I held out and then the Middlesbrough scout drove me home. When I got to the door, he told my granny he had all the necessary forms; all we had to do was sign them. My granny told him, 'Sorry, Neil's going to sign for Aberdeen'. The guy was taken aback and simply drove off. This was the team I'd always supported, that I'd dreamt of playing for, and there was no way I was going to turn up the chance to sign for them.

Actually, the Pittodrie crowd never did give me a hard time. I think if they see you're giving 100% then they will support you, and I was lucky because of my style of play and where I played, right in the heart of the action in mid-field.

When I turned 16, I went full time with Aberdeen. My first wage was £25 a week and you got £10 for your keep. When I started, I was one of the ground staff boys. We had to do what we were told, and that included cleaning the boots of the First team players and laying out their kit. I was given Joe Harper's to look after – my boyhood hero! I was going in and out by bus each day. In fact, when, aged 16, I made my debut against Hamilton, for a Wednesday evening match, I had to go down to the bus station after the game to catch the Newmachar bus. It was odd because there were quite a few people there who'd been at the match and I got some comments from them.

I accepted right from the start I would be leading a different way of life to my contemporaries, that I would have to follow the disciplines of going to bed early and

At the height of his powers.

Now an indispensable member of a great Aberdeen team, Neil Simpson pictured at Pittodrie in the early 1980s.

being moderate with my drinking. In any case, Fergie [Sir Alec Ferguson] was very hot on our drinking habits and instilled a fear of overdoing it into all of us. I never went out on a Friday night, not even to the pictures. I felt it was my resting time, before the Saturday game, and that nothing should get in the way of that. If I was invited to a party, I would just tell them, 'Sorry, can't go,'.

Where my football ability comes from, I'm not sure. There seems to be nothing in my family background that would explain it. You could say I was self-made. Life was quite hard and certainly pretty simple. When my granda died, we had to move to a cottage in the middle of nowhere. It was freezing cold and the toilet was outside. I was out in the country among the dubs and the sharn. I remember once when the ball flew over this drystane dyke and I went to retrieve, I climbed up on the dyke and then jumped down on the other side. I landed, squelch, right into this pool of mud and cow shit; I was just clarted with it all. Disgusting!

I did all the normal things country kids did. In the summer I'd go out barley roguing in the fields for a bit of extra cash; I'd be one of a gang of about 10 and you'd put on these plastic bags round your trousers, because the fields would be soaking wet with the rain or the overnight dew. Then, in the autumn, it was the tattie picking and I'd be out at that.

I know that people claim that lads from the North-east lack something compared to those from the Central Belt, that we might be a bit softer, that we aren't street fighters. I don't buy that. I actually think my rural upbringing has helped me stand on my own two feet, that the values which come from my farming background have given me a sense of hard work and a desire to do a proper job. I think the outdoor life I led, with all the biking backwards and forwards, and the playing out in the fields, had helped me to develop what I've always thought was my greatest asset as footballer and that was my nonstop energy.

I've been fortunate in my career. I've won eight winners' medals with Aberdeen; I've got five Scottish caps. The early Eighties were a great time to be building up a career at Pittodrie. With the players we had and under Fergie, we never expected to lose to anyone, not even to Real Madrid or to Bayern Munich. If we even drew a game then that was to be regarded as a disaster. It was a great team, a great group of players, with a great spirit, under a fantastic manager. We were what Fergie called 'Winners'.

I suppose I missed out on the really big money that came into the game later. We never got the big salaries; it was the bonuses which lifted you above the outside world. Staying at Aberdeen through the Eighties was never going to make any of us millionaires. But then, the glamorous life has never been my scene. My first car was a Marina and I haven't progressed much since. I've had a great life in football, a good childhood here in the North-east, and a wonderful career playing for the team I've always supported. As a boy I'd go to sleep dreaming of playing for the Dons; I'd tremble at the thought of pulling on that red shirt and feeling the white collar round my neck – and then it all came true.

Neil Simpson, born 1961, interviewed 2009: Newmachar

The concert pianist

My career has been in music, as a piano player, tutor and composer. You could attribute some of my music talents to a genetic basis. Although my contact with my mother's father was sketchy – he died when I was only seven – he was Reg Barret-Ayres, Head of Music at Aberdeen University for many years. My paternal grandparents lived latterly nearby. They had a piano and I was fascinated by it from the start. I remember listening to my grandfather touching the keys. It was a battered old upright but, to me, it was a wonderful new toy. I loved the shininess of the keyboard and the shapes of the keys all ranged along it. I was soon running my hands over them, exploring the wondrous sounds I could make.

Round about my fifth birthday I discovered I had perfect pitch. My parents were always very supportive of my music. They not only helped with all the things that go with learning and performing, like taking me to lessons, they also supervised my practices. They were always on hand to offer advice and encouragement. They did push me a little but, later on, I was ready to take the initiative myself and do things off my own bat. Maybe I did have talents, but there were also hours and hours of continuous practice and hard work.

My father has always been into music. He would play me excerpts from standard pieces, complete with comments and questions. He would make up compilations of music and put them on tape. Soon I was listening to music wherever I could find it – on the radio, the television, my father's records. When I had gone through his entire collection, he borrowed more from the university library. I found a whole new world waiting for me to discover; we'd go upstairs of an evening and listen to all the great masters: Beethoven, Sibelius, Bach, Mozart, Vaughan Williams and so on. I enjoyed picking out where the most important features of a piece would be, the notes and keys especially. I became absorbed in the whole system of music; I loved its orderliness and its logic.

I reached the stage where I just wanted to keep on playing and playing, to perfect what I knew I was already good at. By the time I was 10, I'd be involved in two hours of practice a day. I began to take part in local concerts. So early on, I was aware of myself as a performer. I did interviews on local radio. All this helped me to realise I possessed unusual talents. I attended the Aberlour House summer school, for 'gifted children'; there was a television feature.

I lapped it all up. But my parents were careful not to make too much of it: they wanted to help me make the most of myself, but they also held on to the philosophy that I should have as normal a childhood as possible. I was born with cataracts in both eyes. I use special equipment, such as large print texts and a magnifying TV screen. At school I had a telescope so I could read the blackboard.

Despite all this, they insisted I went to the local schools along with all the rest of the kids in the village. They resisted the notion I should go away as a boarder in some specialist music school or be registered as 'Partially sighted'. On this point, I now realise that it's possible to be over-anxious about the opposite issue of playing up one's disability

Right from very young. The infant Joseph Long at the keyboard in his Muchalls home.

The mature artist.
Joseph has blossomed into a nationally renowned student, tutor and concert pianist – but still lives in Muchalls.

too much and giving oneself a seemingly negative label. I've since decided to register myself as partially sighted – and found that nobody has regarded me negatively as a result and that, in fact, only benefits have come from it.

It would be wrong to picture me as some half-blind boy who prefers to exist in his own cut-off world of music. What I've done is what I've wanted to do; apart from that, I've led a fairly normal sort of existence.

From an early age, I realised that my musical development would have to involve a lot of extracurricular activity and private tuition. I also realised that I couldn't expect my schoolmates to follow me into my interests. As early as five, I came to grasp that you couldn't go around telling people that such and such a piece is pitched in middle C and get any sort of comprehension. I'd tell a school mate and get the response, 'Do you mean that you're in the middle of the sea?'

Of course, I did experience the Eighties pop scene and I'd analyse it like any other piece of music. I could tell people that a particular piece by the Stranglers was in B minor, that it was in 3/4 time and had a 4/4 bar in the instrumental bridging section. But I quickly learned that pop music doesn't lend itself to that kind of technical discussion, so I soon stopped making analytical comments of that kind. I came to understand that the way I respond to music isn't for most people.

I've come to accept that there are different levels at which people can listen to a piece. When somebody has a go at breaking down a bit of pop in terms of key and note progression, I'll think, 'Well, fine, but why are you bothering to do that? Surely it's not meant to be taken that way'. Pop music isn't high art, but it has its place in the scheme of things. I try to no longer go around devouring every piece I come across in technical terms; I've got over my 'middle of the sea' phase, I hope.

I'm not too pessimistic about the future of serious music. Now downloading, I-pods and the rest mean that there are many other ways of accessing music than going to a concert hall. The main thing is that music is alive and in the world. You've got to start where people are; there's no point in aggressively campaigning for people to change their tastes. We should be trying to turn listening into a more active experience, by encouraging young people to learn an instrument and getting them to discuss ways of interpreting what they hear in terms of their own efforts to play.

The North-east has proved to be a good environment for me. I can give myself a plug here – I tutor at it – but the North of Scotland Music School does a great job. Sometimes people tell me 'I ought to be down in London because that's the hub of things'. My response is, 'What is the hub exactly?' There's little I want to do musically that I can't here in my own home area.

Joseph Long, born 1975, interviewed 2008: Muchalls

Joseph Long has built up a national reputation as a tutor, composer, recitalist and recording artist, notably of works by Chopin, Balakirev, Scriabin, Sibelius and Ravel.

HOME AND AWAY, HERE AND NOW

Evening falls at Portside of Plaidy, the farm where Janet Byth spent much of her girlhood

Here and there: changes in the community

We never speak

In the old days, if you walked down the street you'd always know who everyone was; if you saw someone who was new to you, then you could be sure it was someone up on holiday visiting. Now I can sit at my window here on the High Street and see strange figures passing by on the pavement outside. Every day I'll catch sight of this very tall man coming along wearing a big broad-rimmed hat. John Wayne, I call him, but I couldn't tell you who he is.

We see each other, but we never speak. Just once, when he was about to step off the pavement and I was in my car and had to brake suddenly, we looked each other in the face and exchanged a smile. That silent smile has been the only act of communication between us. That's village life in 2008, I suppose. Sometimes I just wish we could all go back to the old days.

Community life in action.

The Senior Citizens of Cumminestown enjoying an entertainment by Monquhitter WRI, 1960s.

Ally Irvine, born 1926, interviewed 2008: Cuminestown

Before pedestrianisation: Marischal Street, Peterhead, as it was in James Coull's boyhood.

Sounding like a grumpy old man?

We now live in an age of abundance, but the irony of it is that people don't necessarily realise they are well off. It's not like that for today's young people. Yet in some ways I feel sorry for them: they have fewer signposts by which to guide their lives. They seem to drift along in a sea of abundance. And the more they have the more they seem to want – and expect to have. That's one of the weaknesses of the democratic system: no party gets elected by promising to provide less. That's the way it seems to be in the Western world: we have plenty, yet appear to think we are entitled to more and yet more.

I can still remember the sacrifices the previous generation made. My own parents left school at 14 and were condemned to a lifetime of hard manual labour; my generation was enabled to go on at school and then to seek comfortable well-paid jobs far away from the rigours and the dangers they knew. I became a university lecturer; my older brother was a Professor of Engineering at Glasgow University; my younger, a Science teacher in Elgin.

Having been brought up in an era of austerity and effort, I was able to measure the opportunities I received against those of my parents' generation and feel grateful. The Labour government of the immediate post-war world ensured that I would have free health care, that I could go to university on a grant, that I could graduate without debt.

Now when I return to Peterhead it seems like a foreign land. Materially things are greatly improved; the town did well out of its Harbour of Refuge, which has been so attractive to the oil industry. The fishing is down, but there are some oil bases. Marischal Street is now pedestrianised and full of shoppers. It all speaks of abundance, but the young seem less certain, have fewer signposts than we were guided by. Living standards are

Community
support and
the spirit of
sharing and
of showing a
sense of
common
responsibility
have become
much less
evident.

higher, but so is the mountain of debt that bears down upon them as they strive to keep up with the drive to buy newer and ever newer acquisitions. It's an era of the consumer, but because it's a more individualistic age, there is a psychological burden, too. Community support and the spirit of sharing and of showing a sense of common responsibility have become much less evident. How are we to give the young sound values by which to anchor their lives when they are born into such a competitive and materialistic environment? I know from my experience as a warden to a student hall that the young now resent any attempt to establish a framework by which to regulate their lives, but I also know that they seem no happier for all that freedom, no more able to find a purpose in their lives.

And in demanding this freedom to be themselves, as they would put it, they seem to be attempting to cut themselves free from any sense of a past or of roots. It's now all about presentation and about making an impression on the immediate scene. Yet an understanding of where we have come from, a sense of connection to the lives of our parents and of the community that has shaped us, seems to me to be humanly necessary.

Oh dear, I sound like another grumpy old man! I can only quote the old wisdom of Peter Buchan, that talented Peterhead son who left school to go to sea, but who in a later age, would have in all probability risen to the ranks of a university professor: 'Contented weel wi little – as lang's as the neeboring man has less'.

James Coull, born 1935, interviewed 2007: Peterhead

An empty countryside

But the countryside has changed out of all recognition. When I went to school in the mornings, you'd see the smoke going up from every cottar's fire. Always at the same time. If you didn't see the smoke rising, you'd know that something was wrong. The countryside was thick with activity. It's dead now, empty. The first time I realized how quiet the countryside had become was when there was this chap at Catterline who'd bought a car from me, and he couldn't get in to pick it up. So, I said, 'I'll tell you what I'll do. I'll take the car to your house and then I'll walk back to Stonehaven. It'll be a fine, interesting walk for me'. So I went out, delivered the car and walked back from Catterline. Five miles. You know this, I never saw a soul in any of the fields! In my young day, you'd have seen somebody in any of the fields and you could have greeted them, talked with them. And now, if you do happen to see anyone in a field, he'll be stuck inside a tractor and you can't speak at all. The countryside used to be such an interesting place to go into and now it's dead. Just dead.

Only the gulls for company. Ploughing 2010 style, Muchalls.

Eric Brown, born 1935, interviewed 2002: Stonehaven

Mutual respect, that's the key

I have a lot of sympathy for today's younger generation. Our grandson's at Aberdeen College and he's 18. At that age we were both in the thick of it – clubs, dancing, whist drives, church events, youth club, sport – and all laid on locally. But now there's almost nothing like that. What can he do on a Saturday night? Just about the only place he can meet friends is the pub. No wonder it's either a choice between staying in at the playstation or being driven to go to the pub and start drinking.

Saturdays used to be a great day with all sorts of things on the go. I used to love going into the classroom on a Monday morning and devoting the first 10 minutes to chat: 'Did you get a game? What was the score?' Now Saturday morning football in the schools is almost dead and cricket completely so. And with it that kind of link between the generations too. We had a framework we could grow up in, an initiation into adulthood, a common meeting point with the older folk. Now there seems to be a lack of common ground between the generations, almost as if the old regard the young with suspicion and fear. I always make a point of passing the time of day with the younger folk in the village; if I see them of a morning waiting for the school bus I'll stop and chat – and invariably I get a friendly response.

Do you know that in all my years as a Mackie Academy teacher and in a school that hit 1,800 of a population at one point, I can't recall one incident in which a breakdown of order in the classroom even threatened! The mythology has it that there's no discipline in schools nowadays, that youngsters run wild and do as they please. But that's just the myth – meet them, talk to them, show an interest in their point of view, and a completely different picture will emerge.

Young people want to be respected as well, you see: I find you tend to get back what you give. In Johnshaven we've adopted a policy of extending trust to the youth of the village. If you go to the park you won't see a spot of vandalism or misuse. We let the kids know that it's their park as much as it is ours, that they are welcome to use it as freely as any adult. We've got thousands of pounds worth of machinery in there, but nothing's ever been tampered with. Mutual trust, mutual respect, that's what works.

Clark Simpson, born 1935, interviewed 2011: Johnshaven

Passing it on.
Founding Committee of Benholm & Johnshaven Heritage Society, 1990. Back row, left to right: Ann and Edward Foster, Richard Firth, Walter Adam, Joyce Marr. Front: Alec Wallace, Moira McKenzie, Don Marr, Clark Simpson, Tom Kinihan.

Now Saturday morning football in the schools is almost dead and cricket completely so.

A North-east heritage.
Evelyn Hood's maternal grandparents, James and Georgina Young, and family take tea in the garden at Parkhill Stores, Greens, 1918.

End of an era

When I was six, we moved down to East Fife. I remember a sense of loss in leaving the North-east. My grandmother was appalled by the whole idea: to her, Fife was a black country, one dark coalpit after another. She had a horror of such a dirty industrial place, after the clean open land of Aberdeenshire.

But we didn't lose our family contact and, after the war, I was sent north for holidays – out by train to Turriff or on Burnett's bus to Parkhill Stores at Greens, near New Deer. My father's side of the family were an enterprising and adventurous lot who went out all over the world to try anything to make a go of things. As a result I have a lot of cousins in Canada, for instance.

They were very resourceful folk, Buchan people. I think the landscape and the climate must have had a lot to do with it. If you wanted to make something of a small Buchan farm, then you just had to work at it and be ready for whatever the elements threw at you. To do that, you would have to be not only an agriculturalist, but an economist, engineer, blacksmith, joiner, shrewd judge of character, and politician, all rolled into one. They were strong individualists, but they also had a great sense of community and were ready to help one another.

Buchan was an area which would always bring you back to earth. There was this family at Burnside of Greens who had a son called Henry. Henry today would be classed as having learning difficulties. I can remember sitting at a meal round the table with them all and going on about all the wonderful things I was studying at Madras College in St Andrews. I became aware of Henry leaning further and further forward, staring intently at me as I poured forth. This was annoying me so I asked, 'What are you staring at?' 'Ach,' he said, 'A'body says ye spik wi' a bool in yer moo, but I canna see it.'

In those days the era of homemade entertainment and the bothy ballads was still not over. I can remember in the front parlour at Greens with Auntie Peggy at the piano, Sandy Scott on the trumpet and Johnnie Gerrie on the fiddle and singing *The Farmyard o' Delgaty* and many others.

This went on into the Fifties. The arrival of mains electricity and the television spelt

Evelyn enjoys the Arnage gathering, Auchnagatt, 1938.

Preparing for the worst. The infant class complete with gas masks, at Ashley Road School, 1940. The teacher is Miss Spence and Evelyn is the tallest girl in the front row.

its death knell. This was brought home to me one evening when I went to visit Johnnie Gerrie at Little Swanford, Greens. As I approached the house all I could see was darkness and then you caught sight of a wee glimmer of light in the corner. There was Johnnie with two of the farm workers sitting there, gawping at the TV set in the corner. I remember thinking to myself, 'This is it – the end of an era!' The year before you would have seen Tilley lamps and home-made entertainment. The fire would have been aglow and someone might have been playing the piano or the fiddle. And now there they were in silence, staring at some programme being piped into their living room from London.

Evelyn Hood, born 1936, interviewed 2011: Greens, New Deer

Only a place to sleep?

In those days a lot of people were employed on the land and most of the young folk would settle back in the district to work in farming. People would stay in their community; they would take a real interest in all that was going on. Nowadays it's different. I'm on the Community Council and we get quite frustrated at the lack of interest shown by many folk these days. So many seem content to spend their evenings in their own homes now. In the old days, people would be working with each other locally;

A time of respect.
The Alford School prize-giving, 1954. Ian Law is back row, second left, next to Kenny Morgan, sporting his international football cap *(see 'Life in the Community').*

now they commute into the city and don't get back till six, seven o'clock, so it's not surprising they no longer feel such a close part of their community. To many of them, it's a place to sleep, that's all.

I suppose I'm guilty of looking back through rose-coloured specs, but my impression is that life was more agreeable then. Folk weren't so affluent, but they were all in it together. Even the neep howing, which could be a pretty soul-destroying job, your back bent over the drill hour after hour, going up and down the line, well, three of you would be at it together and it could be quite entertaining, with all the backchat.

As a lad, my life was full enough, what with the farm work and the homework from school. Nowadays, kids are forever complaining that they're bored. That's why they commit vandalism, we're told. In the spring we'll be busy putting up hanging baskets and the very next day you'll get a phone call telling you that such and such a display has been wrecked. Why they have this urge to destroy I'm not sure; it's as if anything put in to make the place more attractive acts as a challenge. A few years back we placed that statue of the Black Bull at the entrance to the village and immediately it got defaced with graffiti. But Robbie Gordon, in his wisdom, advised us not to say anything about it, not give it any publicity, and after a while the disfigurement stopped.

We were brought up in a climate of respect for our elders and for those in authority over us. But you know why the respect is no longer there? It's because they've removed

the schoolhouse from the community, they've removed the police house and often the village shop, too. There's nobody left the young can see living among them and respect. When I was at school, Mr Ritchie, the headmaster, stayed next to the school and he could identify all the possible troublemakers and knew their parents well enough to go and tell them.

We looked up to adults in the community. There were the teachers and the bobby. My parents would say, 'Cut that out right now, or I'll get the bobby to you!', and that was quite a scary threat. Even the shopkeeper was on a certain level of respect. He knew all the families, he'd know which ones were running up any debts, which ones always settled their accounts at once and those who had to wait to the end of the week. Now you go off to a supermarket where you pay with a wee bit of plastic to some lassie you don't know, sitting at the checkout.

You could say the same of any North-east community, of course. But what you can also add is that, despite it all, Alford has kept on pulling together and managed to forge ahead. In the 1960s things were going down: the old agricultural and service industries were no longer big employers and the railway had gone. Look at what's been achieved since then: the caravan park and miniature railway at Haughton House; the transport museum on the site of the old station; the Heritage Centre and Charles Murray Room at the old mart; the upgrading of the school to a six-year academy, complete with swimming pool and leisure hall; the dry ski slope… Alford has more in the way of tourist attractions than any like-sized community in the whole of Scotland. So, maybe not just a dormitory town after all, but a place to come to.

Ian Law, born 1939, interviewed 2007: Alford

The young farmer.
At the Turriff Show, watching the judging of an Oxford class of sheep, early 1950s. Ian is centre, his brother, Roy, and father are to his left.

Ian with sister Eva.

It's changing so fast

I feel very fortunate to be living in this part of the world; I look out this window over towards Tarland and Morven and know there's no better view anywhere. But it's changing so fast. A neighbour, Alistair McDonald, who has lived in the same house for 70 years, recalls how his father had to walk three miles to school from the Tillylodge area, every day. There were over 100 pupils then, under two teachers. The school closed in 1964, when the roll was down to 11. The village hall has stood unused for over 40 years. Up the back road there were once 11 black house crofts and now there are only heaps of stones as the Forestry has taken over, and no more than the odd gean or rowan tree to show where whole families once struggled to live out their lives. Not far away is the old manse with its 13 chimneys.

Financially there've been changes. I remember gathering rose hips and getting a penny

a pound for them. A good snared or ferreted rabbit would fetch half-a-crown at the butcher's. A day at the tattie howking earned you five bob – but rowies cost a halfpenny each, Woodbine cigarettes a bob and a petrol three shillings the gallon. The gean trees were abundant and served as a source of income – where have they all gone now?

The Doric's going too. I love poems like *The Whistle* by Charles Murray because they're relevant to a way of life I can still remember. My wife Ethel's father used to 'cut a sappy sucker fae the muckle rodden tree' and fashion a wee whistle out of it. But now, if they wanted a whistle, they'd go to the supermarket and buy one there, 'made in China'. I reckon if you recited *The Whistle* even to people who are local, the great majority wouldn't have a clue what it was about. Not long ago I recited *The Puddock* at a local gathering and a very nice elderly English lady approached me afterwards to compliment me on my rendition: 'I'm afraid I didn't follow all of it, but I did get the bit about the cow being in the paddock.'

The old locals in almost every village are in the minority now. My daughter, Angela, was teaching in a rural primary school and she told me that in her class of 30 there are only five children who were born in the area. The turnover's fantastic: of my 13 adjoining properties, 10 have new owners. I've been here five years and I'm one of the oldest residents. People come in to retire or commute to the town. Twenty years ago, you'd have seen workers in the parks and they would have been local. Now there's just the occasional big machine working them and usually a hired-in figure sitting at the controls, in his air conditioned cab, earphones clamped around his ears and mobile phone at the ready.

I can see yet Big Henry Gray of Cushnie, a great Highland heavyweight, especially at the caber. At hairst time his workers were not amused, having to big his cairt. Normally two sheaves of

a stook were thrown up at a time, but Henry had a lang-taed fork made so he could throw up the hale stook of 12 sheaves. Where are the likes of him now?

The big divide is between the city and the land. Many toonsers will come out on a run, sit in a lay-by with their sandwiches and flasks and imagine they're in the country. For them there's a strangeness about all those parks and trees, the empty spaces. I've had visitors who look upon the country as if it's some kind of art gallery: 'What colour!', they'll say, 'Look at the view!' 'Don't worry,' I tell them, 'there's a good chance it'll still be there tomorrow.' They're looking at the countryside as if it's a huge painting; they are spectators of it all. Mind you, they make me appreciate how fortunate I am.

Douglas Aberdein, born 1938, interviewed 2008: Coull

My generation had the best of it

I believe I inhabited a happier community when I was a boy. Certainly there's a lot more prosperity now and a car on every drive – but all that allows you to do is to buy more and be quicker about it. It doesn't mean you actually see more or do more. Every home has its TV set in the corner, but all that means is that people are having a nightly fix of passive experience, sitting there watching figures on the screen doing their living for them.

I'd say we had the best of it in my generation. Growing up in those post-war years there was little spare cash around, but conditions had improved enough to say that no one ever went without the basics. There was no unemployment, people were now living in decent houses, where running water was being supplied; electricity was reaching out to all the little farm communities. Everyone had enough; now nobody thinks they've enough. So where's your prosperity then? Then, everyone felt himself to be on the same level as those about him and there was none of today's frantic acquisition of more and more goods.

I regret the extent to which children's lives have become so mechanised. We loved playing football at all hours and in most weathers. Now you can watch it non-stop on TV. Playing the game was a shared excitement; now you sit in your own living room and turn on a game any day of the week. It's a surfeit, which means it's lost its savour. That's true for so much today that used to be special. For us sweeties were a real treat; now they are a daily event. The kids of today have so much gear that a present gives them no joy any more.

Materially, life has improved out of sight since my boyhood, but in human terms I couldn't say that people have become richer. Society has become less cohesive, more materialistic and geared to a personal consumption of the world's goods. But that's been a national phenomenon for which the North-east and its people are no more to blame than any other part of Britain. By that criterion I would say that it's done relatively well, that it has retained more stability, greater social cohesion than most.

Charlie Allan, born 1940, interviewed 2006: Methlick

Telling it as it is. The cover to the first volume of Charlie Allan's account of his life upon a North-east farm.

In harmony with the environment?

We now inhabit a digital world. Pupils email their work to teachers and pick up their homework from the class website. All this is a necessary induction into the digital age, of course, but it's difficult not to feel that something has also faded away from a pupil's experience of growing up. In my day our work was to be seen as something out there, in a physical, tangible artefact such as our jotters and our ink exercises. You graduated from the slate to the notebook, to the jotter, to the ink exercise book and felt a certain amount of visible achievement in so doing. The 'thisness' of the world of learning and of experience has begun to fade way – the glow and the pride in going out and bringing home your first LP, putting it on the turntable, fingering its cover,

Climate change?
A common comment by *Grampian Lives* interviewees is that 'winters are not what they used to be'. This early century scene of Strichen would appear to give force to this claim.

stacking it alongside other vinyl LPs on the shelf, watching your collection grow, showing it off to your mates, sharing the whole experience and savouring its 'thisness'. Now, no more.

Of course, you can't put things back in their box; nor should you want to. But I do find myself fretting about the way the world is going, not for my own sake – I'm too old to look ahead to a lengthy future and on the whole I've been able to enjoy a good life – but I'm concerned about what may lie in store for my grandchildren. The digital age marks a shift in culture and human beings can cope with that as they have done in the past. But I fear that the physical environment is threatened to a degree that we simply might not be able to manage or even survive it.

In my young day, there was plenty to worry about – the effects of the war, the Cold War, the nuclear arms race, the succession of social and international crises, such as Suez or the Hungarian Uprising. I can remember vividly – we'd just started a new term at the university – those two weeks in 1962 when we all thought that the world was about to be blown up by Russia and America fighting over the Cuban missile crisis.

But the point is that, difficult though times have been, up to now the situation has always been recoverable. And now my fear is that it's the very fabric of our environment that is under threat. Climate change, the population explosion and the impending global food, water and resources flashpoints that are certain to occur – how will the world recover from all of that?

Large scale industrialised farming has destroyed the agricultural community as we knew it 60 years ago. Commuters now inhabit the old cottar houses and the steadings have been converted into executive homes for accountants and business folk who travel into Elgin, or even Aberdeen, daily, and who use their houses as places to sleep in and to weekend in. Fifty years ago the concept of the parish, each with its own school, its own church, its own hall, was still a living reality; now it's just an area, a stretch of assorted housing developments and agricultural units.

For me, that sums up the larger problem, that human beings are losing the capacity to live in an organic way, in harmony with their environment. Will my grandchildren be able to live their lives in a way that will enable them to enjoy the sort of progressive experiences and benefits that I've done? I devoutly hope it, but I can't be sure.

Richard Bennett, born 1942, interviewed 2011: Torphins

You can't stop the clock

Inverbervie has changed since the Sixties. It's grown in size, but the jute mill has closed down, the fish processing has gone, the council houses are now largely in private hands, the railway has vanished; there's new housing sprouting up wherever you look. But there is still the baker, the Post Office, the paper shop, the church, the Co-op. Change has come, but much still endures – change is built out of the past and on its foundations.

This is something I am always trying to point to in my work as a literary commentator: that change is the great theme of our 19th and 20th century literature. Lewis Grassic Gibbon is a great author because he shows you that change not only happens but that is inevitable, part of the larger historical process. For people of our generation that can be unsettling but the great crime would be to try to stop the clock, to attempt to impose our own past values on the ever changing present.

Ian Campbell, born 1942, interviewed 2011: Inverbervie

> Inverbervie has grown in size, but the jute mill has closed down, the fish processing has gone.

The village shops are going...

When I began at the butcher's, 90% of Auchenblae shopped with us. At the end I would say it was no more than 50%. The trend is more and more towards a one-stop, once a week big shop and that'll be at a supermarket on the edge of town, not at a small place in a wee village.

Back then, I could have put a name and face to 90% of the village – now I go down the street and I see nothing but strangers. In the Fifties and Sixties people still shopped locally; they'd walk down the street and pop into the shops to get their daily needs and stop and chat to one another. Now it's all cars. I fear for our village shop; it's the only one left of the 10 when I came here. If it goes, then Auchenblae will become another of those villages which has lost its shop in recent years – Drumlithie, Fordoun, Luthermuir, Marykirk.

But then, people don't have the same attachment to their village as they used to. Forty years ago there was a lot of employment for them here – sawmills, farming, forestry, wood cutting, the two hotels, the 10 shops, a garage. Now there's nothing. They're here because it's a pleasant place to sleep and to weekend in, not to work and to shop.

My shop had been going as a butcher for 120 years. It was housed in one of the oldest buildings in Auchenblae, built by the Earl of Kintore in 1676. It's still there but, since I gave up the business, standing empty, unwanted. There's a mess of weeds at the front and it all looks a bit depressing – but there you are: the past is the past.

David Hutchison, born 1947, interviewed 2011: Auchenblae

Towards the end. David Hutchison with his partner, Andrew Smith, outside his butcher's shop in Auchenblae just before its closure, after 120 years of service to its community.

Facing the future with confidence.
Rachel Adams, 2012.

They'll grow out of it

At the moment I'm working as a relief care worker with the elderly. I never thought I'd like the work; my first wish was to do something with young children; I love their freshness, their energy, and here I am, with the very old who're no longer capable of looking after themselves. I had thought that taking on personal care with the elderly would repulse me. I started off downstairs in the day care centre, but then I was asked if I would be prepared to go upstairs and into the personal care. I decided to give it a try, and I'm glad I did. The first time I was called on for intimate care, I did find the contact with an old person's body a bit disconcerting. It was quite a shock to see how much the body deteriorates over the course of a lifespan, but it's all part of life. And I'm glad to be able to give them the level of respect they deserve. It's lovely to be able to talk with them and to hear their stories of the old days.

I know my generation's got a bad name for behaviour – binge drinking, drugs and so on. But I would say that it's only one section that goes to that kind of excess. There's such a range of behaviour and attitudes that you shouldn't make easy generalisations. My own feeling is that mine is a 'fun' generation and that can lead to some selfish, anti-social behaviour. But I think the older generation can be too worried about such things. What's really happening, I think, is that young people who go out and drink and indulge in rowdy behaviour on the streets are really doing it to make their own mark, to say, 'Look, we are the new generation and here we are – you'd better realise that!' Most of them will grow out of it. In fact, I bet a lot of the older people who shake their heads at what they're doing, did much the same at their age. It's simply their time; they will grow older, settle down – and then another generation will come onto the stage and they'll worry about them.

Rachel Adams, born 1990, interviewed 2008: Kinneff

Councillor at 18

So here I am, at the age of 18 and still at school, a full member of the Stonehaven Community Council. On occasion the discussion can just seem to go round and round and I can be sitting there feeling that this is all very well, but what about some action! But on the whole, I feel my presence is valued as providing a fresh viewpoint.

The older members – some of them – can give the impression that because they've dealt with the same recurring issues for so long now, they have become sceptical that any new proposal will simply run into the ground like all the rest before it. For example, I feel the Council needs to hear that, yes, the proposal to build a College of Further Education outpost next to the Academy would be real step forward. They can appear to see a new proposal like that in terms of its problems rather than its advantages. From my experience, it would be a great advantage to have a practical, vocationally-directed alternative to secondary education. So when some members grumble that the area was

On the whole, I feel my presence is valued as providing a fresh viewpoint.

The young councillor.
Jenni Keenan and Dunnottar Castle, 2011.

intended for school sports, I can assure them that Mackie would still be left with a huge field for that purpose and that nobody would be deprived. An inside view like that is important for the Council to hear, I think.

Often the younger generation is seen as a challenge; we're often seen as the section of society that's responsible for litter, for noise and for underage drinking. But there've been efforts to tackle the litter problem: the school has formed an environmental team which goes out and collects litter in the town. But the bad things do tend to stick in the mind and this can lead to reluctance to approve new projects in case they are simply abused – yet look at the skateboard park and how well that has been taken up.

I can't deny that there are bad incidents, but it's a small minority and it's valuable for the rest of us – the majority who're not like that – to have the opportunity to put these issues in their wider perspective.

Jenni Keenan, born 1992, interviewed 2010: Stonehaven

'The experience made me grow up.'
Bill as a 19-year-old (left) entrusted with the driving of a V-wagon in Berlin, 1949.

The soldiers' tale: stories of National Service

The first taste of army life.
Bill McRae among the new Gordon Highlanders recruits, Fort George, 1949.

The experience made me grow up

I was called up for my National Service in 1949 and was posted out to Berlin with the First Gordon Highlanders. There I was, a country loon from Maud, someone who'd seen nothing of the big world apart from the odd day trip into Aberdeen. I was very quiet and very shy. And then I found myself in Berlin, having to mix with all sorts. You got plenty banter about where you came from, about being from the back of beyond and speaking in a funny accent, but you learned how to take it and to give it back.

The experience made me; it made me grow up. There you were driving a lorry in Berlin, having to pick your way through the heaps of rubble piled up by the sides of the streets. The damage to that city, especially made by the Russians at the end of the war, was horrendous. Before I'd gone away, the most exciting events in my life was a Saturday night out with my pals. I had been well looked after at home: my mother would press my suit for me, she would shine up my shoes.

I learned to stand on my own feet; I learned discipline. National Service was a very good experience, but I'm not sure it would work the same nowadays. The orders we were given could be annoying, but we obeyed them without question. The NCO would order you to get a haircut: you'd be standing to attention and he would come round your back and ask if he was hurting you. You'd say, 'No, sir,' and he'd come back with, 'Well, I ought to be – I'm standing on your hair!' That was his way of telling you to go off and get a really short haircut.

In the Army you were chased everywhere; you were never let off with anything. Would young men accept all that today? I'm not sure. At the end of my career at RAF Buchan I was chatting to the CO about all the changes I'd seen in my time there. We agreed the biggest one was discipline. 'Yes,' he told me, 'Nowadays my hands are tied. If you punish a man and he takes exception to it, then he'll be writing to his MP and I'll likely as not get it in the neck.' It's not like it was.

William McRae, born 1930, interviewed 2007: Maud and Berlin

> National Service was a very good experience, but I'm not sure it would work the same nowadays.

I got discipline all right

When I was called up in 1953 for my National Service and had to spend 10 weeks at the Bridge of Don barracks, I got discipline all right. I remember an old major at the end of it standing on the parade ground and telling us, 'We're proud of you loons today'. And I remember thinking, 'Why? All we've done for the past 10 weeks is learn bloody marching and bloody saluting'.

But when we got to Malaya I realised what it was all about – discipline! You'd find yourself in the jungle, fighting an invisible enemy, wading through the swamps soaking and sweating, with a 40-pound pack on your back and the leeches sucking at you till you could scarcely put one leg in front of another – and it was the discipline we'd had drilled into us back home which got us through. That old Major had known what he was talking about, all right. I'd had to leave my painter's job where I was getting £7.10 a week, and all for a load of bloody saluting, marching and 14 bob. But it was the best training you could get.

That's what's missing nowadays – discipline. The days of National Service have gone. I was speaking with an old Army mate a while back and he was telling me, 'Oh, Ian, ye shid see the auld barracks noo – it's sae sad. Aathin's dirty an untidy; weeds aawye.' But when we were there, everything was kept absolutely clean and tidy. The stones were

Private Stevenson, Gordon Highlander, on leave beside the family car, 1953.

The peace he left behind. The Keith Harmonica band, early 1950s. Ian is front row, third left.

painted white, the brasses were gleaming. You'd never see anyone slouching along, hands in pockets. It was all marching, upright, smart. You'd never be allowed to be idle: there was always something you could be cleaning. So you'd go around with a rag and polish, polish away at your equipment. 'Get on with it!', that was the attitude.

The comradeship among us all was excellent. There was a boy from Newmill out with us. He brought his thrifty home habits with him. He'd come in and say, 'Hey, Ian, hae ye hid a letter frae yer mother the day?' I'd say yes and tell him any news of home that was in it, and then he'd say, 'Can I clean ma beets while I'm here?' That meant that he'd be borrowing my polish and save his own. He also wrote to his mother, but she'd write her letter, send it out to him and then he'd pen the reply on the reverse side of the same paper. Oh, he knew how to save money, he did! And now he's got eight buses and he's worth a fortune. When we were returning to the UK he could hardly get through the customs, his kitbag was that full of tools taken from the Army. He never touched a drop either; all he thought about was saving as much as he could out of our 14 bob a week.

But he was a good comrade; he'd do anything for you. You've got to remember just how hard life was in the country round here back then. People were brought up to respect the value of money. You had to learn how to cope – and that's what it was like in the Army, too.

A long way from Keith. In the jungle, fighting the terrorists, Malaya, 1953.

Ian Stevenson, born 1932, interviewed 2008: Keith and Malaysia

I'd never been out of Scotland before

'd never been out of Scotland and here I was on the train all the way down to London. I landed up in the Army Service Corps. I had three months of initial training and then was selected to drive staff cars attached to the War Office in London. I acted as a sort of chauffeur, ferrying important officers around. Once I encountered Monty – a wee man as brown as a berry.

I had three intensive weeks having to drive a sergeant all over London. He'd instruct me, 'Take me by the quickest route to Westminster Bridge,' or 'There's a traffic jam ahead – find an alternative way to get to Waterloo station'. The idea was never to have to ask the way and never, ever be late.

I was one of a pool of 30 and we all stayed in a barracks at Regent Park. You had your own car to look after and keep immaculately polished and gleaming, inside and out. I worked hard, took a pride in what I was doing and learned to talk when spoken to by all manner of people. Almost without exception those officers were real gentlemen. My accent never created problems; the officers tried to put you at your ease. There was this second lieutenant who was in charge. One evening we got talking and I mentioned my father was having a tough time of it back in Aberdeenshire, struggling to get the harvest in. 'Sounds like a case for harvest leave,' the lieutenant said and arranged for six weeks leave so I could go back north and help on the farm.

Duncan Forbes, born 1936, interviewed 2011: Kininmonth and London

The three new recruits. Duncan Forbes (right) settling into Army life, 1957

'Happy as Larry.' In uniform, 1957

Among the best years of my life

he brown envelope came and instructed me to report to the Bridge of Don barracks. We got our 10 weeks initial training there. That was very tough. The Gordon Highlanders is an infantry unit, so you had to learn how to get through a mile-long march with your kitbag on your back, then, when you'd mastered that, three miles, then six, then nine. I was fairly fit and I managed all that, but some of them were just not up to it and would fall by the wayside. The NCOs would yell at you; you'd feel the spittle in your face but you just had to take their bullyboy tactics, had to learn how to say, 'Yes sir, no sir, three bags full sir!'

I would regard those two years as among the best of my life. You learned to handle yourself, you got very fit, you met plenty of other people from all parts and you saw a bit of the world. I was out in Cyprus, then at Dover, then at NATO HQ at Fontainbleau. My first night in Cyprus a bullet was fired when it was felt that the enemy

Passing out parade. The Bridge of Don Barracks, 1956.

The 1956 intake.
Bill Sinclair with the Gordon Highlanders, Bridge of Don. Bill is third row, fourth left

were creeping in – but it turned out to be a donkey! But we certainly had to go out into the mountains on the hunt for General Grivas.

One thing that did shock me was the number of men who couldn't read or count. They seemed quite normal, not lacking or anything, but couldn't get through a simple instruction or write a letter home. The Army had to give them crash courses. To begin with, you had to be on your guard in the barracks, take care not to leave your belongings lying around. There were some men who would thieve the blades out of your razor, but once you got into your platoon then it was case of being part of close-knit family group. The others became like brothers and you would live and die for each other.

Of course, there is no getting away from the fact that you were being turned into a trained killer. You'd be ordered to run at sacks and knife them with the bayonet attached to your rifle; you'd stick the blade in, twist it and then extract it ready for the next one, all the time uttering some blood-curdling cry. And we had to watch the most horrific films of combat and dying in close action; the idea was to teach you that in war it's you or him, and no messing. Despite all that I would advocate some form of National Service for everyone.

William Sinclair, born 1937, interviewed 2008: Quilquox and Cyprus

The stuff of the North-east

I've come across plenty of laughs

I've come across lots of laughs on my travels round the farms. I once went to this remote croft where an old man had died. His neighbour told his wife, 'De ye ken, Ah think I'd bitter gae an pay ma respects te auld Jock afore he's pit awa into the groon'. So he stepped across to the dead man's croft and announced to his wife that he was offering his condolences and would like to pay his last respects. She showed him through to the room where old Jock was laid out on the bed. He gazed down at the dead man's face and then thought to himself, 'Bit he's lookin sae peaceful, lyin there. In fact, ye cud swear that wis a smile on his face. He's lookin awfu weel fer a deed man.' So he went back to the widow and told her, 'My, my, bit your Jock's lookin awfu weel, lyin there like that'. To which she replied, 'Ah weel, that's because he disna ken fit's happened tae him yet!'

To me that kind of story sums up North-east folk – down to earth humour, people who can poke fun at themselves and at the common events of life, and death. I've got another story, one that happened to us. We were just newly married and living in our rooms at Old Street. There was this old fishwife who came from the coast every week with a creel on her back; she'd go round the doors, selling fish from house to house. She knocked on our door: 'I hear ye're new marrit. Noo here's a wee bitty advice – your boun to hae yer oops an doons – it wudnae be a praper marraige withoot that. Bit I'll tell you this: I aye liked to hae a row wi ma man; ye see, it was awfu fine fan we made up in bed later!'

Jack Benzie, born 1919, interviewed 2008: Huntly

'He's lookin sae peaceful, lyin there. In fact, ye cud swear that wis a smile on his face. He's lookin awfu weel fer a deed man.'

Civic action

I've lived most of my life south of the border now. I've married Beryl, from Ashton-under-Lyne. My two daughters were born and brought up in the south of England. I think my Scottish background has led to a tendency to incorporate socially open attitudes into my behaviour. If people want to see me at work, they don't have to jump through all the hoops they might elsewhere. I sense that this kind of attitude doesn't come quite so naturally to a lot of southern English people. The people here, in St

Montrose born and bred. The High Street as it was during Donald Munro's boyhood, 1950s

Over 20 years in Herts. Donald and wife, Beryl, alongside David and Kathleen Northcroft, St Albans High Street, 2011.

Albans, have learnt to speak to me, but only after they've weighed me up and found me socially acceptable, I suspect. In Scotland, my experience is that we're a bit more ready to talk to all and sundry, without such circumspection. People here tend to be more individually focused – but, of course, this is a generalisation and there are plenty of Scots like that, too. But you will find in Scotland a greater habit of looking at things from a viewpoint of civic responsibility. It's there in a newspaper like the *Scotsman*, the assumption that the way to approach a problem is through civic, public action. And the *P&J* provides a peculiar Northern cement through its huge coverage of local news.

Donald Munro, born 1942, interviewed 2003: Montrose and St Albans

The North-east in action

There's an uncomplimentary song which goes:
Oh Rhynie is a Hieland place.
It disnae suit a Lawland loon.
And Rhynie is a cauld clay hole
It isna like my faither's toun.

Despite these comments, Rhynie with its fine war memorial in the Square and the parish kirk in the background can look beautiful. The memorial is in the form of a great-coated soldier and it fully captures the essence of the First World War sacrifice. This was carved by a North-east man, a young man called Warrack Morrison who'd served his time in the Aberdeen granite yards.

And the parish of Rhynie actually has a proud history. That 'cauld clay hole' has produced a stream of people who have gone out into the world and used their native character and skills to make a real mark.

Think of the roll call of sons who have played a notable part in overseas developments during the 19th century. There's Alexander Mackay – 'Mackay of Uganda' – the son of the local Free Kirk minister and the missionary who devoted his short life to service

The family heritage. John Kemp's father, with two of the ponies he used to transport shooters over the hills above Rhynie.

among the tribes and dangers of Uganda. Then there's George Whitefield Anderson, or 'Anderson Bey', who served in numerous wars and expeditions – Egypt, China, Sudan, Botswana – winning awards for his bravery and leadership. Or China Jonny', John Anderson, who spent 30 years in China combating disease and the opium trade.

Rhynie is also a centre of ancient history. There's the fossil beds, the Rhynie chert beds, where just about the oldest evidence of living forms, dating back over 400 million years when Rhynie was near the Equator and had hot springs, has been discovered. Then there are the various Pictish stones, such as the Rhynie Man, uncovered by a farmer out ploughing. It's an impressive depiction of a man carrying an axe and is about 1,300 years old.

I'm not claiming there is anything unique in all this; I expect that any typical North-east settlement can point to a similar history. And that's the point – Aberdeenshire is full of small rural communities which may appear to be isolated, plain backwaters, but which actually contain stories of real endeavour and history.

I wouldn't dream of suggesting my own history should join this roll call, but like many of my Rhynie predecessors I've used what was developed in me there to forge a career in the wider world. I got a very sound education at home, at Lesmore Primary School and then at the Gordon Schools, Huntly. Then I studied French and German at Aberdeen University. I later joined Guinness and spent many years in Africa, helping develop the business. I loved the experience of different cultures, of trying to speak some of the local languages, and taking in the sights and the smells and the colour of it all.

The community infrastructure in action. Sandy Thomson on the rounds from his Rhynie store, delivering the weekly shop to John's mother at the family croft, Essie, 1960s.

A proud history.
The 'very fine' war memorial, carved by Warrack Morrison, which stands in Rhynie's central square.

I'm not the only one in my family to strike out like this. One worked in a silver mine in Bolivia and was probably killed in an uprising out there. Two of my grandmother's brothers became ranchers in Canada and another worked on the railways in South Africa.

But I've never been sorry that my starting point was Rhynie. I can't really say to what extent my North-east background is special in any way, but I do know it has provided a wealth of achievement. You could claim that the land and the climate demand the growth of particular qualities of character and skill to make a go of it and that these have proved to be highly exportable ones.

It's dangerous to generalise. What I can say is that the environment I grew up in nurtured a sense of self-sufficiency and getting on. The fact that it was essentially a farming community which had managed the combination of seasons, land, beasts, weather, and illness and forged a real community out of it, well, that must have a lot to do with the notable contributions its people have made to the wider world.

Perhaps the language helps – it's so physical and immediate that it cuts through to the heart of things in a way that Standard English often blurs. Then, I remember there was a little old building in the neighbouring croft at Essie where I grew up, called the Schoolie. This goes back to the days before state education, when a community like Rhynie had to see to itself to make sure its young had access to an education. Just think of it, this small, very ordinary croft settlement supporting not just an actual school, but also a library of books, known as the 'Parochial Library'.

And then I remember the times when the threshing mill would go round all the farms and crofts. When it came to our district I was fascinated to see how people from neighbouring farms would all come to lend a hand and how all of them just settled into an allotted task. No fuss, no hesitation. It was as if a tradition, born out of years of hard, uncomplaining work and shared experience, was at work. It was the North-east in action.

John Kemp, born 1944, interviewed 2011: Rhynie

A real country village

A lot of people like Fettercairn because they see it as a real country village. A lot of the English people who've come here to settle feel the same way. There's a lassie who stays on the other side of the Ramsay Arms who comes from Somerset. Her husband was originally from Arbroath, but he went down south as a chef and that's where they met. He was always wanting to come back and she would only agree if he could find her a genuine little village to live in. Well, she came to look at Fettercairn and immediately said, 'That's it! That's where I want to bring up my children'. She's really settled here and just loves it. I speak to other English folk and a lot of them are like her.

Margaret McArthur, born 1945, interviewed 2004: Fettercairn

'A real country village.'
Fettercairn, 2012.

A genuine earthiness

I'm settled in the North-east. There are many things I admire about the people here. When you go out into the country you'll find a real earthiness in people, an appreciation of their place in the scheme of things. I live in New Deer, in the heart of Buchan. There's a real sense of community there, very traditional. A lot of the younger people there wouldn't dream of moving away; the outside world doesn't have that kind of meaning or attraction for them. Maybe that comes from sitting on the same benches as the old men in the village; there's a sense of the place's history, of the generations, of their place in the world. Also of their place in nature. They know about the seasons, the tilling of the soil, the sowing and the harvesting.

There's a lot of continuity in the North-east: when you look at people's faces, the way they walk even, you'll see the same features continued down through the generations. They know that life is stark, that they die, and that between birth and death you work and you play and make out as best you can. They are part of the soil. There's still a stability and strength about the North-east and for me it's a comfortable place to live.

Cathy Macaslan, born 1953, interviewed 2005: Ayrshire and New Deer

The young face of the North-east.
Dorothy Shaw's *(see 'Church Going')* daughter, Jean, among the barley on her father's farm at Maidenfold, Blairs, 1960s.

The book of the North-east

In my fifth year at school I encountered Lewis Grassic Gibbon and *Sunset Song*. The novel spoke to me immediately. It's about growing up, about the tensions between the generations, about discovering who and what you are and how the forces of environment and history feed into that, and all recreated with a lyricism that sweeps you

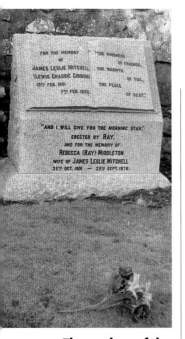

The author of the North-east.
Lewis Grassic Gibbon's memorial stone, Arbuthnott kirkyard.

up in its flow – just the book for someone who is leaving adolescence and going through the same journey.

It's now been adopted as a standard school reader. I'm a bit ambivalent about that. I love to teach it, but it does present its challenges. Although the book is supposedly about 'their' very own North-east, *Sunset Song* demands a certain maturity before it can be fully taken in. The book is so rich and pupils aren't necessarily equipped to meet its treatment of what is too easily assumed to be their own society by virtue of simply growing up in the North-east. You have to have a fair grasp of the politics and the ideologies at work – materialism, Humanism, Presbyterianism – how many 21st century kids know about these?

I can still recognise the constants in human nature, still pick out North-east types that were caught in *Sunset Song:* the workaholic who's the first to get up in the morning to get out into the fields; the pupils at school from a farming background who gaze out of the window, thinking only of what a fine day it is for the ploughing and not a whit about what's in front of them on the desk; the mean and grippy ones; the gossipy and the sly types; the decency beneath the rough and dour exteriors. I do think North-east people still have something of the doggedness he celebrated, the ability to laugh at themselves and not to be carried away by romantic fancies as to what you can expect from life.

William Malcolm, born 1955, interviewed 2009: Aberlour

A land worth fighting for

When I first moved in, 20 years ago, I knew nobody. Once I got in among the people I found them really friendly and warm. But to begin with, it had been hard. For example, we started growing strawberries, the very best organic strawberries you could ever hope to taste. We'd get a glut and rather than see them rot I'd take them down to Stonehaven and try to give them away. It was very difficult. People would be suspicious, or not want to show themselves as greedy or easily taken in. Now, if this had been Dundee, they'd have been flocking around: 'Hey, ye gat ony mair o they strawberries, missus?'

It felt a strange land, bleak and harsh. And the weather! There was always this wind blowing and tugging at you whichever corner you turned, whatever the time of the year. You'd put ornaments on the windowsill, open the window because it looked nice outside and they'd get blown over onto the floor. We put double-glazing in, but we could never keep the draughts out; they just whistled round your feet and chilled your legs. I've always maintained that it's the wind that's made North-east people use 'Fit' instead of saying 'What'. They go outside, the wind takes their throat and then it's 'Fit, fit!' as they puff along; 'Fit, fit!' I think that wind has had a lot to do with

'A land worth fighting for.'
Maggie Fraser's farm, Burnorrachie, Bridge of Muchalls, 2012

the shaping of the people in the North-east. It's such an open country; all the way from the Mearns up to Huntly, it's big open fields with little in the way of trees or hedges. 'Fit, grow trees? You dinna mak money fae trees, ye ken!'

People can be very reserved round here, so deferential that they politely sit back and let others, often from the outside, make all the running. When the link road for the Aberdeen bypass was proposed, we held a meeting in Cookney Hall and folk just sat there and took what the Government was proposing. I would ask them, 'How long have you farmed this land? How much work and sweat have you put into making this land something where crops will grow?' I could see them eyeing me nervously, waiting for me, the woman from Dundee, to say something. 'Will she embarrass us all?', they were thinking. I stood up and told them this was a beautiful land and now it was going to be put under tarmac by order of politicians in Edinburgh. I told them it might not be lush and picturesque, but it has its own bleak, pure beauty, worth the fighting for.

Maggie Fraser, born 1956, interviewed 2008: Dundee and Bridge of Muchalls

The morality of the North-east

My grandparents were all farmworkers or farmers, but my mother's father became a haulage contractor and he ran lorries all over the North-east, over Scotland and England as well. He hired a new lorry driver who'd just been demobbed from the Army in '52, and that driver fell in love with the boss's daughter. So that's how I happen to be here; I've lived in Alford all my life.

There's a certain integrity in values about the North-east. I can't be certain how unique these values are, because the North-east is the only place I've ever lived in, but I'd be prepared to put a lot of money that just about everyone of my vintage would be prepared to tell you that that's just the way we are. There's this work ethic; if you can't afford something, you just can't have it. HP and credit are anathema to most people out in the country. If you can't afford something, wait till you've

saved up. No short cuts, no loans. This springs from the morality of the North-east.

Norman Harper, born 1957, interviewed 2002: Alford

'A brilliant place to grow up in.'
A general view of Gardenstown, 1960s.

Going away showed the value of home

I made an attempt to escape when I left home when I was 17 and went down to Newcastle with a friend. We already knew some people there and I wanted to try life in a big new city. Because of that link, Newcastle was just about the only city that my mother would hear of me going to, so that's where I ended up. We were young girls, brought up in a small Moray Firth fishing village, and couldn't wait to spread our wings. Gardenstown had been a brilliant place to grow up in – so warm and so familiar – but as we got older it was becoming too restrictive and we felt that there was a big exciting world waiting for us. The fact that everyone knew your business and still saw us as just young girls of the village was becoming oppressive. The religious tone to life there tended to make people suspicious of activities such as dancing and – for girls – drinking. Whenever I raised the question of where to go to on a Sunday, I could feel my mother's disapproval weighing down on me.

Newcastle really opened my eyes, all right – but not always in a way that I found comfortable. In the end it made me realise just what I had been fortunate to take for granted back in my own wee fishing village. People in Gardenstown had had to work hard and some must have found things tight at times, but it wasn't till I arrived in Newcastle that I discovered that there were people out there who were really poor. It was then that I began to know what destitution really was. Back home if ever I'd needed anything, then I knew I would be able to go out and get it; in the big city I came across people who couldn't even afford the basics of everyday living like food and warmth, let alone clothes and entertainment.

I had a good enough job there, but my friend got homesick and now I was by myself. I was appalled by the inner city way of life I could see around me. I'd been brought up in what I now realised was a wholesome, secure environment and found the areas I was living in seedy and disturbing. I came across what I can only describe as depravity and destitution. The climax came when I fell ill with a really bad dose of flu and had to stay in bed for three weeks, alone and unable even to let my parents know – no phone in my flat, let alone a mobile, not in those days. Finally I felt just about well enough to totter down to the phone box at the end of the street. I told my parents all that had been happening to me; my father simply said, 'Just come home,'. That's what I'd been waiting to hear.

My mother warned me, 'Don't you go expectin aa'thin to be jist the way it wis,' but I got a warm welcome. It was like the return of the Prodigal Daughter. However, I'd now tasted independence and realised my mother was right – I couldn't expect everything to be just waiting for my return. Not long afterwards I met my future husband and moved into my own home. But my experiences had taught me the value of my Gardenstown upbringing and of a strong family life. I'm now teaching and conducting research into the ethno-musicology at the university; my topic is lullabies and I'm discovering more and more about the real significance of the lullaby in adult as well as a child's life. All that is fascinating, but I'll always be grateful for my Gardenstown childhood and the rich family life that helped to nurture me there.

Irene Watt, born 1957, interviewed 2011: Gardenstown

> Newcastle made me realise what I had been fortunate to take for granted back in my own wee fishing village.

A sense of belonging

I started life in Paisley but when I was three we moved to Stonehaven and that's where I was brought up. My parents were Glaswegians and that made them different from North-east ones. I see Glasgow as a vibrant colourful city and Glaswegians as warm extrovert folk, easy to chat to. These are generalisations, I know, but there does seem a real contrast between the inhabitants of the two places. After all, North-east folk are not exactly famous for their bubbliness, for presenting a sense of joie de vivre to the outside world!

My parents always loved their Glasgow, but they also came to love Stonehaven. My mother will tell you the story of their arrival in Stonehaven. It was the end of March and the day they moved in there was snow. Then they woke up the next morning to find the wind had shifted round and that the sun was shining and the snow completely melted away. They were able to have a picnic in the garden, there outside their very own door – and this was their first home with its own garden. To them that summed up the kind of place they had come to: a small community which had the feel of the sea and the countryside about it, a lovely open place to bring up young children.

They were always conscious of a difference. Glasgow folk are more inclined to come out and to take you on; North-east people will stand back and be wary of a new situation. Nowadays, I go round old folks' centres and lead singing sessions. One of my tasks is to

A timeless Stonehaven beauty spot: Dunnottar Woods as they were in the 1920s – and are now.

encourage people to use music as a way of sharing common experiences. Last week I was at the Stonehaven Resources Centre, running a workshop for older people. Most of them were in their 80s. Well, when I started off by inviting them to come out with memories of the kind of songs they would have heard as children, it was like drawing teeth. They wouldn't even give me a title, let alone sing any examples.

But that's the way North-east folk are and I just accept it. It's not that they aren't interested, it's just they are wary about showing too much commitment to a stranger. The lady who was organising the event remarked as I was leaving, 'You know what'll happen now. As soon as you've gone and they're enjoying their cup of tea, they'll be bubbling away nineteen to the dozen about all the old songs. But they'll wait till you're not there!'

Something you notice about North-east people is that they have a deep-seated sense of belonging, one that has roots to it. I've got it too: I've lived spells in Glasgow, London, Iona, but I've always felt North-east. For me there's been the awareness of the sea always near me, but for others it appears to be the land. There are two distinct communities, a coastal and a rural one, but what brings them together is that they each have this sense of the elements around them. There's only one real city in the region and North-east folk can't go very far before they are in the midst of the land. They have this awareness of being surrounded by natural open spaces and that gives them more of a feel for a slower, more reserved way of dealing with life than you have in a large, busy conurbation such as Glasgow, where you tend to see crowds of people around you and your dealings are with them, rather than with nature.

Fiona Squires, born 1962, interviewed 2007: Glasgow and Stonehaven

My wee Kincardineshire village

I was brought up in Coatbridge. My memories are of being brought up in a close-knit, caring family. But it was also something of a wild place, back in the Seventies and Eighties. The Catholic-Protestant divide was very marked and ran right through everything you did and everywhere you went. At that period it was also being inflamed by the troubles in Northern Ireland. The town had acted as an overspill for Glasgow and the people had imported their sectarian culture with them, one which spread and was then driven on by the intense rivalry between Rangers and Celtic.

I lived in a smallish Protestant enclave in what was a predominately Catholic town; my family had had strong ties on my mother's side, including links with the Orange Order, whereas my father, who had been brought up as a Catholic in Fort William, despised religion in general and the Catholic church in particular because of the many beatings he had received at the hands of the priests. At that time, I saw Rangers and Protestantism as my tribe, its people as my people.

All this created a tense atmosphere with fights, bottles and a few stabbings. You went about constantly on the lookout that you might take the wrong turning, get challenged

and end up being set upon. There was a strong gang culture, based on area and on religion – and the two went together. You had to become a fighter to survive and you had to learn how to live on your wits. Coatbridge was a tough, tough place to be a young lad in. But there was a lot to be said for it. Among your own folk there was a warmth, a generosity, a sense of loyal support freely given. We worked hard, we drank hard and we fought hard.

In 1982, the week before my 18th birthday, I moved up to Newtonhill. I found it something of a small parochial fishing village, lacking in the openness and immediate warmth of the Central Belt. I was a very angry young man at that time, distraught at the recent death of my father. I was brash and loud mouthed compared to the local lads and, as the new 'Weegie' in the village, eager to make my presence felt. The local pub was the Newton Arms and I started to go there regularly. Not everyone took to my sharp Glaswegian ways. Betty, the landlady, never did become overfond of me. Her pub was cold and draughty, so I'd say things like, 'Hey, Betty – would you mind opening the door and letting some heat in?'

I was introduced to Derek McKenzie who ran the local football team. 'Ach, ye're a right big loon – you'll mak a useful centre-half for the team.' 'Loon'? I took that as an insult; here was this guy only just introduced to me and already calling me some sort of meathead. I'd go around asking people, 'What are you? Protestant or Catholic?' and when they replied, 'I dinna ken – never thought much aboot it,' I was incredulous. In the Central Belt that was the vital clue to their whole identity and to the kind of relationship you could expect to have with them – and here were all these North-east folk not concerned about it at all.

I've now been in the North-east for 30 years and am well settled. But I must confess that I still have a pang or two for the old days. I was down in Glasgow the other week and took in the craic and the buzz and couldn't help but make a comparison. In Glasgow you can stroll into a pub and strike up a conversation with a complete stranger and make a pal for life. Up here, I found it difficult to make friends. Maybe my accent made people

Loyalty to the tribe.
The Orange Order on the march, Coatbridge, 1970s.

'Always a Ger.'
Eric McNeil's front window on the Saturday of Rangers' debut match in the Third Division, versus Peterhead – which they just managed to draw, August 2012.

An in-your-face sort of approach that doesn't go down too well with your average Aberdonian.

wary of me, maybe it's the fact that I'm used to a fast-paced delivery and an in-your-face sort of approach that doesn't go down too well with your average Aberdonian. He prefers to take things more slowly, to weigh things up, to go canny. Maybe it's the agricultural and fishing background compared to the industrial ethos of the Central Belt, where people work together en masse and you have to show a quick wit and hold your own. And, for sure, the rivalry between Rangers and Aberdeen hasn't helped.

But once the folk round here get to know you, then you can trust them with your life. What I will say is that the friends I've made over the past 30 years have become friends for life, just as loyal as any of my fellow Weegies. I'm certainly not sorry I made the move; I love living in my wee secure Kincardineshire village. But I'll always support the Gers!

Eric McNeil, born 1964, interviewed 2012: Coatbridge and Muchalls

A sense of belonging

I've since spent time in large cities, both as a social worker and as a minister. I worked in London, in Glasgow. The experience was enriching, but it has enabled me to conclude that I am more at home in a rural community. When I was at the Wellington Church, Glasgow, I had a phone call from the university chaplain. A young couple from Dufftown were in the city to attend their young baby daughter at the Yorkhill Children's Hospital and they had just lost her. Here they were complete strangers in a large city and bereaved; could I go and be with them?

'A close-knit community.' Dufftown, 1960s.

I knew the family quite well and went to offer what support I could. I then followed them back up to Dufftown to conduct the funeral service at Mortlach Church. It was a desperately sad occasion, but one thing struck me as I looked around the church: the whole of the village seemed to be there, if not every inhabitant then at least one person from each household. That made me aware of something which till then I'd simply taken for granted – that a rural area like Dufftown has such a close-knit, supportive spirit, that it's a community where people know and look out for each other.

I knew then that I was meant for a rural parish. In Glasgow and in London I'd been in the midst of large shifting populations, of a great mix of people from all corners of the earth. In many ways that was all to the good, a lively, exciting, human melting pot. But you couldn't know your neighbour even, let alone who might live in the next street. The pavements were full of strangers. In Dufftown you'd stop and talk and find out about the latest small events and needs; in the city, life was far too anonymous for that kind of personal contact.

Ian Murray, born 1970, interviewed 2011: Dufftown